READING

Basic

Intermediate

Advanced*

Expert*

LISTENING

Basic*

Intermediate*

Advanced*

Expert*

* To be released

Informative passages

HACKERS APEX READING includes informative and interesting passages on a variety of topics, such as science, art, and history.

Useful online study materials

HACKERS APEX READING provides access to quality online study materials at HackersBook.com. These include streaming audio recordings of all passages accessible through QR codes in the book.

HACKERS

APEX READING for the TOEFL iBT®

Intermediate

Preface

Preface

Thank you for purchasing HACKERS APEX READING for the TOEFL iBT Intermediate. The TOEFL iBT is a highly challenging exam, so it is important to select an effective study guide. All of us at Hackers Language Research Institute are confident that this publication will be an invaluable resource as you prepare for the TOEFL iBT.

HACKERS APEX READING for the TOEFL iBT is a series of comprehensive study guides for students planning to take the TOEFL iBT or for those wanting to improve their general English reading skills. This series includes four books that progress in difficulty. Students can begin at the level that matches their current abilities and then move on to the higher ones. All of the books in this series provide step-by-step question-solving strategies for every TOEFL question type. These are based on thorough research and years of instructional experience. Each book also includes informative and interesting passages that enable students to improve their English reading skills and expand their background knowledge at the same time. Furthermore, students will receive access to quality online study materials that are designed to help them get the most out of the books in this series. Key features of HACKERS APEX READING for the TOEFL iBT books include:

- Detailed explanations and question-solving strategies for all TOEFL Reading question types
- A large number of high-quality TOEFL Reading passages and questions
- Two full-length TOEFL Reading tests
- Vocabulary exercises to review essential vocabulary that appeared in the passages
- An answer book with Korean translations and lists of key vocabulary
- Access to streaming audio recordings of all passages through QR codes
- Access to supplementary study materials online (www.HackersBook.com)

Thank you again for choosing HACKERS APEX READING for the TOEFL iBT Intermediate, and we wish you all the best whether you are preparing to take the TOEFL iBT in the near future or simply hoping to develop your English reading skills overall.

Table of Contents

How to Use This Book

1 Understand the Question Type

Each chapter includes an Overview page that provides essential information about the featured question type and key strategies for answering it. Make sure you fully understand the strategies before moving on to the Example section, which provides a short passage with one or two questions to apply the key strategies to.

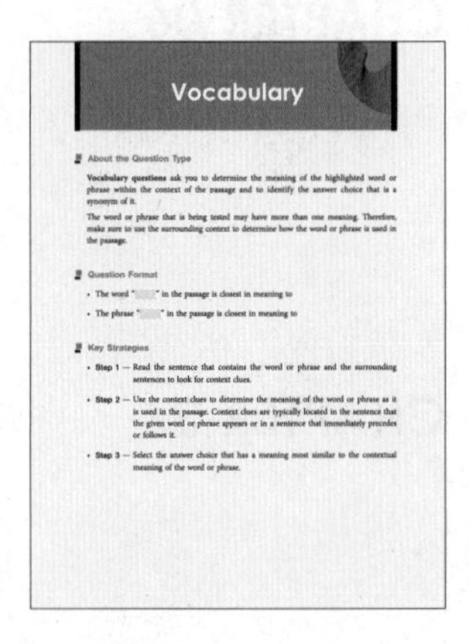

Vocabulary

About the Question Type

Vocabulary questions ask you to determine the meaning of the highlighted word or phrase within the context of the passage and to identify the answer choice that is a synonym of it.

The word or phrase that is being tested may have more than one meaning. Therefore, make sure to use the surrounding context to determine how the word or phrase is used in the passage.

Question Format

- The word "____" in the passage is closest in meaning to
- The phrase "____" in the passage is closest in meaning to

Key Strategies

- Step 1 — Read the sentence that contains the word or phrase and the surrounding sentences to look for context clues.
- Step 2 — Use the context clues to determine the meaning of the word or phrase as it is used in the passage. Context clues are typically located in the sentence that the given word or phrase appears or in a sentence that immediately precedes or follows it.
- Step 3 — Select the answer choice that has a meaning most similar to the contextual meaning of the word or phrase.

2 Improve Your Skills with Reading Practice Exercises

Each chapter includes four Reading Practice exercises. These will help you become more familiar with the featured question type, as well as other question types. Each exercise is accompanied by a vocabulary quiz so that you can review the key vocabulary from the passage.

Reading Practice 4

Answer Book p. 14

The History of Vatican City

Vatican City, the home of the pope and the headquarters of the Roman Catholic Church, is an independent city-state. It only occupies about 100 acres of territory near the center of Rome, but it has its own government, of which the pope is the absolute monarch. The 800 people who reside within Vatican City are either clergy or members of the Swiss Guard, the small army that defends the state. The Vatican does not collect taxes to pay for its expenses; rather, tourism, merchandising, and contributions pay the city's bills. To have a tiny sovereign state enclosed entirely within a larger nation is a unique arrangement. How did it come to be?

The Vatican became the center of the Catholic Church in AD 324. This is the year when a public building called a basilica was constructed by the first Christian emperor of Rome, Constantine I. The site of the basilica is believed to be the grave of the Apostle Peter, who is considered the church's first pope. Saint Peter's Basilica has always been a holy place for the Catholic people. It is also one of the largest churches in the world. The basilica's dome is one of the most recognizable architectural features in all of Italy. It is a popular destination for pilgrims and tourists.

The Vatican's status as a government was a source of tension with the surrounding governments for centuries. From the eighth century until 1870, the Vatican was not just a religious center but the seat of power for political entities called the Papal States. The boundaries of the Papal States varied over a period of hundreds of years, but at one point or another much of present-day Italy was subject to rule by the pope. When Italy unified under the rule of King Victor Emmanuel II in 1860, the era of political power for the pope appeared to be ending. Indeed, in 1870, Italy declared war on the Papal States and claimed all territory outside the walls of Vatican City. The tension between Italy and Vatican City was finally resolved with the rise of Prime Minister Benito Mussolini. In 1929, Mussolini signed an agreement that recognized Vatican City as a sovereign entity. The church was paid $92 million to compensate for the loss of the Papal States.

Glossary

Papal States: territories of central Italy that were directly governed by the pope from 756 to 1870

3 Take the iBT Reading Test

Each chapter includes an iBT Reading Test, which consists of a longer passage and 10 questions that are similar to those that appear on the TOEFL iBT. Taking this test will enable you to improve your reading comprehension skills and prepare for the TOEFL iBT.

iBT Reading Test

Answer Book p. 15

TOEFL Reading

The First Whale

→ Considering that all animals evolved from sea creatures during the Cambrian age more than 400 million years ago, one might imagine that whales are directly descended from an underwater species. But nature seldom progresses that simply. In reality, the cetacean family, which today consists of whales, dolphins, and porpoises, apparently originated some fifty million years ago with a four-legged, wolf-like mammal.

→ In the early 1980s, a team of paleontologists discovered the collection of fossils in the northern part of Pakistan and immediately recognized that it included a long skull similar to that of a whale. They named this creature Pakicetus meaning "Pakistan whale." Later, it was found that the creature's skull had a bony wall around the inner ear that enabled it to hear underwater. This constituted a striking link between land mammals and contemporary whales.

As more fossils were discovered, scientists pieced together the creature's habitat and means of subsistence. Pakicetus divided its time between the shore and the sea. Its long legs ended in webbed feet that made it a natural swimmer. It also had powerful teeth that likely gave it the ability to tear the flesh of fish and small animals, which it could reach with a twist of its flexible neck. The animal's molars showed evidence of scraping that suggests it ground its teeth when it chewed. At the back end of the creature was a long tail.

→ The fossil record suggests that descendants of Pakicetus evolved over the next fifteen million years to enhance their water-friendly features. The webbed feet gradually morphed into flippers. Eventually, the aquatic baleen whale emerged. Over a period of about thirty-five million years, whales grew larger and larger, growing from twenty feet to an average of forty feet in length. The increase in size likely occurred so the whales could evade large predators in the sea. A Such an occurrence is a common phenomenon in evolution; it is thought that animals that evolve over a long period of time generally tend to get larger. B Even so, the process has had an extreme effect on whales. C That this monstrous creature is descended from the diminutive Pakicetus is a wonder of nature. D

Glossary

molar: a tooth at the back of the mouth for grinding food

4 Review Essential Vocabulary

At the end of each chapter is a Vocabulary Review, which includes questions on essential vocabulary from the chapter. You will be able to easily memorize the vocabulary words by seeing them in sentences with various contexts.

Vocabulary Review

5 Evaluate Your Progress with Actual Tests

The book includes two Actual Tests, which are full-length reading tests that include passages and questions that closely match what appears on the TOEFL iBT. They provide an excellent opportunity to apply the skills you have learned and evaluate your progress.

Actual Test 1

Horses in Agricultural Work

6 Check the Answer Book

The Answer Book specifies the correct answer choice for all questions and provides Korean translations of all passages and questions. It also includes a list of key vocabulary words from each passage with definitions.

Vocabulary

About the TOEFL iBT

What Is the TOEFL iBT?

The TOEFL (Test of English as a Foreign Language) iBT (Internet-Based test) includes Reading, Listening, Speaking, and Writing sections to comprehensively assess English ability. Although most tasks require the application of only one of these skills, some require the use of two or more. The TOEFL iBT is designed to measure a student's capacity to use and understand English at a university level and is, therefore, much more difficult than many other English proficiency tests.

TOEFL iBT Structure

Section	No. of passages and questions	Time (min.)	Score	Notable Features
Reading	• 3-4 Passages • 10 Questions/Passage	54-72	30	• Each passage is approximately 700 words long.
Listening	• 2-3 Conversations • 5 Questions/Conversation • 3-4 Lectures • 6 Questions/Lecture	41-57	30	• Speakers have various accents, including American, British, Australian, etc.
10-minute break				
Speaking	• 1 Independent Task • 3 Integrated Tasks	17	30	• Independent Tasks ask you to state your opinion about a specific topic. • Integrated Tasks ask you to provide a response based on reading and listening content.
Writing	• 1 Integrated Task • 1 Independent Task	50	30	• Integrated Tasks ask you to provide a response based on reading and listening content. • Independent Tasks ask you to write about a specific topic.
Total Time: Approximately 3 hours 30 minutes / Total Score: 120				

TOEFL iBT Reading Section

The TOEFL iBT Reading Section evaluates a student's ability to read and comprehend English texts that are comparable to those encountered in a typical first- or second-year university class. Although the passages cover a wide variety of academic topics, there is no requirement to be familiar with the subject matter. The information in the passage is all that is needed to answer the questions.

TOEFL iBT Reading Question Types

Question Type	Description	Score	No. of Questions (per passage)
Vocabulary	Choose the answer choice that is closest in meaning to the given word or phrase.	1	1-2
Reference	Choose the answer choice that the given word or phrase refers to.	1	0-2
Sentence Simplification	Choose the answer choice that accurately and completely summarizes the key information in the given sentence.	1	0-1
Fact & Negative Fact	Choose the answer choice that restates (Fact) or contradicts (Negative Fact) the relevant information in the passage.	1	2-7
Inference	Choose the answer choice that can be inferred based on the relevant information in the passage.	1	1-2
Rhetorical Purpose	Choose the answer choice that best describes the function of a specific piece of information in relation to the immediate context or the passage as a whole.	1	1-2
Sentence Insertion	Choose the answer choice that corresponds to the correct location in the passage to insert the given sentence. Each possible location in the passage is marked by a square [■].	1	1
Summary	Choose three answer choices that best summarize the main points of the passage.	2	0-1
Category Chart	Choose the answer choices that match the given categories.	3	0-1

CHAPTER 01

Vocabulary

Vocabulary

About the Question Type

Vocabulary questions ask you to determine the meaning of the highlighted word or phrase within the context of the passage and to identify the answer choice that is a synonym of it.

The word or phrase that is being tested may have more than one meaning. Therefore, make sure to use the surrounding context to determine how the word or phrase is used in the passage.

Question Format

- The word "   " in the passage is closest in meaning to
- The phrase "   " in the passage is closest in meaning to

Key Strategies

- **Step 1** — Read the sentence that contains the word or phrase and the surrounding sentences to look for context clues.
- **Step 2** — Use the context clues to determine the meaning of the word or phrase as it is used in the passage. Context clues are typically located in the sentence that the given word or phrase appears or in a sentence that immediately precedes or follows it.
- **Step 3** — Select the answer choice that has a meaning most similar to the contextual meaning of the word or phrase.

Example

Answer Book p. 2

Mediterranean Sea Trade

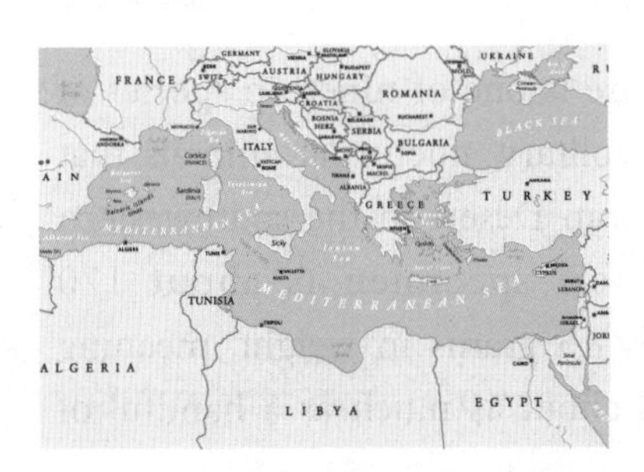

Although the Mediterranean Sea is connected to the Atlantic Ocean, it is almost completely enclosed by land. Throughout history, it has played a central role in the rise of Western civilization. Powerful countries struggled with each other to have full use of it because of its importance to trade. Thus, numerous societies attempted to colonize the coastline.

Two of the earliest civilizations to do so were the Greek city-states and Phoenicia, whose merchants used the sea extensively as a highway for commerce. Later, however, the region was taken over by the Romans, who went on to control the sea and its coastal regions for the next 400 years. They called the Mediterranean *Mare Nostrum*, or "Our Sea." As the Roman Empire was largely concentrated in coastal areas, the Mediterranean was extremely significant for the Romans' commerce and naval development.

After Rome collapsed in AD 476, countries continued to struggle for supremacy as the region switched hands many times. Today, the Mediterranean Sea's control resides largely with the European Union, and it still represents one of the largest areas for commerce in the world.

1 The word "enclosed" in the passage is closest in meaning to

(A) characterized
(B) centered
(C) surrounded
(D) developed

2 The word "supremacy" in the passage is closest in meaning to

(A) position
(B) dominance
(C) liberation
(D) aptitude

Reading Practice 1

Answer Book p. 2

Adaptation of the Rock Pocket Mouse

The rock pocket mouse is one of nineteen species of pocket mice. They are solitary, nocturnal animals that live all around the Sonoran Desert in the southwestern United States. A typical specimen is about 170 millimeters and roughly 15 grams in weight, meaning this tiny mouse weighs about as much as a handful of paper clips.

While there appears to be nothing special in particular about these rodents, evolutionary biologists have been quite intrigued by the species and have conducted numerous studies on their fur color since the early 1930s. The most common variety of this species has a sandy, light-colored coat. This color pattern helps them blend in with the desert rocks and sand where they live.

However, populations of rock pocket mice that have a darker coloring have also been found in nearby areas. Scientists discovered that these groups lived on strips of the desert where the ground was covered in dark patches of volcanic rock called basalt which was formed by lava flows from volcanic eruptions thousands of years ago. Seeing this, scientists combed through the data compiled from both light and dark-colored populations to search for any specific gene that may have caused the difference. After thorough analysis, a mutation in a certain gene turned out to be the determiner of coat color.

A gene mutation is any change in the DNA sequence of a gene. Gene mutations can alter the structure of the resulting protein, which can change the way it functions. In the case of the rock pocket mice, a direct association was discovered between the mutated gene and coat color. Mice that possessed it had more melanin while the mice with no gene mutation remained lighter. The primary cause of the mutation was found to be what biologists call selective pressure, which affects an organism's ability to survive in a given environment. For rock pocket mice, the color of the environment pressured the gene to mutate in the mice living on the basalt to help them camouflage better, ensuring higher survival rates and better protection from predators. It is a prime example of adaptation through natural selection.

Glossary

· melanin: a dark brown pigment in the skin, hair, and eyes in animals and humans

1 The word "intrigued" in the passage is closest in meaning to

(A) terrified
(B) perplexed
(C) elevated
(D) fascinated

2 The phrase "combed through" in the passage is closest in meaning to

(A) arranged neatly
(B) searched carefully
(C) summarized completely
(D) tested extensively

3 According to paragraph 3, some rock pocket mice populations

(A) occupy land covered with thick vegetation patches
(B) live in areas that once had active volcanoes
(C) include both light and dark-colored individuals
(D) lack a gene found in members of other groups

4 The word "it" in the passage refers to

(A) resulting protein
(B) direct association
(C) mutated gene
(D) coat color

5 According to paragraph 4, rock pocket mice have differently colored coats because

(A) the amount of melanin increased in the light-colored mice
(B) survival rates were higher for camouflaged mice
(C) gene mutations in dark-colored mice had no effect
(D) predators were deterred by the difference in color

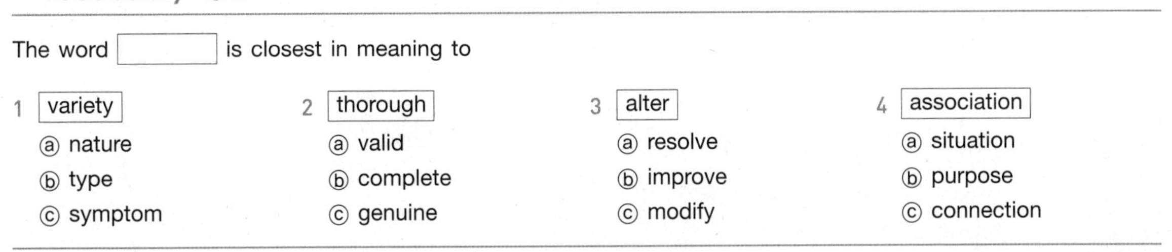
• Vocabulary Quiz •

The word [ ] is closest in meaning to

1 variety	2 thorough	3 alter	4 association
ⓐ nature	ⓐ valid	ⓐ resolve	ⓐ situation
ⓑ type	ⓑ complete	ⓑ improve	ⓑ purpose
ⓒ symptom	ⓒ genuine	ⓒ modify	ⓒ connection

Reading Practice 2

Answer Book p. 3

How Hearing Works

When we hear something, it happens in a split second, and we recognize it instantly. Yet despite this speedy reaction, the process of hearing is quite complicated. Sound waves first enter the ear canal and strike the eardrum, causing it to vibrate. The vibrations then move along to the bones in the middle ear. As the eardrum vibrates, so do these bones, and this sets the fluid of the cochlea, a snail-shaped structure in the inner ear, in motion. As the fluid moves in the cochlea in a wave-like manner, the alternating changes in pressure stimulate the hair cells. As these cells move up and down, they transform the vibration into an electrical signal that is carried to the brain and turned into sounds that we understand.

Hearing well depends on the entire system working together so that sound can reach the brain and be processed without disruption. Thus, if a person has a hearing problem, the specific type depends on which part of the auditory system is not responding well. For example, if you have a problem in the outer or middle ear, it usually means there is an inefficient transfer of vibrations from the eardrum to the cochlea. Generally, this affects the volume of what you hear, so sound can seem muted and low. This is called conductive hearing loss because sound vibrations are not being conducted efficiently. With this kind of hearing issue, a bone conduction hearing device is used in place of traditional hearing aids. The device transfers sound by bone vibration directly to the cochlea. This is necessary because the cochlea is still working normally but simply not receiving enough information via its connection with the middle ear.

On the other hand, if a problem occurs in a part of the system between the cochlea and the brain, it is called sensorineural hearing loss. In this case, sound is not processed after reaching the cochlea either because of damaged hair cells or because of defects in the auditory pathway leading to the brain. This type of hearing loss is due to constant exposure to loud noises or simply because of aging. Sometimes, surgery can help remedy the situation, but in most cases, a conventional hearing aid is used to fix it.

Glossary

· eardrum: a thin membrance that separates the outer ear from the middle ear

1 The word "complicated" in the passage is closest in meaning to

(A) complex
(B) immediate
(C) random
(D) accurate

2 According to paragraph 1, which of the following is NOT true of properly functioning hearing?

(A) Sounds waves first travel through the ear canal.
(B) Hair cells convert vibrations into electrical signals.
(C) Pressure changes carry sounds directly to the brain.
(D) Vibrations cause fluid in the cochlea to move.

3 The word "disruption" in the passage is closest in meaning to

(A) corruption
(B) interruption
(C) protection
(D) destruction

4 According to paragraph 2, conductive hearing loss occurs because

(A) vibrations are not transferred to the cochlea efficiently
(B) the brain processes sound other than speech
(C) the cochlea fails to interpret vibrations
(D) damaged hair cells prevent sound from reaching the brain

5 The word "it" in the passage refers to

(A) problem
(B) system
(C) cochlea
(D) brain

• Vocabulary Quiz •

The word [ ] is closest in meaning to

1 processed
ⓐ exceeded
ⓑ handled
ⓒ removed

2 auditory
ⓐ hearing
ⓑ sensing
ⓒ feeling

3 constant
ⓐ variable
ⓑ significant
ⓒ continuous

4 remedy
ⓐ explain
ⓑ address
ⓒ describe

Reading Practice 3

Answer Book p. 4

Rise and Fall of Tenochtitlan

Tenochtitlan was once one of the greatest cities in the Aztec Empire. It was founded by the Mexica people around AD 1325 after they left their homeland of Aztlan in response to what they believed was a command from their god, Huitzilopochtli. According to legend, Huitzilopochtli directed them to build the city in the place where they saw an eagle perched on a cactus, eating a snake. They saw this vision on an island in Lake Texcoco, where they eventually settled. 5

The early years for the Mexica were difficult as they tried to build up their new home. The people lived in small huts, the sacred temple for Huitzilopochtli was made of perishable material. The city even had to pay regular tribute to the neighboring city of Azcapotzalco, which ruled over them. Their challenging life began to change when the Tenochtitlan ruler, Itzcoatl, detected infighting and political instability at Azcapotzalco. He took the opportunity to form alliances with other smaller cities and eventually gained Tenochtitlan its independence. 10

From those humble beginnings, Tenochtitlan became the center of the empire over the next 80 years. Now, the Mexica people were receiving tribute and conquering nearby regions. The city grew in wealth and power as well as in infrastructure. The residents had enough material to build an aqueduct that brought in potable water from the lake and a proper temple dedicated to both Huitzilopochtli and Tlaloc, the god of rain and fertility. The city's wealth, ample natural resources, and strategic position on the lake boosted its trade market, making it an economic and political powerhouse. 15 20

Unfortunately, the golden age of Tenochtitlan would come to an end when the Spanish conqueror Hernán Cortés landed in Mexico in 1519. The arrival of the Spanish signaled the downfall of the Aztec Empire. Cortés was initially greeted warmly by the Mexica and given gifts of gold. They hoped that the signs of respect would please him and he would leave them in peace. Of course, knowing so much gold was available in the city only increased Cortés's desire to conquer it. He returned several months later with an army of 700 soldiers and 70,000 native troops who had allied themselves with the Spanish. They laid siege to Tenochtitlan for 93 days—burning, looting, and destroying everything they could—until the Mexica finally surrendered on August 13, 1521. 25

Glossary

· loot: to steal things during a violent event (war, riot, etc.)

1 According to the passage, the city in Lake Texcoco was established because the Mexica

(A) needed a capital for their newly independent society
(B) sought shelter from infighting and political instability
(C) renamed Azcapotzalco after defeating it in war
(D) were following the orders of a mythical being

2 The word "alliances" in the passage is closest in meaning to

(A) unions
(B) truces
(C) admirations
(D) monopolies

3 The word "ample" in the passage is closest in meaning to

(A) abundant
(B) excessive
(C) unique
(D) attractive

4 In paragraph 3, the author's explanation of the rise of Tenochtitlan mentions all of the following EXCEPT

(A) conquests of neighboring regions
(B) the availability of drinking water
(C) a conversion to a new religion
(D) success at trading natural resources

5 The word "them" in the passage refers to

(A) the Spanish
(B) the Mexica
(C) gifts of gold
(D) signs of respect

• Vocabulary Quiz •

The word [ ] is closest in meaning to

1 command	2 sacred	3 dedicated	4 downfall
ⓐ sign	ⓐ holy	ⓐ isolated	ⓐ influence
ⓑ order	ⓑ grand	ⓑ assembled	ⓑ dignity
ⓒ burden	ⓒ main	ⓒ devoted	ⓒ collapse

Reading Practice 4

Answer Book p. 4

America's First Movie Theater

The Nickelodeon was the first commercial movie theater to open in the United States. During the early 1900s, this type of storefront theater became a popular entertainment facility due to the public's growing interest in film. Soon, more than 8,000 theaters were popping up across the country.

Before then, movies themselves were minor distractions at vaudeville shows, which featured a variety of different types of entertainment, and were not considered substantial enough to warrant their own facilities. This is because a film, at the time, was merely a collection of "shadow" images—such as a couple dancing or a man sneezing—that were shown between vaudeville acts. As a result, it was almost like a commercial, if commercials only consisted of moving images with no plot or narrative. However, it was not long before it occurred to some clever innovators to tell a story with them. As film and projection techniques advanced, so did the excitement for this new form of entertainment.

It was Harry Davis, a vaudeville organizer, who saw an opportunity and decided to devote an entire theater exclusively for showing films. He bought a machine called a cinematograph and set up chairs and a screen in a storefront on Smithfield Street in downtown Pittsburgh. He decided his first showing would be a film that already had some popularity: *The Great Train Robbery*, a ten-minute film about outlaws robbing a train. He and his brother-in-law opened the Nickelodeon, as he dubbed it, on June 19, 1905, to a delighted public.

They took in over 400 customers on the first day and more than 1,000 on the next. Everyone was eager to get in on the experience, and the Nickelodeon was the ideal venue. First of all, since the movie did not require live performers, no breaks were needed. This allowed Davis to keep the theater open from eight in the morning until midnight, with multiple shows every hour. It also meant he could keep admission fees low. Whereas it cost a pricey twenty-five cents to go to a vaudeville show, the theater on Smithfield Street only charged five cents so that anyone could attend. In fact, that's where Davis got the name for his theater; he combined the price of admission, a nickel, with the Greek word for theater, *odeon*.

Glossary

· vaudeville: a theatrical entertainment featuring a mixture of acts by comedians, singers, dancers, and magicians

1 The word "substantial" in the passage is closest in meaning to

(A) extravagant
(B) significant
(C) permanent
(D) innovative

2 The word "them" in the passage refers to

(A) vaudeville acts
(B) commercials
(C) moving images
(D) clever innovators

3 According to paragraph 2, early movies

(A) combined various entertainment forms
(B) were designed to sell a product
(C) were minor parts of a longer show
(D) competed with vaudeville performances

4 The word "exclusively" in the passage is closest in meaning to

(A) easily
(B) surely
(C) directly
(D) only

5 According to the passage, which of the following is NOT true about the Nickelodeon?

(A) Thousands of similar storefront theaters emerged after it opened.
(B) It charged less than the price that it cost to attend a vaudeville show.
(C) The first movie that was shown at it was already somewhat well-known.
(D) It was kept open 24 hours because there was no need for live performers.

• Vocabulary Quiz •

The word [ ] is closest in meaning to

1 warrant
ⓐ transmit
ⓑ justify
ⓒ attain

2 commercial
ⓐ advertisement
ⓑ prediction
ⓒ currency

3 dubbed
ⓐ shifted
ⓑ linked
ⓒ named

4 venue
ⓐ event
ⓑ part
ⓒ place

Answer Book p. 5

TOEFL Reading

The Origin of Land Plants

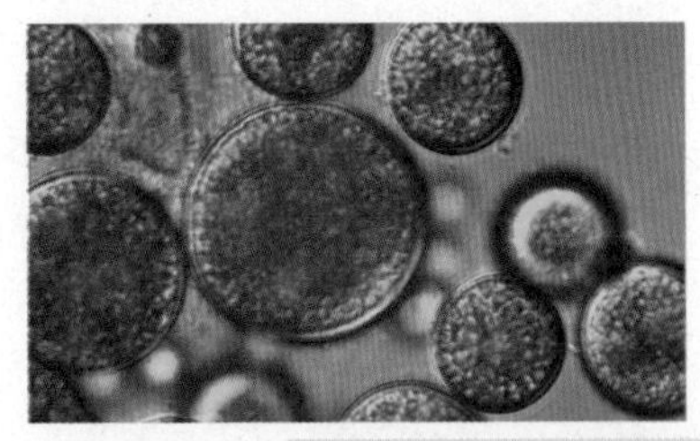

➡ A billion years ago, the earth's continents were nearly devoid of life. Apart from limited quantities of bacteria and fungi, the land was rocky and barren. The only complex life was underwater. Then, about half a billion years ago, plant life began to appear on the land, eventually covering 5 the surface with soil and producing forests, swamps, and shrublands. Plants filled the planet with oxygen through the process of photosynthesis, and consequently, animals began to emerge from the depths of the sea. But where did these land plants come from?

Scientists believe that plants evolved from freshwater green algae, which performed 10 photosynthesis long before complex life found its way ashore. Algae are aquatic organisms that are descended from single-cell species much like amoeba. These single-cell organisms gained the ability to perform photosynthesis by consuming oceanic bacteria that also had the ability to convert carbon dioxide into oxygen.

➡ Algae gradually evolved to survive on land. In order to do so, the way that the 15 organisms reproduce changed. Instead of releasing embryos into water, as algae continue to do today, land plants began growing embryos inside themselves. The plants developed a cuticle—a layer that could retain water within the organism—now that they no longer had constant direct access to water. Further, plants developed pores in their leaves that allowed them to exchange carbon dioxide for oxygen without losing water. Finally, vascular tissue 20 evolved to transport water throughout the plant after receiving it through the roots.

➡ There has been some debate as to which freshwater algae species gave rise to land plants. The leading candidate was complex green algae, which resemble plants in that they have long branching bodies. **A** However, recent genetic analysis of various algae species revealed that single-cell algae species have much more in common with early species of 25 land plants. **B** While this hypothesis is difficult to test, researchers now suspect that these simple organisms began to grow outside of ponds and streams, evolving into moss, shrubs, and even trees. **C** Thus, the evolution of land plants was more circuitous than scientists had assumed. **D**

Glossary
vascular tissue: a plant tissue that transports water

Volume Review Help Back Next

1 The word "devoid" in the passage is closest in meaning to

(A) dense
(B) diverse
(C) lacking
(D) robust

2 Which of the sentences below best expresses the essential information in the highlighted sentence in the passage? *Incorrect* choices change the meaning in important ways or leave out essential information.

(A) Because animals came from the sea, plants pumped oxygen into the atmosphere.
(B) Since the earth was filled with oxygen by the plants, animals moved out of the oceans.
(C) As the earth became oxygenated, animal ancestries emerged from the ocean floor.
(D) Despite the arrival of animals, photosynthesis resulted in animal evolution.

3 In paragraph 1, the author's description of the continents one billion years ago mentions which of the following?

(A) Animals evolving from algae
(B) Bacteria on land before plants
(C) Fungi performing photosynthesis
(D) Soil resulting from plant life

Paragraph 1 is marked with an arrow [➡].

4 The word "descended" in the passage is closest in meaning to

(A) prepared
(B) removed
(C) originated
(D) replicated

5 The word "they" in the passage refers to

Ⓐ organisms
Ⓑ algae
Ⓒ embryos
Ⓓ plants

6 According to paragraph 3, algae evolved into plants in each of the following ways EXCEPT

Ⓐ developing a layer to retain water
Ⓑ becoming capable of containing embryos
Ⓒ forming pores that facilitated reproduction
Ⓓ transporting water from the roots to the plant

Paragraph 3 is marked with an arrow [➡].

7 The word "hypothesis" in the passage is closest in meaning to

Ⓐ experiment
Ⓑ theory
Ⓒ trial
Ⓓ doubt

8 According to paragraph 4, single-cell algae are the most likely organisms to have

Ⓐ competed with early land plants
Ⓑ grown first outside of freshwater
Ⓒ developed long branching bodies
Ⓓ included genes sequenced by scientists

Paragraph 4 is marked with an arrow [➡].

9 Look at the four squares [■] that indicate where the following sentence could be added to the passage.

Scientists presumed that this physical similarity was an indication that these algae and plants had a shared ancestry.

Where would the sentence best fit?

Click on a square [■] to add the sentence to the passage.

10 **Directions:** An introductory sentence for a brief summary of the passage is provided below. Complete the summary by selecting the THREE answer choices that express the most important ideas in the passage. Some sentences do not belong in the summary because they express ideas that are not presented in the passage or are minor ideas in the passage. **This question is worth 2 points.**

Drag your answer choices to the spaces where they belong.
To remove an answer choice, click on it. To review the passage, click on **View Text**.

Once, life was limited to underwater environments, but eventually land plants evolved.

•

•

•

Answer Choices

Ⓐ Soil was a result of the evolution of plants on the earth.

Ⓑ Plants are descended from freshwater green algae.

Ⓒ In order to survive on land, algae had to adapt in several ways.

Ⓓ Plants have pores that allow gases to be processed while water remains constant.

Ⓔ For years, scientists believed that single-cell algae evolved into complex algae.

Ⓕ Scientific opinions have changed regarding which algae species were the original ancestors of land plants.

Answer Book p. 5

Vocabulary Review

A. Fill in the blanks with the appropriate words from the box.

nocturnal	challenging	surrender
humble	access	barren

1 The land was ____________ with little vegetation due to the lack of rainfall this year.

2 Despite her ____________ background, she will one day be president of the country.

3 The exam was quite ____________ and most of the students failed.

4 The army would not ____________ even though they were losing the battle.

5 Owls are ____________ birds, hunting at night and sleeping during the day.

6 You need a key card if you want ____________ to the building.

B. Choose the closest meaning for each highlighted word or phrase.

7 The airline's first priority is to ensure the safety of all its passengers.
(A) announce (B) inspect (C) encompass (D) guarantee

8 All the office supplies arrived on time apart from the copy paper.
(A) exceeding (B) including (C) excluding (D) following

9 The small nation finally gained its independence after years of oppression.
(A) liberty (B) esteem (C) honor (D) virtue

10 The crowd at the music festival consisted of mostly teenage girls.
(A) approved (B) detached (C) comprised (D) supported

11 The circuitous route the bus followed resulted in a very long trip.
(A) groundless (B) indirect (C) advantageous (D) ingenious

12 She tries to devote several hours each week to volunteer work.
(A) detach (B) submit (C) commit (D) expand

13 The recent increase in oil price has caused economic instability in many countries.
(A) insecurity (B) growth (C) consumption (D) depression

14 When a product has defects, especially safety issues, a product recall is issued.
(A) spaces (B) flaws (C) interests (D) features

CHAPTER 02

Reference

Reference

About the Question Type

Reference questions ask you to identify what the highlighted word or phrase refers to in the passage.

The highlighted word or phrase is usually a pronoun (*it*, *they*, *this*, *which*, etc.). The correct answer choice will be the noun that the highlighted word or phrase refers to. The incorrect answer choices will be nouns that appear in the preceding sentences but are not referred to by the highlighted word or phrase.

Question Format

- The word " " in the passage refers to
- The phrase " " in the passage refers to

Key Strategies

- **Step 1** — Read the sentence that contains the highlighted word or phrase and the sentences that immediately precede it.
- **Step 2** — Find the noun that the highlighted word or phrase refers to. Determining whether the highlighted word or phrase is singular or plural can make it easier to identify its referent.
- **Step 3** — Substitute your answer choice for the highlighted word or phrase, and confirm that it makes sense.

Example

Answer Book p. 6

Vaccinations

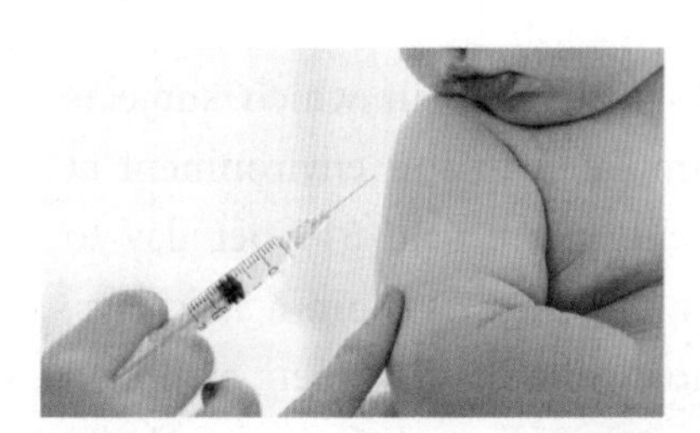

Vaccination was not introduced in the West until 1796, although it had been used in ancient times in China, India, and Persia. In fact, long before anyone had heard of bacteria and viruses, it had been observed that survivors of certain diseases did not catch them again. This observation was put into practice by the Chinese through an early form of vaccination called variolation, which was carried out as early as the tenth century. The method aimed to prevent smallpox by exposing healthy people to matter from the lesions caused by the disease, by putting it under the skin. Variolation caused mild illness and, although it could occasionally cause death, smallpox rates were reported to be lower in populations that tried it.

Western medicine caught up with its Eastern equivalent when British doctor Edward Jenner discovered that a mild disease called cowpox made patients immune to the much deadlier disease smallpox. Much like variolation, vaccination worked by exposing patients to a form of the disease they wished to prevent. Alongside aggressive testing and pharmaceutical care, this treatment has become a basic component of every public health strategy.

Glossary

· lesion: a diseased or injured area in the body

1 The word "it" in the passage refers to

(A) method
(B) smallpox
(C) matter
(D) disease

2 The phrase "this treatment" in the passage refers to

(A) variolation
(B) vaccination
(C) testing
(D) care

Reading Practice 1

Answer Book p. 7

The Stanford Prison Experiment

The Stanford Prison Experiment was a 1971 psychological study in which subjects were randomly divided into guards and prisoners in a simulated prison environment at Stanford University. The participants, undergraduate students, were paid $15 per day to be confined to or to guard three cells, each housing three prisoners. Within a few days, the guards were engaging in aggressive and abusive behavior while the prisoners exhibited symptoms of severe anxiety and emotional distress. The guards abused their powers to the point that the experiment had to be eventually stopped, days before it was scheduled to end.

The experiment revealed how people willingly conform to the social roles they are expected to play even if doing so means harming other people. In other words, if people are given power over others, they will abuse that power. And people who are put into situations where they are powerless will be driven to obedience. The findings of the experiment were widely reported in the media and became a fixture of psychology textbooks. They have also been the subject of numerous books, movies, television programs, and documentaries.

Despite the experiment's established position among the most important studies in social science history, there have been repeated complaints about flaws in its design and implementation. For one thing, the participants were all white middle-class males. The lack of demographic diversity among the participants calls into question its validity with regard to humanity as a whole. The experiment also failed to realistically simulate a prison environment, leading many to question the study's value as a representation of behavior in a typical penal institution.

The most significant criticisms of the experiment concern violations of scientific ethics. A 2015 study published in the journal *American Psychologist* revealed recordings of the researchers instructing the guards to behave aggressively toward the prisoners. The researchers even admitted that they were motivated by the desire to receive press attention. Instead of slipping automatically into an oppressive social role, many of the guards resisted the researchers' directions. Moreover, one of the prisoners confessed to faking emotional distress in order to get out of the experiment. Many psychologists have recommended that the experiment be removed from textbooks.

Glossary

· penal institution: an institution where persons are imprisoned for punishment (e.g. a prison)

1 According to paragraph 1, participants in the Stanford Prison Experiment were

(A) employees of a prominent university
(B) provided with financial compensation
(C) patients with mental disorders
(D) allowed to choose their roles

2 The phrase "conform to" in the passage is closest in meaning to

(A) reject
(B) obey
(C) blame
(D) apply

3 The word "They" in the passage refers to

(A) people
(B) situations
(C) findings
(D) textbooks

4 The word "its" in the passage refers to

(A) experiment
(B) lack
(C) diversity
(D) question

5 According to the passage, the Stanford Prison Experiment was criticized for all of the following EXCEPT

(A) its narrow demographic focus
(B) the unethical behavior of the experimenters
(C) its failure to reproduce prison conditions
(D) the practice of recording the students

• **Vocabulary Quiz** •

The word [ ] is closest in meaning to

1 confined
ⓐ imprisoned
ⓑ liberated
ⓒ reformed

2 distress
ⓐ flaw
ⓑ pain
ⓒ disorder

3 implementation
ⓐ destruction
ⓑ enthusiasm
ⓒ operation

4 oppressive
ⓐ outgoing
ⓑ hopeless
ⓒ brutal

Reading Practice 2

Answer Book p. 8

Warning Coloration

Many animals avoid predators by hiding, while others ward off would-be threats by making themselves as conspicuous as possible. Animals in the former group use camouflage to blend into their surroundings. Animals in the latter group use a tactic called warning coloration, whereby brightly colored skin or distinctive fur markings signal to predators that an animal is harmful or has a disgusting taste. Predators that eat one of these animals remember the experience and learn to avoid repeating it.

The defensive mechanisms used by animals with warning coloration vary widely. The striking white and black stripes of the skunk are easily recognizable by other animals, allowing them to avoid this creature's foul-smelling emissions. The brilliant blue, red, yellow, and green colors of the poison dart frog alert other animals to its deadly toxic secretions. The blue-ringed octopus is a sea creature with a similar strategy: its blue rings light up and glow to warn others of its powerful venom. In the insect kingdom, butterflies and ladybugs utilize colorful exteriors to communicate the fact that they make a distinctly unappetizing meal.

Warning coloration is such an effective evolutionary strategy that other animals with no defensive mechanism sometimes mimic the distinctive coloration of other creatures. British naturalist Henry Walter Bates discovered in the mid-nineteenth century that some insects exhibit startling colors even though they do not have harmful effects to back them up. For instance, the yellowjacket fly has the striking yellow coloring of a wasp but has no sting. This is called Batesian mimicry, and it works best when the animals with defensive mechanisms outnumber those without.

The other type of warning coloration imitation is Müllerian mimicry, named for German zoologist Fritz Müller. Müllerian mimicry differs from Batesian mimicry because all species involved are unpleasant to predators. In Müllerian mimicry, one or more animal species develop similar colorations in order to increase the chances that predators will recognize their dangerous properties. Each of these species is either toxic or inedible by predators. Predators may only encounter one species, while others are protected because they look similar.

Glossary

· mimicry: the external resemblance of an organism to another organism

1 The word "conspicuous" in the passage is closest in meaning to

(A) hazardous
(B) transparent
(C) noticeable
(D) attractive

2 Which of the following is NOT an example of a defense mechanism possessed by an animal that employs warning coloration?

(A) Deadly venom
(B) Poisonous secretions
(C) Unpleasant smells
(D) Hard exteriors

3 The word "them" in the passage refers to

(A) animals
(B) insects
(C) colors
(D) effects

4 According to paragraph 3, animals that use Batesian mimicry

(A) are harmless to predators
(B) are distasteful to certain predators
(C) cooperate with species with similar properties
(D) mimic the colors of predators

5 The word "their" in the passage refers to

(A) species
(B) colorations
(C) chances
(D) predators

• Vocabulary Quiz •

The word [ ] is closest in meaning to

1 ward off
ⓐ upset
ⓑ deter
ⓒ confuse

2 distinctly
ⓐ clearly
ⓑ briefly
ⓒ mainly

3 startling
ⓐ promising
ⓑ overwhelming
ⓒ shocking

4 properties
ⓐ traits
ⓑ weapons
ⓒ sections

Reading Practice 3

Answer Book p. 8

Dime Novels

Dime novels were short books printed on cheap paper and sold for five to ten cents. Dominated by adventure stories, they were immensely popular in the United States in the late 1800s. The format owed its existence to the emergence of cheap paper and advances in printing technology, which made it profitable to produce 100-page serial tales and sell them at prices nearly everyone could afford.

The content of dime novels was commercially driven. In the beginning, they focused on the exotic lives of Native Americans, a topic of great fascination to the American public. As the Native Americans moved to reservations and out of the public view, dime novels changed their focus to the equally lucrative subjects of cowboys and crime. Eventually, the books covered other genres like romance. Writers hired to pen dime novels understood that they were expected to focus on exciting storylines, not character development or narrative experimentation. Dime novel publishers paid well, so they attracted top-notch writers such as Upton Sinclair, Jack London, and Louisa May Alcott.

While dime novels were not innovative, they did help to foster a more literate populace. When the format emerged, literacy rates were already rising as a result of educational reforms and enforcement of mandatory school attendance for people of all social classes. There were other factors at play as well. Oil lamps were making it easier to read at night. More people were starting to commute by train and streetcar, giving them time to read. Civil War soldiers on both sides had to be entertained during boring days of inaction. All lower-class readers needed was affordable reading material with stories that were accessible to the masses. Dime novels filled that void.

If the lower class devoured dime novels with delight, moralists in the middle class worried about their corrupting influence. Many considered the books a guilty pleasure. Some went so far as to describe them as "literary poison" and "evil reading" objecting especially to their depictions of criminals and assertive women. Yet far from teaching immorality, dime novels always featured protagonists who did the right thing when faced with moral dilemmas. The same complaints have been made about the numerous entertainments influenced by dime novels, including pulp fiction, comic books, and video games.

Glossary

- reservation: an area of land set apart for a special purpose (as for the use of Native Americans)
- pulp fiction: a fiction dealing with sensational subjects, often printed on poor quality paper

1 The word "they" in the passage refers to
(A) Native Americans
(B) genres
(C) writers
(D) dime novels

2 According to paragraph 2, established authors wrote dime novels because
(A) their conventional novels received promotion with a mass audience
(B) publishers of these works paid their writers generously
(C) they were permitted to experiment with new narrative forms
(D) the opportunity to write adventure stories appealed to them

3 The word "mandatory" in the passage is closest in meaning to
(A) associated
(B) monitored
(C) required
(D) scheduled

4 According to paragraph 3, all of the following contributed to increased literacy rates EXCEPT
(A) the availability of lighting
(B) the use of new transportation methods
(C) the need for entertainment during war
(D) the sale of secondhand books

5 The word "their" in the passage refers to
(A) the lower class
(B) dime novels
(C) moralists
(D) the middle class

• Vocabulary Quiz •

The word [ ] is closest in meaning to

1 lucrative	2 top-notch	3 affordable	4 immorality
ⓐ expensive	ⓐ outstanding	ⓐ genuine	ⓐ corruption
ⓑ profitable	ⓑ contemporary	ⓑ inexpensive	ⓑ confusion
ⓒ offensive	ⓒ prolific	ⓒ convenient	ⓒ damage

Reading Practice 4

Answer Book p. 9

Why the South Lost the Civil War

The American Civil War was a challenging time for the country. The total American deaths from the war exceeded those of World War I and World War II combined. Political divisions tore entire communities apart, sometimes making brothers enemies of one another, and these were so deep that the two sides could not avoid military conflict. Slavery is often given as the primary reason for the war. Yet disputes over the type of governance were equally important. Generally, the Union supported a robust centralized government, while the Confederacy favored a more democratic system based on states' rights. Ultimately, the former won the war, and the reasons for the Confederacy's loss can be viewed through internal and external factors.

There are some plausible explanations for the internal-cause argument. First, because the war was waged primarily in the South, Southerners grew very weary of war. They witnessed the burning of their towns and the destruction of their homes and farms by Union troops. Seeing these events firsthand led to feelings of low morale, and by 1865, many began to vehemently oppose the war. Some Confederate soldiers even began to desert the army. Also, the institution of slavery itself hurt the Confederate cause. Thousands of slaves fled to the North, and some of them joined the war effort. The slave migration directly strengthened the Union army by more than 100,000 men. Finally, the economy of the Confederate states was based on labor-intensive agriculture. As a result, its industrial and technological capabilities were not very advanced.

Still, experts generally agree that the main reasons for the defeat of the Confederate states by the Union states were external. The Union was simply superior in military, economic, and industrial resources. It had a population of 18.5 million, approximately three times the number of soldiers, and considerably more money in the bank. Also, prior to the start of the war, it manufactured 97 percent of the country's firearms and had a fully developed factory infrastructure. More directly, the military might and winning strategies of the Union army created a series of victories that the South could not overcome. Thus, the majority of modern historians believe that the South was destined to lose the war regardless of any internal issues of the Confederacy.

Glossary

- the Union: the group of Northern states that remained part of the US during the Civil War
- the Confederacy: the 11 Southern states that separated themselves from the US during the Civil War

1 The word "these" in the passage refers to

(A) deaths
(B) political divisions
(C) communities
(D) enemies

2 The word "robust" in the passage is closest in meaning to

(A) trustworthy
(B) powerful
(C) subordinate
(D) efficient

3 The word "many" in the passage refers to

(A) Southerners
(B) Union troops
(C) events
(D) feelings

4 According to paragraph 2, why were the South's industrial and technological abilities limited?

(A) It had a farming economy built on manual workers.
(B) It lost a significant amount of slave labor to the North.
(C) It refused to adopt practices that were common in the North.
(D) It devoted minimal economic resources to the war effort.

5 Which of the following is NOT mentioned as an external factor for the defeat of the Confederate states?

(A) The larger population of the Union
(B) The Union's monetary reserves
(C) The military strategy of the Union
(D) The Union's superior firearm designs

• Vocabulary Quiz •

The word [ ] is closest in meaning to

1 disputes
ⓐ conflicts
ⓑ boundaries
ⓒ strikes

2 weary
ⓐ annoyed
ⓑ tired
ⓒ depressed

3 vehemently
ⓐ especially
ⓑ unusually
ⓒ fiercely

4 manufactured
ⓐ discovered
ⓑ exchanged
ⓒ produced

Answer Book p. 10

TOEFL Reading

Natural and Synthetic Diamonds

➡ Natural diamonds are more expensive than synthetic diamonds, even though they share the same chemical composition. What distinguishes the two is that the former were forged millions of years ago in the heat of the earth's mantle. They ascended through volcanic eruption and were mined in one of three ways. In alluvial mining, diamonds are sifted from sand in riverbeds and coasts. In underground mining, explosives are used to extract diamonds in a tunnel. Marine mining utilizes machines to collect diamonds from the ocean floor. Synthetic diamonds, on the other hand, are grown in a laboratory. 5

It can be impossible to tell a mined diamond from a laboratory-made diamond by looking at it. With both kinds, the diamond's quality is appraised by the 4Cs—cut, clarity, carat, and color. A well-cut or faceted diamond sparkles, offering the greatest brilliance and value. The clarity of the diamond can also affect the brilliance, as naturally occurring imperfections, called inclusions, might obstruct the path of light through a diamond. Size is measured in carat weight, where one carat is 200 mg. Diamonds may also have color tones, and the rarity of a particular color affects the price of the diamond. Natural blue diamonds are particularly scarce and therefore greatly valued. 10 15

➡ Synthetic diamonds are colored through a process called irradiation. Irradiated diamonds are colorless diamonds that have been treated with a special combination of radiation and intense heating to bring forth a wide spectrum of rich, fancy colors. The treatment creates a permanent color change, and it leaves no harmful traces of radiation on the diamond. Irradiated diamonds have a significantly lower value than naturally occurring colored diamonds, and they can be detected for what they really are through careful analysis in a properly equipped laboratory setting. 20

➡ Much of the cost of synthetic diamonds comes from the expensive process of cutting them. [A] Because diamond is the hardest substance, the use of another diamond is required to cut it. [B] Diamond cutters in Antwerp first achieved this in 1550. [C] Since then, the diamond has become a fundamental industrial material used to cut, grind, and polish hard substances. [D] In fact, 80 percent of the diamonds mined annually are used in industry, and four times that amount is grown synthetically for industry use—over 500 million carats a year. 25

Glossary
alluvial: of materials deposited by running water

Volume Review Help Back Next

1 The word "forged" in the passage is closest in meaning to

(A) created
(B) discovered
(C) transported
(D) mined

2 According to paragraph 1, which of the following techniques is NOT used to mine diamonds?

(A) Blowing them out of the ground
(B) Drilling into the earth's mantle
(C) Finding them in a river or beach
(D) Removing them from the bottom of the sea

Paragraph 1 is marked with an arrow [➡].

3 Which of the following does NOT affect the value of a diamond?

(A) Weight
(B) Shape
(C) Color
(D) Composition

4 The word "it" in the passage refers to

(A) radiation
(B) spectrum
(C) treatment
(D) change

5 According to paragraph 3, radiation is used on diamonds

Ⓐ to polish the surface
Ⓑ to alter the color
Ⓒ to increase the brilliance
Ⓓ to boost its value

Paragraph 3 is marked with an arrow [➡].

6 It can be inferred from the passage that the color of irradiated diamonds

Ⓐ is limited to a few colors
Ⓑ will not fade
Ⓒ is brighter than naturally colored diamonds
Ⓓ will be radioactive

7 The word "fundamental" in the passage is closest in meaning to

Ⓐ essential
Ⓑ popular
Ⓒ durable
Ⓓ simple

8 According to paragraph 4, industrial diamonds are used to

Ⓐ find gem diamonds
Ⓑ produce irradiated diamonds
Ⓒ judge diamond quality
Ⓓ reshape hard materials

Paragraph 4 is marked with an arrow [➡].

9 Look at the four squares [■] that indicate where the following sentence could be added to the passage.

These include stones, ceramics, metals, and concrete, as well as eyeglasses, gems, and computer chips.

Where would the sentence best fit?

Click on a square [■] to add the sentence to the passage.

10 **Directions:** An introductory sentence for a brief summary of the passage is provided below. Complete the summary by selecting the THREE answer choices that express the most important ideas in the passage. Some sentences do not belong in the summary because they express ideas that are not presented in the passage or are minor ideas in the passage. **This question is worth 2 points.**

Drag your answer choices to the spaces where they belong.
To remove an answer choice, click on it. To review the passage, click on **View Text**.

Diamonds are either natural or man-made.

•

•

•

Answer Choices

Ⓐ All diamonds are formed deep in the earth's crust.

Ⓑ Alluvial mining requires the miner to sift through the sand in rivers.

Ⓒ A diamond's quality is measured using four criteria.

Ⓓ Synthetic diamonds are colored by exposing them to heat and radiation.

Ⓔ Diamond is the hardest substance on the planet.

Ⓕ Both natural and synthetic diamonds are used in various industries.

Answer Book p. 10

Vocabulary Review

A. Fill in the blanks with the appropriate words from the box.

immune	randomly	obedience
complaints	fascination	brilliance

1 You cannot see the ____________ of the gem until it is polished and shined.

2 The captain required complete ____________ from his soldiers at all times.

3 Celebrities are a source of ____________ to many who are captivated by their stardom.

4 The new virus is very dangerous because it is ____________ to vaccinations.

5 Winners were ____________ chosen by picking numbers out of a hat.

6 There were several ____________ from consumers about the product's poor design.

B. Choose the closest meaning for each highlighted word or phrase.

7 You should be more assertive in a meeting if you want your opinion to be heard.
(A) timid (B) appealing (C) enigmatic (D) confident

8 These clothes are half off because of some small imperfections in the stitching.
(A) defects (B) holes (C) tears (D) wounds

9 Residents complained that the new building obstructed the view of the mountains.
(A) altered (B) improved (C) blocked (D) expelled

10 The depiction of the Queen in the portrait looked almost like a photograph.
(A) significance (B) representation (C) dignity (D) exaggeration

11 The theory that life on Earth came from Mars is plausible but not proven.
(A) reasonable (B) specific (C) impressive (D) perfect

12 There was a recognizable improvement in the computer after I upgraded the software.
(A) sudden (B) obvious (C) gradual (D) important

13 Deer have been scarce in this area because of their predators such as wolves.
(A) dull (B) routine (C) urgent (D) rare

14 The new web browser delivers significantly faster search results than the previous one.
(A) sufficiently (B) readily (C) quite (D) relatively

CHAPTER 03

Sentence Simplification

Sentence Simplification

About the Question Type

Sentence Simplification questions ask you to choose the sentence that best summarizes the highlighted sentence in the passage.

Incorrect choices often change the original meaning of the highlighted sentence or leave out essential information. Therefore, make sure that your answer choice paraphrases the key information of the sentence.

Question Format

Which of the sentences below best expresses the essential information in the highlighted sentence in the passage? *Incorrect* choices change the meaning in important ways or leave out essential information.

Key Strategies

- **Step 1** — Read the highlighted sentence in the passage and identify its essential information.
- **Step 2** — Select the answer choice that most accurately paraphrases the essential information of the sentence. Keep in mind that an answer choice that does not fully restate the essential information cannot be the correct one.

Example

Answer Book p. 11

Discovering Gravitation

A number of early physicists contributed to the acceptance of gravitation as a natural and universal force. [1]Ancient Greek philosophers thought that the motions of the stars and planets were completely unrelated to events on Earth. Galileo was one of the first physicists to agree with the Copernican view that Earth orbited around the Sun. This was in contradiction to the established view held from ancient times. Most people believed that the planets and stars revolved around Earth. Johannes Kepler took the research of his mentor, Tycho Brahe, to formulate the laws of planetary motion known as Kepler's Laws. Kepler was able to show that the planets moved in elliptical paths around the Sun. [2]The stage was now set for Sir Isaac Newton to describe a more general law that governs gravitational forces. His observations of the motion of the Moon, the tides, and even comets helped him develop the universal law of gravitation.

Glossary

· Copernican: of the astronomical theories of Nicolaus Copernicus

1 Which of the sentences below best expresses the essential information in the highlighted sentence in the passage?

(A) Ancient Greeks did not believe the stars and planets moved on their own.
(B) The stars and planets move without regard to things that happen on Earth.
(C) Events on Earth dictate the motions of the stars and planets, contrary to the opinion of Greek philosophers.
(D) According to the ancient Greeks, earthly events were not affected by stellar and planetary ones.

2 Which of the sentences below best expresses the essential information in the highlighted sentence in the passage?

(A) Sir Isaac Newton could now offer a comprehensive principle of gravity.
(B) Sir Isaac Newton was forced to revise his law of gravitational forces.
(C) The theory of gravitational forces was accepted by Sir Isaac Newton.
(D) That gravity followed a set rule was initially rejected by Sir Isaac Newton.

Reading Practice 1

Answer Book p. 12

Edward Hopper

The painter Edward Hopper is considered one of the most notable members of the American Realism art movement. Certainly, his depictions of ordinary urban settings fit into that movement's emphasis on everyday people rather than the rich and famous. [1]Yet his ability to infuse his subjects with subtle melancholy places him in the tradition of the Symbolists, who saw little point in objectively reproducing reality without exposing their own subjective feelings. For Hopper, a depiction of a woman looking out a high-rise window in his 1926 *Eleven A.M.* was not only a study in light and shadow but also an opportunity to express his own loneliness. Similarly, the simple late-night diner scene in his 1942 classic *Nighthawks* became a commentary on war-era anxiety. 5

Hopper's focus on the isolation of modern life reflected his own personality. The painter had little interest in small talk, and he disliked discussing his own work. Instead, he preferred to let his art speak for itself, saying that "the whole answer is there on the canvas." [4]His social sphere was largely restricted to the company of his wife of 43 years, Josephine Hopper, an artist herself who also served as his most frequent female model. Although he was a prolific artist, his work was ignored in the art world for many years. 10 15

Josephine's connections in the New York art world helped Hopper to achieve financial success late in life. Although he became devoted to his art as a child, Hopper did not sell his first painting until he was in his 30s or his second painting until 11 years later. After their marriage, Josephine was able to win an exhibition for Hopper in the Brooklyn Museum. This led to his establishment as a major artist toward the end of the Great Depression, when he was around 50 years old. In 1933, the Museum of Modern Art made up for lost time with a retrospective exhibition, something it rarely did for a living artist. Today, Hopper's paintings are highly prized by collectors. In 2018, a 1929 oil painting depicting his courtship of Josephine, *Chop Suey*, sold for a record $92 million. 20

Glossary

· retrospective exhibition: an art exhibit of work that an artist has done in the past

1 Which of the sentences below best expresses the essential information in the highlighted sentence in the passage?

(A) Hopper painted subjects without considering their feelings, just like the Symbolists.
(B) Symbolists believed that showing the feelings of their subjects was more important than realistic depictions.
(C) Hopper's paintings resembled those of Symbolists in that they reflected his own feelings on the subjects.
(D) Despite Hopper's preference for reproducing reality, he enjoyed the paintings of the Symbolists.

2 According to paragraph 1, Hopper is considered an American Realist because he

(A) drew urban locations and people instead of rural ones
(B) was fascinated by people of substantial wealth
(C) preferred to paint regular people living out their daily lives
(D) portrayed life as it appeared rather than as he felt it to be

3 The word "isolation" in the passage is closest in meaning to

(A) solitude (B) obsession (C) affection (D) vitality

4 Which of the sentences below best expresses the essential information in the highlighted sentence in the passage?

(A) Hopper had little contact with artists; he preferred to socialize with female models like his wife Josephine.
(B) Socially, Hopper spent most of his time with his wife, also a painter, who modeled for many of his paintings.
(C) Artist Josephine Hopper was the longtime wife of Edward Hopper, and they posed for each other's paintings.
(D) Hopper's social circle was narrower than that of his wife, Josephine, who insisted on modeling for his work.

5 The word "it" in the passage refers to

(A) establishment
(B) the Great Depression
(C) the Museum of Modern Art
(D) exhibition

• Vocabulary Quiz •

The word [   ] is closest in meaning to

1 notable	2 anxiety	3 restricted	4 prolific
ⓐ prominent	ⓐ suspicion	ⓐ validated	ⓐ productive
ⓑ obscure	ⓑ complexity	ⓑ approved	ⓑ professional
ⓒ experimental	ⓒ worry	ⓒ limited	ⓒ proficient

Reading Practice 2

Answer Book p. 12

The Automobile and Suburbanization

The invention of the automobile contributed to the rise of the suburbs in the early twentieth century. Henry Ford's automobile company began to mass-produce the affordable Model T in 1908. It spread like wildfire across the United States, realizing Ford's dream of manufacturing a car so low in price that the man of moderate means may own one. Cars like the Model T allowed commuters to live further from their place of employment and eliminated restrictions on travel. As a result, people fled the crowded cities in droves, building large single-family homes on spacious properties outside of the city cores.

[3]In addition to providing the transportation necessary for the mass migration to the suburbs, Ford intentionally spurred suburban growth by raising wages and encouraging his workers to move out of the city. To facilitate this suburban development, he moved his automobile factory to Dearborn, a new suburb of Detroit. Suburbs full of industrial workers with cars and disposable incomes sprouted throughout the Midwestern states in the 1920s and '30s. [4]However, critics of suburbanization pointed out that most of the homes belonged to wealthier white-collar workers while manual laborers, particularly African Americans, remained in cities that were increasingly deprived of resources by the exodus to the suburbs.

Because of the increase in the number of cars on the roads, state and local governments responded with massive road-building projects. In the 1950s, the federal government began a major expansion of the interstate highway system. However, this resulted in congestion in the central cities, giving people still more incentive to move to the suburbs.

In the 1990s, suburban growth slowed and urban growth increased as density in the first tier of suburbs reached urban levels, causing some of the suburbs to become cities themselves. In the West, where features of the land often made growth difficult or impossible, suburbs became increasingly dense. However, this was not the case in the South, where there were fewer natural barriers to suburban growth. Moreover, the density of Southern first-tier suburbs was lower, resulting in further spreading of suburbs farther from the cities.

1 The word "spacious" in the passage is closest in meaning to

(A) accessible (B) ample (C) convenient (D) secure

2 According to paragraph 1, people moved to the suburbs because

(A) automobiles were easier to store on spacious properties
(B) it was more affordable to live in the suburbs than in the city
(C) travel restrictions prevented them from driving in the city
(D) the automobile enabled them to make long commutes

3 Which of the sentences below best expresses the essential information in the highlighted sentence in the passage?

(A) Ford funded the growth of the suburbs by increasing the amount of money he paid to his suburban employees.
(B) Ford increased suburban populations not only by making cars but also by paying his workers more and supporting their relocation.
(C) Whereas Ford decided to boost suburban populations, he gave his employees a raise that helped them leave suburbs.
(D) Since he wished to see more people in the suburbs, Ford made the automobiles that suburban life required.

4 Which of the sentences below best expresses the essential information in the highlighted sentence in the passage?

(A) Suburbanization was criticized that African American manual laborers were unfairly treated by the people who moved away from the cities.
(B) People criticized that wealthy homeowners in the suburbs left insufficient resources for manual laborers in the cities.
(C) Those who criticized suburbanization emphasized how it negatively affected the relationships between white-collar and manual workers.
(D) Suburbanization was criticized because it left manual workers in impoverished cities while suburban homes were owned by white-collar.

5 According to paragraph 4, which of the following is true of the South in the 1990s?

(A) Suburban populations grew large enough to become cities.
(B) Suburban expansion was held in check by the lack of resources.
(C) Suburbs extended to at great distances from urban centers.
(D) Suburban growth stalled as people moved back to the cities.

• Vocabulary Quiz •

The word [ ] is closest in meaning to

1 eliminated
ⓐ removed
ⓑ dispersed
ⓒ installed

2 fled
ⓐ observed
ⓑ selected
ⓒ escaped

3 spurred
ⓐ eased
ⓑ pushed
ⓒ revived

4 incentive
ⓐ motivation
ⓑ impulse
ⓒ capacity

Reading Practice 3

Answer Book p. 13

The Allende Meteorite

The Allende meteorite is the oldest meteorite ever discovered on Earth. The automobile-sized meteor crashed into the planet on February 8, 1969. It burnt and broke up upon entry into Earth's atmosphere and leaving scattered fragments near the Mexican city of Pueblito de Allende. Since the impact, some two tons of meteorite have been collected and analyzed. By measuring the ratio of isotopes in the meteorite, scientists estimated that the object was about 4.57 billion years old, making it older than Earth. [2]Prior to its collision with Earth, the Allende meteorite likely escaped the asteroid belt that exists between Mars and Jupiter.

Meteors are relatively small space rocks that enter Earth's atmosphere, often fragments of larger space rocks called asteroids. When they burn up in the atmosphere, they are known as shooting stars. The pieces of the meteor that land on the surface of the planet are called meteorites. Every day, about 25 million meteors bombard Earth. Few of them result in meteorites, and most of the rocks that strike Earth's surface fall into the ocean.

Among those space rock fragments that have been analyzed by scientists, the Allende meteorite is easily the most studied. That is because it was probably created during the formation of the solar system. It is most likely debris from the formation of the planets. By studying these ancient fragments, scientists hope to learn more about the solar system's origins. [5]For example, the substance in the Allende meteorite indicates that the time between the supernova that created the Sun and the formation of the planets may have been relatively short, perhaps only twenty to fifty thousand years.

The space rock contains minerals that have never been found on Earth. That is significant since over 5,000 minerals have been identified on this planet, only 65 of which date back to the creation of the solar system. Scientists have found 19 new minerals in the Allende meteorite samples. These inclusions become embedded inside the meteorite as the rock formed in intense nebular heat, just as Earth minerals are formed in the heat of the planet's core.

Glossary

· isotope: an element that shares the same number of protons but has different numbers of neutrons
· nebular: relating to a dense cloud of interstellar gas and dust

1 The word "scattered" in the passage is closest in meaning to

(A) prepared
(B) designated
(C) spread
(D) absorbed

2 Which of the sentences below best expresses the essential information in the highlighted sentence in the passage?

(A) Either Mars or Jupiter is the most likely source of the asteroid that collided with Earth.
(B) An object passed by Mars and Jupiter before a collision with it and Earth finally occurred.
(C) The Allende meteorite probably broke free from the asteroid belt before reaching our planet.
(D) The asteroid belt is the origin of the meteors that hit the planets in our solar system.

3 According to the passage, scientists dated the Allende meteorite by

(A) tracing the formation of minerals to the origins of the solar system
(B) analyzing isotope compositions in the meteorite
(C) referring to previous studies of meteorites found in the ocean
(D) comparing the Allende meteorite with similar meteorites

4 The word "them" in the passage refers to

(A) asteroids
(B) shooting stars
(C) meteorites
(D) meteors

5 Which of the sentences below best expresses the essential information in the highlighted sentence in the passage?

(A) The Allende meteorite's makeup suggests the Sun and planets formed up to fifty thousand years apart.
(B) The Sun was created in a supernova according to the materials in the Allende meteorite.
(C) For twenty to fifty thousand years, the planets formed following the Sun's supernova.
(D) The Allende meteorite was formed in a supernova twenty to fifty thousand years after the Sun's creation.

• Vocabulary Quiz •

The word [ ] is closest in meaning to

1 fragments
ⓐ conflicts
ⓑ tactics
ⓒ pieces

2 measuring
ⓐ developing
ⓑ calculating
ⓒ removing

3 probably
ⓐ maybe
ⓑ nearly
ⓒ obviously

4 debris
ⓐ mixtures
ⓑ ingredients
ⓒ remains

Reading Practice 4

Answer Book p. 14

The History of Vatican City

Vatican City, the home of the pope and the headquarters of the Roman Catholic Church, is an independent city-state. It only occupies about 100 acres of territory near the center of Rome, but it has its own government, of which the pope is the absolute monarch. The 800 people who reside within Vatican City are either clergy or members of the Swiss Guard, the small army that defends the state. [1]The Vatican does not collect taxes to pay for its expenses; rather, tourism, merchandising, and contributions pay the city's bills. To have a tiny sovereign state enclosed entirely within a larger nation is a unique arrangement. How did it come to be?

The Vatican became the center of the Catholic Church in AD 324. This is the year when a public building called a basilica was constructed by the first Christian emperor of Rome, Constantine I. The site of the basilica is believed to be the grave of the Apostle Peter, who is considered the church's first pope. Saint Peter's Basilica has always been a holy place for the Catholic people. It is also one of the largest churches in the world. The basilica's dome is one of the most recognizable architectural features in all of Italy. It is a popular destination for pilgrims and tourists.

The Vatican's status as a government was a source of tension with the surrounding governments for centuries. From the eighth century until 1870, the Vatican was not just a religious center but the seat of power for political entities called the Papal States. [2]The boundaries of the Papal States varied over a period of hundreds of years, but at one point or another much of present-day Italy was subject to rule by the pope. When Italy unified under the rule of King Victor Emmanuel II in 1860, the era of political power for the pope appeared to be ending. Indeed, in 1870, Italy declared war on the Papal States and claimed all territory outside the walls of Vatican City. The tension between Italy and Vatican City was finally resolved with the rise of Prime Minister Benito Mussolini. In 1929, Mussolini signed an agreement that recognized Vatican City as a sovereign entity. The church was paid $92 million to compensate for the loss of the Papal States.

Glossary

· Papal States: territories of central Italy that were directly governed by the pope from 756 to 1870

1 Which of the sentences below best expresses the essential information in the highlighted sentence in the passage?

(A) Whereas the Vatican does not tax its citizens, it does charge tourists for the privilege of visiting.
(B) The Vatican acquires revenue from visitors, sales, and donations, but it does not receive taxes.
(C) Tourists cover the Vatican's obligations by paying for admission and souvenirs.
(D) The Vatican taxes its residents even though it gets plenty of money from non-residents.

2 Which of the sentences below best expresses the essential information in the highlighted sentence in the passage?

(A) The citizens of Italy were governed by the pope, although the state lines were inconsistent.
(B) The borders of the Papal States, which included large parts of Italy, shifted for centuries.
(C) Throughout its history, Italy allowed much of the territory to be ruled by the pope.
(D) The Papal States were territories in Italy that had constantly fluctuating boundaries.

3 The word "resolved" in the passage is closest in meaning to

(A) settled
(B) returned
(C) concluded
(D) hindered

4 According to paragraph 3, Benito Mussolini signed a document that

(A) acknowledged the independence of a state
(B) demanded compensation for lost territories
(C) created an alliance between two countries
(D) established the role of a nation's leader

5 The author's description of Vatican City mentions all of the following EXCEPT its

(A) origins as a burial place
(B) means of protecting itself
(C) conflicts with neighboring powers
(D) methods of electing rulers

• Vocabulary Quiz •

The word [ ] is closest in meaning to

1 absolute	2 expenses	3 sovereign	4 tension
ⓐ uniform	ⓐ costs	ⓐ autonomous	ⓐ strain
ⓑ complete	ⓑ values	ⓑ principal	ⓑ closeness
ⓒ temporary	ⓒ debts	ⓒ exceptional	ⓒ tolerance

Answer Book p. 15

TOEFL Reading

The First Whale

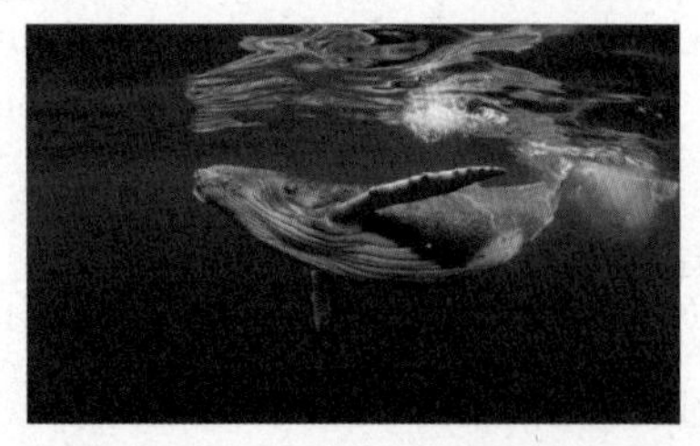

➡ Considering that all animals evolved from sea creatures during the Cambrian age more than 400 million years ago, one might imagine that whales are directly descended from an underwater species. But nature seldom progresses that simply. In reality, the cetacean family, 5 which today consists of whales, dolphins, and porpoises, apparently originated some fifty million years ago with a four-legged, wolf-like mammal.

➡ In the early 1980s, a team of paleontologists discovered the collection of fossils in the northern part of Pakistan and immediately recognized that it included a long skull similar to that of a whale. They named this creature Pakicetus meaning "Pakistan whale." Later, it was 10 found that the creature's skull had a bony wall around the inner ear that enabled it to hear underwater. This constituted a striking link between land mammals and contemporary whales.

As more fossils were discovered, scientists pieced together the creature's habitat and means of subsistence. Pakicetus divided its time between the shore and the sea. Its long legs ended in webbed feet that made it a natural swimmer. It also had powerful teeth that 15 likely gave it the ability to tear the flesh of fish and small animals, which it could reach with a twist of its flexible neck. The animal's molars showed evidence of scraping that suggests it ground its teeth when it chewed. At the back end of the creature was a long tail.

➡ The fossil record suggests that descendants of Pakicetus evolved over the next fifteen million years to enhance their water-friendly features. The webbed feet gradually morphed 20 into flippers. Eventually, the aquatic baleen whale emerged. Over a period of about thirty-five million years, whales grew larger and larger, growing from twenty feet to an average of forty feet in length. The increase in size likely occurred so the whales could evade large predators in the sea. **A** Such an occurrence is a common phenomenon in evolution; it is thought that animals that evolve over a long period of time generally tend to get larger. **B** Even so, the 25 process has had an extreme effect on whales. **C** That this monstrous creature is descended from the diminutive Pakicetus is a wonder of nature. **D**

Glossary
molar: a tooth at the back of the mouth for grinding food

Volume Review Help Back Next

1 According to paragraph 1, which of the following is true of cetaceans?

Ⓐ They walked on land during the Cambrian era.
Ⓑ The only cetaceans living today are whales.
Ⓒ The oldest known cetaceans had four legs.
Ⓓ They emerged from the sea about fifty million years ago.

Paragraph 1 is marked with an arrow [➡].

2 The word "it" in the passage refers to

Ⓐ team
Ⓑ collection
Ⓒ part
Ⓓ Pakistan

3 The word "contemporary" in the passage is closest in meaning to

Ⓐ mature
Ⓑ massive
Ⓒ modern
Ⓓ marine

4 According to paragraph 2, the first Pakicetus skull was linked to modern whales because it

Ⓐ was as large as a modern whale's skull
Ⓑ had an inner ear structure like a whale's
Ⓒ was found in a sea populated by modern whales
Ⓓ had a distinctive bony wall around its teeth

Paragraph 2 is marked with an arrow [➡].

5 Which of the sentences below best expresses the essential information in the highlighted sentence in the passage? *Incorrect* choices change the meaning in important ways or leave out essential information.

- (A) Scientists learned from subsequent fossils where the animal lived and what it ate.
- (B) When they found additional fossils, scientists put pieces of the body together.
- (C) The organism's dwelling place and eating habits emerged over time.
- (D) Scientists searched for fossil fragments in the organism's habitat.

6 Which of the following is NOT mentioned in the author's description of Pakicetus?

- (A) Agile neck
- (B) Strong teeth
- (C) Finned tail
- (D) Webbed feet

7 The word "morphed" in the passage is closest in meaning to

- (A) adopted
- (B) transformed
- (C) exceeded
- (D) functioned

8 According to paragraph 4, whales grew larger over time because

- (A) they consumed very large sea creatures
- (B) their size enabled them to deter predators
- (C) larger animals are better at swimming
- (D) they needed to evade large dinosaurs

Paragraph 4 is marked with an arrow [➡].

9 Look at the four squares [■] that indicate where the following sentence could be added to the passage.

This is illustrated by the blue whale, which weighs approximately 200 tons and is the largest animal ever to occupy the planet.

Where would the sentence best fit?

Click on a square [■] to add the sentence to the passage.

10 **Directions:** An introductory sentence for a brief summary of the passage is provided below. Complete the summary by selecting the THREE answer choices that express the most important ideas in the passage. Some sentences do not belong in the summary because they express ideas that are not presented in the passage or are minor ideas in the passage. **This question is worth 2 points.**

Drag your answer choices to the spaces where they belong.
To remove an answer choice, click on it. To review the passage, click on **View Text**.

It is surprising that whales are descended from land animals.

-
-
-

Answer Choices

Ⓐ The oldest known ancestor of whales was a wolf-like creature.

Ⓑ Whale skulls and Pakicetus skulls share distinct features.

Ⓒ The first Pakicetus fossil was found in a Pakistani sea.

Ⓓ Pakicetus bones taught scientists about its habits.

Ⓔ Whales have flippers that were originally webbed feet.

Ⓕ Pakicetus's descendants evolved to become sea-dwellers.

Answer Book p. 15

Vocabulary Review

A. Fill in the blanks with the appropriate words from the box.

congestion	retrospective	disposable
elliptical	revolved	occurrence

1 People thought the Sun ____________ around the Earth and not the other way around.

2 Many young adults spend most of their ____________ income on hobbies.

3 There is a lot of ____________ on the highway because of the ongoing construction.

4 The gallery held a ____________ exhibit that showed the painter's entire past works.

5 Most planets follow an ____________ path rather than a perfectly circular one.

6 Neck pain is a common ____________ among those who work in an office.

B. Choose the closest meaning for each highlighted word or phrase.

7 Cryptocurrency is steadily gaining acceptance at major financial institutes.
(A) interference (B) contemplation (C) approval (D) devotion

8 A number of excellent students do not have the means to go to a good college.
(A) drive (B) degree (C) wealth (D) chance

9 Mental health is affected negatively when employees are deprived of ample rest.
(A) undergoing (B) enacting (C) lacking (D) needing

10 The guest had to pay $500 to compensate for the damage he caused to the hotel.
(A) concur (B) repay (C) switch (D) object

11 The car was seriously damaged, but no one was injured in the collision.
(A) setback (B) force (C) crash (D) conflict

12 Newton formulated the theory of universal gravitation after watching an apple fall.
(A) estimated (B) provoked (C) discerned (D) developed

13 The festival constituted a way to help the charity and provide fun for the community.
(A) governed (B) pronounced (C) mitigated (D) established

14 The scuba divers emerged from the water as the sun was setting.
(A) surfaced (B) launched (C) retracted (D) wavered

CHAPTER 04

Fact

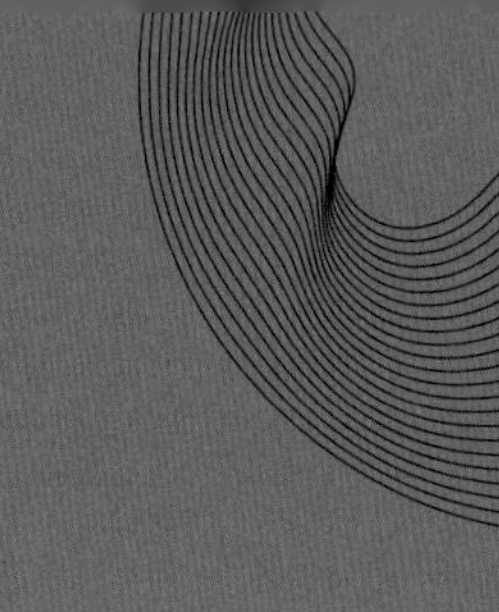

Fact

About the Question Type

Fact questions ask you to identify specific information that is explicitly stated in the passage.

The correct answer choice restates specific information in the passage that directly answers the question. Incorrect answer choices include information that is contradicted by the passage, irrelevant to the question, or not mentioned in the passage.

Question Format

- According to paragraph #, which of the following is true of X?
- According to paragraph #, what/how/why . . . ?
- The author's description/discussion of X mentions which of the following?

Key Strategies

- **Step 1** — Read the question and identify the keywords. If the question indicates a specific paragraph, you can ignore the rest of the passage.
- **Step 2** — Scan the passage for the keywords, and locate the relevant information.
- **Step 3** — Select the answer choice that correctly paraphrases the relevant information in the passage.

Example

Answer Book p. 16

Salamanders and Newts

The newt and the salamander are actually the same animal. The name *salamander* is the scientific term that applies to the fully aquatic and fully terrestrial animals. The name *newt* is affixed to those salamanders that live on land from late summer through winter, entering water to breed in the spring. Often mistaken for lizards due to their long tails, salamanders have frog-like soft, moist skin covering their bodies. They can be as long as six inches but are usually smaller. Their legs are so short that their bellies touch the ground as they crawl. They have no scales, claws, or external ear openings. The majority of salamanders and their larvae are carnivorous, eating insects and small invertebrates. The larvae begin feeding immediately after hatching, devouring tiny aquatic animals. Large adults eat fish, frogs, and other salamanders. Salamanders are chiefly nocturnal, hiding under fallen logs and damp leaf litter during the daylight hours.

Glossary

· invertebrate: an animal that lacks a backbone, such as insects and snails (↔ vertebrate)

1 According to the passage, which of the following is true of the newt?

(A) It is smaller than a salamander.
(B) Its habitat depends on the season.
(C) It moves onto land to breed in the summer.
(D) It has scaly skin like a lizard.

2 The author's description of the salamander mentions which of the following?

(A) The exact length of its tail
(B) The average hours it sleeps at night
(C) Its preferred types of food
(D) Its unusually long legs

Answer Book p. 17

The Roman Road System

The ancient Romans developed a road system that is considered one of the greatest engineering feats of all time. The expression "all roads lead to Rome" was in fact true in that the system of highways linked Rome to the most distant provinces of the Roman Empire. 5 There were over 50,000 miles of paved roads in the territories controlled by Rome.

The roads were efficiently constructed and made to last. Four layers of materials comprised most of the roads. The uppermost layer was made of flat, hard stones, concrete, and pebbles set in mortar. The second layer was made of cement mixed with 10 broken tiles. The third layer had broken stones, sand, cement, and pebbles to make a firm base. The deepest layer was composed of large stones. The roads were constructed in such a way that even in inclement weather, travelers would not experience inconvenience. In fact, roads were crowned; that is, the middle of the road was higher than the sides of the road. This allowed water to run off to the sides where it was caught in gutters that 15 drained the water.

Rome's conquest of Celtic Britain resulted in the building of a network of roads that improved travel in Britain. Primarily, the Romans found a haphazard collection of roads and paths. To facilitate the movement of troops and the flow of trade goods, Rome established a more orderly network of roads. The Romans initially concentrated on 20 the channel ports of Richborough, Dover, and Lympne in order to channel supplies to military centers. Only after these roads had been established did the Romans begin to expand on a network of minor roads. This resulted in the linking of economic centers such as mining towns and pottery centers. The final level of roads constructed by the Romans was at the local level. These connected villas, farms, and villages to larger roads 25 and market towns.

Generally, the Roman roads in Britain were laid out in straight lines, but where obstacles proved hard to remove, the Romans built the road around them. To help travelers find their way, the Romans placed milestones at certain points. The milestones gave travelers the distance remaining to the nearest largest city. The roads were so well 30 built that they survived for centuries, and many modern streets in the United Kingdom were constructed on top of them.

1 The author's description of the uppermost layer of the Roman roads mentions which of the following?

(A) It was mostly composed of cement.
(B) It included holes for drainage.
(C) It combined tiles with cement.
(D) It made a strong and flat surface.

2 According to paragraph 2, the Roman roads were crowned in order to

(A) prevent the roads from flooding
(B) ensure an efficient construction process
(C) help travelers find their way
(D) provide an indication of road length

3 The word "haphazard" in the passage is closest in meaning to

(A) obvious
(B) disorganized
(C) efficient
(D) expansive

4 According to paragraph 3, why did the earliest Roman roads in Britain connect to port cities?

(A) To provide food and equipment to soldiers
(B) To increase trade across the English Channel
(C) To join places of economic importance
(D) To establish additional centers of industry

5 According to paragraph 4, which of the following is NOT true of the Roman roads in Britain?

(A) They provided the foundation of contemporary roads.
(B) They were built to avoid barriers.
(C) They featured markers indicating the distance to destinations.
(D) They mostly followed winding routes.

• Vocabulary Quiz •

The word [ ] is closest in meaning to

1 inclement
ⓐ suitable
ⓑ abrupt
ⓒ harsh

2 orderly
ⓐ distant
ⓑ sturdy
ⓒ organized

3 initially
ⓐ eagerly
ⓑ originally
ⓒ ordinarily

4 obstacles
ⓐ barriers
ⓑ materials
ⓒ processes

Reading Practice 2

Answer Book p. 17

Wampum

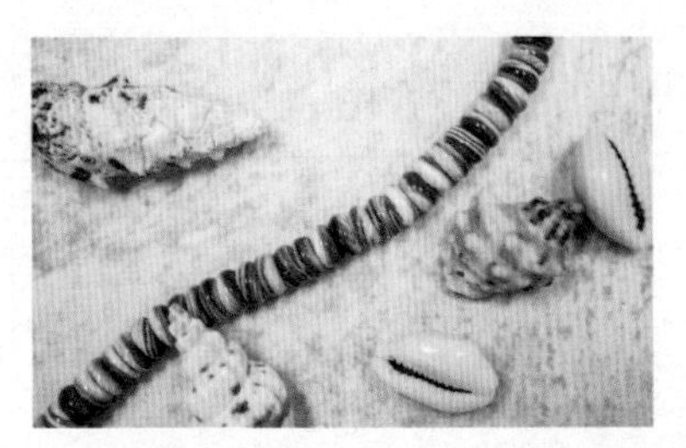

Wampum were beads made by indigenous people in northeastern North America. The beads were made from mollusk shells that were collected from the Atlantic coast, sanded smooth, and drilled. Typically, they were either white or purple and strung together to make belts or other forms of jewelry. Skilled labor was required to make wampum, and they acquired spiritual, historical, and political significance. Thus, they were highly prized by tribal communities. While wampum was sometimes thought to be a Native American currency because it was traded for goods and services, the beads were not used as money until Europeans got involved.

For the natives, the primary value of wampum was spiritual and symbolic. The Iroquois believed it could bring the living in contact with the dead. The Algonquins viewed the colors of the beads as symbols that are similar to the Chinese concept of yin and yang: the white represented lightness and life while the purple stood for darkness and death. In some cultures, wampum belts were also used to mark diplomatic agreements. For instance, the Two Row Wampum Belt depicted a canoe and a European ship to symbolize peace between indigenous people and Dutch colonists.

The Europeans were largely oblivious to the significance of wampum until 1622, when a Dutch trader received them as ransom after taking a native hostage. The Dutch punished the hostage-taker but subsequently began to offer furs in exchange for wampum, which they then traded to other tribes in order to acquire more furs. In this way, the Dutch were able to beat the French to the natives' furs, since the French had no wampum to exchange for them. In 1630, English Puritans also learned to treat wampum as a currency, creating violent rivalries over wampum between the two colonies.

Eventually, however, European traders decided that they preferred to trade furs overseas. Wampum began to lose their value with European consumers; it was great for trading with Native Americans but was worthless when attempting to obtain slaves from Africa or tobacco from the West Indies. The decline in value of wampum left indigenous nations without a vital trade partner. Although wampum had a short run as currency, the term is still used today as slang for money.

Glossary

· mollusk: animals such as clams that have a soft body and that are protected by a shell

1 The author's description of wampum mentions all of the following EXCEPT

(A) The creatures whose shells were used to make it
(B) The place where its materials were collected
(C) The process of producing it
(D) The materials used to string it together

2 According to paragraph 2, the Two Row Wampum Belt symbolized which of the following?

(A) The ability to communicate with the dead
(B) The contrast between lightness and darkness
(C) The achievement of peace with Europeans
(D) The wealth of the indigenous peoples

3 The word "oblivious" in the passage is closest in meaning to

(A) ignorant
(B) addicted
(C) curious
(D) adherent

4 The word "them" in the passage refers to

(A) the Dutch
(B) the French
(C) furs
(D) wampum

5 According to the passage, Europeans stopped trading wampum because it

(A) became more difficult to acquire from the natives
(B) required less skill due to technological advancements
(C) could not be exchanged for forced labor
(D) had less value for acquiring furs from the tribes

• Vocabulary Quiz •

The word [ ] is closest in meaning to

1 significance	2 subsequently	3 obtain	4 decline
ⓐ approval	ⓐ later	ⓐ submit	ⓐ decrease
ⓑ variation	ⓑ often	ⓑ acquire	ⓑ defect
ⓒ meaning	ⓒ before	ⓒ oblige	ⓒ damage

Reading Practice 3

Answer Book p. 18

Smooth Cordgrass

Smooth cordgrass is a tall perennial grass that can reach heights of seven feet. Its underground stems branch out in every direction, while its aboveground stems grow in clumps of ten to forty and are topped with blade-like leaves. It flowers in the fall, at which time it produces seeds covered with spikes. The species thrives in saltwater wetlands where few other plants can survive. Common habitats include marshes, beaches, and tidal flats. Smooth cordgrass demonstrates that a plant can have a positive impact on some ecosystems and threaten the health of others.

On the East Coast of the United States, from Maine to Texas, smooth cordgrass offers numerous benefits. Fiddler crabs find shelter from predators by burrowing in the soft soil where it grows. This allows oxygen to enter the soil and improves drainage. Ribbed mussels attach themselves to the plant's stems and roots, which is also helpful for the soil. Snow geese enjoy consuming the plant's underground stems when they pass through the southeast. Smooth cordgrass also prevents Atlantic beaches from eroding, helps to filter pollutants like nitrogen and phosphorus out of the water, and is responsible for much of the photosynthesis in marsh ecosystems.

On the West Coast, however, smooth cordgrass is considered an invasive species. It was introduced to Washington State in the late 1800s, an unwanted hitchhiker in shipments of oysters from the East Coast. It also arrived as a packing material in westbound shipments. In Washington, the species has outcompeted endangered native plants, resulting in biodiversity losses. Smooth cordgrass is a more recent invader in San Francisco Bay, where it was intentionally introduced by the U.S. Army Corps of Engineers. There, it formed a hybrid with the bay's native plants that has caused numerous problems. For instance, the cordgrass clogs channels, causing flooding in adjacent areas. It also threatens endangered native species of birds and mice by altering the character of the ecosystem.

Eradicating smooth cordgrass from the West Coast is challenging and expensive but possible. In Washington, infestations have been reduced by repeated mowing. Insects called planthoppers have also been released there to reduce seed survival. In San Francisco, about 700 acres of smooth cordgrass have been removed using an herbicide. With the invader diminished, native species are now being reintroduced in the bay.

Glossary

· perennial: living for several years

1 According to paragraph 1, what is a physical feature of smooth cordgrass?
(A) Thick roots
(B) Clustered stems
(C) Broad leaves
(D) Large seeds

2 According to paragraph 2, smooth cordgrass is beneficial on the East Coast because
(A) it provides a food source for crabs and mussels
(B) it improves filtration of water pollutants
(C) its tall blades provide shelter for snow geese
(D) it reduces the quantity of sand on the shore

3 The word "adjacent" in the passage is closest in meaning to
(A) widespread
(B) extensive
(C) nearby
(D) underlying

4 In paragraph 3, the author's discussion of the infestation in Washington mentions that smooth cordgrass
(A) affected an endangered mouse species
(B) had a tendency to reduce water drainage
(C) arrived as a material used for packing
(D) formed a hybrid with several native plants

5 According to paragraph 4, smooth cordgrass can be reduced by all of the following methods EXCEPT
(A) introducing bugs to the ecosystem
(B) applying herbicides to the wetlands
(C) mowing down the grass several times
(D) planting more native plant species

• **Vocabulary Quiz** •

The word [ ] is closest in meaning to

1 shelter	2 consuming	3 outcompeted	4 diminished
ⓐ habitat	ⓐ saving	ⓐ aggravated	ⓐ reduced
ⓑ nourishment	ⓑ finding	ⓑ defeated	ⓑ replaced
ⓒ security	ⓒ eating	ⓒ transformed	ⓒ restored

Reading Practice 4

Answer Book p. 19

The Early Space Race

Direct space exploration became a possibility after World War II. Previously, land-based optical and radio telescopes accomplished much of the space exploration conducted by astronomers. Although these accumulated valuable data, interference from Earth's atmosphere prevented scientists from obtaining accurate information. 5

A major breakthrough occurred in 1957. Russia, then the Union of Soviet Socialist Republics (USSR), launched Sputnik I, the first artificial satellite. It relayed information on cosmic rays, meteoroids, temperature, and air density. Its launch marked the beginning 10 of the Space Age and prodded the United States space program to become more active, thus paving the way for what was to become a space race between the two superpowers. A second satellite was launched by the USSR in the same year. The satellite carried a dog as a passenger, enabling scientists to record physiological data on a living creature in outer space in order to determine whether humans could make the journey. The Explorer 15 I was launched by the United States in 1958, after which a number of satellites were launched by both countries in an ever-continuing quest for information on outer space. As useful as these satellites were in acquiring information, space probes were even more productive.

In the 1960s, both Russia and the United States launched approximately fifty space 20 probes to the Moon. Early space probes were designed only to pass the Moon or to crash-land on it. As technology improved, space probes became capable of making soft landings and more precise maneuvers. By the mid-1960s, the space probes could take pictures and transmit the pictures back before crashing into the Moon. The Soviet space probes, known as Luna, were several months ahead of the American equivalent, the 25 Surveyors, in obtaining data. However, data obtained by the United States space probes were more detailed. In time, thousands of explicitly clear pictures were taken, providing humans with abundant information on the celestial body closest to planet Earth.

As the space probes became more advanced, both nations turned to the objective of putting a man on the Moon. Although both countries competed fiercely to achieve this, 30 the United States was the only country to ever send its people to the Moon.

1 The word "accumulated" in the passage is closest in meaning to

(A) simulated
(B) collected
(C) experimented
(D) resolved

2 According to paragraph 2, which of the following was an accomplishment of the first artificial satellite?

(A) It took pictures of the Moon.
(B) It provided data on meteoroids.
(C) It made a soft landing.
(D) It orbited around the Moon.

3 According to paragraph 2, what was the purpose of putting a dog in flight?

(A) To test the viability of a manned spacecraft
(B) To compare the reactions of a dog to those of a human
(C) To demonstrate that a technology was superior
(D) To provide company for human astronauts

4 Which of the following is NOT a feature of the space probes to the Moon?

(A) Accurate navigation
(B) Ability to land softly
(C) Facility to take pictures
(D) Rapid flights

5 According to paragraph 3, the American Surveyor probes were

(A) able to gather detailed information
(B) developed earlier than Luna
(C) unable to travel all the way to the Moon
(D) limited in terms of the data they obtained

• **Vocabulary Quiz** •

The word [ ] is closest in meaning to

1 prodded	2 maneuvers	3 celestial	4 objective
ⓐ prompted	ⓐ estimates	ⓐ eternal	ⓐ aim
ⓑ examined	ⓑ movements	ⓑ heavenly	ⓑ instance
ⓒ destined	ⓒ calculations	ⓒ boundless	ⓒ pioneer

Answer Book p. 20

TOEFL Reading

Preserving Dance

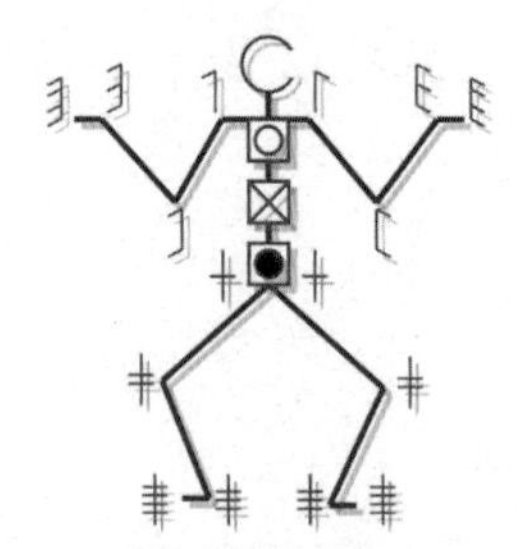

➡ Before humans could communicate through speech or written word, there was movement, and with this movement came dance. Yet the changeable nature of dance made it difficult to preserve with accuracy. From toe to toe, hand to hand, and eye to eye, dance has been transmitted from generation to generation. Human chains 5 of dancers, choreographers, and others involved in its creation and performance have passed down their knowledge of specific dances. For a dance to survive the test of time, there must first be people who can appreciate it and then be willing to learn and remember it. Even when these conditions are met, there is little guarantee of accurate preservation, as with each performance the dance may change. 10

➡ Early attempts to preserve dance relied on written descriptions of the movements. Detailed accounts could not, however, accurately capture the subtleties without inviting subjective interpretations. It is difficult to express in words the form a dancer must assume when jumping or spinning, and harder still to understand these words without having seen the dance. Several attempts were made at creating a system of notation for dance, similar 15 to that in music. The first successful system of notation was Labanotation, developed in 1928 by a dance theorist Rudolf von Laban. The system uses symbols to represent all aspects of human motion, from subtle gestures to transference of weight. Most variations of Labanotation, such as Motif Notation, are simplifications of this method. However, Sutton DanceWriting is a distinct system that uses stick figures to depict motion. The problem with 20 all of these two-dimensional systems of notation is that no matter how intricate they are, they cannot capture the full extent of three-dimensional movement.

➡ Graphical methods have also been employed to record dance. **A** Recently, video has become the standard for recording any dance, as the dance in its entirety can be captured in real time. **B** However, video can only offer one perspective of the dance at one time— 25 that of the cameraperson's. **C** Even with multiple angles, the medium is still in essence two-dimensional. **D** Video also requires expensive equipment and careful preservation, as the tapes may deteriorate with time. Any method of recording dance takes place from the viewpoint of the person recording the dance, and can never be a substitute for knowledge or experience. 30

1 According to paragraph 1, which of the following describes the difficulty of accurately recording dance?

Ⓐ Dances may be performed only rarely.
Ⓑ Dances may be too complicated to understand.
Ⓒ Dances may change with each performance.
Ⓓ Dances may take place too quickly for notation.

Paragraph 1 is marked with an arrow [➡].

2 Which of the sentences below best expresses the essential information in the highlighted sentence in the passage? *Incorrect* choices change the meaning in important ways or leave out essential information.

Ⓐ Unless a dance can be described correctly by those who watch, it will be hard for other dancers to imitate.
Ⓑ Seeing a dance in person makes it easier to understand the difficult motions that the dancer performs.
Ⓒ Only individuals who have taken part in a dance are capable of explaining its various movements accurately.
Ⓓ Both providing a description of a dance and comprehending one without observing it can be challenging.

3 Why does the author mention "Sutton DanceWriting" in the passage?

Ⓐ To present an early way to capture three-dimensional motion
Ⓑ To introduce a notation method with a distinct feature
Ⓒ To criticize an ineffective form of dance notation
Ⓓ To describe an ancient technique of dance notation

4 The word "intricate" in the passage is closest in meaning to

Ⓐ enthusiastic
Ⓑ sophisticated
Ⓒ flawed
Ⓓ compelling

5 According to paragraph 2, which of the following is true of Labanotation?

(A) It converts gestures into symbols.
(B) It simplifies prior systems of notation.
(C) It uses stick figures to represent movements.
(D) It was developed by an expert in music.

Paragraph 2 is marked with an arrow [➡].

6 The word "that" in the passage refers to

(A) standard
(B) video
(C) perspective
(D) dance

7 The word "deteriorate" in the passage is closest in meaning to

(A) progress
(B) expand
(C) degrade
(D) regulate

8 According to paragraph 3, which of the following is true of recorded dance?

(A) It is sometimes difficult to capture in real time.
(B) It is an effective way to offer multiple perspectives.
(C) It cannot replace experience and understanding.
(D) It does not require costly equipment or maintenance.

Paragraph 3 is marked with an arrow [➡].

9 Look at the four squares [■] that indicate where the following sentence could be added to the passage.

Photographs were initially used to offer dancers a visual reference for notational dance.

Where would the sentence best fit?

Click on a square [■] to add the sentence to the passage.

10 **Directions:** An introductory sentence for a brief summary of the passage is provided below. Complete the summary by selecting the THREE answer choices that express the most important ideas in the passage. Some sentences do not belong in the summary because they express ideas that are not presented in the passage or are minor ideas in the passage. **This question is worth 2 points.**

Drag your answer choices to the spaces where they belong.
To remove an answer choice, click on it. To review the passage, click on **View Text**.

The preservation of dance has always been difficult.

-
-
-

Answer Choices

Ⓐ Choreographers have been responsible over the centuries for translating dance into written form.

Ⓑ The earliest method of communicating dance steps was to describe the movements in writing.

Ⓒ Labanotation was developed by Rudolf von Laban, a renowned choreographer.

Ⓓ Systems of dance notation have at times been quite elaborate, yet they are imperfect.

Ⓔ Even video recordings of a dance are not an ideal way of capturing its essence.

Ⓕ Video recordings of dance are limited by the flatness of the recorded images.

Answer Book p. 20

Vocabulary Review

A. Fill in the blanks with the appropriate words from the box.

viewpoints	explicitly	physiological
diplomatic	carnivorous	devoured

1 Stress can cause a __________ effect in the body, not just a mental one.

2 Lions are purely __________ animals and cannot survive on vegetation.

3 He found the cave with no trouble because the map __________ showed its location.

4 My brother and I have different __________ on politics, so we argue often.

5 Although they were enemies before, the nations now have a __________ relationship.

6 The boys were so hungry that they __________ the pizza in just a few minutes.

B. Choose the closest meaning for each highlighted word or phrase.

7 The art museum uses a variety of high-tech methods to preserve ancient works of art.
(A) adjust (B) display (C) identify (D) maintain

8 There was no guarantee that the ancient explorers would return home.
(A) proposition (B) conclusion (C) assurance (D) assistance

9 You can use honey as a substitute for sugar in this cake recipe.
(A) preference (B) addition (C) replacement (D) convenience

10 It was proven that the crime had not been committed intentionally but was an accident.
(A) generally (B) purposely (C) unwittingly (D) consistently

11 Many people take the subway to the city because parking is such an inconvenience.
(A) difficulty (B) investment (C) dedication (D) responsibility

12 The new safety guideline applies to all employees working in the factory.
(A) varies from (B) calls off (C) touches on (D) pertains to

13 You need to watch the film at least twice to catch all the subtleties and humor.
(A) emotion (B) criticism (C) nuances (D) insight

14 This position requires at least three years of on-the-job experience or its equivalent.
(A) rank (B) ability (C) trend (D) equal

CHAPTER 05

Negative Fact

Negative Fact

About the Question Type

Negative Fact questions ask you to identify specific information that is NOT true according to the passage or NOT mentioned in the passage.

These questions usually contain the words *NOT* or *EXCEPT*. Be careful to select the answer choice that includes information that is contradicted by the passage or not mentioned in the passage.

Question Format

- According to paragraph #, which of the following is NOT true of X?
- According to paragraph #, all of the following are true of X EXCEPT
- The author mentions all of the following EXCEPT

Key Strategies

- **Step 1** — Read the question and identify the keywords. If the question indicates a specific paragraph, you can ignore the rest of the passage.
- **Step 2** — Scan the passage for the keywords, and locate the relevant information.
- **Step 3** — Verify each answer choice. Select the answer choice that includes information that is contradicted by the passage or not mentioned in the passage.

Example

Answer Book p. 21

Lighting Up the Eiffel Tower

The original lighting system of the Eiffel Tower consisted only of gas lights because electricity was unavailable at the time. Once this technology became plausible in 1900, electric bulbs replaced the old lights and were placed along the tower's frame to highlight its structure. Later, even more creative lighting was installed for special events. In 1925, a French industrialist rented the tower and put up 250,000 lights to spell out and advertise his brand name for the World's Fair. Sixty years later, the modern form of Eiffel Tower lighting was born. An engineer installed hundreds of 1000-watt bulbs inside the frame as spotlights. Rather than simply illuminating the tower, these made the tower itself seem like a source of light that could be seen from very far away. Several additional innovations have been made in the twenty-first century. As more efficient lighting has become available, the wattage of the bulbs has been reduced, saving energy without any loss in brightness. Also, the tower has been fitted with lighting that can create sparkling effects or specific colors. These upgrades have allowed for the production of magnificent light shows for specific purposes like commemorating important events or anniversaries.

1 All of the following are true about the Eiffel Tower in the 1900s EXCEPT:

(A) The many lights on it were powered by gas.
(B) An entrepreneur used it to advertise his company.
(C) Electric lights were installed on it for the first time.
(D) Spotlights allowed it to be viewed from a great distance.

2 Which of the following is NOT mentioned about the innovations made to the Eiffel Tower in the twenty-first century?

(A) Lights with the ability to sparkle were introduced.
(B) Upgrades have made splendid light shows possible.
(C) Colored lights began to be used on anniversaries.
(D) Energy-saving lights with higher wattage were added.

Reading Practice 1

Answer Book p. 21

The Rust Belt

Known as the Rust Belt, the northeastern part of the United States became reputed for abandoned factories, unemployment, and out-migration. This economic region includes the midwestern states Illinois, Indiana, Michigan, and Ohio, and one northeastern state, Pennsylvania. The Rust Belt was once the dominant industrial region. However, starting in the 1950s, manufacturers began to relocate, causing a decline in population and economic strength. Detroit, home of the nation's auto industry and formerly one of the world's largest manufacturing producers, was affected most deeply by the downtrend.

In general, the rest of the United States prospered by shifting the focus to industries in the service sector. The Rust Belt, however, continued to worsen in the 1970s as automobile and steel manufacturing experienced a decline in its domestic and international markets. Wages not only began to decline but the unemployment rate increased, expanding the number of people who went on welfare.

Toward the mid-1990s, the Rust Belt made an unexpected recovery. The trends in out-migration, wage rate decline, production, crime rate, and unemployment either ceased or reversed direction. Exports increased by 27 percent, which was 5 percent higher than the United States as a whole. Detroit, carrying the name as the Rust Belt's industrial capital, saw a dramatic increase in population. In the first seven years of the 1990s, the metropolitan area's population rose by nearly 5 percent. The average annual pay increased by 7 percent during the period of 1994 to 1996. Detroit also saw a growth in the number of private non-farm businesses in the first five years of the decade. Other areas in the Rust Belt, notably major cities in Ohio, also experienced an uptrend during this period.

However, this proved to be a short-term development rather than a lasting recovery. The 1997 Asian financial crisis elevated the US dollar, reducing demand for American products abroad. In the first decade of the new millennium, the manufacturing sector cut around 1.6 million jobs. A combination of technological advancement and open trade policies that brought in more foreign products negatively impacted the Rust Belt companies.

Glossary

· welfare: a government support for the poor or the unemployed

1 According to paragraph 2, how did the other parts of the United States avoid the economic decline that occurred in the Rust Belt?

(A) By forming economic partnerships
(B) By switching to other industries
(C) By exploiting local market
(D) By increasing domestic demand

2 The word "ceased" in the passage is closest in meaning to

(A) halted
(B) delayed
(C) adjusted
(D) reduced

3 According to paragraph 3, which of the following did NOT occur in the Rust Belt during the 1990s?

(A) The crime rate went down.
(B) The population increased.
(C) There was a rise in exports.
(D) There was a decrease in wages.

4 The word "this" in the passage refers to

(A) the Rust Belt
(B) Ohio
(C) uptrend
(D) period

5 All of the following contributed to the post-millennial decline of the Rust Belt EXCEPT

(A) surging Asian economies
(B) the value of the US dollar
(C) loss of manufacturing jobs
(D) availability of foreign products

• Vocabulary Quiz •

The word [ ] is closest in meaning to

1 reputed
ⓐ well-known
ⓑ criticized
ⓒ involved

2 relocate
ⓐ establish
ⓑ move
ⓒ advance

3 formerly
ⓐ lately
ⓑ previously
ⓒ usually

4 domestic
ⓐ national
ⓑ central
ⓒ global

Reading Practice 2

Answer Book p. 22

Atmospheric Dust

Atmospheric dust occurs as minute particles, which remain suspended by slight wind currents and settle slowly. These dust particles are most common at low altitudes over cities and least common at high altitudes over oceans. Dust particles are very tiny—less than one micron or a thousandth of a millimeter in diameter—and are so light that they are capable of staying airborne for weeks at a time. Dust from a volcanic eruption such as Krakatoa in Indonesia was observed to still be floating in the air three years after the eruption. 5

Atmospheric dust comes from many sources. Winds blowing over dry earth pick up dust from plowed fields, deserts, and roads. Products of combustion, soot from fires, and auto pollution are common sources in industrialized areas. Fine particles of sea salt from distant turbulent oceans, pollen from plants, and meteoric particles are some natural sources. Large seasonal dust storms occur in African deserts and in the Taklimakan and Gobi deserts. Dust from these storms often travels to other regions where it can negatively affect air quality. 10

The airborne nuclei form cloud droplets that develop into clouds. These dust particles are called hygroscopic dust particles, or particles to which water adheres, and they are so small that they cannot be observed without the use of a microscope. The nucleus of each water droplet in a cloud is one of these tiny particles of inorganic or organic dust. The Scottish physicist John Aitken, who invented a device for counting particles in the air in 1880, first correlated dust particles and condensation. As the cloud droplets that form around the nuclei begin to coalesce, they can no longer remain suspended. They then drop to the earth as a form of precipitation. While individual raindrops may not appear particularly large, they are giants compared to cloud droplets. One raindrop is equivalent to one to ten million cloud droplets. 15 20

Atmospheric dust can also affect the earth's climates in another way. It warms the earth's climate system by functioning in a manner similar to greenhouse gases. It absorbs both solar radiation entering the earth's atmosphere and outgoing radiation from the earth's surface, ultimately trapping heat in the atmosphere. 25

Glossary

· soot: a black powder that is formed when something is burned

1 Why does the author mention "Krakatoa" in the passage?

(A) To cite one of the major sources of dust
(B) To show that dust stays in the air for a long time
(C) To explain the process by which dust forms
(D) To compare dust output from volcanoes and farm fields

2 In paragraph 1, the author's description of dust particles mentions which of the following?

(A) Their tendency to plunge to the ground due to light winds
(B) Their concentration just above the surface of the ocean
(C) Their accumulation rate in urban environments
(D) Their low mass that allows them to float

3 In paragraph 2, all of the following are mentioned as sources of atmospheric dust EXCEPT

(A) soil that has been disturbed by plows
(B) remnants of salt from the sea
(C) sandstorms from the desert
(D) fire-resistant materials from factories

4 The word "adheres" in the passage is closest in meaning to

(A) sticks
(B) embraces
(C) relates
(D) vanishes

5 According to paragraph 3, which of the following is NOT true about airborne nuclei?

(A) Clouds are made up of them.
(B) They are mostly inorganic.
(C) They are incredibly small.
(D) They fall to the earth as rain.

• Vocabulary Quiz •

The word [ ] is closest in meaning to

1 minute
ⓐ quick
ⓑ fine
ⓒ rare

2 turbulent
ⓐ rough
ⓑ distant
ⓒ deep

3 particularly
ⓐ relatively
ⓑ especially
ⓒ regularly

4 ultimately
ⓐ finally
ⓑ rapidly
ⓒ greatly

Reading Practice 3

Answer Book p. 23

Ancient Terracotta

Terracotta is a form of ceramic pottery that dates back to prehistoric times and is still used widely today. The name is an Italian term that means "baked earth," a reference to the process that is used to make it. Terracotta begins with a coarse, porous clay that is shaped and then hardened in a special oven at a temperature of 1,000 degrees Celsius. The appeal to ancient sculptors is not difficult to comprehend. Terracotta is a cheaper and easier-to-use medium than bronze or stone. In fact, this material is so convenient that it was used by numerous early cultures around the world.

Terracotta seems to have been made in nearly every corner of the ancient world. The earliest known terracotta sculpture was a four-inch statue of a woman, referred to as the *Venus of Dolni Vestonice*. Found buried in ash in Moravia, now the Czech Republic, it is believed to be around 30,000 years old. Ancient terracotta sculptures also turned up in modern-day Turkey, Romania, Pakistan, Greece, Egypt, and Iraq. Even more far-flung terracotta samples have been attributed to the Nok people of sub-Saharan Africa, who used the technique as early as 1500 BC, and the Olmecs of present-day Mexico, whose culture dates to a similar era. The most impressive terracotta work is the *Terracotta Army*, a collection of 8,000 life-size clay soldiers. It was discovered at the tomb of China's first emperor. Construction of the statues began in 246 BC, requiring the contributions of 720,000 people.

Did all of these different peoples discover terracotta independently? This is a sensitive question. In 2016, a Chinese researcher created controversy by suggesting that the lifelike appearance of the soldiers that make up the *Terracotta Army* suggests the influence of ancient Greek artists. A British art historian went further, claiming that "Western DNA" had been found at the site. The two proposed that cross-cultural interaction between East and West must have started earlier than had previously been recognized. Despite widespread coverage in the press, the theory has been challenged by numerous experts in history, who view it as part of a longstanding tendency to doubt the ability of non-European cultures to produce remarkable works of art on their own.

1 The word "comprehend" in the passage is closest in meaning to

(A) understand
(B) examine
(C) represent
(D) substitute

2 In paragraph 1, the author's description of the process of making terracotta does NOT mention

(A) the comparative hardness
(B) the temperature of the oven
(C) the texture of the clay
(D) the relative cost

3 According to paragraph 2, which of the following is NOT true of early terracotta?

(A) It was used to create full-size representations of people.
(B) It was made on every continent apart from Africa.
(C) More than half a million workers contributed to a Chinese project.
(D) The oldest work was found in Moravia.

4 The word "it" in the passage refers to

(A) coverage
(B) press
(C) theory
(D) history

5 Which of the following can be inferred from paragraph 3 about the *Terracotta Army*?

(A) It proves the influence of the Chinese on ancient Greece.
(B) It exhibits qualities similar to the art of another culture.
(C) It confirms the date of the first East-West interaction.
(D) It includes depictions of individuals of a British origin.

• Vocabulary Quiz •

The word [　　　] is closest in meaning to

1 far-flung	2 sensitive	3 challenged	4 longstanding
ⓐ remote	ⓐ strenuous	ⓐ investigated	ⓐ artificial
ⓑ famous	ⓑ controversial	ⓑ disputed	ⓑ uneven
ⓒ creative	ⓒ amendable	ⓒ assumed	ⓒ lasting

Answer Book p. 24

Mineral Deficiency in Plants

It is commonly understood that plants depend on sunlight and water for survival, but the requirements for flourishing plant life are broader than that. Just like people, plants become unhealthy if they lack proper nutrition. Mineral nutrients are absorbed by plants through their roots and distributed into the organism's cells and tissues. That means that the soil has to be rich in essential nutrients. In cases where the soil is deficient in them, it becomes crucial to apply the missing minerals to the dirt where the plant's roots extend. While plants demand numerous nutrients from their soils, the most common plant deficiencies are of phosphorus, nitrogen, and iron. When plants are missing these substances, they exhibit certain predictable symptoms.

Insufficient phosphorus can also negatively affect all aspects of plant development, including seed germination and blooming. The plant's younger leaves may appear healthy, but the older leaves typically start to take on a purple hue on their undersides due to excess accumulation of anthocyanin, a pigment. Additionally, the tips of the leaves sometimes dry out and appear burnt. These symptoms are a sign that the plant is not receiving enough phosphorous from the soil, diminishing its capacity to conduct photosynthesis.

When ammonium and nitrates are washed away by excessive water, plants may experience the symptoms of nitrogen deficiency. The primary sign of this condition is a yellowing of older leaves and a transition to light green in younger leaves. Some leaves may even acquire a pinkish tint. Growth is also slowed and diminished. The reason these symptoms develop is that nitrogen is essential for plant growth and maturity. They can be prevented by applying fertilizers high in nitrogen such as manure or blood meal.

Iron is a micronutrient, meaning that while it is essential to the health of a plant, it is required in smaller quantities than other nutrients. Iron facilitates the synthesis of enzymes and chloroplast proteins. When the pH level of the soil climbs above 6.5, plants may not be able to access the usually plentiful iron in the soil. The veins of the leaves remain dark green while the rest of the leaf pales. This discoloration progresses to the point where the whole leaf becomes yellow.

Glossary

· germination: the process of a seed of a plant starting to grow

1 The word "flourishing" in the passage is closest in meaning to

(A) fluorescent
(B) perseverant
(C) thriving
(D) exquisite

2 The word "its" in the passage refers to

(A) sign
(B) plant
(C) phosphorous
(D) soil

3 In paragraph 2, the author mentions all of the following about phosphorus deficiency symptoms EXCEPT

(A) darkening of the roots
(B) reduced moisture in the leaves' tips
(C) purple discoloration in the leaves
(D) disturbances in the germination of seeds

4 According to paragraph 3, a lack of nitrogen results in

(A) limited reproduction
(B) slowed growth
(C) reduced photosynthesis
(D) delayed flowering

5 According to paragraph 4, which of the following is NOT true of iron?

(A) It is present in adequate quantities in most soils.
(B) It is not required in very large amounts.
(C) It helps plants process proteins and enzymes.
(D) It turns the whole leaf yellow immediately.

• Vocabulary Quiz •

The word [ ] is closest in meaning to

1 distributed
ⓐ delivered
ⓑ attained
ⓒ regulated

2 deficient
ⓐ irregular
ⓑ extreme
ⓒ lacking

3 crucial
ⓐ impossible
ⓑ impractical
ⓒ essential

4 plentiful
ⓐ essential
ⓑ abundant
ⓒ peculiar

Answer Book p. 24

TOEFL Reading

Song Learning in Birds

Approximately half of the 9,000 existing species of birds learn how to sing. There are many similarities between the learning process of songbirds and language acquisition in human beings. Both seem to involve an innate predisposition to learn a method of communication that is shaped by social influences. 5

➡ Infant songbirds raised in soundproofed chambers in a laboratory emitted a crude but recognizable song that contained elements similar to those of the normal song. Scientists postulated that birds are born with a basic template of what their species' song should sound like. They match this template to the song they hear around them during development until 10 the song they produce is perfected. An isolated bird does not hear the normal song, and so it can only produce the crude template. Young birds prefer to learn the songs of their parents but will learn the songs of other species if the song of their own species is not heard during this critical period.

➡ Young birds that learn a song through electronic mediums, such as cassette tapes 15 and CDs, have a greater tendency to incorporate notes used by other species in the final adult song if they hear a live tutor of another species. They are even capable of ignoring the electronic song of the same species and learning the song of a different species if the live tutor of another species is present in the same environment. This occurs during the sensorimotor phase, when the bird is comparing and practicing the sounds it heard 20 previously.

➡ After much practice and experimentation, the final adult song is established. **A** There are always individual variations that depend on the genetic ability of each individual, as well as the capacity for the individuals to absorb and remember the musical notes heard. **B** As long as they are exposed to an adequate stimulus, all young birds learn how to sing. **C** It 25 is important to note that the process of learning does not end once a bird is fully grown. **D** In some cases, individuals that have reached full maturity will acquire new songs when they change territories.

Glossary

sensorimotor: involving both sensory and motor functions

Volume Review Help Back Next

1 The word "innate" in the passage is closest in meaning to

Ⓐ special
Ⓑ extra
Ⓒ inborn
Ⓓ standard

2 The word "They" in the passage refers to

Ⓐ elements
Ⓑ scientists
Ⓒ birds
Ⓓ species

3 Why does the author mention an "isolated bird" in the passage?

Ⓐ To emphasize the importance of solitude during development
Ⓑ To provide evidence of a basic song template in birds
Ⓒ To argue that song learning is similar to language acquirement
Ⓓ To illustrate the extent of research on songbirds

4 According to paragraph 2, a young bird is best able to learn songs when

Ⓐ it is separated from other birds of its species
Ⓑ its parent is in the same environment
Ⓒ it only hears the songs of other species
Ⓓ its flock migrates to a different territory

Paragraph 2 is marked with an arrow [➡].

5 The word "incorporate" in the passage is closest in meaning to

Ⓐ decide
Ⓑ assemble
Ⓒ modify
Ⓓ combine

6 Which of the sentences below best expresses the essential information in the highlighted sentence in the passage? *Incorrect* choices change the meaning in important ways or leave out essential information.

Ⓐ They can adopt the communication styles of other birds when conditions are perfect.
Ⓑ Different species of birds have different learning abilities with regard to the songs they sing.
Ⓒ Electronic recordings can be ignored by birds when other birds are present.
Ⓓ They can imitate a live song of another species and disregard a recording of one of their own.

7 It can be inferred from paragraph 3 that young birds

Ⓐ prefer to imitate live birds rather than recordings
Ⓑ practice several songs at the same time
Ⓒ learn only the songs sung by others of the same species
Ⓓ ignore birds that produce unusual sounds

Paragraph 3 is marked with an arrow [➡].

8 According to paragraph 4, adult birds can acquire new songs when they

Ⓐ migrate to a different area
Ⓑ interact with birds of other species
Ⓒ listen to young birds experimenting
Ⓓ face competitors for territory

Paragraph 4 is marked with an arrow [➡].

9 Look at the four squares [■] that indicate where the following sentence could be added to the passage.

However, only a few will be capable of a perfect reproduction of the song taught.

Where would the sentence best fit?

Click on a square [■] to add the sentence to the passage.

10 **Directions:** An introductory sentence for a brief summary of the passage is provided below. Complete the summary by selecting the THREE answer choices that express the most important ideas in the passage. Some sentences do not belong in the summary because they express ideas that are not presented in the passage or are minor ideas in the passage. **This question is worth 2 points.**

Drag your answer choices to the spaces where they belong.
To remove an answer choice, click on it. To review the passage, click on **View Text**.

Birds learn to sing in a similar way to humans learning to speak.

-
-
-

Answer Choices

Ⓐ Half of bird species learn to sing birdsongs.

Ⓑ Birds start life with the ability to sing crudely.

Ⓒ Birds develop their songs by listening to others.

Ⓓ A bird's song is finalized when it reaches adulthood.

Ⓔ When isolated, birds do not learn to sing.

Ⓕ Birds can learn to sing from cassette tapes.

Answer Book p. 24

Vocabulary Review

A. Fill in the blanks with the appropriate words from the box.

crude	altitude	insufficient
controversy	unexpected	commemorate

1 The company had __________ funds to purchase the expensive equipment.

2 Scientists were shocked by the __________ discovery of a new virus.

3 The hikers lost in the jungle made a __________ shelter from some branches.

4 The statue was made to __________ the soldiers of the war.

5 The film's depictions of historical events generated __________.

6 The air temperature gets much colder at a higher __________ on the mountain.

B. Choose the closest meaning for each highlighted word or phrase.

7 Everyone agreed that the orchestra gave a magnificent performance last night.
(A) ambivalent (B) ingenious (C) challenging (D) outstanding

8 The new factory affected the town's environment more than local people expected.
(A) elevated (B) conquered (C) disturbed (D) bolstered

9 The fisherman had coarse hands, filled with calluses from years of hard work.
(A) sweaty (B) rough (C) stable (D) careful

10 People did not like the mystery movie because the story was too predictable.
(A) cautious (B) expected (C) violent (D) confusing

11 It has been postulated that there may be some particles moving faster than light.
(A) hypothesized (B) determined (C) disputed (D) disregarded

12 Young learners are usually better than older learners in second language acquisition.
(A) expression (B) display (C) obtainment (D) understanding

13 We will upgrade to a more efficient software system next month.
(A) thorough (B) protected (C) durable (D) effective

14 It was difficult for farms to prosper this year because of the drought.
(A) condense (B) diversify (C) flourish (D) replicate

CHAPTER 06

Inference

Inference

About the Question Type

Inference questions ask you to identify information that is implied but not explicitly stated in the passage.

These questions require you to draw a logical conclusion based on the information in the passage. Be careful to use only the information presented in the passage to select the correct answer choice. Do not draw any conclusion based on what you know about the topic from other sources.

Question Format

- Which of the following can be inferred from paragraph # about X?
- In paragraph #, what does the author imply about X?
- It can be inferred from paragraph # that

Key Strategies

- **Step 1** — Read the question and identify the keywords.
- **Step 2** — Scan the passage for the keywords, and locate the relevant information.
- **Step 3** — Select the answer choice that is a logical conclusion based on the information in the passage.

Example

Answer Book p. 26

Cats in Ancient Egypt

Cats occupied an honored place in ancient Egypt. The Egyptians loved their cats so much that they were believed to worship their feline companions. Cats were more than beloved pets; they were ubiquitous in the rich cultural traditions of the ancient Egyptians. The art of the period reveals the qualities that the Egyptian people so admired. Cats were portrayed as protectors, keeping threatening snakes and scorpions out of Egyptian homes. They were symbols of fertility, often depicted under the chairs of seated women. They were cherished companions in this life and the next; the tombs of the wealthy and important frequently contained mummified felines. However, rather than being objects of worship, cats were believed to have godlike characteristics: intelligence, speed, and power. Their habit of sleeping in the sun reminded the Egyptians of their sun god Ra. It was also believed that some of the Egyptian shape-shifting gods took the form of lions or domestic cats. It is not difficult to understand how people acquired the misunderstanding that cats were considered to be gods in ancient Egypt.

Glossary

· feline: of cats or the cat family

1 The author implies that cats in ancient Egypt

(A) rarely appeared in works of art
(B) hunted household pests
(C) appealed mainly to powerful noblewomen
(D) received protection from religious leaders

2 Which of the following can be inferred about Egyptian tombs?

(A) Their exteriors often featured statues of cats.
(B) They were designed to commemorate the achievements of Egyptians.
(C) Some of them were built for the deceased pets of the wealthy.
(D) Their contents were believed to enter the afterlife.

Reading Practice 1

Answer Book p. 26

The Importance of Biodiversity

Biological diversity is made possible through genetic diversity. Genes control how varied a species can be within the constraints placed on it by the environment. Biologists define a species as a group of similar, related individuals that can breed and produce offspring capable of reproduction. Each individual in a species has a large number of genes. For example, a single bacterium can have 1,000 genes, while a flowering plant can have as many as 400,000 genes. Each gene contains a great store of information, and this genetic material is necessary to sustain healthy and diverse ecosystems.

The species that compose one community can come to have an interdependence on one another. Thus, the loss of a single species can have an enormous impact on an entire ecosystem. This is because it would mean the loss of billions upon billions of bits of information that can help maintain biological diversity. The existence of numerous and diverse populations allows many given species to have the genetic variety to escape extinction in the case that the environment changes. Hence, maintaining biological diversity by preventing the dying out of a species is essential to the survival of living things on Earth.

Yet habitat change has always caused disturbances, including extinctions. For example, in North America, the richness of the natural landscape made European settlers incorrectly believe that they could alter the land as much as they wanted. Their misguided use of the land and forests for raising crops and domestication of animals caused the number of the predators like gray wolves to dwindle. At the same time, their hunting and harvesting of wild animals caused entire species to vanish. Some that did survive were left severely limited in their numbers and genetic diversity. Even the common bison, which once existed in the hundreds of millions, was reduced to a wild population of a few hundred.

Because modern environmental scientists now understand the importance of biological diversity, they increasingly recommend the conservation of species through the protection of ecosystems. Since the last half of the twentieth century, the efforts of conservationists have successfully reintroduced some species to areas that they once had freely roamed. As these species reestablish themselves in the ecosystem, they will recreate the genetic balance needed for optimum ecological diversity.

Glossary

· interdependence: a state of relying on each other

1 The word "constraints" in the passage is closest in meaning to

(A) objectives
(B) communities
(C) restrictions
(D) procedures

2 It can be inferred from paragraph 1 that the members of a species

(A) can exist in only one type of environment
(B) possess the exact same number of genes
(C) exhibit greater biological variation when healthy
(D) can produce fertile young with each other

3 It can be inferred from paragraph 2 that a species faces extinction if it

(A) is composed of a single population group
(B) is made up of individuals with diverse traits
(C) becomes dependent on another species
(D) has too much genetic variety

4 The word "their" in the passage refers to

(A) settlers
(B) animals
(C) predators
(D) gray wolves

5 Why does the author mention "the common bison" in the passage?

(A) To give an example of a wild animal that is very familiar
(B) To show the extent of European's impact on an abundant species
(C) To illustrate that a large population can help a species survive
(D) To identify an animal that Europeans successfully domesticated

• Vocabulary Quiz •

The word [ ] is closest in meaning to

1 diverse	2 compose	3 existence	4 vanish
ⓐ protected	ⓐ utilize	ⓐ creation	ⓐ disappear
ⓑ complex	ⓑ comprise	ⓑ presence	ⓑ survive
ⓒ varied	ⓒ support	ⓒ result	ⓒ scatter

Reading Practice 2

Answer Book p. 27

The Development of Citizenship

The concept of citizenship has not always remained the same through the ages. It first became an important notion in ancient Greece but was limited to a small group within the population. This concept changed from time to time. However, its basic principle—that only citizens were allowed rights and privileges that were denied to the remainder of the population—continued to apply. 5

During the time of the Roman Empire, citizenship was available to all residents who were neither slaves nor foreigners. In Rome, this was approximately 55 percent of the population, whereas the number was around 70 percent for Italy as a whole. These numbers reflect the fact that Rome had a higher number of slaves and foreign-born residents than elsewhere in Italy. In the Roman provinces outside of Italy, Roman 10 citizenship was considerably less common. In the provinces, only certain individuals who had performed an extraordinary service to Rome in a show of loyalty earned citizenship for themselves and their family members.

The laws of almost every country in modern times follow two principles in the determination of a person's citizenship at birth. The first, *jus soli* ("right of soil"), states 15 that any person born within a given territory is automatically a citizen of that territory, with a few exceptions like the children of foreign diplomats. The United States is an example of a country that uses the principle of jus soli. Some countries, however, base citizenship on the second, *jus sanguinis* ("right of blood"). This states that a child acquires the nationality of his or her parents wherever born. This second principle is based on 20 ancestry rather than place of birth.

Neither of these principles, though, is practiced in its pure form in most countries. For example, a child born outside of Canada has Canadian citizenship if either parent was a Canadian at the time of the birth and if the birth was properly registered with the Canadian authorities. Moreover, many modern nations also have a path to citizenship that 25 is not based on birth but on immigration. Immigrants can seek residency in a foreign country, and, once there, they can apply for citizenship if they meet the requirements. Common ways of establishing residency include having a family member or employment sponsor in the country. Also, increasingly, refugees escaping from extreme conditions like abuse or war are immigrating to foreign countries. 30

1 It can be inferred from paragraph 2 that citizenship during the Roman Empire was

(A) accessible for foreigners living in Rome
(B) offered to all residents of Roman territory
(C) not available to slaves
(D) not allowed in Roman provinces

2 Which of the following can be inferred from paragraph 3 about the United States?

(A) It does not automatically grant citizenship to newborns of foreign diplomats.
(B) It recently changed from jus sanguinis to jus soli.
(C) It does not allow dual citizenship for its citizens who are born abroad.
(D) It bases its citizenship model on that of the Roman Empire.

3 The phrase "apply for" in the passage is closest in meaning to

(A) entail
(B) request
(C) perceive
(D) obtain

4 Why does the author discuss Canada in paragraph 4?

(A) To emphasize the need for parents to register their child's birth
(B) To suggest a citizenship model that other nations should follow
(C) To highlight a country with an unusual approach to immigration
(D) To show that countries follow multiple citizenship principles

5 Which of the following is NOT mentioned in paragraph 4 as a way of establishing residency?

(A) Attending an educational institute
(B) Having a relative in the country
(C) Having a work sponsor in the country
(D) Seeking refuge from serious circumstances

• Vocabulary Quiz •

The word [ ] is closest in meaning to

1 notion
ⓐ pledge
ⓑ concept
ⓒ device

2 considerably
ⓐ frequently
ⓑ temporarily
ⓒ significantly

3 determination
ⓐ decision
ⓑ progress
ⓒ source

4 ancestry
ⓐ recovery
ⓑ mystery
ⓒ lineage

Reading Practice 3

Answer Book p. 28

Marcel Duchamp

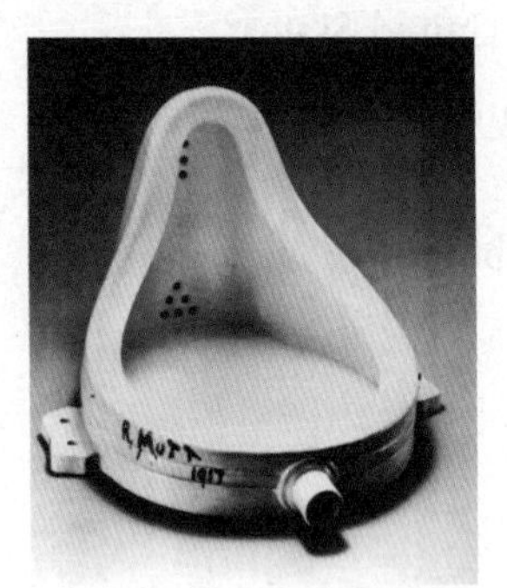

Modern art was founded on revolution, and one of its pivotal figures was French artist Marcel Duchamp. Duchamp spent the majority of his life traveling back and forth between Europe and America, which allowed him to witness avant-garde movements such as Impressionism, Cubism, and Surrealism. This helped to shape his artistic style and vision of what art could be. By the time he reached his early twenties, he had already begun to develop his own unique artistic identity. This was defined by his desire to continually challenge the status quo.

Duchamp was strongly impacted by the horrors of World War I and the associated Dada movement. Dada sought to protest aesthetic art, rational thought, and economic capitalism, all of which its followers blamed for the conflict. It started in Europe, but Duchamp's experience with it occurred primarily in New York, where Dada artists were decidedly less political than in Dada's birthplace. This is evident in Duchamp's increasing interest in pushing boundaries, not exclusively on political grounds but for the purpose of testing the limits of public taste and acceptance.

The earliest of Duchamp's works that demonstrated his creativity and boldness was *Nude Descending a Staircase*. This painting was inspired by the techniques of Cubism as developed by Pablo Picasso and Georges Braque. Like them, Duchamp captured a figure in Cubist form. However, what distinguished his work was the clear sense of dynamic motion in the subject. Though this work is highly admired today, the art world at the time was not ready for it. It generated negative reactions even from Parisian art communities that were accustomed to the unusual. Even the Cubists rejected it as too futuristic.

Perhaps more shocking was Duchamp's pioneering activity in "readymade" art. Readymade works were manufactured objects that were taken from real life and reused as works of art. Duchamp's most famous readymade piece, *Fountain*, was a urinal that he anonymously submitted for an art show in 1917. The work, which must have seemed like a practical joke, was accepted only because no artist who paid the entry fee could be rejected. However, it was never moved to the show area for viewing. Some modern critics consider *Fountain* to be the most groundbreaking artwork of the twentieth century despite the fact that the original is known only from a single photograph.

Glossary

· status quo: the current situation

1 The word "pivotal" in the passage is closest in meaning to

(A) obvious
(B) central
(C) influential
(D) minor

2 According to paragraph 1, which of the following is true of Duchamp's travels?

(A) They occurred primarily in his early twenties.
(B) They introduced him to many different art movements.
(C) They caused him to postpone his study of art.
(D) They led him to develop an interest in political themes.

3 Why does the author mention "New York" in the passage?

(A) To show that Duchamp was unaware of the birthplace of Dada
(B) To explain how the city became a center for Dada art
(C) To highlight what set Duchamp apart from Dada artists in Europe
(D) To emphasize that the Dada movement was not limited to Europe

4 What can be inferred about the subjects of Picasso and Braque?

(A) They were considered strange by their contemporaries.
(B) They were closely copied by Marcel Duchamp.
(C) They appeared more static than the figure in Duchamp's work.
(D) They seemed more lifelike than those of most Cubists.

5 Which of the following can be inferred about Duchamp's *Fountain*?

(A) It received a prize in a competition for artists.
(B) It was initially rejected for inclusion in an art show.
(C) Its creator may have been someone other than Duchamp.
(D) Its original form was never seen by the public.

• Vocabulary Quiz •

The word [ ] is closest in meaning to

1 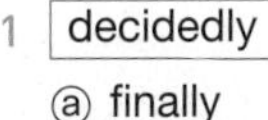 decidedly
ⓐ finally
ⓑ intensely
ⓒ clearly

2 evident
ⓐ obvious
ⓑ secure
ⓒ even

3 grounds
ⓐ burdens
ⓑ reasons
ⓒ changes

4 accustomed to
ⓐ excited with
ⓑ bored with
ⓒ used to

Reading Practice 4

Answer Book p. 28

The First Non-natives to Discover America

When historians discuss the discovery of America, they are typically referring to the discovery of these lands by explorers other than Native Americans, particularly those from across the Atlantic Ocean. Traditionally, school textbooks have perpetuated the notion that Christopher Columbus was the original discoverer. Columbus was the first to reach America, as he stumbled across the continent while seeking a western passage to India in 1492. This idea is now widely acknowledged to be a false claim, but debate continues regarding the first non-natives to land on American soil.

Among the oldest arguments for a pre-Columbian discovery of America gives credit to the Norse. This hypothesis, which first became fashionable in the late 1800s, was originally based on the Vinland Sagas. These sagas are old Icelandic texts that were based on oral traditions. Their authors' descriptions of geography, native customs, and natural resources indicate that they were knowledgeable about America. Yet because they were written down more than two hundred years after the voyages they described, some experts remained skeptical. These skeptics doubted their accuracy and whether America was the destination of the people described in the sagas. Nonetheless, archaeological studies have confirmed that a Norse settlement was established in the Canadian province of Newfoundland. It has been dated to AD 1000, which is long before the voyage of Columbus.

A more recent theory places the date of trans-Atlantic contact far earlier. Some archaeologists contend that Africans traveled to America as early as 2,500 years ago. Proponents of this view emphasize that the statues in Mesoamerica have African features that indicate imported design. Similarly, they presume that the pyramids of Mayan and Aztec cultures reflect pyramid-building knowledge imported from Egypt located in northern Africa. Additional physical evidence that supports this theory comes not from America but from Egypt. After an excavation and analysis of some Egyptian mummies in the 1990s, a German toxicologist detected the presence of cocaine and nicotine. Because both of these narcotics are known to be produced only from American plants, experts deduced that they were brought to Egypt from America. In addition, Mesoamerican oral traditions clearly refer to black-skinned people in America. As the evidence mounts, it becomes clearer that prior generations of historians greatly underestimated the marine navigation capacity of the ancient peoples of Africa.

Glossary

· the Norse: the people of ancient Scandinavia

1 The word "those" in the passage refers to

(A) historians
(B) lands
(C) explorers
(D) Native Americans

2 The word "perpetuated" in the passage is closest in meaning to

(A) rejected
(B) maintained
(C) proposed
(D) proven

3 What can be inferred about the people who put the Vinland Sagas into writing?

(A) They documented American geography during their travels.
(B) They had no direct experience of the journeys they recounted.
(C) They proved the existence of a Norse settlement in Canada.
(D) They included material that contradicts archaeological evidence.

4 Which of the following is NOT mentioned in support of the African trans-Atlantic theory?

(A) Statues with African characteristics
(B) The presence of American drugs in ancient Egypt
(C) Descriptions of Egypt in Mesoamerican oral tradition
(D) Architectural influences from ancient Egypt

5 What can be inferred from paragraph 3 about previous generations of historians?

(A) They assumed that the Mayans and Aztecs came to America from Egypt.
(B) They did not believe that ancient African sailors had the ability to reach America.
(C) They were not aware that Spanish explorers knew about the pyramids.
(D) They concluded that the toxicology results of the mummy analysis were false.

• Vocabulary Quiz •

The word [ ] is closest in meaning to

1 stumbled across	2 fashionable	3 skeptical	4 Proponents
ⓐ bumped into	ⓐ juvenile	ⓐ disrespectful	ⓐ Scholars
ⓑ looked through	ⓑ precise	ⓑ doubtful	ⓑ Advocates
ⓒ pointed out	ⓒ popular	ⓒ conscious	ⓒ Critics

Answer Book p. 29

TOEFL Reading

The Harmful Effects of Pesticides

➡ A pesticide is any substance intended to control, destroy, or repel a pest. There are three general types of pesticides: herbicides, insecticides, and fungicides are designed to kill weeds, insects, and fungi, respectively. Pesticides were once thought of as a miracle cure for hunger, one that was supposed to keep crops free of pests. Scientists now fear that these chemicals are leading to immune system problems, reproductive ailments, birth defects, and higher rates of cancer in people. More than two hundred thousand chemical pesticides have been introduced to the environment in the past fifty years, and most people have at least 250 synthetic industrial chemicals in their bodies that should not be there.

➡ Some of these chemicals were banned in the United States twenty years ago, but they still crop up in supermarket produce. Approximately 99 percent of pesticides miss their intended target and find their way into the surrounding environment. There, the chemicals can embark upon long journeys through water flows, air currents, or food webs, and these can last many months and end thousands of miles from the original location. Most of this dispersed pollution is not strong enough to have an immediate impact on humans, making wildlife the primary victim of these contaminants. Despite the rise in the use of pesticides, crop losses from insect damage have actually doubled in the past fifty years. Insects are adapting through mutation, and the chemicals are inadvertently killing the natural predators of these insects, affecting the natural balance and diversity of the ecosystem.

➡ Many pesticides function as endocrine disrupters, altering the hormonal makeup of wildlife and negatively impacting them behaviorally and anatomically. **A** Behavioral abnormalities have been cited in different species of gulls, and immune suppression has been discovered in beluga whales. **B** Reproductive problems have been discovered in alligators, harbor seals, snapping turtles, and western gulls. **C** Rainbow trout have emerged with rudimentary reproductive organs, and individual western and herring gulls have been observed exhibiting mating behaviors of both genders. **D** In 1995, teenagers in Minnesota discovered frogs with up to six legs, and chemical toxins have been cited as the likely cause. Overall, it is clear that pesticides are affecting the health of humans and wildlife alike, but the solution to these problems is unclear and requires global understanding and cooperation.

Volume Review Help Back Next

1 The word "synthetic" in the passage is closest in meaning to

(A) hazardous
(B) mysterious
(C) novel
(D) artificial

2 According to paragraph 1, which of the following is NOT an intended target of pesticides?

(A) Weeds
(B) Insects
(C) Fungi
(D) Chemicals

Paragraph 1 is marked with an arrow [➡].

3 The word "these" in the passage refers to

(A) long journeys
(B) water flows
(C) air currents
(D) food webs

4 The word "inadvertently" in the passage is closest in meaning to

(A) willfully
(B) accidentally
(C) intentionally
(D) unfortunately

5 Which of the following can be inferred from paragraph 2 about insects?

Ⓐ They are playing a more important role in keeping ecosystems balanced.
Ⓑ They are mutating as they have no natural predators left.
Ⓒ They are leading to the development of new chemicals.
Ⓓ They are becoming more resistant to pesticides.

Paragraph 2 is marked with an arrow [➡].

6 According to paragraph 2, which of the following is true of pesticides that enter the environment?

Ⓐ They are effective only after long-term use.
Ⓑ They can travel by natural pathways.
Ⓒ They are not strong enough to affect wildlife.
Ⓓ They can efficiently kill weeds and insects.

Paragraph 2 is marked with an arrow [➡].

7 The word "exhibiting" in the passage is closest in meaning to

Ⓐ obscuring
Ⓑ repressing
Ⓒ displaying
Ⓓ limiting

8 It can be inferred from paragraph 3 that the issues caused by the use of pesticides

Ⓐ affect only certain regions of the planet
Ⓑ are gradually becoming less severe
Ⓒ are unlikely to be resolved any time soon
Ⓓ have a greater effect on wildlife than people

Paragraph 3 is marked with an arrow [➡].

9 Look at the four squares [■] that indicate where the following sentence could be added to the passage.

This phenomenon is commonly observed among species that inhabit marine or freshwater habitats.

Where would the sentence best fit?

Click on a square [■] to add the sentence to the passage.

10 **Directions:** An introductory sentence for a brief summary of the passage is provided below. Complete the summary by selecting the THREE answer choices that express the most important ideas in the passage. Some sentences do not belong in the summary because they express ideas that are not presented in the passage or are minor ideas in the passage. **This question is worth 2 points.**

Drag your answer choices to the spaces where they belong.
To remove an answer choice, click on it. To review the passage, click on **View Text**.

Once believed to be an innovative agricultural tool, pesticides have proven to be harmful to the environment.

-
-
-

Answer Choices

Ⓐ A small percentage of the pesticides applied in agriculture gets into the water and soil.

Ⓑ The increased use of pesticides has led to less crop loss from insect damage.

Ⓒ Pesticides have been linked to a number of health problems in humans.

Ⓓ The majority of pesticides inadvertently enter nearby ecosystems.

Ⓔ Some of the behavioral changes in animals seem to be natural adaptations rather than negative consequences of pesticide exposure.

Ⓕ Pesticides have resulted in abnormal behavior and anatomy in wildlife.

Answer Book p. 29

Vocabulary Review

A. Fill in the blanks with the appropriate words from the box.

ubiquitous	optimum	privilege
exceptions	underestimate	demonstrate

1 The crowd asked the inventor to __________ how his machine worked.

2 You should use this eye cream every night to get the __________ result.

3 Affordable health care should be a basic right for every citizen and not a __________.

4 All students must follow the dress code and there are no __________.

5 The fashion trend was __________, worn all over the world by teenagers.

6 It is wise not to __________ your competition, no matter how weak they appear.

B. Choose the closest meaning for each highlighted word or phrase.

7 Citizens who are knowledgeable about political issues are more likely to vote.
(A) passionate (B) worried (C) informed (D) perplexed

8 Unfortunately, his misguided attempts to fix the problem only made things worse.
(A) mistaken (B) insistent (C) dramatic (D) lengthy

9 Crops began to dwindle as the drought went on for months.
(A) collapse (B) rebound (C) decline (D) stretch

10 Rural areas are characterized by a dispersed population and the low population density.
(A) estimated (B) concentrated (C) scattered (D) settled

11 The water plant uses many filters to remove contaminants from the river.
(A) fragments (B) disorders (C) pollutants (D) ailments

12 He had a back ailment caused by a sports injury that he got in college.
(A) variation (B) illness (C) corruption (D) exception

13 The research team will embark upon a long journey to the North Pole.
(A) begin (B) resolve (C) announce (D) choose

14 She was born with a genetic abnormality that causes severe skin rashes.
(A) compound (B) principle (C) perception (D) irregularity

CHAPTER 07

Rhetorical Purpose

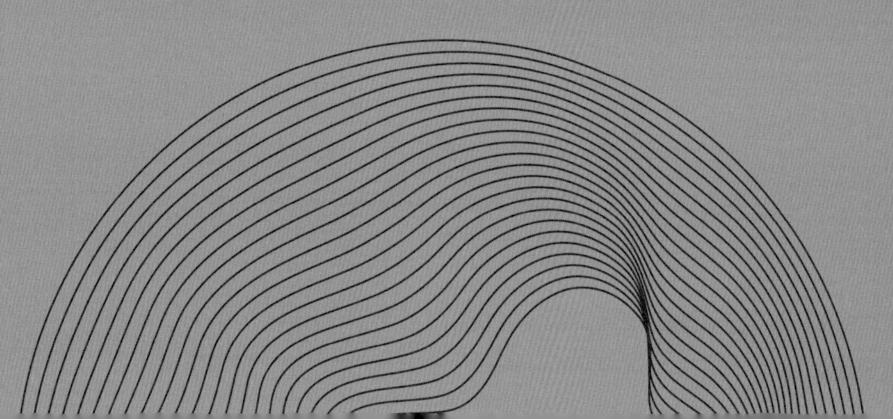

Rhetorical Purpose

About the Question Type

Rhetorical Purpose questions ask you to identify the function of a particular piece of information presented in the paragraph or the passage. Possible functions include explaining a concept, suggesting an option, illustrating a point, making a comparison, and providing an example.

Rhetoric refers to the writing techniques that an author uses to make his or her point effectively. Make sure to understand why the specified piece of information was presented by the author.

Question Format

- Why does the author mention "   " in the passage?
- In paragraph #, the author mentions/discusses/includes "   " in order to

Key Strategies

- **Step 1** — Read the question and locate the specified piece of information in the passage.
- **Step 2** — Use the surrounding context to determine its purpose.
- **Step 3** — Select the answer choice that best describes the rhetorical function of the piece of information.

Example

Answer Book p. 30

Determining Where Earthquakes Occur

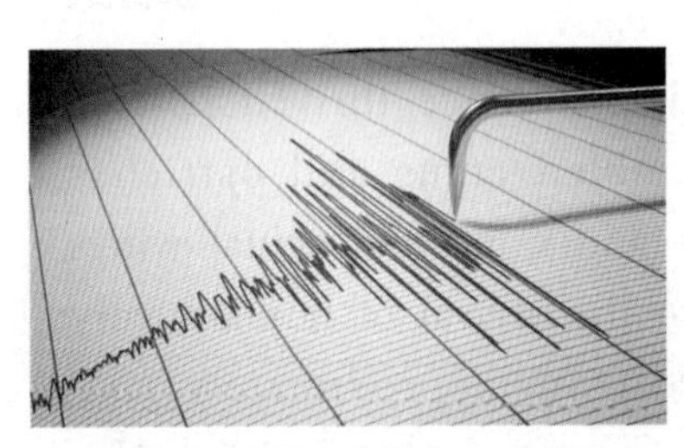

An earthquake is a disturbance that cannot be photographed the way meteorologists can photograph a storm. An earthquake occurs deep inside the earth and can only be felt. Hence, locating an earthquake requires special equipment. Earthquakes may be observed with a network of seismographs, which amplify and record ground motion. The occurrence of an earthquake generates an expanding wave front from the earthquake's hypocenter, or the focus of the earthquake, at a speed of several kilometers per second. As the wave front expands from the hypocenter, it reaches distant seismic stations.

Seismologists use a simple procedure to determine the location and origin time of an earthquake. They obtain this information by using seismographs to record the time at which seismic waves arrive at the stations. The procedure calls for guesswork at the start—the location and origin time are estimated, and then this information is compared with the observed arrival time of the waves at the stations. A series of calculations are then performed until a possible location for the earthquake is identified that is consistent with the speed and distance the waves traveled to reach the stations.

1 Why does the author mention the photographing of a storm by meteorologists in paragraph 1?

(A) To emphasize how far inside the earth earthquakes can occur
(B) To explain how the equipment for measuring earthquakes originated
(C) To offer a contrast to the method used for locating earthquakes
(D) To show the connection between seismology and meteorology

2 Why does the author mention "guesswork" in paragraph 2?

(A) To point out that seismologists are unsure of how to locate an earthquake
(B) To compare how ordinary people and seismologists locate earthquakes
(C) To describe an outdated method for identifying where an earthquake occurs
(D) To explain an initial step in determining the location of an earthquake

Reading Practice 1

Answer Book p. 31

Moa Extinction

Moas were large flightless birds that once thrived in New Zealand. They superficially resembled emus and ostriches, but some could grow much larger and none had actual wings. Estimates of their numbers prior to the arrival of humans vary; scientists propose that anywhere from approximately sixty 5 thousand to more than two million individuals once existed. Now they are known only from a few skeletons and fossilized eggs in museums as all nine species of moa died out around six hundred years ago. Traditionally, scientists debated whether factors such as climate fluctuations and volcanic eruptions contributed to the 10 birds' demise. However, the current consensus is that humans were primarily responsible for their extinction.

When the Polynesian people known as the Maori discovered New Zealand, moas were the largest land animals and the dominant herbivores on the islands. Their only predator was Haast's eagle, which depended on the moas as prey. Otherwise, moas 15 were relatively free from natural enemies. However, this does not mean that they lacked natural vulnerability. For example, their huge eggs were the largest of any bird to date. Yet, despite being eighty times larger than a chicken egg, they were far more prone to break. And because moa females laid only one egg at a time, a broken egg represented a significant loss. Moreover, a newly hatched moa took nearly a decade to reach maturity, 20 so moa populations had low overall reproductive rates.

Still, the moa not only survived but thrived before the arrival of humans. Genetic studies indicate that the last populations were genetically diverse—a sign of strong biological fitness. Perhaps more importantly, according to Maori oral traditions, the moas were once numerous and represented an important source of food for their ancestors. 25 Many of their proverbs also refer to its disappearance, along with that of Haast's eagle. Evidence that moas were hunted to the point of extinction by Maori has been found at numerous archaeological sites throughout New Zealand. Their meat was eaten, their feathers and skins were made into clothing, and their bones were crafted into fish hooks and jewelry. The extinction was hastened when Maori stole the eggs and burnt the forest 30 in which moas lived. Only after two hundred years of human settlement, moas vanished forever.

1 Why does the author mention "a few skeletons and fossilized eggs"?

(A) To suggest that little is known about the behavior of the moa
(B) To show that the moa's original numbers are not possible to confirm
(C) To emphasize that no living moa specimens remain today
(D) To indicate how scientists learned about the moa's appearance

2 The word "demise" in the passage is closest in meaning to

(A) extinction
(B) decrease
(C) evolution
(D) departure

3 According to paragraph 1, all of the following have been proposed as reasons for the moa's extinction EXCEPT

(A) changes in the climate
(B) erupting volcanoes
(C) human activity
(D) competition from herbivores

4 According to paragraph 2, what were TWO characteristics of moa eggs? Choose TWO answers.

(A) They required constant protection against predators.
(B) They took an unusually long time to hatch.
(C) They were the biggest of any bird in history.
(D) They were much more fragile than a chicken egg.

5 Which of the following can be inferred from paragraph 3 about Haast's eagle?

(A) It was never mentioned in Maori proverbs.
(B) It died out as an indirect result of Maori activities.
(C) It was domesticated by the Maori people.
(D) It preyed upon a variety of different organisms.

• Vocabulary Quiz •

The word [ ] is closest in meaning to

1 superficially	2 consensus	3 vulnerability	4 maturity
ⓐ intensely	ⓐ agreement	ⓐ familiarity	ⓐ agreement
ⓑ outwardly	ⓑ explanation	ⓑ weakness	ⓑ retirement
ⓒ rightfully	ⓒ portrayal	ⓒ experience	ⓒ adulthood

Reading Practice 2

Answer Book p. 32

North American Petroglyphs

A petroglyph is a form of rock art that has been practiced for thousands of years. Petroglyphs are distinct from pictographs in that the latter are painted onto rock surfaces while the former are carved into the surface of the rock. The carvings are created with a stone chisel, which scratches the stone in order to uncover a contrasting color of rock under the top layer. Petroglyphs cannot be washed away, so they last a very long time. There are petroglyphs all over the world, but North America contains some particularly remarkable specimens of the ancient art form.

The oldest known petroglyphs in North America were carved in Reno, Nevada between 10,000 and 14,800 years ago. The petroglyphs consist of geometric patterns such as circles and diamonds alongside tree-like shapes carved into a collection of enormous boulders. When the ancient carvings were dated by scientists in 2013, the results were astounding because it had been thought that the earliest humans in North America arrived some 14,000 years ago. This artwork would seem to indicate that the best previous estimates of the arrival of people on the continent may be inaccurate. The petroglyphs could be among the only works of art that the earliest inhabitants of North America left behind.

Another remarkable collection of rock art can be found in Albuquerque, New Mexico's Petroglyph National Monument. There are over 24,000 images carved within the boundary of the monument. Most of them were likely chiseled after AD 1300, but some may reach back as far as 2000 BC. The artists were mostly ancient Pueblo people, although some of the early Spanish settlers in New Mexico added to the carvings beginning in the 1700s. The Spanish influence may have terminated the practice of making petroglyphs after 1680 because the Catholic priests discouraged Puebloans from engaging in the sorts of traditional ceremonies in which the rock carvings were likely created. Still, these depictions of animals, people, stars, spirals, and geometric shapes reflect aspects of the Pueblo people's social customs and religious rites, and they function as a valuable record of their culture.

Glossary

· boulder: a very large rock

1 The author's description of petroglyphs in paragraph 1 mentions all of the following EXCEPT
(A) the distinction between them and other forms of rock art
(B) the instrument used to create the rock carvings
(C) the reason they endure for thousands of years
(D) the types of images depicted in ancient carvings

2 The word "astounding" in the passage is closest in meaning to
(A) satisfying
(B) shocking
(C) convincing
(D) noteworthy

3 The author discusses the date the Reno petroglyphs were created in paragraph 2 in order to
(A) contrast the great age of these works with the more recent petroglyphs
(B) provide evidence that the Reno petroglyphs are the earliest rock carvings in the world
(C) stress that the petroglyphs challenged estimates of the arrival of humans in North America
(D) question the accuracy of the methods used to date the petroglyphs in Reno

4 The word "they" in the passage refers to
(A) depictions
(B) aspects
(C) customs
(D) rites

5 It can be inferred from paragraph 3 that the Spanish discouraged Pueblo ceremonies because
(A) the ceremonies were thought to conflict with Catholic beliefs
(B) the Spanish feared the ceremonies were used to plot wars against them
(C) the Spanish wished to be the only group making petroglyphs
(D) the ceremonies were openly hostile to the Spanish settlers

• Vocabulary Quiz •

The word [ ] is closest in meaning to

1 uncover
ⓐ provoke
ⓑ reveal
ⓒ install

2 specimens
ⓐ samples
ⓑ materials
ⓒ elements

3 estimates
ⓐ documents
ⓑ guesses
ⓒ domains

4 terminated
ⓐ adapted
ⓑ ended
ⓒ incited

Reading Practice 3

Answer Book p. 32

Object Permanence in Infants

Studying the psychological characteristics of infants is obviously more challenging than studying the same qualities in adults because babies are incapable of self-reporting. The researcher faces the same dilemma that parents face when attempting to interpret the thoughts and feelings of a preverbal child: the infant cannot tell you what he or she thinks. Therefore, even longstanding and abundantly tested theories of infant behavior or mental processes are open to criticism. Such is the case with Jean Piaget's famous concept of object permanence, a key facet of the psychologist's 1954 theory of cognitive development.

People who have spent time playing with babies know that young infants naturally become distressed when objects disappear. Games of "peekaboo" or "now you see it, now you don't" are demonstrations of the mental deficit that Piaget observed. Newborns, he suspected, do not realize that objects do not cease to exist when they escape the child's range of vision. Only after a period of a few months do young humans develop the *schema* (basic units of knowledge) required to realize that an object remains permanent even when out of view.

Piaget had a fairly simple method for testing infants' capacity for object permanence. He would put a toy into a baby's line of sight and then hide it. Then he would observe and record the child's reaction to the toy's seeming disappearance. If the child searched for the missing toy, Piaget assumed that he or she had acquired an understanding of object permanence. If, on the other hand, the child became upset about the missing object, he assumed that this pivotal developmental milestone had not yet been attained.

Critics of Piaget's conclusions argued that he underestimated the mental capacities of very young infants. They pointed out that infants who seemingly failed to recognize the continued existence of absent objects may simply have insufficient motor skills to initiate a search for those objects. Or perhaps their memories were not as well developed as those of the children who did conduct searches. It is even possible that the problem was a lack of interest in the toy. In other words, object permanence could be present in the minds of every infant but be concealed by certain variables. Researchers today continue to craft new experiments aimed at correcting these vulnerabilities, but the unavoidable fact is that infants are difficult to study.

Glossary

· preverbal: being before the development of speech

1 Why does the author mention "parents" in paragraph 1?

(A) To suggest that people know their children better than psychologists possibly can
(B) To demonstrate the universality of the struggle to understand babies
(C) To imply that Piaget had an innate bond with the children he studied
(D) To argue that adults too sometimes lack object permanence

2 The word "they" in the passage refers to

(A) games
(B) demonstrations
(C) newborns
(D) objects

3 The word "attained" in the passage is closest in meaning to

(A) achieved
(B) guaranteed
(C) disapproved
(D) identified

4 According to paragraph 3, what did Piaget believe was a sign that a child possessed object permanence?

(A) A negative emotional reaction to the loss of a toy
(B) An effort to find an item that was suddenly removed
(C) An attempt to hide an object that was just acquired
(D) A clear understanding of a researcher's expectations

5 According to paragraph 4, the lack of object permanence in infants can be explained by all of the following EXCEPT

(A) a deficit in physical coordination
(B) indifference to the object that disappeared
(C) overstimulation limiting body movement
(D) an inability to remember the missing toy

• Vocabulary Quiz •

The word [ ] is closest in meaning to

1 attempting
ⓐ trying
ⓑ learning
ⓒ failing

2 criticism
ⓐ negotiation
ⓑ public
ⓒ objection

3 distressed
ⓐ upset
ⓑ glad
ⓒ messy

4 deficit
ⓐ urge
ⓑ disadvantage
ⓒ lack

Reading Practice 4

Answer Book p. 33

The Uncovering of Pompeii

After the eruption of Mt. Vesuvius in AD 79, the town of Pompeii literally vanished. As the years passed, the area became known as *Civitas* or The City. Therefore, the existence of a town there was never totally forgotten. However, Pompeii's cultural 5 and economic significance, and even its name, were. Even locals did not realize that the ancient Roman way of life had been preserved below the surface. The remains lay largely intact for many centuries until a series of excavations revealed Pompeii once again.

The first major rediscovery of Pompeii occurred by accident in 1592. When an 10 Italian architect named Domenico Fontana was building an underground aqueduct in the area, he uncovered ancient walls with paintings and inscriptions. Some work was conducted in the next few years, but a destructive earthquake halted progress in 1631. In the 1680s, the discovery of a stone inscribed with the phrase *Decurio Pompeiis* (town councillor of Pompeii) was wrongly believed to refer to the Roman emperor Pompey the 15 Great. Then, in 1699, Italian archaeologist Giuseppe Macrini asserted that the site was actually Pompeii, but his claim was widely viewed with skepticism. It was not until 1763 that anyone knew with certainty what Fontana had found. In 1763, an archaeological excavation found an inscription that clearly identified the name of the ancient town as Pompeii. 20

Many of the early excavations revealed very little about Pompeii. Charles III of Spain once ordered the removal of debris in order to look for ancient artifacts with which to decorate his palace. However, when no gold or valuables were found, the pits were filled in and left. This type of treasure hunting was typical and caused substantial damage. Even the digs of J.J. Winckelmann and Karl Weber, who are considered the fathers of 25 archaeology, did not avoid creating a mess. However, Weber did uncover the Temple of Fortuna Augusta, a worship site with marble columns and an altar.

In the 1800s and 1900s, excavations became more careful and systematic. They unearthed an amazingly detailed snapshot of daily life and showed that Pompeii was a prosperous city. It was a place where the wealthy lived, and where there were many 30 leisure and entertainment facilities. This is evidenced by the existence of a stadium for gladiator fights and other contests that could seat twenty thousand spectators, a theater where comedies and tragedies were performed, and numerous public and private baths.

1 Why does the author mention "*Civitas*" in the passage?

(A) To show that Pompeii was culturally and economically important
(B) To suggest that local people were familiar with Pompeii's way of life
(C) To emphasize that the name of Pompeii was forgotten
(D) To explain why no excavations were made for many centuries

2 The word "halted" in the passage is closest in meaning to

(A) diminished
(B) stopped
(C) hastened
(D) amended

3 What can be inferred from paragraph 2 about Italian archaeologist Giuseppe Macrini?

(A) He participated in the construction of an aqueduct.
(B) His evidence for a claim about Pompeii was inconclusive.
(C) His excavations revealed a stone with an important inscription.
(D) He inspired other experts to investigate the Pompeii site.

4 According to paragraph 3, which of the following is true of the early excavations of Pompeii?

(A) They resulted in the discovery of many valuable artifacts.
(B) They were abandoned because of their expense.
(C) They were conducted by Italian archaeologists.
(D) They caused much harm to the ancient site.

5 What was NOT mentioned in paragraph 4 in support of Pompeii having many arts and entertainment facilities?

(A) Luxury resorts for wealthy tourists
(B) Arenas large enough for 20,000 viewers
(C) A venue for theatrical performances
(D) Public and private bathing facilities

• Vocabulary Quiz •

The word [ ] is closest in meaning to

1 intact	2 inscribed	3 skepticism	4 unearthed
ⓐ tremendous	ⓐ repelled	ⓐ outlook	ⓐ worked on
ⓑ untouched	ⓑ engraved	ⓑ irony	ⓑ dug up
ⓒ impoverished	ⓒ detected	ⓒ disbelief	ⓒ left out

iBT Reading Test

Answer Book p. 34

TOEFL Reading

The Role of the Brain Stem

The human brain is comprised of several parts that control the various functions of the body. All of the information to and from our body passes through the brain stem. Some scientists consider it a simple part of the brain because some animals have brains that consist entirely of just the brain stem. However, the role of the brain stem is by no means simple, as it is responsible for vital life functions. 5

➡ The upper part of the brain stem is called the midbrain, and it controls involuntary actions. The frontal part of the midbrain influences functions such as vision and auditory perception, while the rear part interfaces with the cerebral cortex and is important for voluntary motor functions. **A** The pons is also a part of the brain stem and is somewhat like a hub for a highway system. **B** For example, information from the ear first enters the brain 10 in the pons, which relays this information to the midbrain and subsequently to other parts of the brain. **C** The pons also affects consciousness and is crucial during deep sleep. **D**

➡ Below the pons and continuous with the spinal cord is the medulla, which transmits nerve signals between the spinal cord and the brain. The medulla is the brain's reflex center and controls automatic responses such as sneezing. Similarly, it manages involuntary 15 muscular activities like respiration and heart contraction. Thus, it is crucial for regulating blood chemistry. For instance, if the blood becomes too acidic, the medulla conveys chemical signals to muscle tissues, causing them to contract and supply more oxygen to the blood. Blockage of blood vessels that leads to a stroke can damage the medulla and result in the loss of the sensation of touch in parts of the body. 20

➡ Due to its proximity to bone structures, the brain stem is susceptible to damage from impact. Nerve fibers in the brain stem do not readily regenerate; hence, injury may result in permanent loss of function. A patient who suffers brain damage may recover, but serious damage to the brain stem is difficult to overcome. In this situation, the brain stem is unable to control the vital functions, and there is virtually no chance of survival. 25

Glossary

stroke: sudden loss of consciousness caused when a blood vessel in the brain is blocked

Volume Review Help Back Next

1 The phrase "by no means" in the passage is closest in meaning to

Ⓐ almost
Ⓑ hardly
Ⓒ ever
Ⓓ slightly

2 Some scientists consider the brain stem simple because

Ⓐ it conveys the most basic information of any part of the brain.
Ⓑ it only performs functions that are not complex.
Ⓒ it constitutes the entire brain of some organisms.
Ⓓ it was formed during the earliest stage of human evolution.

3 Why does the author mention "a hub for a highway system"?

Ⓐ To emphasize the significance of part of the brain
Ⓑ To describe the physical appearance of the brain
Ⓒ To explain the function of a brain component
Ⓓ To describe how the brain stores information

4 According to paragraph 2, which of the following is true of the front of the midbrain?

Ⓐ It is connected to the cerebral cortex.
Ⓑ It is associated with deep sleep.
Ⓒ It is crucial for sleep and consciousness.
Ⓓ It is important for hearing and sight.

Paragraph 2 is marked with an arrow [➡].

5 According to paragraph 3, which of the following is NOT a direct function of the medulla?

Ⓐ Balancing the chemistry of the blood
Ⓑ Regulating breathing
Ⓒ Managing voluntary muscle movements
Ⓓ Controlling the heartbeat

Paragraph 3 is marked with an arrow [➡].

6 According to paragraph 3, which of the following is a possible outcome of damage to the medulla?

Ⓐ Some memory functions can be disrupted.
Ⓑ Blood vessel blockages can lead to stroke.
Ⓒ The blood in the body can become too acidic.
Ⓓ Some body parts can lose their sense of touch.

Paragraph 3 is marked with an arrow [➡].

7 The word "readily" in the passage is closest in meaning to

Ⓐ inevitably
Ⓑ gradually
Ⓒ easily
Ⓓ rapidly

8 Which of the following can be inferred from paragraph 4 about significant damage to the brain stem?

Ⓐ It is usually possible to heal with medical treatment.
Ⓑ It is less serious than other forms of brain damage.
Ⓒ It is highly likely to result in the death of the patient.
Ⓓ It is typically followed by the regeneration of nerve fibers.

Paragraph 4 is marked with an arrow [➡].

9 Look at the four squares [■] that indicate where the following sentence could be added to the passage.

This is because it is responsible for relaxing muscles so that they do not overreact while people are dreaming.

Where would the sentence best fit?

Click on a square [■] to add the sentence to the passage.

10 **Directions:** An introductory sentence for a brief summary of the passage is provided below. Complete the summary by selecting the THREE answer choices that express the most important ideas in the passage. Some sentences do not belong in the summary because they express ideas that are not presented in the passage or are minor ideas in the passage. **This question is worth 2 points.**

Drag your answer choices to the spaces where they belong.
To remove an answer choice, click on it. To review the passage, click on **View Text**.

The brain stem plays a vital role in bodily functions.

•

•

•

Answer Choices

(A) The medulla is the portion of the brain stem that passes information between the brain and spinal cord.

(B) Because of the brain stem's nearness to bone structures, sudden impact can damage it and lead to severe consequences.

(C) Voluntary motor functions are primarily controlled by the cerebral cortex.

(D) The midbrain and the pons each play a variety of important roles in the brain stem.

(E) Injuries to the brain stem are the most common types of brain damage in patients.

(F) The portion of the brain system directly below the medulla is the pons.

Answer Book p. 34

Vocabulary Review

A. Fill in the blanks with the appropriate words from the box.

artifacts	discouraged	fluctuations
generate	assumed	inaccurate

1 There have been many unpredictable weather __________ due to climate change.

2 Brainstorming together can help __________ many creative and interesting ideas.

3 The measurements the scientist took were __________, so he had to take them again.

4 The museum will display the Egyptian __________ for the entire year.

5 Park rangers __________ hikers from going up the mountain because of the storm.

6 She __________ the train would be on time, so she was surprised when it was late.

B. Choose the closest meaning for each highlighted word or phrase.

7 It is typical for blue whales to migrate through the region this time of year.
(A) scarce (B) usual (C) casual (D) basic

8 There are many variables in the experiment that can change in an instant.
(A) factors (B) restrictions (C) borders (D) reactions

9 Most marine animals can detect any kind of disturbance in the water.
(A) pressure (B) dwelling (C) arrangement (D) disruption

10 Blinking is an involuntary action that prevents the eye from drying out.
(A) accidental (B) unconscious (C) effective (D) certified

11 Patients with a weak immune system are more susceptible to pneumonia.
(A) impervious (B) restricted (C) sarcastic (D) vulnerable

12 The millionaire stored his valuables in a safe hidden behind a painting.
(A) assets (B) donations (C) codes (D) reports

13 Large crowds are unavoidable at the beach during the summer in Korea.
(A) inevitable (B) plentiful (C) fundamental (D) extraordinary

14 The creation of environmental laws was hastened by new data on rising sea levels.
(A) unaffected (B) magnified (C) accelerated (D) shielded

CHAPTER 08

Sentence Insertion

Sentence Insertion

About the Question Type

Sentence Insertion questions ask you to identify the best place within a paragraph to insert the given sentence.

To understand the logical connections between sentences, pay attention to words or phrases that indicate the logical relationships between the sentences marked by the squares. These include, among others, conjunctive adverbs such as *however*, *therefore*, *nevertheless*, *yet*, and *moreover*, as well as pronouns like *it*, *they*, *this* and *that*.

Question Format

Look at the four squares [■] that indicate where the following sentence could be added to the passage.

[A given sentence]

Where would the sentence best fit?

Click on a square [■] to add the sentence to the passage.

Key Strategies

- **Step 1** — Read the given sentence and look for transitional words or phrases. Use these to determine the logical relationship between the given sentence and the rest of the paragraph.
- **Step 2** — Determine the location the sentence should be placed in the paragraph.
- **Step 3** — Confirm that the paragraph has a logical flow with the sentence inserted.

Example

Answer Book p. 35

Common Cold

It is a fact that most colds occur more frequently in the fall and winter than in the summer. However, unlike what most people believe, cold weather has little or no direct effect on the development or severity of a cold. ■A The main reason people catch a cold in winter is that they spend more time indoors to get away from the bad weather. ■B Thus, they are in closer proximity to each other, increasing the likelihood of infection risk. ■C Moreover, common cold-causing viruses survive better when the humidity is low, which is the case during the colder months of the year. ■D

Over the course of a single year, individuals in the United States suffer some one billion colds. A large percentage of that is attributed to children who have a lower resistance to viral infection and also come into greater contact with other children at daycare centers and schools. ■A In fact, children catch anywhere from six to ten colds per year, accounting for 190 million missed school days annually. ■B In addition, parents miss 120 million workdays in order to stay home to care for their children. ■C In fact, the economic cost of the common cold exceeds 20 billion dollars over the country. ■D

1 Look at the four squares [■] in paragraph 1 that indicate where the following sentence could be added to the passage.

Less moisture in the air also tends to dry up the lining of the nasal passages, making a person more vulnerable to viral infection.

Where would the sentence best fit?

2 Look at the four squares [■] in paragraph 2 that indicate where the following sentence could be added to the passage.

This loss of manpower has a negative impact on the national economy.

Where would the sentence best fit?

Reading Practice 1

Answer Book p. 36

The Development of Writing Tools

Of all human inventions, writing is one of the greatest. It allows people from all over to record ideas, beliefs, and discoveries and share them across borders and across time. However, it was not always as easy as putting pen to paper to jot something down. In the beginning, the tools used for writing were quite different from what we know today.

In fact, the earliest writing tools did not use pigments at all. **A** The Chinese, for example, carved words into turtle shells or animal bones. **B** Ancient Sumerians used a stylus to make markings in soft clay tablets that could be reused or baked for permanence. **C** Romans had a similar system using wax tablets, which could be easily erased and used again. **D** Marks in bone could not be erased, clay was brittle and difficult to work with, and wax tablets were not heat resistant. As time went on, people found better ways to document their history.

The first evidence of writing with ink comes from ancient Egypt sometime around 3000 BC. Egyptians invented a writing material called papyrus, which was made from thin layers of reed. It was one of the first truly practical and stable surfaces. Fittingly, they also invented the reed pen, which was a length of reed cut to a point that was dipped in ink. Such a rudimentary tool was serviceable but time-consuming to make and annoying to use. This is when a leap in advancement came from Europe: quill pens. Quills were made from the feathers of large birds, and the hollow shaft in the feather could be filled with ink that flowed into the tip. This allowed for longer writing sessions without the hassle of dipping the points, which is why they dominated writing for the longest period in history—over a thousand years.

Another significant development occurred in the nineteenth century as a result of the technological advances of the Industrial Revolution. The availability of resources like steel and the proliferation of machines meant that a new type of pen could be manufactured. Englishman James Perry produced the first metal nib pen in 1819, and, by 1835, his company was producing more than five million of them a year. This simple, cheap, and durable pen paved the way for fountain pens, ballpoint pens, and mechanical pencils, making writing much more convenient.

1 Look at the four squares [■] that indicate where the following sentence could be added to the passage.

Though quite innovative in their own right, these methods had their shortcomings.

Where would the sentence best fit?

2 The word "rudimentary" in the passage is closest in meaning to

(A) exemplary
(B) basic
(C) compulsive
(D) sophisticated

3 The word "they" in the passage refers to

(A) quills
(B) birds
(C) sessions
(D) points

4 In paragraph 3, why does the author mention that quill pens had a hollow shaft?

(A) To criticize a feature of their design that was inconvenient
(B) To explain why they were used for an extended period
(C) To stress that they took a lot of time to produce
(D) To compare them with other types of European pens

5 According to paragraph 4, which of the following is NOT true about metal pens?

(A) They were invented during the Industrial Revolution.
(B) Millions of them were produced by 1819.
(C) They were the precursors to fountain and ballpoint pens.
(D) They were not expensive or fragile.

• Vocabulary Quiz •

The word [ ] is closest in meaning to

1 stable
ⓐ reliable
ⓑ innovative
ⓒ conventional

2 serviceable
ⓐ useful
ⓑ accurate
ⓒ tedious

3 hassle
ⓐ limit
ⓑ bother
ⓒ habit

4 proliferation
ⓐ criticism
ⓑ origin
ⓒ increase

Reading Practice 2

Answer Book p. 36

The Advantages of Aquatic Environments

Approximately 70 percent of our planet is covered in water, which provides many advantages for the aquatic life that inhabits it. While air temperature may fluctuate by up to 20 degrees a day, water temperature remains relatively stable, varying only a few degrees daily. Seasonal fluctuations are also moderate, creating stable year-round conditions. Water constantly bathes the internal and external surfaces of aquatic life forms. As a result, aquatic creatures do not need to develop intricate body-heat maintenance systems or consume significant amounts of fluids like terrestrial animals. They also do not require elaborate respiratory structures for the diffusion of gases. In addition, the density and viscosity of water creates favorable conditions for invertebrates, as the water can provide the support that backbones provide for vertebrates.

Many nutrients and salts are already dissolved in water and can easily be absorbed by aquatic life forms. Microscopic plant and animal life also float in the water. Therefore, many marine creatures, particularly invertebrates, capture their food in a stationary manner through suspension-feeding. This method does not require a significant level of exertion. Organisms such as jellyfish float around and filter their food from the water. Such feeding behavior is extremely rare in terrestrial environments, where web-building spiders are a notable exception. The spider's web functions much like a net, in that it is used to passively catch insects so that the spider does not have to actively search for prey. Aquatic suspension-feeders have a filter system in their bodies that functions in a similar manner, offering them an advantage over terrestrial suspension-feeders.

Reproduction is also considerably easier in water than on land. Sponges reproduce asexually, creating gemmules, or little packets of various cells. **A** These packets eventually grow into adult sponges in a few months. **B** In sexual reproduction, the female might lay many eggs, millions for certain species, and wait for them to be fertilized by a male. **C** The fertilized eggs can be left on their own to mature in the water, while terrestrial animals must fertilize internally and carry the embryo around for several months. **D**

Glossary

· viscosity: the property of liquid that determines how fast or slow it flows

1 Which of the following is NOT a characteristic of water advantageous to supporting life?

(A) Temperature
(B) Density
(C) Transparency
(D) Viscosity

2 The word "stationary" in the passage is closest in meaning to

(A) active
(B) organized
(C) permanent
(D) unmoving

3 It can be inferred from paragraph 2 that aquatic suspension-feeders

(A) expend little energy searching for food
(B) construct web-like structures to capture prey
(C) employ less effective methods than spiders
(D) consume only microscopic plant matter

4 The word "them" in the passage refers to

(A) sponges
(B) eggs
(C) millions
(D) species

5 Look at the four squares [■] that indicate where the following sentence could be added to the passage.

As a result, land animals pay a higher physical cost to produce new offspring.

Where would the sentence best fit?

• Vocabulary Quiz •

The word [ ] is closest in meaning to

1 maintenance
ⓐ distribution
ⓑ conservation
ⓒ automation

2 diffusion
ⓐ spread
ⓑ limit
ⓒ mixture

3 favorable
ⓐ insufficient
ⓑ ambiguous
ⓒ advantageous

4 eventually
ⓐ loosely
ⓑ ultimately
ⓒ probably

Reading Practice 3

Answer Book p. 37

The Inuit Way of Life

The Inuit are the indigenous people of the Arctic regions of Greenland, Canada, and the United States. For thousands of years, they met the challenges of living in a severe environment. Keeping to specific territories, clusters of family groups used skill and ingenuity to survive. Some groups consisted of no more than a dozen members, while others, in the more productive areas of the Arctic, had as many as a few hundred. These were politically autonomous groups with no official form of government and no single leader to make all of the decisions.

Most of the Inuit's activities were centered on the sea because it provided them with many resources. At times, they did make forays inland, but these were conducted during certain seasons and only to obtain food staples such as caribou meat. The manner in which the Inuit lived revealed that they considered themselves a part of the environment, and they respected nature as a result. They took only what they needed, and the animals they killed became food, clothes, tools, and other supplies.

Their way of living, however, was challenged when European explorers journeyed into their territories in the eighteenth century. The newcomers believed that nature was something to be conquered, and the rich lands and sea provided an abundance of resources they hoped to take advantage of. It was not difficult for whalers and other traders to exploit the area as it was so expansive. The Arctic people thus found themselves forced to cope with the influx of new settlers and their activities.

By the beginning of the twentieth century, life for the Inuit had changed drastically. **A** They could no longer hunt for food due to overfishing and overhunting and were forced to barter for goods with Western traders. **B** Becoming more dependent on others meant that they lost much of their former self-sufficiency. **C** In addition, newly formed governments in the area viewed the Inuit as barbaric and naive. **D** While this did benefit the Inuit in some ways—providing better healthcare and job opportunities—much of their traditional way of life and cultural heritage was unfortunately lost.

Glossary

· foray: an initial attempt outside one's usual area

1 The word "ingenuity" in the passage is closest in meaning to
(A) optimism
(B) cleverness
(C) strength
(D) heritage

2 Why did the author mention the Inuit's "forays inland" in the passage?
(A) To describe the ignorance of the Inuit
(B) To show the resilience of the Inuit
(C) To provide an example of a challenge the Inuit faced
(D) To identify another source of food for the Inuit

3 What can be inferred from paragraph 2 about the Inuit and animals?
(A) The Inuit used the whole animal without waste.
(B) The animals the Inuit liked best were the ones from land.
(C) The Inuit killed more animals than they needed.
(D) An animal was the most sacred being to the Inuit.

4 According to paragraph 3, which of the following is true?
(A) The Inuit served as guides for many of the early European explorers.
(B) The Inuit viewed their environment as an enemy to be defeated.
(C) Whalers and traders were able to profit from the Arctic region due to its vastness.
(D) The new settlers in the Arctic region provided significant benefits to the Inuit.

5 Look at the four squares [■] that indicate where the following sentence could be added to the passage.
As such, they established many different kinds of programs that promoted the assimilation of the Inuit into more "civilized" culture.
Where would the sentence best fit?

• **Vocabulary Quiz** •

The word [ ] is closest in meaning to

1 severe
ⓐ hidden
ⓑ harsh
ⓒ broad

2 cope with
ⓐ overcome
ⓑ absorb
ⓒ regard

3 drastically
ⓐ scarcely
ⓑ immensely
ⓒ recently

4 barter
ⓐ replicate
ⓑ indicate
ⓒ exchange

Reading Practice 4

Answer Book p. 38

The Industrial Revolution's Environmental Impact

Around 1760, the world began to undergo an irrevocable change. A number of important innovations, including steam power and new methods to produce textiles and iron, sparked the Industrial Revolution. The move from an agricultural economy to an industrial one changed the fundamental structures of society—the way people worked, lived, and played. Yet along with the alterations to society, the Industrial Revolution also radically transformed the planet and not for the better. As one historian put it, "With few exceptions, the world's modern environmental problems began with or were greatly exacerbated by the Industrial Revolution."

One of the biggest consequences was the decline in air quality, and the biggest culprit was coal. The Industrial Revolution was powered by it, leading to huge quantities of smoke being pumped into the atmosphere. Copious amounts of particulate matter rose drastically, creating a perpetual haze over cities. Respiratory illness and a higher death rate quickly followed from all of the smog. **A** In addition, carbon dioxide—a byproduct of burning coal—caused an unnatural rise in global temperatures. **B** Of course, the earth has gone through cooling and warming periods in the past, but these changes usually occurred gradually and naturally over millennia. **C** However, the Industrial Revolution introduced a sudden burning of fossil fuels, triggering a dramatic warming of the climate over a very short period of time. **D** These changes have led to mass extinctions, rising sea levels, and unpredictable and severe weather patterns.

Other nonrenewable resources that were used as fuels, such as oil and gas, had their own issues. These energy sources are derived from beneath the earth's crust, so ecosystems above the ground have largely evolved in their absence. With their introduction to the surface from drilling, though, the toxins that were released have, in essence, poisoned the biosphere, causing an immense loss in the biodiversity of both plants and animals. Contaminated soil and water also caused crops to suffer severely.

Since the first factory opened, the earth has been heading toward an environmental tipping point. If it hits the threshold, the collapse of all natural systems could occur with no hope of turning back. Such an impact does not extend merely to the land, seas, and air but to future generations who may one day inherit an unlivable planet.

Glossary

· particulate matter: a mixture of fine dust and liquid droplets suspended in air

1 The word "exacerbated" in the passage is closest in meaning to

(A) worsened
(B) stabilized
(C) measured
(D) proceeded

2 Look at the four squares [■] that indicate where the following sentence could be added to the passage.

As a result, life on the plant had sufficient time to make the necessary adjustment to the new climate conditions.

Where would the sentence best fit?

3 Which of the following is NOT mentioned in paragraph 2 as a consequence of the increased use of coal?

(A) A worsening of the air quality
(B) An increase in respiratory diseases
(C) A decline in urban population size
(D) A rise in global temperatures

4 The word "their" in the passage refers to

(A) fuels
(B) issues
(C) sources
(D) ecosystems

5 According to paragraph 3, which of the following is true of oil and gas drilling?

(A) It consumes a large amount of energy.
(B) It negatively affects agricultural activities.
(C) It has a greater impact on plants than animals.
(D) It reduces available water supplies in a region.

• **Vocabulary Quiz** •

The word [ ] is closest in meaning to

1 irrevocable	2 perpetual	3 triggering	4 inherit
ⓐ careless	ⓐ continual	ⓐ observing	ⓐ challenge
ⓑ improper	ⓑ resilient	ⓑ causing	ⓑ receive
ⓒ permanent	ⓒ impressive	ⓒ completing	ⓒ preserve

Answer Book p. 39

TOEFL Reading

The Medici and the Renaissance

➡ The very mention of the Renaissance brings to mind artists with meticulous technique who were capable of producing photorealistic portraiture. There is no denying that art advanced by leaps and bounds during the fifteenth and sixteenth centuries, nowhere more than in Florence, Italy. However, it is easy to overlook the extent to which art during this period was inevitably linked to money, religion, and politics. This is the complicated legacy of the Medici, a banking family from Florence who used their fortune to commission art that helped to cement their own dominance.

➡ The Medici funded the artistic Renaissance in part as a marketing strategy for the family bank, which was founded by Giovanni de' Medici in 1397. [A] Giovanni's son, Cosimo the Elder, established Florence as the cultural center of Europe, which was good for business. [B] Artists like Leonardo da Vinci and Michelangelo visited the Medici homes, lending the bankers legitimacy as leading intellectual figures. [C] The art the bankers commissioned was opulent and was often made of valuable materials. [D] Portraits of family members were common, spreading the family's reputation.

➡ Much of the Renaissance artwork commissioned by the Medici had religious themes, and doing this served the purpose of compensating for their religiously questionable banking practices. Charging interest on loans was forbidden by the teachings of religious leaders. The Medici family, which produced four Catholic popes, technically obeyed Christian laws but pushed their limits by profiting on currency exchanges in foreign trade. It was in the family's best interests to portray themselves as a pious family incapable of violating religious principles. Moreover, some of the Medici may have been uncertain of their standing in heaven, since theologians were divided on the morality of their banking policies. For both reasons, commissioning biblical paintings with Medici family members inserted therein was sensible.

➡ The Medici were also powerful political figures who ruled Florence for generations, another reason to invest heavily in art. Family portraits, such as images of Medici matriarch Eleonora of Toledo posing next to her son, the heir to the Medici dynasty, functioned as political propaganda. They projected the family's power, suggested that the dynasty would continue, and bolstered a politically advantageous reputation for cultural refinement.

Volume Review Help Back Next

1 The word "meticulous" in the passage is closest in meaning to

Ⓐ impressive
Ⓑ careful
Ⓒ expressive
Ⓓ gorgeous

2 According to paragraph 1, the art of the fifteenth and sixteenth century

Ⓐ made significant advancements
Ⓑ had limited aesthetic value
Ⓒ generated great wealth for artists
Ⓓ was criticized by religious leaders

Paragraph 1 is marked with an arrow [➡].

3 Which of the following is NOT mentioned in paragraph 2 as evidence of the Medici's cultural prominence?

Ⓐ The famous artists who called on the Medici in person
Ⓑ The Medici's tendency to commission paintings of themselves
Ⓒ The improvements to Florence's architecture paid for by the Medici
Ⓓ The expensive and impressive quality of Medici-sponsored art

Paragraph 2 is marked with an arrow [➡].

4 Which of the sentences below best expresses the essential information in the highlighted sentence in the passage? *Incorrect* choices change the meaning in important ways or leave out essential information.

Ⓐ The Medici commissioned religious art to make up for their dubious business methods.
Ⓑ Because the Medici were suspicious characters that few trusted, they invested heavily in Biblical paintings.
Ⓒ It made the Medici look better that they were involved in the production of sacred artwork.
Ⓓ The Medici were unsure they were not violating Christian principles in their banking practices.

5 The word "their" in the passage refers to

Ⓐ loans
Ⓑ leaders
Ⓒ popes
Ⓓ laws

6 According to paragraph 3, the Medici made a profit by

Ⓐ selling artwork to wealthy galleries
Ⓑ raising taxes on the people of Florence
Ⓒ exchanging the currencies of other countries
Ⓓ establishing the official bank of the Catholic Church

Paragraph 3 is marked with an arrow [➡].

7 The word "bolstered" in the passage is closest in meaning to

Ⓐ boosted
Ⓑ depended
Ⓒ succeeded
Ⓓ defined

8 It can be inferred from paragraph 4 that the Medici commissioned portraits of Eleanora of Toledo because

Ⓐ she was exceptionally beautiful
Ⓑ they wanted her to reign over Florence
Ⓒ they wanted their family to retain power
Ⓓ she convinced the men in the family to do so

Paragraph 4 is marked with an arrow [➡].

9 Look at the four squares [■] that indicate where the following sentence could be added to the passage.

For example, one bronze bust of Cosimo by the sculptor Cellini features priceless silver eyes.

Where would the sentence best fit?

Click on a square [■] to add the sentence to the passage.

10 **Directions:** An introductory sentence for a brief summary of the passage is provided below. Complete the summary by selecting the THREE answer choices that express the most important ideas in the passage. Some sentences do not belong in the summary because they express ideas that are not presented in the passage or are minor ideas in the passage. **This question is worth 2 points.**

Drag your answer choices to the spaces where they belong.
To remove an answer choice, click on it. To review the passage, click on **View Text**.

The Medici were a family of Florence whose riches powered the Renaissance.

•

•

•

Answer Choices

(A) The Medici family bank received positive publicity for its association with art.

(B) Michelangelo was a guest at the Medici home and was hired to create art for the family.

(C) The Medici used portraits to advance their political dominance in Florence.

(D) Renaissance artists were reluctant to become involved professionally with wealthy bankers.

(E) Christian laws prevented the Medici from charging interest on loans.

(F) Sponsoring religious paintings was a way of compensating for the Medici's immoral family business.

Answer Book p. 39

Vocabulary Review

A. Fill in the blanks with the appropriate words from the box.

proximity	resistance	pave
naive	byproduct	absence

1 When he was young, he had the __________ belief that all people were good.

2 I live in close __________ to the subway station, so it is easy for me to get to work.

3 In the __________ of adults, kids can get into all kinds of trouble on their own.

4 Sawdust is a __________ of woodworking that can cause respiratory problems.

5 If patients develop a __________ to the drug, they will no longer feel its effects.

6 This amazing discovery will __________ the way for new vaccines to be made.

B. Choose the closest meaning for each highlighted word or phrase.

7 Although the cut on her arm was deep, she reported feeling only moderate pain.
(A) mild (B) suitable (C) transient (D) compliant

8 She was an impulsive girl who did not think about the consequences of her actions.
(A) representations (B) repercussions (C) properties (D) threats

9 A barrier was erected to protect the brittle sculpture from the visitors of the gallery.
(A) ancient (B) valuable (C) fragile (D) minute

10 Winning the finals would cement the team's reputation as an unbeatable force.
(A) crush (B) seal (C) haul (D) invent

11 The opulent house was filled with antiques and famous works of art.
(A) luxurious (B) innumerable (C) honorable (D) everlasting

12 Visitors to the zoo are forbidden from feeding or touching the animals.
(A) dismissed (B) distinguished (C) impeded (D) prohibited

13 Because of recent robberies, he made the sensible decision to install security cameras.
(A) main (B) expert (C) quick (D) wise

14 The small country won the war and finally became an autonomous nation.
(A) important (B) independent (C) immutable (D) irreversible

CHAPTER 09

Summary

Summary

About the Question Type

Summary questions ask you to complete a summary of the passage by selecting the three out of six sentences that best express the major ideas in the passage.

Correct answer choices are restatements of the main idea of one or more paragraphs in the passage. Incorrect answer choices often express inaccurate information, minor points (examples, supporting ideas, etc.), or details that are not mentioned in the passage.

Question Format

Directions: An introductory sentence for a brief summary of the passage is provided below. Complete the summary by selecting the THREE answer choices that express the most important ideas in the passage. Some sentences do not belong in the summary because they express ideas that are not presented in the passage or are minor ideas in the passage. **This question is worth 2 points.**

Drag your answer choices to the spaces where they belong.
To remove an answer choice, click on it. To review the passage, click on **View Text**.

[An introductory sentence]
•
•
•

Answer Choices

Key Strategies

- **Step 1** — Read the introductory sentence that represents the main idea of the passage.
- **Step 2** — Scan the passage to see if each answer choice is supported by the passage.
- **Step 3** — Select the three answer choices that express the major ideas in the passage.

Example

Answer Book p. 40

Testing on Zebrafish

Zebrafish are tiny, striped fish native to South Asia that are closely related to minnows. They might seem to share few characteristics with humans, but, in fact, zebrafish and people share about 70 percent of their genes. The little finned creatures also have a lot of the same body parts found in a human being. Because of this similarity, zebrafish are replacing mice as the most preferred animal species for medical experimentation. Mice are more closely related to humans from an evolutionary perspective; both species are mammals. But zebrafish are far cheaper to collect and store, and their genetic resemblance to people makes it comparatively easy to manipulate their genes in an effort to study human diseases and treatments. Moreover, zebrafish have some useful differences from people. They reproduce quickly and in large numbers, making for quick multigenerational studies. Their translucent bodies make it possible to witness the growth of embryos as it occurs. Of course, zebrafish are poor models for human diseases that affect organs such as the lungs because the little fish lack those parts. But for genetic mutations, zebrafish provide a surprisingly fertile testing ground to evaluate drug efficacy. They are quickly becoming popular models for research in biomedical fields, both contributing to reducing testing on other animals and facilitating the development of new drugs.

1 **Directions:** An introductory sentence for a brief summary of the passage is provided below. Complete the summary by selecting the THREE answer choices that express the most important ideas in the passage.

Zebrafish can be better as a testing species than mice.

(A) Zebrafish bear a surprising genetic resemblance to human beings.
(B) Mice are mammals, so they are closer to mirroring the human genome.
(C) The genetic closeness with people makes it useful to modify zebrafish genes.
(D) Humans have a closer evolutionary relationship to mice than they do to zebrafish.
(E) In spite of the zebrafish's differences from people, they have many features suitable for research.
(F) Studying zebrafish is more ethical than studying rodents because they are less highly evolved.

Reading Practice 1

Answer Book p. 41

Huygens Lands on Titan

Titan is the largest moon orbiting Saturn. Until January 14, 2005, when a NASA-designed probe called *Huygens* landed on its surface, scientists knew little about Titan due to its distance from Earth and a thick, cloudy atmosphere that obscured its geological characteristics. Fly-by missions are of little use in studying Titan; the best way to explore the moon is to send a spacecraft plunging toward its surface. The *Huygens* mission was an enormously successful first step toward unraveling Titan's mysteries.

NASA's uncertainty about the Titan surface terrain meant that a successful landing was far from a foregone conclusion. In fact, the plan was for *Huygens* to gather most or all of its data in a 2.5-hour descent through Titan's atmosphere. Although radio telescopes indicated that there was probably a solid surface to land on, NASA's engineers could not predict whether the surface would support the probe or whether it would encounter any number of potential perils. The scientists placed bets on what *Huygens* would find on Titan. Ice? Liquid? Tar? One participant jokingly gambled on "eaten by sea monsters."

The freefall into Titan's airspace allowed *Huygens* to ascertain the chemical composition of its atmosphere. The probe found mostly nitrogen and methane, confirming the scientists' expectations. It found only small amounts of argon, a gas that is much more abundant in the Sun, leading NASA to suspect that Titan was not formed at the beginning of the solar system. Rather, it is probable that Titan gained its atmosphere from meteorite impacts into it when it was first forming. Earth may have been formed in the same way. *Huygens* also noticed molecules called tholins that suggest the chemical building blocks of life are present in Titan's atmosphere. While Titan itself does not host life, the presence of tholins there is a positive sign in the search for life elsewhere other than Titan.

In the end, *Huygens* landed gently on a soft substance, sending back 100 remarkable images of beach-like terrain. Titan, it turns out, is the only known body in the solar system containing liquid. Although there is no water, liquid hydrocarbons apparently flow through rivers carved into Titan's surface. *Huygens* did not directly spot any of this liquid, but it snapped photos of winding riverbeds. Titan's surface shows signs of flooding, as well as methane rain erosion. Unfortunately, *Huygens* was only able to explore Titan for 72 minutes before its batteries expired.

1 The word "its" in the passage refers to

(A) Titan
(B) Saturn
(C) NASA
(D) *Huygens*

2 Why does the author mention "radio telescopes"?

(A) To establish the futility of trying to study Titan's surface from Earth
(B) To discuss technologies that have not been developed but could be useful
(C) To explain why scientists suspected that Titan has a surface to land on
(D) To reveal the source of scientists' knowledge that Titan has liquid

3 Which of the following was NOT discovered during *Huygens*'s descent through Titan's atmosphere?

(A) The chemical building blocks of life are present on Titan.
(B) Liquid hydrocarbons flow through rivers on Titan.
(C) The atmosphere is dominated by nitrogen and methane.
(D) Titan's atmosphere resulted from collisions with meteorites.

4 **Directions:** An introductory sentence for a brief summary of the passage is provided below. Complete the summary by selecting the THREE answer choices that express the most important ideas in the passage.

The *Huygens* mission provided information about Titan's surface that could not be obtained from afar.

(A) Titan is about one billion miles away from Earth, making it impossible to reach by a manned mission.
(B) Titan is covered by clouds, which made planning the *Huygens* probe's landing challenging.
(C) Scientists placed bets on the likely surface characteristics that *Huygens* would encounter on Titan.
(D) *Huygens* gathered data about Titan's gases during its descent through the atmosphere.
(E) Titan's gases provide information about the formation of Earth early in the solar system's history.
(F) After landing, *Huygens* revealed that Titan is the only body other than Earth to contain liquid.

• Vocabulary Quiz •

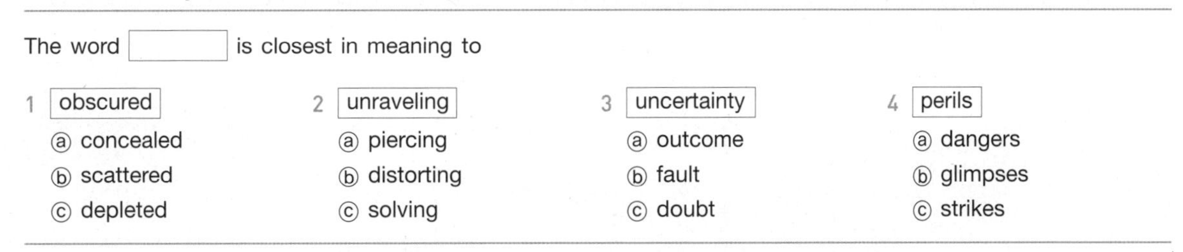

The word [ ] is closest in meaning to

1 obscured
ⓐ concealed
ⓑ scattered
ⓒ depleted

2 unraveling
ⓐ piercing
ⓑ distorting
ⓒ solving

3 uncertainty
ⓐ outcome
ⓑ fault
ⓒ doubt

4 perils
ⓐ dangers
ⓑ glimpses
ⓒ strikes

Reading Practice 2

Answer Book p. 42

Early Banking

Before there were banks, there was banking. As civilization began to rely on various forms of currency, the need arose for the three main banking services: lending, record-keeping, and storage of financial resources. Often the earliest institutions to offer these services were religious in nature. The ancient Babylonians required individuals—and even the royal family—to make regular contributions to the gods, payable in the form of grain and livestock. When the temples collected a surplus of these products, they began to loan them out. By 2000 BC, the temples were also accepting deposits of gold and charging a percentage of the deposit for the service.

The first civilization to move banking out of the temple and into private buildings was the Romans. In 352 BC, a Roman public bank was founded to manage the debts of the poor in an effort to prevent social unrest, particularly during times of war. These public bankers, known as the *mensarii*, were empowered by government officials to confiscate land when citizens were unable to pay their debts. The mensarii also accepted deposits and evaluated the authenticity and value of coins.

The bulk of the banking in the Middle Ages was provided by merchant banks. The Italian region of Lombardy became a major hub for this industry. Many of the bankers during this period were Jewish merchants who came to Italy to escape persecution by the Spanish. It was a natural profession for them because they were not bound to the Christian usury laws that prevented lenders from charging interest on loans. This gave them the freedom to take on high-risk loans and purchase the right to sell grain before it was harvested.

Public banking, which had receded after the fall of Rome, reemerged in western Europe during the twelfth century. The Bank of Venice, which was established in 1157, was the first public banking institution in the modern sense. King Henry II of England began to tax his people to support the Crusades. Over time, the royal powers of Europe began to offer loans at a price they dictated themselves. These practices evolved slowly into modern banking by the eighteenth century.

Glossary

· the Crusades: a series of medieval military expeditions made by Europeans to recover the Holy Land from the Muslims

1 According to paragraph 1, banking first started in ancient Babylon because

(A) religious leaders started to loan goods that had been donated to the gods
(B) the temples kept records of grain possessed by the people who worshiped there
(C) people needed a place to store their gold while they traveled
(D) foreigners escaping religious persecution offered loans in the temples

2 The word "their" in the passage refers to

(A) public bankers
(B) mensarii
(C) government officials
(D) citizens

3 According to paragraph 3, all of the following is true of Jewish merchants in the Middle Ages EXCEPT

(A) they were able to collect interest on loans
(B) they fled religious discrimination
(C) they were punished for violating usury laws
(D) they purchased the rights to grain in advance

4 **Directions:** An introductory sentence for a brief summary of the passage is provided below. Complete the summary by selecting the THREE answer choices that express the most important ideas in the passage.

The provision of banking services preceded the first banking institutions.

(A) The temples in early civilizations served as the earliest banking institutions.
(B) In ancient Babylon, the royal family was required to make offerings of grain and animals.
(C) The first government-run banks were founded by the Romans.
(D) The mensarii could take over plots of land if citizens had debts they could not pay.
(E) Merchant banks performed the functions of banking during the Middle Ages.
(F) King Henry II turned to taxation to pay the expenses incurred during the Crusades.

• Vocabulary Quiz •

The word [ ] is closest in meaning to

1 confiscate
ⓐ steal
ⓑ fund
ⓒ seize

2 profession
ⓐ task
ⓑ job
ⓒ act

3 bound
ⓐ submitted
ⓑ persuaded
ⓒ obligated

4 receded
ⓐ recited
ⓑ faded
ⓒ objected

Answer Book p. 42

Raccoon Takeover

With its captivating black face mask, intelligent eyes, and bushy striped tail, the raccoon is a disarmingly adorable creature native to North America. Charmed humans have transported these animals to numerous locations around the world, and they always regret the decision. Raccoons were introduced to Germany in the 1930s by admirers of their distinctive fur. They are now spreading to every corner of Europe, plus parts of the Middle East. In the 1970s, Japanese children convinced their parents to import some 1,500 of the animals per month after a cute cartoon raccoon became popular on television. Most of the pet raccoons were released into the wild after threatening their owners with dangerous behavior. Now they wreak $300,000 worth of agricultural damage in Japan on an annual basis.

Raccoons have proven themselves to be shockingly adaptable creatures. Originally, they lived around rivers, which explains their odd habit of dunking their food in water before eating. Now they live everywhere, overtaking rural, urban, and suburban areas with equal ease. The omnivores can eat almost anything, from nuts and berries to rodents and turtles. They are disturbingly fond of tearing into garbage bags and dining on all kinds of human delicacies. Raccoons are smarter than other similarly sized animals, have nimble forepaws that easily win access to attics and chimneys, and are capable of withstanding a wide array of climate conditions. They are comfortable in warm weather, and, when winter is on the way, they simply accumulate fat.

Raccoons are notoriously difficult to remove once they have entered a region. The city of Toronto spent millions of dollars designing and producing supposedly raccoon-proof trash cans, only to find that the animals were able to get into them. When they are removed through trapping and hunting, the species' population numbers tend to rebound within a year. That's due to their capacity for rapid reproduction, with females giving birth up to eight times a year.

Due to global warming, raccoons are likely to become even more ubiquitous around the world. They are expected to invade the delicate forests of northern Canada, Europe, and Asia. That could be catastrophic from an ecological perspective since the resilient scavengers eat everything and tend to outcompete every native species they encounter. Cute though they are, raccoons pose a dilemma for which the world has yet to find an effective solution.

1 The word "They" in the passage refers to

(A) humans
(B) locations
(C) raccoons
(D) admirers

2 According to paragraph 2, which of the following is NOT true of raccoons?

(A) They eat both plants and animals.
(B) They can survive in a range of temperatures.
(C) They prefer cities to rural areas.
(D) They outsmart comparably sized species.

3 According to the passage, raccoons are expected to spread to the forests of northern Canada because

(A) they migrate north during the summer
(B) average temperatures will rise
(C) northern residents enjoy them as pets
(D) the forests tend to have many rivers

4 **Directions:** An introductory sentence for a brief summary of the passage is provided below. Complete the summary by selecting the THREE answer choices that express the most important ideas in the passage.

Raccoons have spread from North America by endearing themselves to humans.

(A) A television program in Japan featured raccoons as characters.
(B) Raccoons are capable of survival under a variety of conditions.
(C) Raccoons have dexterous forepaws that are used to gain access to structures.
(D) Permanent removal of raccoons is a challenge that has yet to be realized.
(E) Toronto spent too much on expensive garbage cans that did not work.
(F) Raccoons are anticipated to further spread into fragile ecosystems.

• Vocabulary Quiz •

The word [   ] is closest in meaning to

1 adaptable	2 nimble	3 withstanding	4 capacity
ⓐ rundown	ⓐ agile	ⓐ enduring	ⓐ expectancy
ⓑ careful	ⓑ silky	ⓑ detecting	ⓑ ability
ⓒ versatile	ⓒ rugged	ⓒ performing	ⓒ function

Reading Practice 4

Answer Book p. 43

The Acropolis

The literal meaning of *acropolis* is "the highest point in the town," and nearly every city in ancient Greece had one. However, this term is generally used in modern times to refer to the Acropolis of Athens, which is an ancient collection of temples and other buildings occupying four hills overlooking the city of Athens. The Acropolis features over twenty archaeological remains, including the Parthenon, a 23,000-square-foot temple dedicated to the goddess Athena, and the Theatre of Dionysus, a performance space where works by the great tragic poets of Greece were staged.

The earliest records of architectural development at the Acropolis date back to the Bronze Age civilization of the Mycenaeans. The Mycenaean kings constructed palaces there around 1400 BC, which were fortified by 26-foot walls. The remains of one of those walls stand at the southwest end of the Acropolis, the most significant representation of this period to survive to the present day. In addition to functioning as a royal residence, the Acropolis also provided a center for the worship of Demeter, the goddess of fertility and nature.

Most of the structures at the Acropolis were decimated by the Persians in 480 BC, but Athenian ruler Pericles reconstructed the citadel about three decades later during Athens' Golden Age. After a series of military victories, some 200 cities in the Aegean region paid Athens enormous sums to protect them, and that wealth funded the massive construction effort. It was during this period that the Parthenon, the crown jewel of the Acropolis, was built. The temple was half the size of a football field, and it was surrounded by 46 towering marble columns.

The Acropolis endured centuries of war and shifting political circumstances following the fall of ancient Greece in 146 BC. Under the Holy Roman Empire, many of its temples became Christian churches. Under the rule of the Turks, they became mosques and were used to store ammunition. The Venetians attacked the Acropolis in 1687, leaving the Parthenon open to looting and vandalism. It was not until 1822 that Greece became an independent nation and began the time-consuming work of excavation and restoration. Today, the Acropolis is a popular tourist attraction.

Glossary

· citadel: a fortified structure built in ancient times to defend against enemies

1 The author's description of the Parthenon mentions that it

(A) covers an area greater than a football field
(B) was used to worship Demeter
(C) features almost fifty outer columns
(D) was destroyed by the Persians

2 The word "they" in the passage refers to

(A) circumstances
(B) temples
(C) centuries
(D) Turks

3 According to paragraph 4, which of the following is NOT true of the Acropolis?

(A) Its temples were used by multiple religions over the centuries.
(B) The structures there were used to store military supplies.
(C) It was damaged during a war with another European power.
(D) The site was excavated while under Turkish rule.

4 **Directions:** An introductory sentence for a brief summary of the passage is provided below. Complete the summary by selecting the THREE answer choices that express the most important ideas in the passage.

The Acropolis is home to numerous temples and other structures of archaeological interest.

(A) The Parthenon was designed for the worship of the goddess Athena.
(B) Ancient Greek playwrights had their works performed at the Acropolis.
(C) The history of the Acropolis began with the Mycenaean civilization.
(D) During the Golden Age of Athens, many structures were built at the Acropolis.
(E) Military victories created great wealth in the city of Athens during the Golden Age.
(F) The Acropolis changed hands and religious leadership many times after the fall of Greece.

• Vocabulary Quiz •

The word [ ] is closest in meaning to

1 remains
ⓐ intrusions
ⓑ figures
ⓒ debris

2 fortified
ⓐ assuaged
ⓑ guarded
ⓒ ignited

3 circumstances
ⓐ conditions
ⓑ subtleties
ⓒ compromises

4 restoration
ⓐ recombination
ⓑ redistribution
ⓒ reconstruction

Answer Book p. 44

TOEFL Reading

The History of Ballet

➡ The nobility of Renaissance Italy entertained important visitors with music, mime, and dance. These court shows, called *spectacles*, were magnificent celebrations that often included hundreds of performers. Florentine noblewoman Catherine de' Medici brought court dancing with her to France when she married King Henry II. During this period, Catherine commissioned a spectacle for the celebration of the marriage of the Duke of Joyeuse to Marguerite of Lorraine. This is looked upon as the birth of ballet. It was an epic piece that lasted over five hours and, unlike modern ballet, included elements of vocal performance.

➡ Another influential figure in the development of ballet was King Louis XIV of France, who began the transition of the dance from court entertainment to a profession. Interested in ballet from an early age, Louis encouraged others to work at perfecting the art and making dance respectable. Louis performed in ballets with roles considered worthy of his exalted position. Foremost among these was the *Ballet de la Nuit*, in which he appeared as the Sun King, also a nickname he gave himself. His court devoted much of their energy to dance, achieving greater proficiency in both choreography and composition. In 1661, Louis formally established ballet as a professional theatrical art when he created the Royal Academy of the Dance, the world's first ballet school. Past his physical prime, Louis retired in 1669, allowing more capable and talented dancers to take lead roles.

By the late seventeenth century, the foundations of modern ballet were established. Ballet masters began to codify their teaching methods by systemizing the five foot positions of ballet and by making attempts to create a dance notation similar to that of music. **A** In addition, costumes were adapted to allow for more intricate footwork, and the ballerina, the female dancer, achieved greater renown. **B** Up to this time, many restrictions were placed on the art of ballet. **C** Free-flowing movements, jumps, and lifts were considered socially unacceptable. **D** Variations for effect could be made only through changing floor patterns or tempo. At this time, ballet continued to be a combination of dance, singing, and music, with the emphasis usually on singing. By 1760, however, ballet masters began to question the unwanted restrictions and rigid protocol of their art left over from the days when it was part of court entertainment.

Volume | Review | Help | Back | Next

1 The word "This" in the passage refers to

Ⓐ period
Ⓑ spectacle
Ⓒ marriage
Ⓓ Duke

2 According to paragraph 1, which of the following is true of the *spectacles*?

Ⓐ Only royalty were permitted to attend.
Ⓑ Mime was first performed there.
Ⓒ They featured a wide variety of acts.
Ⓓ They were first created by Catherine de' Medici.

Paragraph 1 is marked with an arrow [➡].

3 What can be inferred from paragraph 1 about ballet?

Ⓐ Ballet is often performed at weddings.
Ⓑ Today's ballet does not include singing.
Ⓒ Ballet was a popular form of entertainment in Italy
Ⓓ The average ballet lasts over five hours.

Paragraph 1 is marked with an arrow [➡].

4 The word "transition" in the passage is closest in meaning to

Ⓐ expectation
Ⓑ comparison
Ⓒ shift
Ⓓ celebration

5 The word "proficiency" in the passage is closest in meaning to

Ⓐ regression
Ⓑ competence
Ⓒ trend
Ⓓ rhythm

6 Which of the following is NOT true about King Louis XIV?

Ⓐ He retired from dance due to an illness.
Ⓑ His love of dancing began in his childhood.
Ⓒ He founded the first ballet school.
Ⓓ He helped develop ballet into a profession.

7 It can be inferred from paragraph 2 that King Louis XIV

Ⓐ taught at the Royal Academy of Dance until his retirement
Ⓑ was the first professional dancer
Ⓒ played the lead role in his ballets
Ⓓ choreographed and composed the *Ballet de la Nuit*

Paragraph 2 is marked with an arrow [➡].

8 Which of the sentences below best expresses the essential information in the highlighted sentence in the passage? *Incorrect* choices change the meaning in important ways or leave out essential information.

Ⓐ The movements in ballet were too limited for some dancers.
Ⓑ Dance professionals felt that ballet was too restrictive due to its origins.
Ⓒ As of the mid-eighteenth century, ballet had faded in favor among dance fans.
Ⓓ Restraints were placed on ballet performances for members of the court.

9 Look at the four squares [■] that indicate where the following sentence could be added to the passage.

Marie de Camargo, one of the first ballerinas, was famous for her jumps and innovative movements.

Where would the sentence best fit?

Click on a square [■] to add the sentence to the passage.

10 **Directions:** An introductory sentence for a brief summary of the passage is provided below. Complete the summary by selecting the THREE answer choices that express the most important ideas in the passage. Some sentences do not belong in the summary because they express ideas that are not presented in the passage or are minor ideas in the passage. **This question is worth 2 points.**

Drag your answer choices to the spaces where they belong.
To remove an answer choice, click on it. To review the passage, click on **View Text**.

Ballet began as an entertainment for aristocrats in Italian society.

-
-
-

Answer Choices

Ⓐ A performance arranged by Catherine de' Medici is considered the origin of ballet.

Ⓑ The art form of ballet gained greater importance under King Louis XIV.

Ⓒ Louis acquired a nickname when he had a major role in the *Ballet de la Nuit.*

Ⓓ Ballet movements were systematized during the 1600s.

Ⓔ Most female roles were danced by men until the late nineteenth century.

Ⓕ The development of a notation system placed limitations on ballet choreography.

Answer Book p. 44

Vocabulary Review

A. Fill in the blanks with the appropriate words from the box.

overlooked	similarities	persecution
efficacy	captivating	attraction

1 The two languages are closely related and share many ___________.

2 The Eiffel Tower in Paris is the city's most popular tourist ___________.

3 Doctors say the ___________ of the medicine is about 95 percent.

4 The house at the top of the hill ___________ the entire valley below.

5 In the past, some people suffered ___________ because of different religious beliefs.

6 She was a ___________ actress who stole the audience's attention.

B. Choose the closest meaning for each highlighted word or phrase.

7 Photo-editing software can be used to manipulate various elements of an image.
(A) present (B) select (C) alter (D) eliminate

8 Environmentalists believe that the effects of climate change may be catastrophic.
(A) oppressive (B) fleeting (C) inexplicable (D) disastrous

9 I did not agree with his perspective on how to improve the product.
(A) transition (B) viewpoint (C) conclusion (D) optimism

10 Several experts verified the authenticity of the old artifact that he found in the cave.
(A) genuineness (B) sustainability (C) extravagance (D) attractiveness

11 The animated series features many adorable characters that children like.
(A) cute (B) new (C) small (D) smart

12 When more energy is consumed than needed, your body will store the surplus.
(A) variety (B) profit (C) excess (D) combination

13 Some areas have been invaded by fire ants, a venomous insect with a sting.
(A) preserved (B) approached (C) defeated (D) infested

14 The police are trying to ascertain what happened and who might be responsible.
(A) collect (B) compare (C) determine (D) explore

CHAPTER 10

Category Chart

Category Chart

About the Question Type

Category Chart questions ask you to complete a table by placing the relevant information in the appropriate categories.

When reading the passage, try to identify what is being compared or contrasted, and recognize the important information for each category.

Question Format

Directions: Select the appropriate phrases from the answer choices and match them to the type to which they relate. **This question is worth 3 points.**

Drag your answer choices to the spaces where they belong.
To remove an answer choice, click on it. To review the passage, click on **View Text**.

Answer Choices	Category 1
	• • •
	Category 2
	• •

Key Strategies

- **Step 1** — Check the categories in the table.
- **Step 2** — Scan the passage and identify the important information for each category.
- **Step 3** — Select the answer choices that best paraphrase the important information in the passage for each category. Answer choices that include information from the passage that is unrelated to the categories can be eliminated.

Example

Answer Book p. 45

Lake Formation

Lakes are large bodies of water surrounded by land. They can be found in a wide variety of sizes, shapes, and depths, and they can contain fresh as well as salt water. It is possible to classify them by the way they were formed. Tectonic lakes, for instance, are created 5 when movements of the plates that form the earth's crust create rifts or depressions in the ground that are subsequently filled with water. Tectonic lakes are usually steep in slope. They tend to be formed in groups, and they are generally very deep compared to other lakes. Examples of tectonic lakes include the Caspian Sea and the Aral Sea. As deep as tectonic lakes can 10 be, lakes caused by glacial activity often cover a much larger area. The Great Lakes in North America are glacial lakes formed during the last ice age when large bodies of ice called glaciers moved gradually over the landscape, leaving basins and valleys behind. Other ways that lakes are formed include volcanic activity, sinkholes, landslides, and erosion caused by rivers. Additionally, some lakes are formed after meteorites from outer 15 space crash into the land. These crater lakes include Ungava Lake in Quebec.

1 **Directions:** Select the appropriate phrases from the answer choices and match them to the type of lakes to which they relate.

Answer Choices	Tectonic Lakes
(A) Were created from volcanoes (B) Feature steep slopes (C) Were caused by landslides (D) Tend to form in groups (E) Have a greater area (F) Include the Great Lakes (G) Are extremely deep	• • • **Glacial Lakes** • •

Reading Practice 1

Answer Book p. 46

Classifying the Arts

The word *art* is an attempt to classify a collection of vastly different human endeavors under a single broad umbrella term. Consequently, there is no correct definition of the word *art*. It is up to people to decide what they wish the word to describe. What makes this difficult is the fact that people cannot seem to agree on what they want the word to describe; they agree only that they want it to describe lots of things that seem to have little in common. Could one word be used to describe Monet's paintings, Mozart's symphonies, Joyce's *Ulysses*, and Shakespeare's *King Lear*? It would seem that such a word is already applied so broadly as to become almost meaningless. And yet we feel instinctively that there is something shared by all of these things and not by, say, picnic baskets, toilet paper, and maple syrup. When pursuing a definition of art, it is useful to distinguish between fine arts and applied arts.

The only purpose of fine art is to give aesthetic pleasure. Consider the *Mona Lisa*, Leonardo da Vinci's most famous painting. It serves no utilitarian function. One cannot do anything with it except appreciate its beauty, lifelike accuracy, and masterful brushwork. Now think of a coffee mug bearing the image of the *Mona Lisa*, the kind one might find in a museum gift shop. The picture on the mug may be an exact reproduction of the painting, but the mug is not fine art because it is intended to provide a container for hot beverages. It has a purpose other than its exhibition of aesthetic beauty.

The *Mona Lisa* coffee mug is an example of the applied arts. This category of art is designed to serve a specific function. Usually the objects in this grouping are intended to be sold for commercial purposes. They may be beautiful, but they are also useful. For example, a luxury car might be described as a "work of art," but surely its primary purpose is to transport people. Fashion falls into the same category, as it is created by artistic designers and sold to cover the purchaser's body in an aesthetically pleasing manner. Also among the applied arts is production art, which includes the creation of mass-produced commercial works such as movies and the component disciplines that make them possible, such as costume design, special effects, and set design.

1 According to paragraph 1, defining art is difficult because

(A) people use the word to describe different things
(B) certain objects clearly don't fit any definition of art
(C) the term does not include objects that are not aesthetically pleasing
(D) fine arts are often confused with applied arts

2 The word "them" in the passage refers to

(A) fine arts
(B) applied arts
(C) movies
(D) disciplines

3 According to the passage, which of the following is NOT an applied art?

(A) Clothing
(B) A gift shop coffee mug
(C) Set design
(D) Symphonies

4 **Directions:** Select the appropriate phrases from the answer choices and match them to the type of arts to which they relate.

Answer Choices	Applied Arts
(A) Serves a useful purpose	•
(B) Has little monetary value	•
(C) Designed to give pure aesthetic pleasure	•
(D) Difficult to reproduce	**Fine Arts**
(E) Often made for commercial reasons	
(F) Serves no utilitarian function	•
(G) Includes movies and other production art	•

• **Vocabulary Quiz** •

The word [ ] is closest in meaning to

1 endeavors
ⓐ confinements
ⓑ undertakings
ⓒ speculations

2 instinctively
ⓐ intuitively
ⓑ fervently
ⓒ reluctantly

3 accuracy
ⓐ dependence
ⓑ precision
ⓒ conclusion

4 masterful
ⓐ radical
ⓑ hollow
ⓒ skilled

Reading Practice 2

Answer Book p. 46

Placental Mammals and Marsupials

Mammals are animals that have a spine, are covered in hair or fur, and generally give birth to their offspring rather than laying eggs. Within this broad classification are two smaller groups: placental mammals and marsupials. The key difference between these two groups of mammals is the way that their young develop. 5

Placental mammals are distinguished by the fact that they have a well-developed placenta, which is an organ in the mother's womb that provides nourishment to a developing fetus. Because placentals provide more nourishment to their young in the womb, they have large babies that are well developed and less dependent on their mothers than their marsupial counterparts. Placental mammals are born with fewer teeth than marsupials, and they have two sets of teeth during their lifetimes instead of just one. They also have higher metabolic rates. They account for the majority of modern mammal species alive today. Humans are placental mammals, and so are whales, cats, and horses. 10 15

Although marsupials also have a placenta, their offspring develop outside their bodies in a pouch. The marsupial placenta provides nutrition in the earliest stages of the pregnancy, and the fetus is only attached to it for a very brief period of time. When they are born, marsupial babies are blind with no ears or back legs, features that emerge while they are in the mother's pouch. Marsupials drink their mothers' milk for a long time compared to placental mammals, which only lactate for several months. It is worth noting that young marsupials use their strong front legs and keen sense of smell to find their way from the mother's birth channel into the pouches. Kangaroos are the most famous of all marsupials; others include opossums and koalas. They are mostly found in Australia although the fossil record shows that they were once more widespread. 20 25

Despite their differences, placental mammals and marsupials have quite a bit in common. Both groups consist of warm-blooded, air-breathing animals that produce milk for their young. The key distinction between them is the marsupial's use of a pouch to develop offspring that are visible to the outside world.

Glossary

· fetus: the unborn offspring of an animal

1 According to paragraph 1, which of the following is NOT true of both marsupials and placental mammals?

(A) Both are mammals.
(B) Both are covered in hair.
(C) Both have only a few young.
(D) Both have spines.

2 Which of the sentences below best expresses the essential information in the highlighted sentence in the passage?

(A) Placentals have larger, better developed, and more independent offspring than marsupials.
(B) Since placentals eat more in the womb, they grow larger than their marsupial equivalents.
(C) Whereas placentals nourish their young in the womb, marsupials have dependent babies.
(D) The wombs of placentals contain more nourishment than do those of marsupials.

3 The author's description of marsupials mentions their

(A) brief attachment to the placenta
(B) lengthy period of lactation in the womb
(C) strong and stumpy hind legs at a young age
(D) mothers' method of transport to the pouch

4 **Directions:** Select the appropriate phrases from the answer choices and match them to the type of animals to which they relate.

<table>
<tr><th>Answer Choices</th><th>Placental Mammals</th></tr>
<tr><td rowspan="3">(A) Are cold-blooded creatures
(B) Give birth to undeveloped babies
(C) Give birth to larger babies
(D) Nourish offspring in the womb for a long period
(E) Nourish offspring in a pouch
(F) Develop three sets of teeth in their lifetimes
(G) Develop two sets of teeth in their lifetimes</td><td>•
•
•</td></tr>
<tr><td>Marsupials</td></tr>
<tr><td>•
•</td></tr>
</table>

• **Vocabulary Quiz** •

The word [ ] is closest in meaning to

1 classification
ⓐ categorization
ⓑ generalization
ⓒ explanation

2 nourishment
ⓐ expansion
ⓑ potency
ⓒ nutrition

3 keen
ⓐ neat
ⓑ acute
ⓒ feeble

4 distinction
ⓐ sequence
ⓑ difference
ⓒ influence

Reading Practice 3

Answer Book p. 47

Veblen and Giffen Goods

The law of demand states that there is an inverse relationship between the price of goods and the quantity that consumers buy. In other words, if the price of goods is high, fewer goods will be sold. And, correspondingly, it is when prices are at their lowest that goods virtually fly off the shelves. This is, of course, why stores put products on sale. They are willing to sacrifice some revenue from each individual item because their total revenue will be greater based on the increased number of items they sell. However, Veblen goods and Giffen goods are an exception to this rule. 5

Veblen goods defy the law of demand because a certain amount of status is attached to the purchase of some exceptionally high-priced products. The phenomenon was discovered by the nineteenth-century economist Thorstein Veblen. He theorized that certain luxury goods are purchased because their high price is perceived as an indication of higher quality. Let's say that a new model of sports car is introduced at a price that is competitive with the price of a compact car. At first, the car follows the law of demand, with sales increasing in response to the affordable sticker price. Then, as the quality of the car becomes well established, the manufacturer begins to inflate the costs. When prices reach a certain threshold, the car begins to acquire prestige with affluent customers, and demand increases with the price. Veblen goods are positional goods, which means they are valued for their limited available supply, like a painting by Leonardo da Vinci. 10 15

On the other end of the spectrum are Giffen goods, which are named for the statistician Robert Giffen. He noted that the law of demand does not apply when staple goods are necessary and there are no cheaper alternatives. In this case, consumers will buy more of this type of good when the price increases rather than less. Consider a household with a limited food budget that consumes mainly bread and meat. As bread is much cheaper than meat, it would account for the bulk of the budget. If the price of bread increased, the household would still need to ensure that it had sufficient food. To do this, it would increase spending on the cheapest staple and reduce spending on the more expensive one. In effect, an increase in the cost of bread would force the household to buy more of it. 20 25

Glossary

· sticker price: a manufacturer's suggested retail price of a new automobile

1 The word "They" in the passage refers to

(A) goods
(B) shelves
(C) stores
(D) products

2 According to paragraph 2, the manufacturer of the sports car sells more units because

(A) middle-class consumers view the car as a status symbol
(B) the supply of the vehicle increases with its price
(C) prices decrease until consumers can afford the cars
(D) a more expensive product is seen as having higher status

3 Which of the following can be inferred from paragraph 3 about Giffen goods?

(A) Their prices tend to vary significantly.
(B) Their prices increase during times of recession.
(C) They are more popular with poorer consumers.
(D) They are usually available in limited quantities.

4 **Directions:** Select the appropriate phrases from the answer choices and match them to the type to which they relate.

<table>
<tr><th>Answer Choices</th><th>Veblen Goods</th></tr>
<tr><td rowspan="3">(A) Usually luxury products
(B) Lack cheaper alternatives
(C) Follow the law of demand
(D) Perceived to be high in quality
(E) Usually staple goods
(F) Tend to be put on sale frequently
(G) Valued for their limited supply</td><td>•
•
•</td></tr>
<tr><td>Giffen Goods</td></tr>
<tr><td>•
•</td></tr>
</table>

• Vocabulary Quiz •

The word [ ] is closest in meaning to

1 inverse
ⓐ precise
ⓑ concrete
ⓒ opposite

2 correspondingly
ⓐ accordingly
ⓑ conversely
ⓒ alternatively

3 revenue
ⓐ status
ⓑ income
ⓒ expense

4 exceptionally
ⓐ temporarily
ⓑ unusually
ⓒ absolutely

Reading Practice 4

Answer Book p. 48

The Dream Interpreters

Austrian psychiatrist Sigmund Freud is considered the father of psychoanalysis, and at one time he saw in his younger colleague Carl Jung a professional heir. When the pair first met in 1907, they talked for 13 hours about their shared interests in psychoanalysis. These included using dreams as a tool for unlocking the secrets of a patient's unconscious mind. For both, dreams contained symbols that could help patients to resolve their mental issues. Their mutual admiration dimmed by 1913, however, as Jung diverged from his teacher's theories in several important ways.

Freud thought that dreams were mostly caused by the repression of unconscious wishes. They were a manifestation of the *id*. This is a component of the human mind driven by base desires that are largely unknown to the conscious mind, which Freud called the *ego*. The raging cravings of the id were repressed in waking life by the judgmental *superego*, which channeled its desires into socially acceptable behaviors. In dreams, the id was free to fulfill its wishes in coded images. These images were identifiable symbols that were consistent for all people. If a wife dreamed of shooting a man to death, for example, Freud would tell her that she secretly hated her husband.

Jung was more concerned with the function of dreams. The younger psychiatrist believed that dreams are the bridge between the conscious and unconscious mind. Disdaining Freud's attempts to build a sort of dictionary of fixed dream symbols, Jung felt the symbols that emerge in dreams can vary in meaning depending on the person and the context. Moreover, while the spiritual power of the unconscious was important to Jung, Freud believed all spiritualism to be delusional. In the example above, Jung would say that the woman's shooting dream probably did not represent a hidden desire regarding her husband. Instead, her spirit might have been sending her a message regarding her feelings toward herself. In the end, Jung separated himself from Freud, developing his own enduring school of psychoanalysis.

Glossary

· spiritualism: a philosophical notion that the world is made up of spirit rather than material

1 According to paragraph 1, both Freud and Jung saw dreams as

(A) useful for treating patients
(B) incompatible with spirituality
(C) restrained by social conventions
(D) containing universal symbols

2 The word "its" in the passage refers to

(A) mind
(B) ego
(C) id
(D) superego

3 The author's description of Jung's view of dreams does NOT mention

(A) the connection between the unconscious and consciousness
(B) the emphasis on spiritualism
(C) causes of personal desires
(D) the contextual nature of symbols

4 **Directions:** Select the appropriate phrases from the answer choices and match them to the psychologist to which they relate.

Answer Choices	Freud
(A) Thought dreams were immoral (B) Believed dreams fulfilled repressed desires (C) Focused on the causes of dreams (D) Focused on the purpose of dreams	• • •
(E) Said dreams predict future criminal activity	**Jung**
(F) Opposed fixed interpretations of symbols (G) Identified the meanings of specific images	• •

• Vocabulary Quiz •

The word [ ] is closest in meaning to

1 heir
ⓐ adviser
ⓑ successor
ⓒ trainer

2 dimmed
ⓐ closed
ⓑ bonded
ⓒ faded

3 manifestation
ⓐ embodiment
ⓑ improvement
ⓒ development

4 Disdaining
ⓐ Disapproving
ⓑ Debating
ⓒ Restraining

Answer Book p. 49

TOEFL Reading

The Atmospheres of Earth and Mars

➡ An atmosphere is a layered envelope of gases that surrounds a planet. This bubble of gases, which extends from the planet's surface, is held together by gravity. While an atmosphere seems to be a requirement for life, having one does not guarantee that life will develop. In determining the viability of life on a particular planet, some key considerations are the atmosphere's temperature, gaseous composition, and density. These factors help to explain why Earth is teeming with life and why its neighbor Mars appears to be barren. 5

Whereas Earth retains precious warmth because it has a greenhouse atmosphere that traps the heat emanating from its surface, Mars has a much weaker greenhouse effect. Earth consequently maintains a 59-degree average temperature at its surface, while Mars averages a deadly minus 80 degrees Fahrenheit. Mars's temperatures also fluctuate much more widely 10 than Earth's, ranging at the equator from 70 degrees during the day to minus 100 degrees at night.

The greenhouse effect is created by the presence of the planet's atmosphere. **A** Greenhouse gases such as carbon dioxide absorb the Sun's radiation, capturing heat like a blanket over the planet. **B** These gases do not have to dominate the atmospheric 15 composition to create a greenhouse effect. **C** Mars's atmosphere is 95 percent carbon dioxide, a greenhouse gas, and Earth's is 71 percent nitrogen, which is not a greenhouse gas. **D** So why does Mars have a weaker greenhouse effect?

➡ The reason is the density of Mars's atmosphere, which is 100 times thinner than Earth's. This thin atmosphere provides little protection against radiation from the constant 20 impact of space particles like solar winds and cosmic rays. However, this may not have been the case billions of years ago. The evidence accumulated by robotic and aerial space missions supports the hypothesis that Mars once had water flowing on its surface. If so, Mars probably had a thicker atmosphere that may have been stripped away by solar winds or by a collision with a large space object. Fortunately for the 8.7 million species on Earth, 25 our atmosphere is protected from solar winds by a robust magnetic field, a feature that Mars lacks.

1 Which of the sentences below best expresses the essential information in the highlighted sentence in the passage? *Incorrect* choices change the meaning in important ways or leave out essential information.

Ⓐ Life can emerge without a planetary atmosphere since the two are not interdependent.
Ⓑ Some planets have atmospheres and no life, but no planet has life and no atmosphere.
Ⓒ Guarantees of life do not exist on any planet, but atmospheres preclude its presence.
Ⓓ Although life sometimes appears with an atmosphere, there is no such requirement.

2 The word "teeming" in the passage is closest in meaning to

Ⓐ vacant
Ⓑ delicate
Ⓒ abundant
Ⓓ sensible

3 According to paragraph 1, the gases surrounding a planet hold together because

Ⓐ gravitational force is exerted upon them
Ⓑ they trap the Sun's radiation in the atmosphere
Ⓒ the atmosphere is thick enough to hold them
Ⓓ they are distributed in several layers

Paragraph 1 is marked with an arrow [➡].

4 The word "its" in the passage refers to

Ⓐ Mars
Ⓑ effect
Ⓒ Earth
Ⓓ temperature

5 Which of the following is NOT true of Earth's greenhouse effect?

Ⓐ It warms the atmosphere.
Ⓑ It is stronger than that of Mars.
Ⓒ It is created by the presence of nitrogen.
Ⓓ It is made possible by the density of the atmosphere.

6 The word "impact" in the passage is closest in meaning to

Ⓐ collision
Ⓑ succession
Ⓒ exposure
Ⓓ outcome

7 The author discusses water on Mars in paragraph 4 in order to

Ⓐ provide evidence that Mars once hosted life despite its thin atmosphere
Ⓑ explain the foundation for a hypothesis about the past condition of Mars's atmosphere
Ⓒ refute a statement made earlier in the passage about the prospects of life on Mars
Ⓓ demonstrate that the atmosphere on Mars has not changed in billions of years

Paragraph 4 is marked with an arrow [➡].

8 According to paragraph 4, Earth has a thicker atmosphere than Mars because

Ⓐ there are fewer greenhouse gases
Ⓑ the atmosphere absorbs solar winds
Ⓒ it is surrounded by a magnetic field
Ⓓ it is a younger planet than Mars

Paragraph 4 is marked with an arrow [➡].

9 Look at the four squares [■] that indicate where the following sentence could be added to the passage.

They can do this because they are transparent to sunlight but opaque to infrared radiation.

Where would the sentence best fit?

Click on a square [■] to add the sentence to the passage.

10 Directions: Select the appropriate phrases from the answer choices and match them to the type to which they relate. **This question is worth 3 points.**

Drag your answer choices to the spaces where they belong.
To remove an answer choice, click on it. To review the passage, click on **View Text**.

Answer Choices	Earth's Atmosphere
Ⓐ Is composed primarily of oxygen	•
Ⓑ Is protected by a magnetic shield	•
Ⓒ Has an average temperature of 59 °F	•
Ⓓ Is dominated by carbon dioxide	**Mars's Atmosphere**
Ⓔ Is 100 times thinner	
Ⓕ Has a strong greenhouse effect	•
Ⓖ Is too thin to support weather	•

Answer Book p. 49

Vocabulary Review

A. Fill in the blanks with the appropriate words from the box.

meaningless	aesthetic	sacrificed
ranging	mutual	appreciated

1 People of all ages, __________ from 10 years old to 80, participated in the charity walk.

2 She __________ many things in her personal life in order to succeed in her career.

3 Although the two athletes were rivals, they had a __________ respect for one another.

4 The writer felt his novel was __________, but others saw it as an important work.

5 The library building looked beautiful after some __________ improvements were made.

6 The gallery visitors __________ the beauty of the artist's paintings.

B. Choose the closest meaning for each highlighted word or phrase.

7 The CEO and his counterpart from the other firm discussed the possibility of a merger.
(A) equivalent (B) competitor (C) phenomenon (D) representative

8 The company began to inflate its prices after a sudden increase in production costs.
(A) reflect (B) diminish (C) escalate (D) reduce

9 The sand on the beach retains the heat of the sun long into the evening.
(A) produces (B) keeps (C) reacts (D) adjusts

10 The lighthouse was not visible for several hours because of the dense fog.
(A) available (B) reliable (C) portable (D) perceptible

11 The viability of the species is dependent on its habitat being protected.
(A) benefit (B) output (C) survival (D) defense

12 Most women who are pregnant have cravings for unusual food combinations.
(A) tactics (B) desires (C) peaks (D) gestures

13 The nation finally rose up against the political repression and became a free state.
(A) compulsion (B) revolution (C) disintegration (D) suppression

14 The strong scent that emanated from the flowers attracted many honeybees.
(A) emerged (B) displayed (C) conducted (D) absorbed

Actual Test

Actual Test 1

Answer Book p. 50

TOEFL Reading

Passage 1

Horses in Agricultural Work

Since their domestication around 4000 BC, horses have been employed by humans for a variety of purposes, including for food, transportation, and agriculture. With wooden and metal devices attached to their bodies, these large mammals are able to cultivate farmland at speeds that surpass human capabilities. Their strong tractive force significantly boosts the rate at which a field can be prepared or harvested. However, their use as agricultural tools took place gradually and changed over time. 5

➡ At first, oxen were traditionally favored by humans as they shifted towards agrarian societies. Oxen have a greater muscle mass and can pull heavier weights than horses, although they are considerably slower. Due to this early preference, the yoke for fieldwork was designed for bovine anatomy rather than that of a horse. Attempts to make yokes more 10 suitable for horses began with the invention of the Chinese breast-strap in 481 BC, an innovation that was eventually introduced to Europe and modified into a full-throat collar. By AD 1100, the full-throat collar lacked the original torso straps and instead consisted of a pair of curved wooden pieces that were tied together with leather. These were thickly padded underneath, which reduced the pressure on the animal's windpipe by spreading the weight of 15 a pulled load evenly across its shoulders. These changes allowed horses to apply 50 percent more power to any given task compared to previous collars.

➡ The social and economic effects of this development in medieval Europe were far-reaching. A direct result was an increase in the efficiency and crop yields of peasant farmers. While horses necessitated time-consuming care, as their hooves required fitted shoes and 20 careful cleaning, their faster pace made them more profitable than oxen. This improvement stimulated the European economy, as farmers became wealthy and began to specialize in other areas, such as trade. Additionally, the food surplus from larger crop yields allowed populations to expand, as small farms could support greater numbers of people than in earlier eras. 25

➡ Despite its benefits, the era of efficient horse-driven farming eventually came to an end. This was initially due to the advent of the steam engine in the United Kingdom in the 1840s. [A] Over time, steam-powered harvesting machines gained popularity. [B] Similarly, tractors rapidly gained dominance on American farms with the spread of mechanization in the 1940s and started to replace horses. [C] Cheap fuel costs and low-interest federal loans enabled 30 American farmers to invest in modern technology, resulting in animals being almost entirely phased out of agriculture. [D]

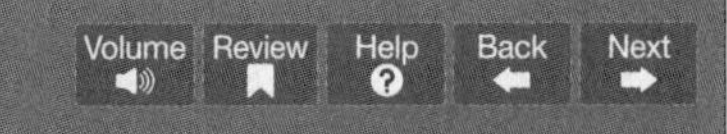

➡ In recent years, following the widespread interest in environmental protection and energy conservation, smallholding farmers have been returning to the use of horses as farming tools, leading to a revival in horse-based agriculture. Advocates proclaim that horses are inexpensive as they eat grass and require less maintenance. In contrast, tractors require constant refueling, recurrent maintenance, and costly part replacements. Moreover, although the animals have a lower efficiency than tractors, they do not emit noxious gases. 35

1 The word "surpass" in the passage is closest in meaning to

Ⓐ support
Ⓑ discover
Ⓒ exceed
Ⓓ widen

2 The word "that" in the passage refers to

Ⓐ preference
Ⓑ yoke
Ⓒ fieldwork
Ⓓ anatomy

3 The word "modified" in the passage is closest in meaning to

Ⓐ designed
Ⓑ altered
Ⓒ deceived
Ⓓ characterized

4 According to paragraph 2, oxen were originally preferred over horses for farming because

Ⓐ they were capable of pulling greater weights
Ⓑ they could carry passengers for longer distances
Ⓒ they could be trained at a faster rate
Ⓓ they were proven to grow more rapidly

Paragraph 2 is marked with an arrow [➡].

5 Which of the sentences below best expresses the essential information in the highlighted sentence in the passage? *Incorrect* choices change the meaning in important ways or leave out essential information.

(A) Horses needed greater effort but generated higher income than oxen.
(B) Horses could move objects, while oxen were more efficient for transport.
(C) Although farmers preferred horses, their maintenance costs were higher than those of oxen.
(D) Horse farming involved fitting shoes that oxen did not require.

6 According to paragraph 3, what impact did the full-throat horse collar have on medieval Europe?

(A) It allowed peasants to expand the sizes of their farms.
(B) It caused wealthy farmers to purchase more oxen.
(C) It led to the growth of the population.
(D) It promoted the trade of horses between farmers.

Paragraph 3 is marked with an arrow [➡].

7 What can be inferred from paragraph 4 about steam engine machinery?

(A) It was popular only within the United Kingdom.
(B) Its inventor was inspired by the work of horses.
(C) Its use in farming occurred in the United Kingdom first.
(D) It was rejected by farmers immediately after its creation.

Paragraph 4 is marked with an arrow [➡].

8 According to paragraph 5, all of the following are negative aspects of tractor farming EXCEPT

(A) repeated fuel costs
(B) harmful gas emissions
(C) expensive repairs
(D) limited efficiency

Paragraph 5 is marked with an arrow [➡].

9 Look at the four squares [■] that indicate where the following sentence could be added to the passage.

As a result, the number of working horses on English farms decreased by 97 percent.

Where would the sentence best fit?

Click on a square [■] to add the sentence to the passage.

10 **Directions:** An introductory sentence for a brief summary of the passage is provided below. Complete the summary by selecting the THREE answer choices that express the most important ideas in the passage. Some sentences do not belong in the summary because they express ideas that are not presented in the passage or are minor ideas in the passage. **This question is worth 2 points.**

Drag your answer choices to the spaces where they belong.
To remove an answer choice, click on it. To review the passage, click on **View Text**.

Horse farming methods evolved over time only to become outdated in the twentieth century, but they have seen a revival due to environmental concerns.

•

•

•

Answer Choices

(A) Horses were not the first animal to be used to advance agricultural productivity.

(B) The Chinese were the first to utilize horses to their full extent in the fifth century.

(C) Developments of the yoke were instrumental in the history of horse-based agriculture.

(D) Small farms in the modern era can gain numerous advantages by returning to horse farming.

(E) The wealth generated by horse farming allowed farmers to become merchants.

(F) Steam engine machinery began to displace horses from agricultural work.

Answer Book p. 50

Answer Book p. 51

TOEFL Reading

Passage 2

What Causes Wildfires to Spread

➡ Scientific scrutiny of wildfires has intensified as more wildfires are encountered due to climate change. Yet, regardless of their frequency, their rate of spread is always dependent on the same factors. The first and most important of these is the availability of fuel. Anything that is combustible in the environment represents fuel. This includes trees and underbrush, as well as many manmade structures and items. Every material has a temperature at which 5 it will burst into flames. This temperature is known as the flash point. For example, if wood is heated to its flash point of 300 degrees Celsius, it begins to release colorless hydrocarbon gases that mix with the air's oxygen and combusts. Once the initial combustion occurs, a fire expands according to the type of propellant that surrounds it. A limited fuel source will cause a new wildfire to expand slowly and burn with low intensity. However, a plentiful one will 10 result in rapid movement and extremely intense heat.

➡ Weather conditions also play a significant role in how quickly a wildfire expands, and the two most relevant variables are humidity and wind. During times of drought, a wildfire can be started even by a small spark or a single lightning strike. However, in wetter conditions, a more substantial or sustained heat source is needed for wildfire expansion. Similarly, stronger 15 winds are associated with more rapid spread. **A** Moreover, wind can set the direction of the fire, sometimes moving it to areas where the greatest destruction can occur. **B** A characteristic of wildfires that was first noted by researchers in the early 1990s is that large, violent wildfires can generate their own winds, known as fire whirls. **C** Fire whirls result from the vortices created by the heat of the fire. **D** These are capable of feeding a fire and are 20 often strong enough to disperse material a vast distance.

➡ In addition, the land itself is an important determinant of the speed at which a wildfire develops. In particular, topography that is flat or gently sloping is far less likely to perpetuate wildfires than heavily sloping land. Because heat rises, fires tend to move uphill far quicker than downhill or across a flat surface, and they have longer flame lengths. The extent of 25 advancement of a wildfire is also impacted by a slope's aspect, which is the direction it faces, as a north-facing slope will dry out and heat up more slowly than a south-facing one. These facts, in combination with an understanding of the available fuel nearby, should be considered when building in areas that are prone to wildfires. Experts recommend planting trees and shrubs at different intervals depending on the steepness of a property. While a few 30 meters between fuel sources may be enough space to create a fire break on flat terrain, a steep slope requires a minimum of ten meters to provide a protective barrier.

11 The word "scrutiny" in the passage is closest in meaning to

Ⓐ consensus
Ⓑ knowledge
Ⓒ investigation
Ⓓ dispute

12 The word "one" in the passage refers to

Ⓐ type
Ⓑ propellant
Ⓒ fuel source
Ⓓ new wildfire

13 According to paragraph 1, what happens if wood is heated to its flash point?

Ⓐ It begins to store hydrocarbons.
Ⓑ It starts to release smoke.
Ⓒ It consumes oxygen from the air.
Ⓓ It lets out colorless gases.

Paragraph 1 is marked with an arrow [➡].

14 Why does the author mention "a small spark or a single lightning strike" in the passage?

Ⓐ To indicate the two most common causes of wildfires in the environment
Ⓑ To emphasize that wildfires can start easily in conditions of low humidity
Ⓒ To highlight the need for a sustained heat source to maintain most wildfires
Ⓓ To suggest that wildfires rarely occur unless local conditions are extremely dry

15 According to paragraph 2, which of the following is true of fire whirls?

Ⓐ They arise from the center of the wildfire.
Ⓑ They can make a fire much hotter.
Ⓒ They can scatter matter a long way.
Ⓓ They limit the supply of oxygen to the fire.

Paragraph 2 is marked with an arrow [➡].

16 Which of the sentences below best expresses the essential information in the highlighted sentence in the passage? *Incorrect* choices change the meaning in important ways or leave out essential information.

Ⓐ Because a northern slope will get drier and hotter more slowly than a southern slope, a slope's aspect also influences how far a wildfire spreads.
Ⓑ Another impact on the advancement of a wildfire is which way that a slope faces.
Ⓒ Due to the differences in how north-facing and south-facing slopes impact wildfires, it is difficult to determine how far any particular wildfire will advance.
Ⓓ Although a slope's orientation toward the north or south has some influence on whether or not a wildfire forms, it has little effect on how it spreads.

17 The word "prone" in the passage is closest in meaning to

Ⓐ immune
Ⓑ susceptible
Ⓒ hazardous
Ⓓ resilient

18 What can be inferred from paragraph 3 about shrubs and trees in building areas?

Ⓐ Burning some of them in a controlled manner will reduce the frequency of wildfires.
Ⓑ They should never be planted in regions where wildfires are common.
Ⓒ Spacing them less than ten meters apart on a steep slope can increase fire risk.
Ⓓ They should be placed a maximum of three meters apart on flat terrain.

Paragraph 3 is marked with an arrow [➡].

19 Look at the four squares [■] that indicate where the following sentence could be added to the passage.

This is because wind supplies a fire with additional oxygen, causing it to move faster.

Where would the sentence best fit?

Click on a square [■] to add the sentence to the passage.

20 **Directions:** An introductory sentence for a brief summary of the passage is provided below. Complete the summary by selecting the THREE answer choices that express the most important ideas in the passage. Some sentences do not belong in the summary because they express ideas that are not presented in the passage or are minor ideas in the passage. **This question is worth 2 points.**

Drag your answer choices to the spaces where they belong.
To remove an answer choice, click on it. To review the passage, click on **View Text**.

The rate of spread of wildfires is determined by several things.

•
•
•

Answer Choices

(A) The features of the land contribute to the speed at which wildfires spread.

(B) Climate change has resulted in more wildfires being encountered in the natural environment.

(C) The availability of fuel is the most important factor in determining whether a wildfire will spread.

(D) Because wind supplies oxygen to wildfires, strong winds result in faster movement.

(E) How fast a wildfire advances depends on weather-related factors like wind and moisture levels.

(F) Wildfires tend to travel downhill at a faster rate than they move up a slope.

Answer Book p. 51

Answer Book p. 53

TOEFL Reading

Passage 3

Development of the US National Government

The year 1763 marked the high point in friendly relations between Great Britain and the American colonies. For more than 150 years, the colonies had been developing their own social, economic, and governmental institutions. However, beginning in 1764, members of the British Parliament passed several acts that placed numerous restrictions on the colonists causing bitter protests by them. As a result, in the fall of 1774, representatives from each of thirteen colonies except Georgia met at the First Continental Congress at Philadelphia. Then, on July 4, 1776, the Second Continental Congress declared its freedom from Great Britain in the Declaration of Independence. With independence declared, it was necessary for the new states to form some type of central authority, but sentiment for a strong government, nevertheless, was not great.

➡ The former colonists were reluctant to establish a powerful national government. Carefully guarding their new independence, representatives to the Continental Congress created a loosely structured legislature that protected the liberty of the individual states at the expense of the nation. [A] Up until this point, the only central government agency had been the Continental Congress. [B] In 1781, this organization was replaced by the first true national government. [C] It was organized under an agreement known as the Articles of Confederation, which had been sanctioned by all the states. [D]

➡ The disorganized federal government created by the Articles quickly demonstrated some glaring weaknesses. The lack of a strong central authority made the government only a league of loosely tied states that were virtually independent nations. Congress could not collect taxes, regulate commerce, or settle disputes among the states. Its work was further handicapped by the people's lack of feeling for national unity. Most Americans still owed their first loyalties to their home state. In addition, the almost four million residents of the new nation were widely scattered from Maine to Georgia. Transportation and communication were poor between settlements and worse between states. The central government also lacked control over foreign affairs, allowing individual states to send envoys to other countries.

To address the government's weaknesses, delegates from each state were sent to Philadelphia in 1787 for the Constitutional Convention. They drafted the United States Constitution, under which the country has been governed ever since, creating the permanent United States Constitution. By June 1788, nine out of the thirteen states had ratified the Constitution, making it the new law of the land. To this day, the original seven articles of the Constitution have remained intact. However, twenty-seven amendments have been added to the original document, greatly expanding its scope.

Volume Review Help Back Next

Questions 21-24 of 30

21 Why does the author mention several acts passed by the British Parliament?

Ⓐ To suggest that the colonists overreacted in their acts of protest
Ⓑ To explain why the colonies had been developing their own culture and economy
Ⓒ To highlight the original model on which the new American government was based
Ⓓ To give the reason for the assembling of the First Continental Congress

22 The word "them" in the passage refers to

Ⓐ members
Ⓑ restrictions
Ⓒ colonists
Ⓓ protests

23 The word "sanctioned" in the passage is closest in meaning to

Ⓐ approved
Ⓑ rejected
Ⓒ nominated
Ⓓ doubted

24 According to paragraph 2, which of the following is true of the Continental Congress's legislature?

Ⓐ It failed to gain control of government until 1781.
Ⓑ It refused to grant voting rights to all states.
Ⓒ It guarded states' freedom at the country's expense.
Ⓓ It established a strongly centralized government.

Paragraph 2 is marked with an arrow [➡].

25 According to paragraph 3, which of the following is true of the majority of Americans in the eighteenth century?

Ⓐ Their trust in the Articles of Confederation was low.
Ⓑ They believed that federal leaders were corrupt.
Ⓒ Their primary loyalty was to their own state.
Ⓓ They complained about the poor transportation.

Paragraph 3 is marked with an arrow [➡].

26 According to paragraph 3, in dealing with the states, Congress had difficulty with all of the following EXCEPT

Ⓐ gathering taxes
Ⓑ building an army
Ⓒ administering trade
Ⓓ resolving conflicts

Paragraph 3 is marked with an arrow [➡].

27 The word "permanent" in the passage is closest in meaning to

Ⓐ frequent
Ⓑ lasting
Ⓒ intentional
Ⓓ transient

28 Which of the following can be inferred about the United States Constitution?

Ⓐ It guaranteed various civil rights for Americans.
Ⓑ The majority of proposed amendments to it have passed.
Ⓒ The support of all states was not necessary to make it law.
Ⓓ It was unpopular with people in most parts of the country.

29 Look at the four squares [■] that indicate where the following sentence could be added to the passage.

However, no meaningful change resulted because the agreement simply legalized the activities that the Continental Congress had already been doing.

Where would the sentence best fit?

Click on a square [■] to add the sentence to the passage.

30 **Directions:** An introductory sentence for a brief summary of the passage is provided below. Complete the summary by selecting the THREE answer choices that express the most important ideas in the passage. Some sentences do not belong in the summary because they express ideas that are not presented in the passage or are minor ideas in the passage. **This question is worth 2 points.**

Drag your answer choices to the spaces where they belong.
To remove an answer choice, click on it. To review the passage, click on **View Text**.

After 150 years of British rule, the American colonists formed an independent government.

-
-
-

Answer Choices

(A) American colonists protested in reaction to the restrictions imposed upon them by the British Government.

(B) In 1763, there was a friendly relationship between Great Britain and the thirteen American colonies.

(C) The colonists were wary of creating a very strong government as they wanted to protect their independence.

(D) When delegates were in Philadelphia attempting to solve problems with the government, they created the US Constitution.

(E) Of the original seven articles of the Constitution, only a small number have not been altered or removed.

(F) Soon after the establishment of the government by the Articles of Confederation, the weaknesses of the new government became obvious.

Answer Book p. 53

Answer Book p. 54

TOEFL Reading

Passage 1

The History of the Library of Congress

➡ Since its creation, the Library of Congress has been a part of the legislative branch of the American government. The institution was established by the fledgling republic as it prepared to move its capital from Philadelphia to Washington DC. On April 18, 1800, President John Adams approved legislation that appropriated money to purchase books that were deemed necessary for the use of Congress. The initial collection consisted of 740 volumes and three maps that were ordered from England and arrived in 1801. They were stored in the US Capitol Building, the Library's first home. 5

The philosophy and ideals of the Library can be traced back to Thomas Jefferson, who believed that the power of intellect could shape a free and democratic society. As a man who stated he could not live without books, he took a keen interest in the Library of Congress and its collection while he was president. Throughout his presidency, he personally recommended books for the Library, and he appointed the first two librarians of Congress. **A** In 1814, the British army invaded the city of Washington and burned down the Capitol Building, destroying the Library of Congress and its 3,000 volumes in the process. **B** Jefferson offered to sell his personal library, the largest and finest in the country, to the Congress to start a new library. **C** The purchase of Jefferson's 6,487 volumes was approved in 1815. **D** 10 15

➡ Over time, the administration and operations of the Library of Congress have been governed by various laws. The first of these was established in 1802. The 1802 measure created the post of librarian of Congress and gave Congress the authority to establish the Library's budget as well as its rules and regulations. It also formally made the appointment of the librarian of Congress a presidential responsibility and permitted the president and vice president to borrow books. Later, this privilege was extended to most government agencies, including the judiciary. A separate law department was approved in 1832, along with a budget to purchase law books under the guidance of the chief justice of the United States. In 1887, a new law granted Congress the power to confirm the president's selection of the Librarian of Congress. In addition, it gave the librarian sole responsibility for making the Library's rules and regulations and appointing its staff. 20 25

Since the middle of the twentieth century, the Library has undergone substantial expansion and diversification. A major reason was the strong interest in international affairs after the two world wars and an associated desire to know more about the world. An increased budget allowed the Library to begin to amass a wide array of foreign materials. Its Asian-languages collection alone includes nearly two million items, the largest such collection outside Asia. In addition to its vast material collections, the Library has numerous digital collections, some of 30

which are available online. It also hosts special events like talks and concerts and serves as the country's official copyright office. 35

1 The word "fledgling" in the passage is closest in meaning to

Ⓐ nascent
Ⓑ democratic
Ⓒ mature
Ⓓ distinctive

2 Which of the following can be inferred about the Library of Congress's original collection?

Ⓐ Its maps were rare and valuable.
Ⓑ Its books were selected by John Adams.
Ⓒ It was stored in Philadelphia.
Ⓓ It was shipped from overseas.

3 It can be inferred from paragraph 1 that the Library of Congress

Ⓐ was originally the idea of John Adams
Ⓑ was created for the president to use
Ⓒ is no longer located in the US Capitol Building
Ⓓ has become part of the judicial branch of government

Paragraph 1 is marked with an arrow [➡].

4 The word "its" in the passage refers to

Ⓐ the United States
Ⓑ Congress
Ⓒ the librarian
Ⓓ the Library

5 According to paragraph 3, the law of 1802 included all of the following measures EXCEPT

Ⓐ giving the president power to appoint the librarian of Congress
Ⓑ giving congress the right to set the library's budget
Ⓒ allowing the president and vice president to borrow books
Ⓓ extending borrowing privileges to the judiciary

Paragraph 3 is marked with an arrow [➡].

6 Which of the following is true of the 1887 law?

Ⓐ It gave the chief justice the power to set the budget for purchasing books.
Ⓑ It transferred control of rules and regulations to the librarian of Congress.
Ⓒ It provided additional funding for the hiring of more staff for the Library.
Ⓓ It confirmed the librarian of Congress as a member of the legislature.

7 The word "amass" in the passage is closest in meaning to

Ⓐ discard
Ⓑ accumulate
Ⓒ restore
Ⓓ incorporate

8 Why does the author mention the Library's "Asian-languages collection" in the passage?

Ⓐ To explain the reason some collections are not available online
Ⓑ To give an example of one of its biggest digital collections
Ⓒ To emphasize that it is the largest library outside of Asia
Ⓓ To highlight its extensive collection of foreign materials

9 Look at the four squares [■] that indicate where the following sentence could be added to the passage.

This more than doubled the holdings that were originally lost.

Where would the sentence best fit?

Click on a square [■] to add the sentence to the passage.

10 **Directions:** An introductory sentence for a brief summary of the passage is provided below. Complete the summary by selecting the THREE answer choices that express the most important ideas in the passage. Some sentences do not belong in the summary because they express ideas that are not presented in the passage or are minor ideas in the passage. **This question is worth 2 points.**

Drag your answer choices to the spaces where they belong.
To remove an answer choice, click on it. To review the passage, click on **View Text**.

The Library of Congress has been part of the US legislature since its founding.

-
-
-

Answer Choices

Ⓐ As interest in international affairs diminished after the world wars, the role of the Library was reduced.

Ⓑ Thomas Jefferson helped establish the ideology of the Library and was highly supportive of it.

Ⓒ The Library of Congress has grown significantly and become much more diverse since the mid 1900s.

Ⓓ Approval for the funding to establish the Library came in 1800 when John Adams was president.

Ⓔ Originally, the Library was open only to members of government, but it was later opened to the public.

Ⓕ A variety of regulations have shaped the functioning and management of the Library over the years.

Answer Book p. 54

The Evolution of American Theater

American theater can trace its origins to the middle of the eighteenth century when theater companies produced shows in downtown New York. These early theaters typically included performances of William Shakespeare's plays and a few operas. As real estate prices became too great, theater owners began to move to midtown Manhattan, where the Theater District was formed. This area gave rise to the famous Broadway musicals, which added dance and original music to tell a story. Once established, theater quickly became a pervasive part of American life.

New York's Broadway established itself as the capital of the American theater industry in the nineteenth century. Large theaters were built to satisfy increasing demand, and this growth attracted bigger productions and more famous performers. Many businesses tried to cash in on this success by moving to the Theater District, further fueling the growth of the industry. By the early twentieth century, Times Square was teeming with theaters, restaurants, and shops—a seamless merger of arts entertainment and commercial enterprise.

➡ Yet as Broadway theater became an increasingly popular medium of entertainment, it also became very expensive to stage productions there. When a producer rented a theater, he got only a building with seats and utilities. All of the lights, props, costumes, sound equipment, and scenery had to be acquired. The financial burden inevitably influenced the type of production undertaken, so Broadway produced mostly proven plays and extravagant musicals. As a consequence, New York theater developed Off-Broadway venues, where productions were staged in smaller playhouses. These more intimate venues attracted blue-collar audiences, which previously could afford only cheaper balcony seats in the Broadway theaters. Off-Broadway also produced a wider range of performances and gave lesser-known actors a chance to become professionals. Still, in some cases, successful Off-Broadway shows eventually moved to Broadway. This move made their actors and producers eligible to be considered for the prestigious Tony Awards.

➡ Despite rapid growth and some success, Off-Broadway productions and performers continued to experience significant challenges. Furthermore, there was increasing recognition of the disparity in artistic value between Broadway and Off-Broadway productions. For example, even if a popular rock band sold more tickets than a Mozart concert, it was unlikely that they would be considered more artistically important than Mozart. **A** Even when Off-Broadway productions were in demand, they often could not sustain themselves through ticket sales alone. **B** Thus, in 1965, the National Endowment for the Arts (NEA) was established as an independent agency of the federal government. **C** The theater industry,

specifically the performers in smaller Off-Broadway productions, received funding from the NEA, which in turn received its funding from donations and tax dollars. **D** The NEA also subsidized tickets both On- and Off-Broadway. As a result, both venues continued to attract audiences to buy tickets for their performances and maintained their unique identities within the American Theater industry. 35

11 The word "pervasive" in the passage is closest in meaning to

(A) extensive
(B) limited
(C) purposeful
(D) stinging

12 The word "fueling" in the passage is closest in meaning to

(A) maintaining
(B) withdrawing
(C) stimulating
(D) compensating

13 Which of the following was NOT a factor in Broadway's early growth?

(A) High demand for theaters
(B) Large productions
(C) Influx of businesses
(D) Greater artistic value

14 According to paragraph 3, which of the following is indicated about the Tony Awards?

(A) They were accompanied by a large financial prize.
(B) They were given to the producer of the most popular musical.
(C) They were awarded only for Broadway productions.
(D) They were reserved for shows with lesser-known actors.

Paragraph 3 is marked with an arrow [➡].

15 It can be inferred that compared to Broadway productions, Off-Broadway productions

(A) were cheaper to produce
(B) attracted larger audiences
(C) were performed more frequently
(D) featured more actors

16 Why does the author mention "a popular rock band" in the passage?

(A) To describe the types of performances that typically appeared Off-Broadway
(B) To show that there was no direct link between commercial success and artistic worth
(C) To emphasize the declining interest in classical music among the public
(D) To highlight the growing demand for pop music in Broadway productions

17 The word "their" in the passage refers to

(A) venues
(B) audiences
(C) tickets
(D) performances

18 According to paragraph 4, why did the NEA fund Off-Broadway productions?

(A) Off-Broadway productions were not popular.
(B) Off-Broadway ticket prices were too high.
(C) Off-Broadway productions could not sustain themselves.
(D) Broadway productions refused to fund Off-Broadway productions.

Paragraph 4 is marked with an arrow [➡].

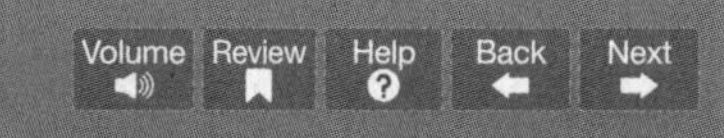

19 Look at the four squares [■] that indicate where the following sentence could be added to the passage.

The institution was created to recognize and support projects of artistic excellence.

Where would the sentence best fit?

Click on a square [■] to add the sentence to the passage.

20 **Directions:** An introductory sentence for a brief summary of the passage is provided below. Complete the summary by selecting the THREE answer choices that express the most important ideas in the passage. Some sentences do not belong in the summary because they express ideas that are not presented in the passage or are minor ideas in the passage. **This question is worth 2 points.**

Drag your answer choices to the spaces where they belong.
To remove an answer choice, click on it. To review the passage, click on **View Text**.

From the eighteenth century onwards, theater has played an important role in American life.

-
-
-

Answer Choices

Ⓐ Early productions in American theater were limited as theaters primarily focused on opera and the plays of Shakespeare.

Ⓑ Broadway became the center of American theater in the nineteenth century, and a thriving arts entertainment industry developed there.

Ⓒ Despite funding from the National Foundation for the Arts, Off-Broadway productions were unable to become financially practical.

Ⓓ Off-Broadway productions continued to face difficulties despite some success, so financial aid from the government was required.

Ⓔ Only a few theater companies could afford to operate on Broadway because the cost of rent was very expensive.

Ⓕ The great expense of staging Broadway productions led to the development of Off-Broadway venues that were smaller.

Answer Book p. 55

Answer Book p. 56

TOEFL Reading

Passage 3

The Birth and Death of Stars

➡ A star starts out as an enormous cloud of gas and dust. Star formation occurs when the cloud begins to condense under its own gravity. The cloud fragments fuse into stellar clouds known as protostars. If the mass of a protostar is large enough, gas and dust eventually collect into a giant ball and the temperature at the center reaches about fifteen million degrees. At this point, nuclear fusion begins and the ball of gas and dust starts to glow. Nuclear fusion supplies fuel to the star by combining hydrogen atoms to form helium. 5

➡ After a new star has begun its life, its evolution is not entirely foreseeable, but its destiny usually is determined by its mass. The most massive stars, which are also the biggest and hottest, last only for millions of years. This is because they tend to exhaust their fuel sources more quickly. Medium-sized stars, such as the Sun, can survive for even billions of years, and small stars like red dwarfs sometimes burn for tens of billions of years before they use up their fuel. The color of the star depends on its temperature—hotter stars are bluer, and cooler stars are redder. 10

➡ Throughout their lives, stars counteract the inward pull of the force of gravity with the outward pressure created by nuclear reactions. Once the star has burned about 10 percent of its hydrogen, helium atoms start to get in the way of hydrogen fusion, and the nuclear reaction stops. Without the outward pressure generated from these reactions to offset the force of gravity, the outer layers of the star begin to collapse inward, increasing temperature and pressure. This forces helium to fuse, and the newly generated heat temporarily counteracts gravity while the outer layers of the star are pushed outward. The star can expand up to a hundred times larger than its original size. If this occurs, the star becomes a red giant. Fortunately, the Sun will not reach this stage for another five billion years. 15 20

➡ Once a star reaches the red giant stage, it either collapses slowly or quickly. **A** For a star the size of the Sun, this stage will last for about two billion years. **B** A slow collapse yields a planetary nebula, and the core cools to become a white dwarf. **C** If the star is five or more times as massive as the Sun, the red giant will collapse quickly and result in a spectacular explosion called a supernova. **D** The core of the supernova may form a dense neutron star or an even denser black hole. It is not always clear which is formed, as most scientific knowledge of stellar evolution is derived from theory rather than observation. All stages of stellar life currently exist in the universe, and astronomical research continues to reveal more clues about stars every day. 25 30

21 The word "condense" in the passage is closest in meaning to

Ⓐ amplify
Ⓑ compress
Ⓒ extend
Ⓓ evolve

22 According to paragraph 1, the formation of a star requires

Ⓐ an equal amount of hydrogen and dust
Ⓑ a nearby star exerting gravitational forces
Ⓒ an adequate supply of hydrogen atoms
Ⓓ a protostar of sufficiently large mass

Paragraph 1 is marked with an arrow [➡].

23 The word "foreseeable" in the passage is closest in meaning to

Ⓐ believable
Ⓑ reliable
Ⓒ available
Ⓓ predictable

24 Which of the following can be inferred from paragraph 2 about the life of stars?

Ⓐ The largest and hottest stars typically have the shortest life spans.
Ⓑ The Sun will eventually become a red dwarf after billions of years.
Ⓒ Red dwarfs increase in size once they begin to run out of fuel.
Ⓓ Most stars exhaust all of their fuel before they can grow in size.

Paragraph 2 is marked with an arrow [➡].

25 According to paragraph 3, what happens after a star's nuclear reaction stops?

Ⓐ Gravity causes multiple nuclear reactions.
Ⓑ The star's outer layers start to fall in.
Ⓒ The temperature and pressure decline.
Ⓓ Hydrogen in the star turns to helium.

Paragraph 3 is marked with an arrow [➡].

26 The word "derived" in the passage is closest in meaning to

Ⓐ extracted
Ⓑ insulted
Ⓒ obstructed
Ⓓ transported

27 According to paragraph 4, which of the following is NOT true of a supernova?

Ⓐ It results from the collapse of a red giant.
Ⓑ Its core may become a neutron star.
Ⓒ It arises from a planetary nebula.
Ⓓ Its core might form a black hole.

Paragraph 4 is marked with an arrow [➡].

28 According to paragraph 4, which stage will the Sun remain at for approximately two billion years?

Ⓐ A red giant
Ⓑ A white dwarf
Ⓒ A neutron star
Ⓓ A black hole

Paragraph 4 is marked with an arrow [➡].

29 Look at the four squares [■] that indicate where the following sentence could be added to the passage.

This chilly remnant of a stellar core can be hard to detect even with a telescope as it produces very little visible light.

Where would the sentence best fit?

Click on a square [■] to add the sentence to the passage.

30 **Directions:** An introductory sentence for a brief summary of the passage is provided below. Complete the summary by selecting the THREE answer choices that express the most important ideas in the passage. Some sentences do not belong in the summary because they express ideas that are not presented in the passage or are minor ideas in the passage. **This question is worth 2 points.**

Drag your answer choices to the spaces where they belong.
To remove an answer choice, click on it. To review the passage, click on **View Text**.

Stars form from giant clouds of gas and dust and begin to undergo nuclear fusion if conditions are right.

-
-
-

Answer Choices

(A) The length of the red giant stage of a star depends on whether its collapse is slow or quick.

(B) It is usually possible to determine the approximate temperature of a star by observing its color.

(C) Stars' nuclear reactions create outward pressure that works against gravity's inward force throughout the stars' life.

(D) Once a star is born, its fate is typically dictated by its mass, though its development is not totally foreseeable.

(E) No matter how much energy a star has in its core, it cannot overcome the force of gravity forever and will eventually die.

(F) Because of the size and age of the Sun, it will probably never become a red giant in its lifetime.

Answer Book p. 56

MEMO

Instructors Who Contributed to This Book

Seoul
Christy Choi CNC Academy
Lee Hyunah Lee Eunjae English Institute
Wi Yeajee GB STUDY Gilbut Academy

Gyeonggi
Cho Eunhye Eden Academy
Chong Phildoo Jeong Sang Language School
Isla Lee Gwanggyo Chungdahm Institute
Kang Minjung YLP Kim Jinsung English Academy
Kim Minseong Rededu
Lee Changseok Junghyun English
Lee Jihye Lykeion Language Forum

Daejeon
Lee Sunggu Narin Academy
Oh Jihyun YoungJae's Kkum

Busan
Hwangbo Youkyung Centum EiE/TOPIA
Jeong Yumi Kookje Language Institute
Jung Hokyung A+ Academy
Kim Seojeen Kateyale Academy
Kwon Eunyoung Centum EiE/TOPIA
Lee Hayoung Centum EiE/TOPIA

Gyeongsang
Jung Kyounghee Cambridge English Language Institute

|H|A|C|K|E|R|S|

APEX READING for the TOEFL iBT® Intermediate

April 7, 2022

Hackers Language Research Institute
23, Gangnam-daero 61-gil, Seocho-gu, Seoul, Korea
Inquiries publishing@hackers.com

ISBN 978-89-6542-470-3 (53740)

Printed in South Korea

2 3 4 5 6 7 8 9 10 28 27 26 25 24 23 22

HACKERS

APEX READING for the TOEFL iBT®

Intermediate

Answer Book

HACKERS

APEX READING for the TOEFL iBT®

Intermediate

Answer Book

CHAPTER 01
Vocabulary

Example

본문 p.13

1 (C) 2 (B)

지중해 무역

비록 지중해가 대서양에 연결되어 있지만, 그것은 거의 완전히 육지로 둘러싸여 있다. 역사를 통틀어, 그것은 서양 문명의 번영에 중심적인 역할을 해왔다. 강대국들은 무역에 있어서 그것의 중요성 때문에 그것의 완전한 사용권을 확보하기 위해 시로 싸웠다. 따라서, 많은 사회들이 그 해안 지대를 식민지로 만들려고 시도했다.

그렇게 한 최초의 두 문명은 그리스의 도시 국가들과 페니키아로, 그곳의 상인들은 그 바다를 상업을 위한 통로로 광범위하게 이용했다. 그러나, 이후 그 지역은 로마인들에게 점령당했고, 그들은 이후 400년 동안 그 바다와 그것의 해안 지역을 지배했다. 그들은 지중해를 '마레 노스트룸', 즉 "우리의 바다"라고 불렀다. 로마 제국이 주로 해안 지역에 집중되어 있었기 때문에, 지중해는 로마인들의 상업과 해군의 발전에 있어서 매우 중요했다.

서기 476년에 로마가 무너진 이후, 그 지역은 여러 차례 주인이 바뀌었고 국가들은 계속해서 패권을 두고 싸웠다. 오늘날, 지중해의 지배권은 주로 유럽 연합에 있으며, 그것은 여전히 세계 최대의 상업 지역 중 하나에 해당한다.

connect 동 연결하다 enclosed 형 둘러싸인
civilization 명 문명, 문명지 struggle 동 싸우다 numerous 형 많은
attempt to ~하려고 시도하다 colonize 동 식민지로 만들다
merchant 명 상인 extensively 부 광범위하게 commerce 명 상업
control 동 지배하다; 명 지배권 coastal 형 해안의
concentrate 동 집중하다 extremely 부 매우 naval 형 해군의
collapse 동 무너지다 supremacy 명 패권, 우위
switch hands 주인이 바뀌다 reside 동 ~에 있다
the European Union 유럽 연합 represent 동 ~에 해당하다

1 지문의 단어 "enclosed"와 의미가 가장 비슷한 것은?
(A) 특징지어진
(B) 집중된
(C) 둘러싸인
(D) 발달된

2 지문의 단어 "supremacy"와 의미가 가장 비슷한 것은?
(A) 위치
(B) 지배
(C) 해방
(D) 적성

Reading Practice 1

본문 p.14

1 (D) 2 (B) 3 (B) 4 (C) 5 (B)

Vocabulary Quiz
1 ⓑ 2 ⓑ 3 ⓒ 4 ⓒ

바위주머니쥐의 적응

바위주머니쥐는 19종의 주머니쥐 중 하나이다. 그들은 미국 남서부의 소노란 사막 도처에 사는 단독 생활하는 야행성 동물이다. 전형적인 표본은 대략 170밀리미터이고 무게가 대략 15그램인데, 이는 이 작은 쥐가 종이 클립 한 움큼만큼의 무게가 나간다는 것을 의미한다.

이 설치류들에게 유달리 특별한 점은 없어 보이지만, 진화 생물학자들은 이 종에 상당히 흥미를 느꼈고 1930년대 초부터 그들의 털 색깔에 대한 많은 연구를 수행해 왔다. 이 종의 가장 흔한 품종은 모래 색깔의 밝은색 털을 가지고 있다. 이 색깔 무늬는 그들이 사는 사막의 바위와 모래에 뒤섞이는 것을 돕는다.

그러나, 인근 지역에서 더 어두운색을 가진 바위주머니쥐 개체군도 발견되었다. [3]과학자들은 이 무리들이 수천 년 전의 화산 분출에서 나온 용암의 흐름에 의해 형성된, 현무암이라고 불리는 화산암의 어두운 부분들로 땅이 덮여 있었던 사막의 좁고 긴 지역에서 살았다는 것을 발견했다. 이것을 보고, 과학자들은 이러한 차이를 초래했을지도 모르는 어느 특정한 유전자를 찾기 위해 밝은색과 어두운색의 개체군 둘 다에서 수집된 정보를 샅샅이 뒤졌다. 철저한 분석 후, 특정 유전자의 돌연변이가 털 색깔의 결정 요인이라는 것이 밝혀졌다.

유전자 돌연변이는 유전자의 DNA 서열의 어떤 변화이다. 유전자 돌연변이는 그 결과물인 단백질의 구조를 변화시킬 수 있으며, 이는 그것이 기능하는 방식을 바꿀 수 있다. 바위주머니쥐의 경우, 돌연변이 된 유전자와 털 색깔 간의 직접적인 연관성이 발견되었다. 유전자 돌연변이가 없는 쥐가 계속 더 밝았던 것에 반해, 그것을 가진 쥐는 더 많은 흑색소를 가지고 있었다. 돌연변이의 주된 원인은 생물학자들이 선택압이라고 부르는 것으로 밝혀졌는데, 이것은 주어진 환경에서 생물의 생존 능력에 영향을 미친다. [5]바위주머니쥐들에게, 환경의 색은 현무암 위에서 사는 쥐들이 더 잘 위장하도록 돕기 위해 유전자가 변이하도록 압력을 가했고, 이는 더 높은 생존율과 포식동물로부터의 더 나은 보호를 보장했다. 그것은 자연 선택을 통한 적응의 좋은 사례이다.

species 명 (생물 분류상의) 종 solitary 형 단독 생활하는
nocturnal 형 야행성의 typical 형 전형적인 specimen 명 표본
rodent 명 (쥐·다람쥐 등의) 설치류 intrigued 형 흥미를 느끼는
conduct 동 수행하다 variety 명 품종 population 명 개체군
strip 명 좁고 긴 지역 patch 명 부분, 조각 basalt 명 현무암
comb through 샅샅이 뒤지다 compile 동 수집하다
gene 명 유전자 thorough 형 철저한 mutation 명 돌연변이
determiner 명 결정 요인 sequence 명 서열, 순서
alter 동 변화시키다 association 명 연관성
melanin 명 흑색소, 멜라닌 selective pressure 선택압
camouflage 명 위장하다 ensure 동 보장하다

1 지문의 단어 "intrigued"와 의미가 가장 비슷한 것은?
(A) 겁에 질린
(B) 당혹한
(C) 고상한
(D) 매료된

2 지문의 어구 "combed through"와 의미가 가장 비슷한 것은?
(A) 깔끔하게 정리했다
(B) 면밀히 살펴보았다
(C) 완전히 요약했다
(D) 광범위하게 시험했다

3 3단락에 따르면, 어떤 바위주머니쥐 개체군은
(A) 울창한 초목으로 덮인 땅에 거주한다
(B) 한때 활화산이 있었던 지역에 산다
(C) 밝은 개체와 어두운 개체를 둘 다 포함한다
(D) 다른 무리의 구성원들에서 발견되는 유전자가 없다

4 지문의 단어 "it"이 가리키는 것은?
(A) 결과물인 단백질
(B) 직접적인 연관성
(C) 돌연변이 된 유전자
(D) 털 색깔

5 4단락에 따르면, 바위주머니쥐가 다양한 색의 털을 가진 것은
(A) 밝은색 쥐에서 흑색소의 양이 증가했기 때문이다
(B) 위장된 쥐의 생존율이 더 높았기 때문이다
(C) 어두운색 쥐의 유전자 돌연변이가 아무런 영향을 미치지 않았기 때문이다
(D) 포식동물들이 색의 차이에 의해 방해받았기 때문이다

Reading Practice 2

본문 p.16

1 (A) 2 (C) 3 (B) 4 (A) 5 (A)

Vocabulary Quiz

1 ⓑ 2 ⓐ 3 ⓒ 4 ⓑ

청각이 작동하는 방식

우리가 무언가를 들을 때, 그것은 순식간에 일어나고, 우리는 그것을 즉시 인식한다. 그러나 이러한 빠른 반응에도 불구하고, 청각의 과정은 꽤 복잡하다. [2A]음파는 먼저 귓구멍으로 들어와 고막을 때려 그것이 진동하게 한다. 그런 다음 그 진동은 중이의 뼈로 이동한다. [2D]고막이 진동하면, 뼈도 진동하고, 이것은 내이의 달팽이 모양 구조인 달팽이관의 액체를 움직이게 한다. 그 액체가 달팽이관 안에서 파도처럼 움직이면, 번갈아 일어나는 압력의 변화가 유모세포를 자극한다. [2B]이 세포들은 위아래로 움직이면서 진동을 뇌로 전달되는 전기 신호로 변환해 우리가 이해하는 소리로 바꾼다.

잘 듣는 것은 소리가 중단 없이 뇌에 도달하여 처리될 수 있도록 함께 작동하는 전체 체계에 달려 있다. 따라서, 어떤 사람이 청각에 문제가 있다면, 그 특정 유형은 청각 체계의 어느 부분이 잘 반응하고 있지 않은지에 달려 있다. [4]예를 들어, 만약 당신이 외이 또는 중이에 문제가 있다면, 그것은 보통 고막에서 달팽이관으로 진동의 비효율적 전달이 있다는 것을 의미한다. 일반적으로, 이것은 당신이 듣는 음량에 영향을 미치기 때문에 소리가 약하고 낮게 느껴질 수 있다. 소리의 진동이 효율적으로 전도되지 않고 있기 때문에 이것은 전음성 난청이라고 불린다. 이러한 종류의 청각 문제에는, 기존의 보청기 대신 골전도 청각 장치가 사용된다. 그 장치는 뼈 진동을 통해 소리를 달팽이관에 직접 전달한다. 이는 달팽이관은 여전히 정상적으로 작동하지만 단지 중이와의 연결을 통해 충분한 정보를 받지 못하기 때문에 필요하다.

반면에, 만약 달팽이관과 뇌 사이의 체계에 문제가 발생하면, 그것은 감각신경성 난청이라고 불린다. 이 경우, 손상된 유모세포 때문에 또는 뇌로 이어지는 청각 경로의 결함 때문에 소리가 달팽이관에 도달한 뒤 처리되지 않는다. 이러한 유형의 난청은 큰 소음에의 지속적인 노출이나 단순히 노화 때문이다. 때로는, 수술이 상황을 해결하는 데 도움을 줄 수 있지만, 대부분의 경우, 이를 해결하기 위해 기존의 보청기가 사용된다.

hearing 명 청각, 듣기, 청력 in a split second 순식간에
instantly 부 즉시 reaction 명 반응 complicated 형 복잡한
ear canal 귓구멍, 외이도 eardrum 명 고막 middle ear 중이
cochlea 명 달팽이관 alternating 형 번갈아 일어나는
hair cell 유모세포 process 동 처리하다 disruption 명 중단
inefficient 형 비효율적인 transfer 명 전달; 동 전달하다
muted 형 (소리가) 약한 conductive hearing loss 전음성 난청
conduct 동 (소리·열을) 전도하다 bone conduction 골전도
hearing aids 보청기 sensorineural hearing loss 감각신경성 난청
defect 명 결함 exposure 명 노출 remedy 동 해결하다
conventional 형 기존의, 전통적인

1 지문의 단어 "complicated"와 의미가 가장 비슷한 것은?
(A) 복잡한
(B) 즉각적인
(C) 무작위의
(D) 정확한

2 1단락에 따르면, 다음 중 제대로 기능하는 청각에 관해 사실이 아닌 것은?
(A) 음파는 먼저 귓구멍을 통해 이동한다.
(B) 유모세포는 진동을 전기 신호로 변환한다.
(C) 압력 변화는 소리를 직접 뇌로 전달한다.
(D) 진동은 달팽이관의 액체를 움직이게 한다.

3 지문의 단어 "disruption"과 의미가 가장 비슷한 것은?
(A) 부패
(B) 중단
(C) 보호
(D) 파괴

4 2단락에 따르면, 전도성 난청은
(A) 진동이 달팽이관으로 효율적으로 전달되지 않기 때문에 일어난다
(B) 뇌가 말이 아닌 소리를 처리하기 때문에 일어난다
(C) 달팽이관이 진동을 해석하지 못하기 때문에 일어난다
(D) 손상된 유모세포는 소리가 뇌에 도달하는 것을 막기 때문에 일어난다

5 지문의 단어 "it"이 가리키는 것은?
(A) 문제
(B) 체계
(C) 달팽이관
(D) 뇌

Reading Practice 3 본문 p.18

1 (D) 2 (A) 3 (A) 4 (C) 5 (B)

Vocabulary Quiz

1 ⓑ 2 ⓐ 3 ⓒ 4 ⓒ

테노치티틀란의 흥망성쇠

테노치티틀란은 한때 아즈텍 제국의 가장 큰 도시들 중 하나였다. [1]그것은 멕시카족에 의해, 그들이 그들의 신 우이칠로포츠틀리의 명령이라고 믿었던 것에 대한 응답으로 고향인 아즈틀란을 떠난 후, 서기 1325년경에 세워졌다. 전설에 따르면, 우이칠로포츠틀리는 그들이 독수리가 선인장 위에 앉아 뱀을 잡아먹는 것을 목격한 자리에 도시를 건설하도록 지시했다. 그들은 텍스코코 호수에 있는 섬에서 이 환상을 목격했고, 마침내 그곳에 정착했다.

멕시카족의 초기 몇 년은 그들이 새로운 주거지를 짓기 위해 노력했기 때문에 힘겨웠다. 그 민족은 작은 오두막에서 살았고, 우이칠로포츠틀리를 위한 신성한 신전은 부패하기 쉬운 자재로 만들어졌다. 이 도시는 심지어 그들을 통치했던 이웃 도시 아즈카포찰코에 정기적인 공물을 바쳐야 했다. 테노치티틀란의 통치자 이츠코아틀이 아즈카포찰코의 내분과 정치적 불안정을 감지했을 때, 그들의 힘든 삶이 바뀌기 시작했다. 그는 다른 더 작은 도시들과 동맹을 맺을 기회를 잡았고 결국 테노치티틀란은 독립을 얻었다.

이 초라한 시작에서부터, 테노치티틀란은 이후 80년 동안 그 제국의 중심지가 되었다. [4A]그 당시에, 멕시카족은 공물을 받았으며 인근 지역을 정복하고 있었다. 그 도시는 사회 기반 시설뿐만 아니라 부와 권력 측면에서도 성장했다. [4B]주민들은 호수에서 식수를 끌어오는 수로와, 우이칠로포츠틀리와 비와 다산의 신인 틀랄록 둘 다에게 바쳐진 제대로 된 신전을 지을 충분한 자재를 가지고 있었다. [4D]그 도시의 부, 풍부한 천연자원, 호수에서의 전략적인 위치는 그것의 무역 시장을 신장시켰고, 그것을 경제적, 정치적 실세로 만들었다.

불행하게도, 테노치티틀란의 황금기는 스페인 정복자 에르난 코르테스가 1519년에 멕시코에 상륙했을 때 끝나게 되었다. 그 스페인인의 도착은 아즈텍 제국 멸망의 전조가 되었다. 코르테스는 처음에 멕시카족에게 따뜻하게 환영받았고 금으로 된 선물들을 받았다. 그들은 이 존경의 표시가 그를 기쁘게 하여 그가 그들을 평화롭게 내버려 두기를 바랐다. 당연하게도, 그 도시에 그렇게 많은 금이 있다는 것을 알게 된 것은 그것을 정복하려는 코르테스의 열망을 키울 뿐이었다. 그는 몇 달 후 700명의 군인과 스페인군과 동맹을 맺은 70,000명의 원주민 군대를 이끌고 돌아왔다. 그들은 1521년 8월 13일에 멕시카족이 마침내 항복할 때까지 93일 동안 그들이 할 수 있는 한 모든 것들을 불태우고, 약탈하고, 파괴하면서 테노치티틀란을 포위 공격했다.

in response to ~에 대한 응답으로 command 명 명령
perch 동 (새가) 앉다 vision 명 환상, 환영 hut 명 오두막
sacred 형 신성한 perishable 형 부패하기 쉬운
pay tribute to ~에게 공물을 바치다 challenging 형 힘든
instability 명 불안정 alliance 명 동맹 independence 명 독립
humble 형 초라한 conquer 동 정복하다
infrastructure 명 사회 기반 시설 aqueduct 명 수로
dedicate 동 바치다 ample 형 풍부한 boost 동 신장시키다
downfall 명 멸망 ally oneself with ~와 동맹을 맺다
lay siege to ~을 포위 공격하다 loot 동 약탈하다
surrender 동 항복하다

1 지문에 따르면, 텍스코코 호수에 그 도시가 건립된 것은 멕시카족이
(A) 그들의 새로이 독립한 사회를 위한 수도가 필요했기 때문이다
(B) 내분과 정치적 불안정으로부터 피난처를 찾았기 때문이다
(C) 전쟁에서 아즈카포찰코를 패배시킨 후 그곳에 새로운 이름을 붙였기 때문이다
(D) 신화적 존재의 명령을 따르고 있었기 때문이다

2 지문의 단어 "alliances"와 의미가 가장 비슷한 것은?
(A) 연합
(B) 휴전
(C) 감탄
(D) 독점

3 지문의 단어 "ample"과 의미가 가장 비슷한 것은?
(A) 풍부한
(B) 과도한
(C) 독특한
(D) 매력 있는

4 다음 중 3단락에서 테노치티틀란의 부흥에 대한 글쓴이의 설명이 언급하지 않은 것은?
(A) 주변 지역의 정복
(B) 식수의 이용 가능성
(C) 새로운 종교로의 개종
(D) 천연자원 무역의 성공

5 지문의 단어 "them"이 가리키는 것은?
(A) 그 스페인인
(B) 멕시카족
(C) 금으로 된 선물들
(D) 존경의 표시

Reading Practice 4 본문 p.20

1 (B) 2 (C) 3 (C) 4 (D) 5 (D)

Vocabulary Quiz

1 ⓑ 2 ⓐ 3 ⓒ 4 ⓒ

미국 최초의 영화관

니켈로디언은 미국에서 개장한 최초의 상업 영화관이었다. 1900년대 초반 동안, 영화에 대한 대중의 관심 증가로 인해 이러한 종류의 상점 앞 극장은 인기 있는 오락 시설이 되었다. [5A]얼마 지나지 않아, 전국에 8,000개 이상의 극장이 생겨나고 있었다.

그전까지, 영화 자체는 여러 가지의 다양한 종류의 오락을 선보이는 보드빌 쇼의 사소한 오락거리였고, 그것들만의 시설을 타당하게 만들 만큼 충분히 중요하게 여겨지지 않았다. [3]이는 그 당시의 영화가 보드빌의 막간에 상영되는, 춤추는 커플이나 재채기하는 남성 같은 "그림자" 이미지들의 모음에 불과했기 때문이다. 그 결과, 만약 광고가 줄거리나 서술 없이 움직이는 이미지로만 구성된다면, 그것은 거의 광고와 같았다. 그러나, 머지않아 몇몇 영리한 혁신가들이 그것들로 이야기를 전달할 수 있다고 생각하게 되었다. 영화와 영사 기술이 발전함에 따라, 이

새로운 형태의 오락에 대한 흥미 또한 함께 발전했다.

기회를 포착하고 오직 영화 상영만을 위해 극장 전체를 할애하기로 결정한 것은 바로 보드빌 기획자인 해리 데이비스였다. 그는 영사기라고 불리는 기계를 구입했고 피츠버그 시내의 스미스필드 거리에 있는 상점 앞에 의자와 화면을 설치했다. 5C그는 그의 첫 상영작을 이미 어느 정도 인기 있었던 영화로 결정했는데, 그것은 '대열차 강도'라는, 기차를 터는 무법자들에 관한 10분짜리 영화였다. 1905년 6월 19일에 그와 그의 처남은 매우 기뻐하는 대중에게 그가 이름을 붙인 니켈로디언을 공개했다.

그들은 첫날에 400명 이상의 관객을, 그다음 날에는 1,000명 이상의 관객을 받았다. 모두가 그 체험에 참여하고 싶어 했으며, 니켈로디언은 이상적인 장소였다. 우선, 영화는 라이브 공연자가 필요 없었기 때문에, 휴식이 필요 없었다. 이것은 데이비스가 매시간 여러 번의 상영으로 아침 8시부터 자정까지 극장을 계속 열 수 있게 해주었다. 이것은 또한 그가 입장료를 낮게 유지할 수 있다는 것을 의미했다. 5B보드빌 쇼를 관람하는 데 25센트라는 값비싼 비용이 들었던 반면에, 스미스필드 거리의 이 극장은 누구나 참석할 수 있도록 5센트만을 청구했다. 사실, 여기에서 데이비스는 그의 극장의 이름을 얻었는데, 그는 입장료인 니켈과 극장을 뜻하는 그리스어 단어인 '오데온'을 결합했다.

commercial 형상업의; 명광고　storefront 형상점 앞의
facility 명시설　pop up 생겨나다　distraction 명오락거리
vaudeville 명보드빌(음악·무용이 섞인 희가극)
feature 동선보이다, 다루다　substantial 형중요한, 가치 있는
warrant 동타당하게 만들다　consist of ~으로 구성되다
plot 명줄거리　narrative 명서술　projection 명영사, 영상
devote 동할애하다　exclusively 부오직
cinematograph 명영사기　outlaw 명무법자
dub 동이름을 붙이다　get in on ~에 참여하다　venue 명장소
admission fee 입장료　pricey 형값비싼　charge 동청구하다
nickel 명니켈(5센트짜리 동전)

1 지문의 단어 "substantial"과 의미가 가장 비슷한 것은?
(A) 사치스러운
(B) 중요한
(C) 영속적인
(D) 혁신적인

2 지문의 단어 "them"이 가리키는 것은?
(A) 보드빌의 막
(B) 광고
(C) 움직이는 이미지
(D) 영리한 혁신가들

3 2단락에 따르면, 초기 영화는
(A) 다양한 오락 형태를 결합했다
(B) 상품을 팔기 위해 고안되었다
(C) 더 긴 쇼의 사소한 일부였다
(D) 보드빌 공연과 경쟁했다

4 지문의 단어 "exclusively"와 의미가 가장 비슷한 것은?
(A) 쉽게
(B) 틀림없이
(C) 직접적으로
(D) 오직

5 지문에 따르면, 다음 중 니켈로디언에 관해 사실이 아닌 것은?
(A) 그곳이 개장한 후 비슷한 수천 개의 상점 앞 극장이 생겨났다.
(B) 보드빌 쇼에 참석하는 데 드는 비용보다 적은 금액을 청구했다.
(C) 그곳에서 상영된 첫 영화는 이미 어느 정도 유명했다.
(D) 라이브 공연자가 필요 없었기 때문에 24시간 열려 있었다.

iBT Reading Test

본문 p.22

1 (C)	2 (B)	3 (B)	4 (C)
5 (D)	6 (C)	7 (B)	8 (B)
9 (A)	10 (B), (C), (F)		

육상 식물의 기원

10억 년 전, 지구 대륙에는 생명체가 거의 없었다. 3박테리아와 균류의 얼마 안 되는 양을 제외하면, 육지는 바위투성이었고 황량했다. 유일한 복잡한 생명체는 물속에 있었다. 그러다 약 5억 년 전에, 육지에 식물이 나타나기 시작했고, 마침내 지표면을 흙으로 덮고 숲, 늪, 관목 지대를 형성했다. 식물은 광합성 과정을 통해 지구를 산소로 채웠고, 그 결과 바다 깊은 곳에서 동물이 출현하기 시작했다. 하지만 이 육상 식물들은 어디에서 왔을까?

과학자들은 식물이 민물 녹조류에서 진화했다고 생각하는데, 이 녹조류는 복잡한 생명체가 해안으로 나오기 훨씬 전에 광합성을 수행했다. 조류는 아메바와 매우 유사한 단세포 종의 후손인 수생 생물이다. 이 단세포 생물은 역시 이산화탄소를 산소로 전환하는 능력이 있는 해양 박테리아를 섭취함으로써 광합성을 수행하는 능력을 얻었다.

조류는 육지에서 생존하기 위해 점차 진화했다. 그렇게 하기 위해, 그 생물들이 번식하는 방식이 바뀌었다. 6B오늘날까지 조류가 계속하는 방식대로 배아를 물속에 방출하는 대신, 육상 식물들은 그것들 내부에서 배아를 성장시키기 시작했다. 6A그것들이 더 이상 지속적으로 직접 물과 접촉하지 않았기 때문에, 그 식물들은 생물 내부에 물을 보유할 수 있는 층인 큐티클을 발달시켰다. 게다가, 식물은 잎에 수분을 잃지 않고 이산화탄소를 산소와 교환할 수 있게 해주는 기공을 발달시켰다. 6D마침내, 관다발 조직은 뿌리를 통해 물을 전달받은 후 식물 전체에 운반하도록 진화했다.

어느 민물 조류 종이 육상 식물을 발생하게 했는지에 대해서 약간의 논쟁이 있었다. 유력한 후보는 복잡한 녹조류였는데, 그것은 가지를 뻗는 긴 몸체를 가지고 있다는 점에서 식물과 유사했다. **과학자들은 이 물리적 유사성이 이 조류와 식물이 공통된 조상을 갖는다는 것을 나타낸다고 추정했다.** 그러나, 최근 다양한 조류 종의 유전자 분석은 단세포 조류 종이 초기 육상 식물 종과 훨씬 더 많은 공통점을 갖는다는 것을 드러냈다. 8이 가설은 검증하기 어렵지만, 연구자들은 이 단순한 생물이 연못과 개울 밖에서 자라기 시작하여 이끼, 관목, 심지어 나무로 진화했다고 추정한다. 따라서 육상 식물의 진화는 과학자들이 가정했던 것보다 더 우회적이었다.

be devoid of ~이 없다　apart from ~을 제외하면
fungus 명균류, 곰팡이류　barren 형황량한　complex 형복잡한
swamp 명늪　shrubland 명관목 지대
photosynthesis 명광합성　algae 명조류　ashore 부해안으로
aquatic organism 수생 생물　be descended from ~의 후손이다
convert 동전환하다　reproduce 동번식하다
embryo 명배아, 태아　retain 동보유하다　access 명접촉, 접근

pore 명 기공, 구멍　vascular tissue 관다발 조직
give rise to ~을 발생하게 하다　candidate 명 후보
hypothesis 명 가설　suspect 동 추정하다　circuitous 형 우회적인

1 지문의 단어 "devoid"와 의미가 가장 비슷한 것은?
(A) 밀집한
(B) 다양한
(C) 없는
(D) 튼튼한

2 아래 문장 중 지문 속의 음영된 문장의 핵심 정보를 가장 잘 표현한 것은? 오답은 문장의 의미를 크게 바꾸거나 핵심 정보를 생략한다.
(A) 동물이 바다에서 왔기 때문에 식물은 대기로 산소를 내보냈다.
(B) 지구가 식물에 의해 산소로 채워졌기 때문에, 동물이 해양 밖으로 이동했다.
(C) 지구에 산소가 공급되면서 해저에서 동물의 조상이 출현했다.
(D) 동물의 등장에도 불구하고, 광합성은 동물의 진화를 초래했다.

3 다음 중 1단락에서 글쓴이가 10억 년 전 대륙에 관해 묘사하는 것은?
(A) 조류에서 진화한 동물들
(B) 식물보다 먼저 육지에 있었던 박테리아
(C) 광합성을 하는 균류
(D) 식물로 인해 생겨난 토양

4 지문의 단어 "descended"와 의미가 가장 비슷한 것은?
(A) 준비된
(B) 제거된
(C) 유래된
(D) 복제된

5 지문의 단어 "they"가 가리키는 것은?
(A) 생물들
(B) 조류
(C) 배아
(D) 식물들

6 3단락에 따르면, 다음 중 조류가 식물로 진화한 방법이 아닌 것은?
(A) 물을 보유하는 층을 발달시킨 것
(B) 배아를 품을 수 있게 된 것
(C) 번식을 촉진했던 기공을 형성한 것
(D) 뿌리에서 식물로 물을 운반한 것

7 지문의 단어 "hypothesis"와 의미가 가장 비슷한 것은?
(A) 실험
(B) 이론
(C) 시험
(D) 의심

8 4단락에 따르면, 단세포 조류는
(A) 초기 육상 식물과 경쟁했던 생물일 가능성이 가장 높다
(B) 가장 먼저 민물 밖에서 자랐던 생물일 가능성이 가장 높다
(C) 가지를 뻗는 긴 몸체를 발달시켰던 생물일 가능성이 가장 높다
(D) 과학자들에 의해 배열된 유전자를 포함했던 생물일 가능성이 가장 높다

9 네 개의 네모[■]는 다음 문장이 삽입될 수 있는 곳을 나타내고 있다.

과학자들은 이 물리적 유사성이 이 조류와 식물이 공통된 조상을 갖는다는 것을 나타낸다고 추정했다.

이 문장은 어디에 들어가는 것이 가장 적절한가?

10 지시: 지문 요약을 위한 도입 문장이 아래에 주어져 있다. 지문의 가장 중요한 내용을 나타내는 보기 3개를 골라 요약을 완성하라. 어떤 문장은 지문에 언급되지 않은 내용이나 사소한 정보를 나타내므로 요약에 포함되지 않는다. **이 문제는 2점이다.**

한때, 생명체는 수중 환경에 국한되었지만, 결국 육상 식물이 진화했다.
· (B) 식물은 민물 녹조류의 후손이다.
· (C) 육지에서 생존하기 위해, 조류는 여러 가지 방식으로 적응해야 했다.
· (F) 어느 조류 종이 육상 식물의 원래 조상인지에 관한 과학적 의견이 바뀌었다.

(A) 토양은 지상에서 식물이 진화한 결과이다.
(D) 식물은 수분이 일정하게 유지되는 동안 기체가 처리될 수 있게 하는 기공을 가지고 있다.
(E) 수년간, 과학자들은 단세포 조류가 복잡한 조류로 진화했다고 믿었다.

Vocabulary Review 본문 p.26

1 barren　2 humble　3 challenging
4 surrender　5 nocturnal　6 access
7 (D)　8 (C)　9 (A)　10 (C)
11 (B)　12 (C)　13 (A)　14 (B)

CHAPTER 02
Reference

Example 본문 p.29

1 (C)　2 (B)

예방 접종

예방 접종은 고대에 중국, 인도, 페르시아에서 이용되었음에도 불구하고, 1796년이 되어서야 서양에 도입되었다. 사실, 누군가가 세균과 바이러스에 대해 알기 훨씬 전부터, 특정 질병의 생존자들은 다시 그것들에 걸리지 않는다는 것이 관찰되어 왔다. 이 관찰은 중국인들에 의해 인두 접종이라고 불리는 초기 형태의 예방 접종을 통해 실시되었는데, 이것은 일찍이 10세기에 수행되었다. 그 방법은 건강한 사람들을 그 질병에서 기인한 환부의 물질에 노출시키도록 그것을 피부 아래에 넣음으로써 천연두를 예방하는 것을 목표로 했다. 인두 접종은 가벼운 질환을 일으켰고, 간혹 사망을 초래할 수 있었지만, 그것을 시도한 집단에서 천연두 발병률이 더 낮은 것으로 보고되었다.

서양 의학은 영국 의사 에드워드 제너가 우두라고 불리는 가벼운 질병

이 환자들을 훨씬 더 치명적인 질병인 천연두에 면역이 되게 만든다는 것을 발견했을 때 동양의 것을 따라잡았다. 인두 접종과 마찬가지로, 예방 접종 또한 환자들을 그들이 예방하고자 하는 질병의 형태에 노출시킴으로써 작용했다. 적극적인 검사 및 약물을 쓰는 간호와 함께, 이 치료법은 모든 공중 보건 전략의 기본적인 구성 요소가 되었다.

vaccination 명예방 접종　observation 명관찰
put ~ into practice ~을 실시하다　variolation 명인두 접종
aim 동~을 목표로 하다　smallpox 명천연두　expose 동노출시키다
matter 명물질, 성분　lesion 명환부　mild 형가벼운
occasionally 부간혹　medicine 명의학
catch up with ~을 따라잡다　equivalent 명대응하는 것
cowpox 명우두　immune 형면역이 된　deadly 형치명적인
aggressive 형적극적인, 공격적인　pharmaceutical 형약물을 쓰는
treatment 명치료법　component 명구성 요소　strategy 명전략

1 지문의 단어 "it"이 가리키는 것은?
(A) 방법
(B) 천연두
(C) 물질
(D) 질병

2 지문의 어구 "this treatment"가 가리키는 것은?
(A) 인두 접종
(B) 예방 접종
(C) 검사
(D) 간호

Reading Practice 1

본문 p.30

1 (B)　2 (B)　3 (C)　4 (A)　5 (D)

Vocabulary Quiz

1 ⓐ　2 ⓑ　3 ⓒ　4 ⓒ

스탠퍼드 감옥 실험

스탠퍼드 감옥 실험은 1971년의 한 심리학 연구로, 그 실험에서 실험 대상자들은 스탠퍼드 대학교의 모의 감옥 환경에서 무작위로 간수들과 죄수들로 나뉘었다. [1]대학생인 참가자들은 감금되거나 각각 세 명의 죄수를 수용하는 세 개의 감방을 감시하는 대가로 하루에 15달러를 받았다. 며칠 안에, 간수들은 공격적이고 폭력적인 행동에 가담했던 반면, 죄수들은 심한 불안과 정서적 고통의 증상을 보였다. 그것이 끝나기로 예정되었던 것보다 며칠 전에, 실험이 결국 중단되어야 했을 정도로 간수들은 그들의 권력을 남용했다.

그 실험은 비록 그렇게 행동하는 것이 다른 사람들을 해치는 것을 의미할지라도, 사람들이 그들이 할 것이라고 예상되는 사회적 역할에 얼마나 기꺼이 순응하는지를 드러냈다. 다시 말해, 만약 사람들에게 다른 사람들에 대한 권력이 주어진다면, 그들은 그 권력을 남용할 것이다. 그리고 무력한 상황에 놓인 사람들은 복종하게 될 것이다. 그 실험의 결과는 언론에 널리 보도되었으며 심리학 교과서의 고정 주제가 되었다. 그것들은 또한 수많은 책, 영화, 텔레비전 프로그램, 다큐멘터리의 소재가 되어 왔다.

사회 과학 역사상 가장 중요한 연구들 사이에서 그 실험의 확고한 지위에도 불구하고, 그것의 설계와 실행에서의 결함에 대한 반복된 비난이 있었다. 첫 번째로, 참가자들이 모두 중산층의 백인 남성들이었다는 것이었다. [5A]참가자들 사이의 인구 통계학적 다양성의 결여는 인류 전체에 대한 그것의 타당성에 의문을 제기한다. [5C]그 실험은 또한 감옥 환경을 현실성 있게 모방하는 데 실패하여, 많은 사람들이 전형적인 교도 시설에서의 행동 표현으로서 그 연구가 갖는 가치에 대해 의문을 제기하게 했다.

[5B]그 실험에 대한 가장 중대한 비판은 과학 윤리 위반에 관한 것이다. '아메리칸 사이콜로지스트'지에 실린 2015년의 한 연구는 간수들이 죄수들에게 공격적으로 행동하도록 지시하는 연구원들의 녹음을 공개했다. 그 연구원들은 심지어 그들이 언론의 관심을 받고 싶은 욕구에 자극받았다고 인정했다. 억압적인 사회적 역할에 무의식적으로 빠져드는 대신, 많은 간수들이 연구원들의 지시에 저항했다. 게다가, 죄수들 중 한 명은 실험에서 빠져나오기 위해 감정적 고통을 가장했다고 자백했다. 많은 심리학자들은 그 실험이 교과서에서 삭제되어야 한다고 권고해왔다.

psychological 형심리학의　subject 명실험 대상
randomly 부무작위로　participant 명참가자
confine 동감금하다　house 동수용하다　engage in ~에 가담하다
abusive 형폭력적인　exhibit 동보이다　distress 명고통
abuse 동남용하다　willingly 부기꺼이
conform to ~에 순응하다　obedience 명복종
fixture 명고정물, 붙박이　complaint 명비난
implementation 명실행, 이행　demographic 형인구 통계학적인
diversity 명다양성　call ~ into question ~에 의문을 제기하다
validity 명타당성, 유효성　penal institution 교도 시설
ethics 명윤리, 도덕　oppressive 형억압적인　fake 동가장하다

1 1단락에 따르면, 스탠퍼드 감옥 실험의 참가자들은
(A) 유명한 대학의 직원들이었다
(B) 금전적 보상을 제공받았다
(C) 정신 질환 환자들이었다
(D) 그들의 역할을 선택할 수 있었다

2 지문의 어구 "conform to"와 의미가 가장 비슷한 것은?
(A) 거부하다
(B) 복종하다
(C) 비난하다
(D) 지원하다

3 지문의 단어 "They"가 가리키는 것은?
(A) 사람들
(B) 상황
(C) 결과
(D) 교과서

4 지문의 단어 "its"가 가리키는 것은?
(A) 실험
(B) 결여
(C) 다양성
(D) 의문

5 지문에 따르면, 다음 중 스탠퍼드 감옥 실험에 대한 비판이 아닌 것은?
(A) 좁은 인구 통계학적 초점
(B) 실험자들의 비윤리적 행동

(C) 감옥 환경을 재현하는 것의 실패
(D) 학생들을 녹음하는 행위

Reading Practice 2 본문 p.32

1 (C) 2 (D) 3 (C) 4 (A) 5 (A)

Vocabulary Quiz

1 ⓑ 2 ⓐ 3 ⓒ 4 ⓐ

경계색

많은 동물들이 숨어서 포식동물을 피하는 반면, 다른 동물들은 스스로를 가능한 한 눈에 잘 띄게 함으로써 장래의 위협을 피한다. 전자의 집단에 속한 동물들은 그들의 주변 환경에 뒤섞이기 위해 위장술을 사용한다. 후자의 집단에 속한 동물들은 경계색이라고 불리는 전략을 사용하는데, 이는 밝은색 피부나 독특한 털 무늬가 포식동물에게 동물이 해롭거나 역겨운 맛이 난다는 신호를 보내는 것이다. 이러한 동물들 중 하나를 먹은 포식동물은 그 경험을 기억하여 그것을 반복하는 것을 피하는 법을 학습한다.

경계색을 가진 동물들에 의해 사용되는 방어 기제는 매우 다양하다. 2C스컹크의 뚜렷한 흑백 줄무늬는 다른 동물들에 의해 쉽게 인식될 수 있고, 이는 그들이 이 생물의 악취가 나는 배출물을 피할 수 있게 한다. 2B독화살개구리의 화려한 파란색, 빨간색, 노란색 및 초록색은 다른 동물들에게 그것의 치명적인 유독한 분비물에 대해 경고한다. 2A푸른고리문어는 비슷한 전략을 가진 바다 생물이며, 그것의 파란 고리는 다른 동물들에게 강력한 독에 대해 경고하기 위해 환해져 빛이 난다. 곤충의 왕국에서, 나비와 무당벌레는 그들이 확실히 맛이 없는 식사라는 사실을 전달하기 위해 알록달록한 외관을 활용한다.

경계색은 매우 효과적인 진화 전략이기 때문에 방어 기제가 없는 다른 동물들은 때때로 다른 생물들의 독특한 천연색을 모방한다. 4영국의 동식물 연구가인 헨리 월터 베이츠는 19세기 중반에 몇몇 곤충들이 그것들을 뒷받침하는 해로운 효과를 가지고 있지 않음에도 불구하고 놀랍도록 선명한 색들을 보인다는 것을 발견했다. 예를 들어, 노랑재킷파리는 말벌의 선명한 노란색을 띠지만 침은 가지고 있지 않다. 이것은 베이츠 의태라고 불리며, 방어 기제가 있는 동물들이 그렇지 않은 동물들보다 수가 더 많을 때 가장 잘 작용한다.

다른 종류의 경계색 모방은 독일 동물학자 프리츠 뮐러의 이름을 딴 뮐러 의태이다. 뮐러 의태는 관련된 모든 종이 포식동물에게 불쾌감을 주기 때문에 베이츠 의태와 다르다. 뮐러 의태에서, 하나 이상의 동물 종은 포식동물이 그들의 위험한 특성을 인식할 가능성을 높이기 위해 서로 비슷한 천연색들을 발달시킨다. 이 각각의 종은 유독하거나 포식동물이 먹을 수 없다. 포식동물은 한 종만을 마주칠지 모르지만, 다른 종들은 그것들이 서로 비슷하게 보이기 때문에 보호된다.

warning coloration 경계색 predator 명포식동물
ward off ~을 피하다 conspicuous 형눈에 잘 띄는
camouflage 명위장술 blend into ~에 뒤섞이다
surroundings 명주변 환경 tactic 명전략 distinctive 형독특한
defensive mechanism 방어 기제 recognizable 형인식될 수 있는
emission 명배출물 secretion 명분비물 distinctly 부확실히
exterior 명외관, 외부 unappetizing 형맛이 없는
naturalist 명동식물 연구가 startling 형놀랍도록 선명한
wasp 명말벌 mimicry 명의태, 흉내
outnumber 동~보다 수가 더 많다 property 명특성
inedible 형먹을 수 없는 encounter 동마주치다

1 지문의 단어 "conspicuous"와 의미가 가장 비슷한 것은?
(A) 위험한
(B) 투명한
(C) 눈에 띄는
(D) 매력적인

2 다음 중 경계색을 이용하는 동물이 갖는 방어 기제의 예시가 아닌 것은?
(A) 치명적인 독
(B) 독성 분비물
(C) 불쾌한 냄새
(D) 단단한 외피

3 지문의 단어 "them"이 가리키는 것은?
(A) 동물들
(B) 곤충들
(C) 색들
(D) 효과

4 3단락에 따르면, 베이츠 의태를 사용하는 동물들은
(A) 포식동물에게 무해하다
(B) 특정한 포식동물에게 불쾌한 맛이 난다
(C) 비슷한 성질을 가진 종과 협력한다
(D) 포식동물의 색들을 모방한다

5 지문의 단어 "their"가 가리키는 것은?
(A) 종
(B) 천연색
(C) 가능성
(D) 포식동물

Reading Practice 3 본문 p.34

1 (C) 2 (B) 3 (C) 4 (D) 5 (B)

Vocabulary Quiz

1 ⓑ 2 ⓐ 3 ⓑ 4 ⓐ

다임 소설

다임 소설은 값싼 종이에 인쇄되어 5에서 10센트에 팔린 짧은 책이었다. 모험 이야기가 주를 이루었으며, 그것들은 1800년대 후반에 미국에서 엄청나게 인기가 있었다. 그 형식은 값싼 종이의 등장과 인쇄 기술의 발전 덕분에 존재할 수 있었는데, 이는 100페이지짜리 연재물을 제작하고 그것들을 거의 모든 사람들이 살 수 있는 가격에 파는 것을 수익성 있게 만들었다.

다임 소설의 내용은 상업 주도적이었다. 처음에, 그것들은 미국 대중에게 큰 매력이 있는 주제인 미국 원주민들의 이국적인 삶에 초점을 맞췄다. 미국 원주민들이 원주민 보호 구역으로 이주하여 대중의 시야에서 벗어남에 따라, 다임 소설은 카우보이와 범죄라는 마찬가지로 수익성이 좋은 주제들로 초점을 바꾸었다. 마침내, 그 책들은 로맨스 같은 다

른 장르들을 다루었다. 다임 소설을 집필하도록 고용된 작가들은 그들이 등장인물의 발전이나 서사적인 실험이 아니라 흥미진진한 줄거리에 집중할 것으로 기대된다는 것을 알았다. [2]다임 소설 출판사들이 후하게 보수를 주었기 때문에, 그들은 업턴 싱클레어, 잭 런던, 루이자 메이 올콧과 같은 최고의 작가들을 끌어들였다.

비록 다임 소설이 혁신적이지는 않았지만, 그것들은 더 많은 읽고 쓸 줄 아는 대중을 육성하는 데 도움을 주었다. 이 형식이 등장했을 때, 식자율은 교육 개혁과 모든 사회 계층의 사람들에 대한 의무 학교 출석 시행의 결과로 인해 이미 상승하고 있었다. 다른 요소들도 작용하고 있었다. [4A]석유등은 밤에 읽는 것을 쉽게 해 주었다. [4B]더 많은 사람들이 기차와 전차로 통근하기 시작했고, 이는 그들에게 독서할 시간을 주었다. [4C]남북전쟁 양측 군인들은 휴전기의 지루한 나날들 동안 즐길 것이 필요했다. 모든 하층민 독자들이 필요로 했던 것은 대중이 이해하기 쉬운 줄거리가 있는 적절한 가격의 읽을거리였다. 다임 소설이 그 빈자리를 채웠다.

하류층이 다임 소설을 즐겁게 탐독했다면, 중산층의 도덕주의자들은 그것들의 비도덕적인 영향력에 대해 걱정했다. 많은 사람들이 그 책을 떳떳하지 않은 즐거움으로 여겼다. 어떤 이들은 특히 그것들의 범죄자와 적극적인 여성의 묘사에 반대하면서 그것들을 "문학적 독약"과 "사악한 독서"라고 표현하기까지 했다. 그러나 부도덕성을 가르치는 것과는 거리가 멀게도, 다임 소설은 도덕적 딜레마에 직면했을 때 옳은 일을 하는 주인공들을 항상 등장시켰다. 싸구려 통속 소설, 만화책, 비디오 게임을 포함해서 다임 소설의 영향을 받은 수많은 오락물에 대해서도 같은 비난이 제기되어 왔다.

dominate 통 주를 이루다　immensely 부 엄청나게
existence 명 존재　emergence 명 등장　profitable 형 수익성 있는
commercially 부 상업적으로　fascination 명 매력
reservation 명 원주민 보호 구역　lucrative 형 수익성이 좋은
pen 통 (글을) 쓰다　narrative 형 서사적인　top-notch 형 최고의
foster 통 육성하다　literate 형 읽고 쓸 줄 아는　populace 명 대중
literacy rate 식자율(국민 중 글을 아는 사람들의 비율)
mandatory 형 의무의, 강제의　at play 작용하고 있는
commute 통 통근하다　affordable 형 적절한 가격의
accessible 형 이해하기 쉬운　void 명 빈자리　devour 통 탐독하다
guilty pleasure 떳떳하지 않은 즐거움　depiction 명 묘사
assertive 형 적극적인　immorality 명 부도덕성
protagonist 명 주인공　pulp fiction 싸구려 통속 소설

1 지문의 단어 "they"가 가리키는 것은?
(A) 미국 원주민들
(B) 장르들
(C) 작가들
(D) 다임 소설

2 2단락에 따르면, 저명한 작가들이 다임 소설을 쓴 것은
(A) 그들의 전통적인 소설들이 일반 대중에게 홍보되었기 때문이다
(B) 이 작품들의 출판사들이 작가들에게 돈을 후하게 지불했기 때문이다
(C) 새로운 서사 형식을 실험하는 것이 허용되었기 때문이다
(D) 모험 이야기를 쓸 수 있는 기회가 흥미를 끌었기 때문이다

3 지문의 단어 "mandatory"와 의미가 가장 비슷한 것은?
(A) 관련된
(B) 감시받는
(C) 필수의
(D) 예정된

4 3단락에 따르면, 다음 중 식자율 증가에 기여한 것이 아닌 것은?
(A) 조명의 이용 가능성
(B) 새로운 교통 수단 이용
(C) 전쟁 중 오락의 필요성
(D) 헌 책의 판매

5 지문의 단어 "their"가 가리키는 것은?
(A) 하류층
(B) 다임 소설
(C) 도덕주의자들
(D) 중산층

Reading Practice 4

본문 p.36

1 (B)　2 (B)　3 (A)　4 (A)　5 (D)

Vocabulary Quiz

1 ⓐ　2 ⓑ　3 ⓒ　4 ⓒ

남북 전쟁에서 남부가 패배한 이유

미국 남북 전쟁은 국가적으로 힘든 시기였다. 이 전쟁으로 인한 총 미국인 사망자는 제1차 세계 대전과 제2차 세계 대전의 사망자를 합친 것보다 많았다. 정치적 분열은 공동체 전체를 분열시켰고, 때로는 형제를 서로의 적으로 만들기도 했는데, 이것들이 너무 심각해서 양측은 군사적 충돌을 피할 수 없었다. 노예 제도는 종종 이 전쟁의 근본적인 이유로 제시된다. 그러나 통치 방식의 유형에 관한 분쟁도 똑같이 중요했다. 일반적으로, 북부 연방은 강력한 중앙집권적 정부를 지지한 반면, 남부 연맹은 주의 권리에 기반한 더 민주적인 체제를 선호했다. 결국, 전자가 그 전쟁에서 승리했으며, 남부 연맹의 패배 이유는 내부적 요인과 외부적 요인을 통해 살펴볼 수 있다.

내부적 원인이라는 주장에 대한 몇 가지 그럴듯한 설명이 있다. 첫째로, 그 전쟁이 주로 남부에서 벌어졌기 때문에, 남부 사람들은 전쟁에 매우 진절머리가 나게 되었다. 그들은 북부 연방군에 의해 그들의 마을이 불타고 그들의 집과 농장이 파괴되는 것을 목격했다. 이러한 사건들을 직접 목격하는 것은 사기 저하의 분위기로 이어졌고, 1865년에 이르러서는 많은 사람들이 전쟁에 격렬하게 반대하기 시작했다. 일부 남부 연맹 군인들은 심지어 탈영하기 시작했다. 또한, 노예 제도 자체가 남부 연맹의 대의명분에 해를 끼쳤다. 많은 노예들이 북부로 도망쳤고, 그들 중 일부는 전쟁에 참여했다. 이 노예 이주는 북부 연방군을 10만 명 이상 직접적으로 증원했다. [4]마지막으로, 남부 연맹 주들의 경제는 노동 집약적인 농업에 기반을 두었다. 그 결과, 그것의 산업 및 기술적 역량은 그다지 발전되지 않았다.

그럼에도 불구하고, 전문가들은 북부 연방주들에 의한 남부 연맹주들의 패배의 주된 이유가 외부적이었다는 것에 대체로 동의한다. 북부 연방은 단순히 군사, 경제, 산업 자원 측면에서 우월했다. [5A/5B]그곳은 1,850만 명의 인구와 대략 3배 더 많은 군인 수를 가지고 있었고, 은행에 상당히 더 많은 자금을 보유하고 있었다. 또한, 전쟁이 시작되기 이전까지, 그것은 국가 총기의 97퍼센트를 생산했으며, 충분히 발전된 공장 기반 시설을 가지고 있었다. [5C]보다 직접적으로는, 북부 연방군의 군사력과 승리 전략이 남부가 극복할 수 없었던 일련의 승리를 가져왔다.

따라서, 대다수의 현대 역사학자들은 남부 연맹의 내부적 문제와 무관하게, 남부가 전쟁에서 패배할 운명이었다고 믿는다.

challenging 형 힘든　exceed 동 ~보다 많다　division 명 분열
tear ~ apart ~을 분열시키다　military 형 군사적인
slavery 명 노예 제도　dispute 명 분쟁　governance 명 통치 방식
the Union (남북 전쟁의) 북부 연방　robust 형 강력한
the Confederacy (남북 전쟁의) 남부 연맹　internal 형 내부적인
external 형 외부적인　plausible 형 그럴듯한
wage 동 (전쟁 등을) 벌이다　grow weary of ~에 진절머리가 나다
vehemently 부 격렬하게　desert the army 탈영하다
cause 명 대의명분, 이상　strengthen 동 증원하다
considerably 부 상당히　manufacture 동 생산하다
overcome 동 극복하다　be destined to ~할 운명이다
regardless of ~과 무관하게

1 지문의 단어 "these"가 가리키는 것은?
(A) 사망자
(B) 정치적 분열
(C) 공동체
(D) 적

2 지문의 단어 "robust"와 의미가 가장 비슷한 것은?
(A) 신뢰할 수 있는
(B) 강력한
(C) 종속된
(D) 효율적인

3 지문의 단어 "many"가 가리키는 것은?
(A) 남부 사람들
(B) 북부 연방군
(C) 사건들
(D) 분위기

4 2단락에 따르면, 남부의 산업 및 기술 역량은 왜 제한되었는가?
(A) 육체노동 근로자들에 기반한 농업 경제를 가지고 있었다.
(B) 북부에 노예 노동력의 상당 부분을 빼앗겼다.
(C) 북부에서 일반적인 관습들을 채택하기를 거부했다.
(D) 전쟁에 최소한의 경제적 자원만을 쏟아부었다.

5 다음 중 남부 연맹 주들의 패배의 외부적 요인으로 언급되지 않은 것은?
(A) 북부 연방의 더 많은 인구
(B) 북부 연방의 금전적인 유보금
(C) 북부 연방의 군사 전략
(D) 북부 연방의 우월한 총기 설계

iBT Reading Test

본문 p.38

1 (A)　2 (B)　3 (D)　4 (C)
5 (B)　6 (B)　7 (A)　8 (D)
9 (D)　10 (C), (D), (F)

천연 및 인조 다이아몬드

천연 다이아몬드는 그것들이 같은 화학적 구성을 공유함에도 불구하고, 인조 다이아몬드보다 더 비싸다. 이 둘을 구분 짓는 것은 전자가 지구 맨틀의 열기 속에서 수백만 년 전에 만들어졌다는 것이다. 그것들은 화산 폭발을 통해 상승했고 세 가지 방법 중 하나의 방법으로 채굴되었다. [2C]충적 채굴에서, 다이아몬드는 강바닥과 해안의 모래에서 걸러진다. [2A]지하 채굴에서는, 갱도의 다이아몬드를 추출하기 위해 폭발물이 사용된다. [2D]해양 채굴은 해저에서 다이아몬드를 채집하기 위해 기계를 사용한다. 반면에, 인조 다이아몬드는 실험실에서 형성된다.

보는 것을 통해 채굴된 다이아몬드와 실험실에서 만들어진 다이아몬드를 구분하는 것은 불가능할 수 있다. [3A/3B/3C]두 종류 모두에서, 다이아몬드의 품질은 컷, 투명도, 캐럿 및 색상의 4C로 평가된다. 잘 잘리거나 깎인 다이아몬드는 반짝이는데, 이는 최고의 광채와 가치를 부여한다. 다이아몬드의 투명도 또한 광채에 영향을 미칠 수 있는데, 이는 함유물이라 불리는 자연적으로 발생하는 결함이 다이아몬드를 통과하는 빛의 경로를 방해할 수 있기 때문이다. 크기는 캐럿 무게로 측정되며, 여기서 1캐럿은 200밀리그램이다. 다이아몬드는 또한 색조가 있을 수 있고, 특정 색상의 희귀성은 다이아몬드 가격에 영향을 미친다. 천연의 블루 다이아몬드는 특히 희귀하기 때문에 매우 가치가 높다.

인조 다이아몬드는 방사선 처리라고 불리는 과정을 통해 착색된다. [5]방사선 처리된 다이아몬드는 넓은 스펙트럼의 풍부하고 화려한 색상을 내기 위해 방사선과 고열의 특수한 조합으로 처리된 무색 다이아몬드이다. [6]이 처리는 영구적인 색상 변화를 일으키며, 그것은 다이아몬드에 유해한 방사선 흔적을 남기지 않는다. 방사선 처리된 다이아몬드는 자연적으로 발생한 유색 다이아몬드보다 현저히 낮은 가치를 지니며, 적절한 장비를 갖춘 실험실 환경에서 면밀한 분석을 통해 그것들의 정체가 확인될 수 있다.

인조 다이아몬드 비용의 상당 부분은 그것들을 절단하는 값비싼 과정에서 발생한다. 다이아몬드는 가장 단단한 물질이기 때문에, 그것을 자르기 위해서는 다른 다이아몬드의 사용이 필요하다. 1550년에 앤트워프에서 다이아몬드 연마공들이 처음으로 이것에 성공했다. [8]그 이후로, 다이아몬드는 단단한 물질들을 자르고, 갈고, 윤을 내기 위해 사용되는 필수적인 산업 재료가 되었다. **이것들은 안경, 보석, 컴퓨터 칩뿐만 아니라 돌, 도자기, 금속, 콘크리트를 포함한다.** 실제로 연간 채굴되는 다이아몬드의 80퍼센트가 산업에서 사용되며, 그 양의 4배인 연간 5억 캐럿 이상이 산업용으로 인조로 형성된다.

synthetic 형 인조의, 합성한　composition 명 구성
distinguish 동 구분 짓다　forge 동 만들다　ascend 동 상승하다
alluvial 형 충적의, 흙·모래가 퇴적된　sift 동 (체로) 거르다
explosive 명 폭발물, 폭약　extract 동 추출하다
appraise 동 평가하다　clarity 명 투명도　brilliance 명 광채
imperfection 명 결함　inclusion 명 함유물　obstruct 동 방해하다
scarce 형 희귀한　irradiation 명 방사선 처리　radiation 명 방사선
bring forth ~을 내다, 가져오다　permanent 형 영구적인
significantly 부 현저히　substance 명 물질
fundamental 형 필수적인　polish 동 윤을 내다

1 지문의 단어 "forged"와 의미가 가장 비슷한 것은?
(A) 생성되다
(B) 발견되다
(C) 수송되다
(D) 채굴되다

2 1단락에 따르면, 다음 중 다이아몬드를 채굴하는 기법이 아닌 것은?

(A) 땅밖으로 폭파시키기
(B) 지구의 맨틀 속으로 구멍 뚫기
(C) 강이나 해변에서 찾기
(D) 해저에서 옮기기

3 다음 중 다이아몬드의 가치에 영향을 주는 것이 아닌 것은?
(A) 무게
(B) 모양
(C) 색상
(D) 구성

4 지문의 단어 "it"이 가리키는 것은?
(A) 방사선
(B) 스펙트럼
(C) 처리
(D) 변화

5 3단락에 따르면, 다이아몬드에 방사선이 사용되는 것은
(A) 표면에 윤을 내기 위해서이다
(B) 색상을 바꾸기 위해서이다
(C) 광채를 더하기 위해서이다
(D) 그것의 가치를 높이기 위해서이다

6 지문에서 방사선 처리된 다이아몬드의 색상에 관해 추론할 수 있는 것은?
(A) 몇 가지 색상으로 제한된다
(B) 바래지 않을 것이다
(C) 천연 색상 다이아몬드보다 더 빛난다
(D) 방사능을 띨 것이다

7 지문의 단어 "fundamental"과 의미가 가장 비슷한 것은?
(A) 필수적인
(B) 인기 있는
(C) 내구성 있는
(D) 간단한

8 4단락에 따르면, 산업용 다이아몬드는
(A) 다이아몬드 보석을 찾기 위해 사용된다
(B) 방사선 처리된 다이아몬드를 생산하기 위해 사용된다
(C) 다이아몬드의 품질을 심사하기 위해 사용된다
(D) 단단한 물질의 형태를 바꾸기 위해 사용된다

9 네 개의 네모[■]는 다음 문장이 삽입될 수 있는 곳을 나타내고 있다.
이것들은 안경, 보석, 컴퓨터 칩뿐만 아니라 돌, 도자기, 금속, 콘크리트를 포함한다.
이 문장은 어디에 들어가는 것이 가장 적절한가?

10 **지시**: 지문 요약을 위한 도입 문장이 아래에 주어져 있다. 지문의 가장 중요한 내용을 나타내는 보기 3개를 골라 요약을 완성하라. 어떤 문장은 지문에 언급되지 않은 내용이나 사소한 정보를 나타내므로 요약에 포함되지 않는다. **이 문제는 2점이다.**

다이아몬드는 천연 또는 인공이다.
- (C) 다이아몬드의 품질은 네 가지 기준을 이용하여 측정된다.
- (D) 인조 다이아몬드는 그것들을 열과 방사선에 노출시킴으로써 착색된다.
- (F) 천연 및 인조 다이아몬드는 모두 다양한 산업에서 사용된다.

(A) 모든 다이아몬드는 지각 깊은 곳에서 형성된다.
(B) 충적 채굴은 광부가 강의 모래를 거르는 것을 필요로 한다.
(E) 다이아몬드는 지구에서 가장 단단한 물질이다.

Vocabulary Review

본문 p.42

1 brilliance		2 obedience	3 fascination
4 immune		5 randomly	6 complaints
7 (D)	8 (A)	9 (C)	10 (B)
11 (A)	12 (B)	13 (D)	14 (C)

CHAPTER 03
Sentence Simplification

Example

본문 p.45

1 (D) 2 (A)

중력 발견

많은 초기 물리학자들은 중력을 자연과 우주의 힘으로 받아들이는 것에 기여했다. [1]고대 그리스 철학자들은 별과 행성의 운동이 지구의 일들과 완전히 무관하다고 생각했다. 갈릴레오는 지구가 태양 주위의 궤도를 돈다는 코페르니쿠스의 견해에 동의한 최초의 물리학자들 중 한 명이다. 이것은 고대부터 확립된 관점과 상반되었다. 대부분의 사람들은 행성들과 별들이 지구 주위를 돈다고 믿었다. 요하네스 케플러는 케플러의 법칙으로 알려진 행성 운동의 법칙을 공식화하기 위해, 그의 스승인 티코 브라헤의 연구를 수행했다. 케플러는 행성들이 타원형의 경로로 태양 주위를 움직인다는 것을 증명할 수 있었다. [2]그때, 중력을 지배하는 더 일반적인 법칙을 설명하기 위한 무대가 아이작 뉴턴 경에게 마련되었다. 달, 조류, 심지어 혜성의 움직임에 대한 그의 관찰은 그가 만유인력의 법칙을 발전시키는 데 도움을 주었다.

gravitation 명 중력 physicist 명 물리학자
contribute to ~에 기여하다 acceptance 명 받아들임
universal 형 우주의 motion 명 운동, 움직임 completely 부 완전히
unrelated to ~과 무관한 orbit 동 (천체의) 궤도를 돌다
in contradiction to ~과 상반되는 established 형 확립된
revolve 동 돌다 mentor 명 스승, 멘토 formulate 동 공식화하다
planetary 형 행성의 elliptical 형 타원형의 govern 동 지배하다
observation 명 관찰 comet 명 혜성
the universal law of gravitation 만유인력의 법칙

1 아래 문장 중 지문 속의 음영된 문장의 핵심 정보를 가장 잘 표현한 것은?
(A) 고대 그리스인들은 별과 행성이 스스로 움직인다고 믿지 않았다.
(B) 별과 행성은 지구에서 일어나는 일들과 무관하게 움직인다.

(C) 그리스 철학자들의 의견과 달리, 지구의 일들은 별과 행성의 운동에 영향을 준다.
(D) 고대 그리스인들에 따르면, 지구의 일들은 별과 행성의 일들에 영향받지 않는다.

2 아래 문장 중 지문 속의 음영된 문장의 핵심 정보를 가장 잘 표현한 것은?

(A) 그때 아이작 뉴턴 경은 중력에 대한 포괄적 법칙을 제공할 수 있었다.
(B) 아이작 뉴턴 경은 그의 중력 법칙을 수정하도록 강요받았다.
(C) 중력 이론은 아이작 뉴턴 경에 의해 받아들여졌다.
(D) 중력이 일정한 규칙을 따른다는 것은 처음에 아이작 뉴턴 경에 의해 거부되었다.

Reading Practice 1

본문 p.46

1 (C) 2 (C) 3 (A) 4 (B) 5 (C)

Vocabulary Quiz

1 ⓐ 2 ⓒ 3 ⓒ 4 ⓐ

에드워드 호퍼

화가 에드워드 호퍼는 미국 사실주의 미술 운동의 가장 주목할 만한 구성원 중 한 명으로 여겨진다. [2]확실히, 평범한 도시 환경에 대한 그의 묘사는 부유하고 유명한 사람들보다 평범한 사람들에 대한 그 운동의 강조와 들어맞는다. [1]그러나 대상에 미묘한 우울감을 불어넣는 그의 능력이 그를 상징주의자들의 전통에 속하게 했는데, 그들은 자신의 주관적인 감정을 드러내지 않은 채 현실을 객관적으로 재현하는 것에는 거의 의미가 없다고 보았다. 호퍼에게 있어서, 그의 1926년 작 '오전 11시'에서의 고층 건물 창밖을 내다보는 여성의 묘사는 빛과 그림자에 대한 습작이었을 뿐만 아니라 그 자신의 외로움을 표현할 기회이기도 했다. 유사하게, 그의 1942년의 명작인 '밤을 지새우는 사람들'의 단순한 심야 식당 풍경은 전쟁 시대의 불안감에 대한 해설이 되었다.

현대 생활의 고립에 대한 호퍼의 집중은 그 자신의 성격을 반영했다. 이 화가는 잡담에 거의 관심이 없었고, 자신의 작품에 대해 이야기하는 것을 싫어했다. 대신, 그는 "모든 답은 화폭 위에 있다"라고 이야기하면서, 그의 예술이 스스로 말하게 하는 것을 선호했다. [4]그의 사회적 영역은 43년간 그의 아내였던 조세핀 호퍼와 함께 있는 것으로 대체로 한정되었는데, 그녀는 그녀 자신이 화가이면서도 그의 가장 빈번한 여성 모델 역할을 했다. 비록 그는 다작하는 화가였지만, 그의 작품은 오랜 세월 동안 예술계에서 무시당했다.

뉴욕 예술계에서의 조세핀의 연줄은 호퍼가 말년에 재정적인 성공을 거두는 데 도움을 주었다. 그는 어린 시절부터 예술에 전념했지만, 호퍼는 30대가 되어서야 첫 번째 그림을 팔았고, 11년이 지나서야 두 번째 그림을 팔았다. 그들의 결혼 이후, 조세핀은 호퍼를 위해 브루클린 미술관에서의 전시회를 얻어낼 수 있었다. 이것은 대공황이 끝날 무렵에 그의 주류 화가로서의 정착으로 이어졌는데, 이때 그는 50세 즈음이었다. 1933년, 뉴욕 현대미술관은 회고전을 열어 잃어버린 시간에 대해 보상해 주었는데, 이는 그것이 살아있는 예술가를 위해서는 거의 하지 않는 것이었다. 오늘날, 호퍼의 그림들은 수집가들에 의해 높이 평가받는다. 2018년에는, 그의 조세핀에 대한 구애를 묘사한 1929년의 유화 '찹 수이'가 기록적인 9천2백만 달러에 팔렸다.

notable 형 주목할 만한 depiction 명 묘사 ordinary 형 평범한
urban 형 도시의 emphasis 명 강조 infuse 동 불어넣다
subtle 형 미묘한 melancholy 명 우울감 objectively 부 객관적으로
reproduce 동 재현하다 subjective 형 주관적인
loneliness 명 외로움 commentary 명 해설 anxiety 명 불안감
isolation 명 고립 reflect 동 반영하다 personality 명 성격
restrict 동 한정하다 prolific 형 다작하는 exhibition 명 전시회
make up for ~에 대해 보상하다 retrospective 형 회고의

1 아래 문장 중 지문 속의 음영된 문장의 핵심 정보를 가장 잘 표현한 것은?

(A) 상징주의자들처럼, 호퍼는 그들의 감정을 고려하지 않고 대상을 그렸다.
(B) 상징주의자들은 대상의 감정을 보여주는 것이 사실적인 묘사보다 더 중요하다고 믿었다.
(C) 호퍼의 그림들은 그것들이 대상에 대한 그 자신의 감정을 반영했다는 점에서 상징주의자들의 그림과 닮았다.
(D) 현실을 재현하는 것에 대한 호퍼의 선호에도 불구하고, 그는 상징주의자들의 그림들을 즐겼다.

2 1단락에 따르면, 호퍼가 미국 사실주의 화가로 여겨지는 것은 그가

(A) 시골의 것들 대신에 도시의 장소와 사람들을 그렸기 때문이다
(B) 막대한 부를 가진 사람들에게 매료됐기 때문이다
(C) 일상의 삶을 사는 보통 사람을 그리는 것을 선호했기 때문이다
(D) 삶을 그가 느끼는 대로가 아니라 보이는 대로 묘사했기 때문이다

3 지문의 단어 "isolation"과 의미가 가장 비슷한 것은?

(A) 고독
(B) 집착
(C) 애착
(D) 활력

4 아래 문장 중 지문 속의 음영된 문장의 핵심 정보를 가장 잘 표현한 것은?

(A) 호퍼는 예술가들과 거의 교류하지 않았고, 그는 그의 아내 조세핀과 같은 여성 모델들과 어울리는 것을 선호했다.
(B) 사회적으로, 호퍼는 대부분의 시간을 화가이자 그의 많은 그림에 모델이 되었던 아내와 함께 보냈다.
(C) 화가 조세핀 호퍼는 에드워드 호퍼와 오랜 세월을 함께한 아내였고, 그들은 서로의 그림을 위한 모델이 되어주었다.
(D) 호퍼의 사교계는 계속해서 그의 작품의 모델을 한 아내 조세핀의 사교계보다 좁았다.

5 지문의 단어 "it"이 가리키는 것은?

(A) 정착
(B) 대공황
(C) 뉴욕 현대미술관
(D) 전시회

Reading Practice 2

본문 p.48

1 (B) 2 (D) 3 (B) 4 (D) 5 (C)

Vocabulary Quiz

1 ⓐ 2 ⓒ 3 ⓑ 4 ⓐ

자동차와 교외화

자동차의 발명은 20세기 초반 교외의 성장에 기여했다. 헨리 포드의 자동차 회사는 1908년에 저렴한 모델 T를 대량 생산하기 시작했다. 그것은 미국 전역으로 삽시간에 퍼져 나갔으며, 이는 적당한 재산을 가진 사람이면 한 대를 소유할 수 있을 정도로 저렴한 가격의 자동차를 생산하겠다는 포드의 꿈을 실현시켰다. [2]모델 T와 같은 자동차들은 통근자들이 직장에서 먼 곳에서 살 수 있게 해 주었고 여행에 대한 제약을 없앴다. 그 결과, 사람들은 붐비는 도시를 줄지어 벗어나, 도심 외곽의 넓은 토지에 대형 단독 주택을 지었다.

[3]교외로의 대규모 이주에 필요한 교통수단을 제공하는 것에 더해, 포드는 임금을 인상하고 그의 직원들을 도시 밖으로 이주하도록 장려함으로써 의도적으로 교외 성장을 자극했다. 이러한 교외 발전을 촉진하기 위해, 그는 그의 자동차 공장을 디트로이트의 새로운 교외인 디어본으로 옮겼다. 1920년대와 30년대에 자동차와 마음대로 쓸 수 있는 소득을 가진 산업 노동자로 가득 찬 교외가 중서부 주들 전역에 생겨났다. [4]하지만, 교외화의 비판자들은 대부분의 주택이 더 부유한 화이트칼라 노동자 소유인 반면, 육체노동자, 특히 아프리카계 미국인들은 교외로의 대이동으로 인해 점점 더 자원을 빼앗긴 도시에 남았다고 지적했다.

도로 위 자동차 수의 증가로 인해, 주 정부와 지방 정부는 대규모 도로 건설 사업으로 대응했다. 1950년대에는, 연방 정부가 주간 고속도로 체계의 대규모 확장을 시작했다. 그러나, 이것은 중심 도시에서의 혼잡을 초래했고, 사람들에게 교외로 이동할 훨씬 더 많은 동기를 부여했다.

1990년대에, 제1 단계 교외의 인구 밀도가 도시 수준에 도달함에 따라, 교외의 성장은 둔화되고 도시의 성장은 증대되었는데, 이는 일부 교외 자체가 도시가 되게 했다. 서부에서는, 지형의 특성이 종종 성장을 어렵거나 불가능하게 하여, 교외는 점점 더 밀집되었다. 그러나, 남부에서는 그렇지 않았는데, 이곳에서는 교외 성장에 대한 자연적인 장벽이 적었다. [5]게다가, 남부의 제1 단계 교외의 인구 밀도는 낮았으며, 이는 도시로부터 더 먼 곳까지의 교외 확장을 초래했다.

suburbanization 명 교외화(도시에서 주변으로의 인구 확산)
contribute to ~에 기여하다　rise 명 성장, 상승　suburbs 명 교외
mass-produce 동 대량 생산하다　affordable 형 (가격이) 저렴한
spread like wildfire 삽시간에 퍼져 나가다　manufacture 동 생산하다
moderate 형 적당한　means 명 재산　commuter 명 통근자
eliminate 동 없애다　flee 동 벗어나다　in droves 줄지어
spacious 형 넓은　property 명 토지, 부동산
intentionally 부 의도적으로　spur 동 자극하다
facilitate 동 촉진하다　disposable 형 마음대로 쓸 수 있는
manual laborer 육체노동자　be deprived of ~을 빼앗기다
exodus 명 대이동, 탈출　interstate 형 주간의, 주와 주 사이의
congestion 명 혼잡　incentive 명 동기　tier 명 단계

1 지문의 단어 "spacious"와 의미가 가장 비슷한 것은?
(A) 접근 가능한
(B) 넓은
(C) 편리한
(D) 안전한

2 1단락에 따르면, 사람들이 교외로 이동한 것은
(A) 넓은 토지에 자동차를 보관하는 것이 더 쉬웠기 때문이다
(B) 도시보다 교외에 사는 것이 더 저렴했기 때문이다
(C) 여행의 제약이 그들이 도시에서 운전하는 것을 막았기 때문이다
(D) 자동차가 그들이 더 먼 거리를 통근할 수 있게 했기 때문이다

3 아래 문장 중 지문 속의 음영된 문장의 핵심 정보를 가장 잘 표현한 것은?
(A) 포드는 교외 근로자들에게 지급하는 금액을 인상함으로써 교외의 성장에 자금을 지원했다.
(B) 포드는 자동차 제조하는 것뿐만 아니라 직원들에게 더 많은 급여를 주고 그들의 이주를 지원함으로써 교외 인구를 증가시켰다.
(C) 포드가 교외 인구를 증가시키기로 결심했던 것에 반해, 그는 직원들이 도시를 떠나는 데 도움이 되는 임금 인상을 했다.
(D) 그가 교외에서 더 많은 사람들을 보기를 원했기 때문에, 포드는 교외에서의 삶이 필요로 하는 자동차를 만들었다.

4 아래 문장 중 지문 속의 음영된 문장의 핵심 정보를 가장 잘 표현한 것은?
(A) 교외화는 아프리카계 미국인 육체노동자가 도시를 떠난 사람들로부터 부당하게 대우받았다고 비판받았다.
(B) 사람들은 교외의 부유한 집주인들이 도시의 육체노동자에게 불충분한 자원을 남겼다고 비판했다.
(C) 교외화를 비판했던 사람들은 그것이 어떻게 화이트칼라 노동자와 육체노동자 사이의 관계에 부정적으로 영향을 미쳤는지를 강조했다.
(D) 교외화는 교외의 주택들이 화이트칼라 계층의 소유가 되는 동안 육체노동자들을 빈곤한 도시에 남겼기 때문에 비판받았다.

5 4단락에 따르면, 다음 중 1990년대 남부에 관해 사실인 것은?
(A) 교외의 인구가 도시가 될 만큼 충분히 증가했다.
(B) 자원 부족으로 인해 교외의 확장이 제어되었다.
(C) 교외가 도시 중심에서 아주 먼 곳까지 확장되었다.
(D) 사람들이 도시로 되돌아감에 따라 교외 성장이 중단되었다.

Reading Practice 3

본문 p.50

1 (C)　2 (C)　3 (B)　4 (D)　5 (A)

Vocabulary Quiz

1 ⓒ　2 ⓑ　3 ⓐ　4 ⓒ

아엔데 운석

아엔데 운석은 지금까지 지구에서 발견된 가장 오래된 운석이다. 그 자동차 크기의 유성은 1969년 2월 8일에 지구와 충돌했다. 그것은 지구의 대기권에 진입하자마자 불타 부서졌고 멕시코의 푸에블리토 데 아엔데 근처에 흩어진 파편들을 남겼다. 그 충돌 이후, 대략 2톤의 운석이 수집되어 분석되었다. [3]그 운석의 동위원소 비율을 측정함으로써, 과학자들은 그 물체의 나이가 대략 45억 7천만 살이라고 추정했는데, 그것은 지구보다 오래된 것이었다. [2]지구와의 충돌 전에, 아엔데 운석은 화성과 목성 사이에 존재하는 소행성대에서 벗어났을 가능성이 높았다.

유성은 지구의 대기권에 진입한 상대적으로 작은 우주 암석이며, 종종 소행성이라고 불리는 더 큰 우주 암석의 파편이다. 그것들이 대기권에서 타버리면, 그것들은 별똥별로 판명된다. 지구의 표면에 떨어지는 유성의 조각들은 운석이라고 불린다. 매일, 약 2,500만 개의 유성이 지구를 강타한다. 그것들 중 운석이 되는 것은 거의 없으며, 지구 표면에 부딪히는 대부분의 암석은 바다로 떨어진다.

과학자들에 의해 분석되어온 우주 암석의 파편들 중에서, 아엔데 운

석이 분명 가장 많이 연구된 것이다. 이는 그것이 아마 태양계의 형성 과정 중에 만들어졌을 것이기 때문이다. 그것은 행성의 형성 과정에서 나온 잔해일 가능성이 크다. 이 아주 오래된 파편들을 연구함으로써, 과학자들은 태양계의 기원에 대해 더 많이 알기를 희망한다. [5]예를 들어, 아옌데 운석의 물질은 태양을 만든 초신성과 행성들의 형성 사이의 시간이 불과 2만 년에서 5만 년 정도로 비교적 짧았을지도 모른다고 시사한다.

이 우주 암석은 지구에서 전혀 발견된 적이 없는 광물을 포함한다. 5,000개 이상의 광물이 이 행성에서 확인되었고 그중 65개만이 태양계의 생성까지 거슬러 올라가기 때문에 이것은 주목할 만하다. 과학자들은 아옌데 운석의 표본에서 19개의 새로운 광물을 발견했다. 지구의 광물이 지구 핵의 열에서 형성된 것과 마찬가지로, 이 함유물들은 암석이 강한 성운의 열에서 형성될 때 운석 내부에 박히게 된다.

meteorite 명운석 atmosphere 명대기권 scattered 형흩어진
fragment 명파편 impact 명충돌 measure 동측정하다
isotope 명동위원소 estimate 동추정하다 collision 명충돌
asteroid belt 소행성대 bombard 동강타하다 probably 부아마
formation 명형성 (과정) debris 명잔해 indicate 동시사하다
supernova 명초신성 mineral 명광물 significant 형주목할 만한
inclusion 명함유물 embed 동박다 nebular 형성운의

1 지문의 단어 "scattered"와 의미가 가장 비슷한 것은?
(A) 준비된
(B) 지정된
(C) 흩어진
(D) 흡수된

2 아래 문장 중 지문 속의 음영된 문장의 핵심 정보를 가장 잘 표현한 것은?
(A) 화성이나 목성이 지구와 충돌한 이 소행성의 가장 가능성 높은 근원이다.
(B) 물체는 마침내 그것과 지구의 충돌이 일어나기 전에 화성과 목성 옆을 지나갔다.
(C) 아옌데 운석은 우리 행성에 도착하기 전에 아마 소행성대에서 이탈했을 것이다.
(D) 소행성대는 우리 태양계의 행성들과 부딪히는 유성의 기원이다.

3 지문에 따르면, 과학자들은 아옌데 운석의 연대를
(A) 광물의 형성을 태양계의 기원까지 추적함으로써 측정했다
(B) 운석의 동위원소 구성을 분석함으로써 측정했다
(C) 바다에서 발견된 운석에 대한 이전 연구를 참조함으로써 측정했다
(D) 아옌데 운석을 유사한 운석들과 비교함으로써 측정했다

4 지문의 단어 "them"이 가리키는 것은?
(A) 소행성
(B) 별똥별
(C) 운석
(D) 유성

5 아래 문장 중 지문 속의 음영된 문장의 핵심 정보를 가장 잘 표현한 것은?
(A) 아옌데 운석의 구성은 태양과 행성들이 5만 년까지의 간격으로 생성되었음을 시사한다.
(B) 아옌데 운석에 있는 물질들로 보아, 태양은 초신성에서 형성되었다.
(C) 2만 년에서 5만 년 사이에, 태양의 초신성을 뒤따라 행성들이 형성되었다.
(D) 아옌데 운석은 태양의 생성 이후 2만 년에서 5만 년 사이에 초신성에서 형성되었다.

Reading Practice 4

본문 p.52

1 (B) 2 (B) 3 (A) 4 (A) 5 (D)

Vocabulary Quiz

1 ⓑ 2 ⓐ 3 ⓐ 4 ⓐ

바티칸 시국의 역사

교황의 거주지이자 로마 가톨릭교회의 본거지인 바티칸 시국은 독립된 도시 국가이다. 그것은 로마 중심부 근처의 약 100에이커의 영토만을 차지하지만, 교황이 절대 군주인 자치 정부를 가지고 있다. [5B]바티칸 시국 안에 거주하는 800명의 사람들은 성직자이거나 그 국가를 방어하는 작은 군대인 스위스 근위대원들이다. [1]바티칸은 그곳의 경비를 지불하기 위해 세금을 걷지 않으며, 그 대신, 관광, 상품 판매, 기부금이 그 도시의 경비를 지불한다. 작은 주권 국가가 더 큰 국가 안에 완전히 에워싸여 있는 것은 독특한 배치이다. 그것은 어떻게 일어났을까?

서기 324년에 바티칸은 가톨릭교회의 중심지가 되었다. 이 연도는 로마의 첫 번째 기독교도 황제였던 콘스탄티누스 1세에 의해 대성당이라고 불리는 공공건물이 건축된 해다. [5A]대성당의 터는 교회의 첫 번째 교황으로 여겨지는 사도 베드로의 무덤이었던 자리로 여겨진다. 성 베드로 대성당은 가톨릭 신자들에게 항상 성지였다. 그것은 또한 세계 최대의 교회 중 하나이기도 하다. 대성당의 돔은 이탈리아 전역에서 가장 눈에 띄는 건축적 특징 중 하나이다. 그것은 순례자와 관광객들에게 인기 있는 행선지이다.

[5C]바티칸의 정부로서의 지위는 수 세기 동안 주변 정부들과의 갈등의 원인이었다. 8세기부터 1870년까지, 바티칸은 단순한 종교적 중심지가 아니라 교황령이라고 불리는 정치적 독립체들을 대표하는 권력의 중심지였다. [2]교황령의 경계는 수백 년의 기간에 걸쳐 달라졌지만, 오늘날의 이탈리아의 많은 부분이 한 번쯤은 교황의 통치를 받았다. 1860년에 비토리오 에마누엘레 2세 국왕의 통치 아래 이탈리아가 통일되었을 때, 교황의 정치 권력 시대는 끝나는 것처럼 보였다. 실제로, 1870년에, 이탈리아는 교황령에 전쟁을 선포하고 바티칸 시국의 장벽 밖의 모든 영토를 차지했다. 이탈리아와 바티칸 시국 사이의 갈등은 베니토 무솔리니 총리의 등장과 함께 마침내 해결되었다. [4]1929년에, 무솔리니는 바티칸 시국을 주권을 가진 독립체로 인정하는 협정에 서명했다. 교회는 교황령의 상실을 보상하는 9천2백만 달러를 지불받았다.

pope 명교황 headquarters 명본거지, 본부
independent 형독립된 city-state 명도시 국가
occupy 동차지하다 absolute 형절대의 monarch 명군주
clergy 명성직자 expense 명경비, 비용
merchandising 명상품 판매 sovereign 형주권을 가진
enclose 동에워싸다 arrangement 명배치, 배열
basilica 명(가톨릭) 대성당 apostle 명사도
recognizable 형눈에 띄는 destination 명행선지
pilgrim 명순례자 tension 명갈등, 긴장 entity 명독립체
Papal States 교황령 boundary 명경계 be subject to ~을 받다
resolve 동해결하다 compensate for ~을 보상하다

1 아래 문장 중 지문 속의 음영된 문장의 핵심 정보를 가장 잘 표현한 것은?

(A) 바티칸은 시민들에게 세금을 부과하지 않지만, 관광객들에게 방문의 특권에 대한 요금을 청구한다.

(B) 바티칸은 방문객, 판매 및 기부에서 수익을 얻지만, 세금은 받지 않는다.

(C) 관광객들은 입장과 기념품에 대해 지불함으로써 바티칸의 채무를 충당한다.

(D) 바티칸은 비거주민에게 많은 돈을 받음에도 불구하고 거주민들에게 세금을 부과한다.

2 아래 문장 중 지문 속의 음영된 문장의 핵심 정보를 가장 잘 표현한 것은?

(A) 국경선이 불규칙적이기는 했지만 이탈리아의 시민들은 교황의 지배를 받았다.

(B) 이탈리아의 넓은 부분을 포함했던 교황령의 국경선은 수 세기 동안 바뀌었다.

(C) 역사에 걸쳐, 이탈리아는 영토의 대부분을 교황의 통치를 받게 했다.

(D) 교황령은 끊임없이 변동하는 경계를 가진 이탈리아 내부의 영토였다.

3 지문의 단어 "resolved"와 의미가 가장 비슷한 것은?

(A) 해결되다
(B) 반환되다
(C) 결론나다
(D) 방해받다

4 3단락에 따르면, 베니토 무솔리니가 서명한 문서는

(A) 국가의 독립을 인정했다
(B) 상실된 영토에 대한 배상을 요구했다
(C) 두 국가 간의 동맹을 맺었다
(D) 국가 지도자의 역할을 확립했다

5 다음 중 글쓴이가 바티칸 시국에 관해 묘사하지 않는 것은?

(A) 무덤으로서의 기원
(B) 스스로를 보호하는 수단
(C) 주변 세력과의 갈등
(D) 통치자를 선출하는 방법

iBT Reading Test

본문 p.54

1 (C) 2 (B) 3 (C) 4 (B)
5 (A) 6 (C) 7 (B) 8 (B)
9 (C) 10 (A), (B), (F)

최초의 고래

4억 년도 더 전의 캄브리아기 동안에 모든 동물이 바다 생물에서 진화했다는 점을 고려하면, 누군가는 고래가 직접적으로 수중 생물의 후손이라고 생각할 것이다. 그러나 자연은 좀처럼 그렇게 단순하게 발달하지 않는다. [1]실제로, 오늘날 고래, 돌고래, 알락돌고래로 이루어진 고래류는 약 5천만 년 전에 네 다리를 가진 늑대를 닮은 포유류에서 기원한 것 같다.

1980년대 초, 한 고생물학자 팀은 파키스탄 북부 지역에서 화석 더미를 발견했고 즉시 그것이 고래의 것과 유사한 긴 두개골을 포함하고 있다는 것을 인지했다. 그들은 이 생물에 "파키스탄의 고래"를 의미하는 파키세투스라는 이름을 붙였다. [4]이후, 그 생물의 두개골이 내이 주변에 그것이 수중에서 들을 수 있게 하는 골벽을 가지고 있다는 것이 밝혀졌다. 이것은 육지 포유류와 현대 고래 사이의 놀라운 연결고리를 형성했다.

더 많은 화석이 발견됨에 따라, 과학자들은 그 생물의 서식지와 생존 수단을 종합했다. 파키세투스는 해안과 바다 사이에서 시간을 나눠 보냈다. [6D]그것의 긴 다리는 그것을 타고난 유영동물로 만든 물갈퀴가 달린 발로 끝났다. [6A/6B]그것은 또한 그것에게 물고기와 작은 동물들의 살을 찢는 능력을 주었을 강한 이빨을 가지고 있었는데, 그것은 유연한 목을 비틀면 그것들에 닿을 수 있었다. 그 동물의 어금니는 그것이 씹을 때 이빨을 갈았다는 것을 시사하는 긁힌 흔적을 보였다. 그 생물의 뒤쪽 끝에는 긴 꼬리가 있었다.

화석 기록은 파키세투스의 후손들이 이후 1500만 년에 걸쳐 물과 친화적인 특성을 강화하기 위해 진화했다는 것을 시사한다. 물갈퀴가 달린 발은 점차 지느러미발로 변했다. 마침내, 물속에 사는 수염고래가 등장했다. 약 3천5백만 년의 기간에 걸쳐, 고래는 점점 더 커져서, 길이가 20피트에서 평균 40피트로 커졌다. [8]고래가 바다에서 큰 포식자를 피할 수 있도록 크기가 증가했을 가능성이 있다. 그러한 일은 진화에서 흔한 현상으로, 오랜 시간에 걸쳐 진화하는 동물은 일반적으로 더 커지는 경향이 있다고 여겨진다. 그렇기는 하지만, 이 과정은 고래에게 극단적인 영향을 끼쳤다. **이것은 대왕고래에 의해 설명되는데, 그것은 약 200톤의 무게가 나가며, 지금까지 지구상에 거주한 동물들 중 가장 크다.** 이 거대한 생명체가 아주 작은 파키세투스의 후손이라는 것은 자연의 경이로움이다.

evolve 통 진화하다 creature 명 생물
be descended from ~의 후손이다 cetacean family 고래류
porpoise 명 알락돌고래 apparently 부 ~인 것 같은
originate 통 기원하다 mammal 명 포유류
paleontologist 명 고생물학자 fossil 명 화석 skull 명 두개골
bony wall 골벽 constitute 통 형성하다 contemporary 형 현대의
habitat 명 서식지 subsistence 명 생존 webbed 형 물갈퀴가 달린
tear 통 찢다 flesh 명 살 morph 통 변하다 flipper 명 지느러미발
emerge 통 등장하다 occurrence 명 일, 사건
monstrous 형 거대한 diminutive 형 아주 작은

1 1단락에 따르면, 다음 중 고래류에 관해 사실인 것은?

(A) 캄브리아기 동안 육지를 걸었다.
(B) 오늘날 살아 있는 유일한 고래류는 고래이다.
(C) 가장 오래된 것으로 알려진 고래류는 다리가 네 개였다.
(D) 약 5천만 년 전에 바다에서 나왔다.

2 지문의 단어 "it"이 가리키는 것은?

(A) 팀
(B) 더미
(C) 지역
(D) 파키스탄

3 지문의 단어 "contemporary"와 의미가 가장 비슷한 것은?

(A) 성숙한
(B) 거대한
(C) 현대의
(D) 해양의

4 2단락에 따르면, 최초의 파키세투스 두개골이 현대의 고래와 연관되는 것은 그것이
(A) 현대 고래의 두개골만큼 컸기 때문이다
(B) 고래의 것과 같은 내이 구조를 가졌기 때문이다
(C) 현대 고래들이 사는 바다에서 발견되었기 때문이다
(D) 이빨 주위에 독특한 골벽을 가지고 있었기 때문이다

5 아래 문장 중 지문 속의 음영된 문장의 핵심 정보를 가장 잘 표현한 것은? 오답은 문장의 의미를 크게 바꾸거나 핵심 정보를 생략한다.
(A) 과학자들은 이후의 화석으로부터 그 동물이 어디에 살았고 무엇을 먹었는지 알게 되었다.
(B) 그들이 추가적인 화석을 발견했을 때, 과학자들은 몸의 조각들을 짜맞추었다.
(C) 그 생물의 거주지와 식습관은 시간이 지남에 따라 나타났다.
(D) 과학자들은 그 생물의 서식지에서 화석 조각을 찾았다.

6 다음 중 글쓴이가 파키세투스에 관해 묘사하지 않는 것은?
(A) 민첩한 목
(B) 강한 이빨
(C) 지느러미가 있는 꼬리
(D) 물갈퀴가 달린 발

7 지문의 단어 "morphed"와 의미가 가장 비슷한 것은?
(A) 채택했다
(B) 변했다
(C) 초과했다
(D) 기능했다

8 4단락에 따르면, 고래가 시간이 지남에 따라 더 크게 자란 것은
(A) 그들이 매우 큰 바다 생물들을 섭취했기 때문이다
(B) 그들의 크기가 포식자들을 막을 수 있게 해주었기 때문이다
(C) 더 큰 동물들이 수영을 더 잘하기 때문이다
(D) 그들이 큰 공룡들을 피할 필요가 있었기 때문이다

9 네 개의 네모[■]는 다음 문장이 삽입될 수 있는 곳을 나타내고 있다.
이것은 대왕고래에 의해 설명되는데, 그것은 약 200톤의 무게가 나가며, 지금까지 지구상에 거주한 동물들 중 가장 크다.
이 문장은 어디에 들어가는 것이 가장 적절한가?

10 **지시:** 지문 요약을 위한 도입 문장이 아래에 주어져 있다. 지문의 가장 중요한 내용을 나타내는 보기 3개를 골라 요약을 완성하라. 어떤 문장은 지문에 언급되지 않은 내용이나 사소한 정보를 나타내므로 요약에 포함되지 않는다. **이 문제는 2점이다.**

고래가 육지 동물의 후손이라는 것은 놀랍다.
· (A) 알려진 고래의 가장 오래된 조상은 늑대를 닮은 생물이었다.
· (B) 고래의 두개골과 파키세투스의 두개골은 뚜렷한 특징을 공유한다.
· (F) 파키세투스의 후손들은 진화해서 바다에서 사는 동물이 되었다.

(C) 최초의 파키세투스 화석은 파키스탄 바다에서 발견되었다.
(D) 파키세투스의 뼈는 과학자들에게 그것의 습성에 대해 알려주었다.
(E) 고래는 원래 물갈퀴가 달린 발이었던 지느러미를 가지고 있다.

Vocabulary Review

본문 p.58

1 revolved		2 disposable	3 congestion
4 retrospective		5 elliptical	6 occurrence
7 (C)	8 (C)	9 (C)	10 (B)
11 (C)	12 (D)	13 (D)	14 (A)

CHAPTER 04
Fact

Example

본문 p.61

1 (B) 2 (C)

도롱뇽과 영원

영원과 도롱뇽은 실제로는 같은 동물이다. '도롱뇽'이라는 이름은 완전히 수생이면서도 완전히 육생인 이 동물에 쓰이는 과학 용어이다. [1]'영원'이라는 이름은 늦여름부터 겨울까지 육지에서 살다가, 봄에는 번식하기 위해 물로 들어가는 도롱뇽에 붙여진 이름이다. 긴 꼬리 때문에 종종 도마뱀으로 오인되는 도롱뇽은 개구리와 비슷한, 그들의 몸을 감싸는 부드럽고 촉촉한 피부를 가지고 있다. 그들은 길이가 6인치까지 길어질 수 있지만, 보통은 더 작다. 그들의 다리는 너무 짧아서 그들이 기어가는 동안에 그들의 배가 땅에 닿는다. 그들은 비늘, 발톱, 또는 외부의 귓구멍이 없다. [2]대다수의 도롱뇽과 그들의 유충은 육식성이며, 곤충과 작은 무척추동물들을 먹는다. 유충은 부화 직후 먹이를 먹기 시작하며, 작은 수생 동물들을 먹어 치운다. 큰 성체는 물고기, 개구리, 다른 도롱뇽을 먹는다. 도롱뇽은 대체로 야행성이며, 낮 시간에는 쓰러진 통나무와 축축한 낙엽 아래에 숨어 있는다.

salamander 명 도롱뇽 newt 명 영원(도롱뇽목 영원과의 동물)
term 명 용어 apply to ~에 쓰이다, 적용되다 aquatic 형 수생의
terrestrial 형 육생의 affix 동 붙이다 breed 동 번식하다
belly 명 배, 복부 crawl 동 기어가다 scale 명 비늘 claw 명 발톱
external 형 외부의 larva 명 유충 carnivorous 형 육식성의
invertebrate 명 무척추동물 hatch 동 부화하다
devour 동 먹어 치우다 nocturnal 형 야행성의 damp 형 축축한
leaf litter 낙엽

1 지문에 따르면, 다음 중 영원에 관해 사실인 것은?
(A) 도롱뇽보다 작다.
(B) 서식지가 계절에 따라 결정된다.
(C) 여름에 번식하기 위해 육지로 이동한다.
(D) 도마뱀처럼 비늘로 덮인 피부를 가지고 있다.

2 다음 중 글쓴이가 도롱뇽에 관해 묘사하는 것은?
(A) 꼬리의 정확한 길이
(B) 밤에 평균적으로 잠을 자는 시간
(C) 선호하는 음식의 종류
(D) 비정상적으로 긴 다리

Reading Practice 1

본문 p. 62

1 (D) 2 (A) 3 (B) 4 (A) 5 (D)

Vocabulary Quiz

1 ⓒ 2 ⓒ 3 ⓑ 4 ⓐ

로마의 도로 체계

고대 로마인들은 역사상 가장 위대한 공학적 업적 중 하나로 여겨지는 도로 체계를 발전시켰다. "모든 길은 로마로 통한다"라는 표현은 이 도로 체계가 로마를 로마 제국의 가장 먼 지방들까지 연결했다는 점에서 실제로 사실이다. 로마에 의해 지배되는 영토에는 50,000마일이 넘는 포장도로가 있었다.

도로는 효율적으로 건설되었고 오래가도록 지어졌다. 네 층의 재료가 대부분의 도로를 구성했다. [1]가장 위층은 평평하고 단단한 돌, 콘크리트, 회반죽에 굳힌 자갈로 만들어졌다. 두 번째 층은 깨진 타일과 섞인 시멘트로 만들어졌다. 세 번째 층은 단단한 기반을 형성하기 위해 깨진 돌, 모래, 시멘트, 자갈을 포함했다. 가장 아래층은 큰 돌로 구성되었다. 도로는 궂은 날씨에도 여행객들이 불편을 겪지 않도록 건설되었다. 실제로, 도로들은 가운데가 높았는데, 다시 말해서, 도로의 중앙이 도로의 측면보다 더 높았다. [2]이것은 물이 측면으로 흐르게 했는데, 여기에서 그것은 물을 빼는 배수로에 닿았다.

켈트족의 영국에 대한 로마의 정복은 영국 내 이동을 개선한 도로망의 건설로 이어졌다. 처음에, 로마인들은 도로와 길의 무계획적인 모음을 발견했다. 군대의 이동과 교역 상품들의 흐름을 용이하게 하기 위해, 로마는 더 질서 있는 도로망을 구축했다. [4]로마인들은 군사 중심지로 보급품을 보내기 위해 처음에는 리치버러, 도버, 림프네의 해협 항구들에 집중했다. 이 도로들이 구축된 이후에서야 로마인들은 작은 도로망을 확장하기 시작했다. 이것은 광산촌이나 도예 중심지와 같은 경제 중심지들의 연결을 가져왔다. 로마인들에 의해 건설된 도로들의 최종 단계는 지역적인 단계였다. 이것들은 저택, 농장, 마을을 더 큰 도로들과 시장이 있는 도시로 연결했다.

[5B]일반적으로, 영국 내의 로마 도로는 직선으로 놓였지만, 장애물이 제거되기 어려운 곳에서는 로마인들은 그것들을 빙 둘러 도로를 건설했다. 여행자들이 길을 찾는 것을 돕기 위해, 로마인들은 특정 지점에 이정표들을 세웠다. [5C]그 이정표들은 여행자들에게 가장 가까운 대도시까지 남은 거리를 알려주었다. [5A]이 도로들은 너무 잘 지어져서 수 세기 동안 존속했고, 영국의 많은 현대 도로들이 그것들 위에 건설되었다.

feat 명 업적 distant 형 (거리가) 먼 province 명 지방, 주
paved road 포장도로 efficiently 부 효율적으로
comprise 동 구성하다 uppermost 형 가장 위의 pebble 명 자갈
mortar 명 회반죽 inclement 형 (날씨가) 궂은
inconvenience 명 불편 crown 동 (도로 등의) 가운데를 높게 하다
gutter 명 (도로의) 배수로 drain 동 (물을) 빼다
haphazard 형 무계획적인 facilitate 동 용이하게 하다
orderly 형 질서 있는 initially 부 처음에 channel 명 해협; 동 보내다
obstacle 명 장애물 milestone 명 이정표

1 다음 중 글쓴이가 로마 도로의 가장 위층에 관해 묘사하는 것은?
(A) 대부분 시멘트로 이루어져 있었다.
(B) 배수를 위한 구멍들을 포함했다.
(C) 타일과 시멘트를 결합했다.
(D) 튼튼하고 평평한 표면을 만들었다.

2 2단락에 따르면, 로마 도로의 가운데가 높았던 것은
(A) 도로가 침수되는 것을 막기 위해서였다
(B) 효율적인 건축 과정을 보장하기 위해서였다
(C) 여행자들이 길을 찾는 것을 돕기 위해서였다
(D) 도로 길이를 알려주기 위해서였다

3 지문의 단어 "haphazard"와 의미가 가장 비슷한 것은?
(A) 명백한
(B) 체계적이지 못한
(C) 효율적인
(D) 광범위한

4 3단락에 따르면, 영국의 초기 로마 도로들은 왜 항구 도시에 연결되었는가?
(A) 군인들에게 식량과 장비를 제공하기 위해
(B) 영국 해협을 가로지르는 무역을 늘리기 위해
(C) 경제적으로 중요한 장소들을 연결하기 위해
(D) 추가적인 산업 중심지들을 구축하기 위해

5 4단락에 따르면, 다음 중 영국의 로마 도로들에 관해 사실이 아닌 것은?
(A) 현대 도로의 기반을 제공했다.
(B) 장애물을 피해 지어졌다.
(C) 목적지까지의 거리를 나타내는 이정표가 특징이었다.
(D) 대부분 구불구불한 경로를 따라갔다.

Reading Practice 2

본문 p. 64

1 (D) 2 (C) 3 (A) 4 (C) 5 (C)

Vocabulary Quiz

1 ⓒ 2 ⓐ 3 ⓑ 4 ⓐ

조가비 구슬

조가비 구슬은 북아메리카 북동부의 토착민들에 의해 만들어진 구슬이었다. [1A/1B/1C]그 구슬은 대서양 연안에서 채취되어 모래로 매끈하게 닦이고 구멍이 뚫린 어패류의 껍데기로 만들어졌다. 일반적으로, 그것들은 흰색이나 보라색이었고 허리띠나 다른 종류의 장신구를 만들기 위해 함께 실로 꿰어졌다. 조가비 구슬을 만들기 위해서는 숙련된 노동이 필요했고, 그것들은 정신적, 역사적, 정치적 중요성을 얻었다. 따라서, 그것들은 부족 사회에게 아주 귀하게 여겨졌다. 조가비 구슬이 상품과 용역으로 거래되었기 때문에 때때로 북미 원주민의 화폐로 여겨지기는 했지만, 그 구슬은 유럽인들이 개입하기 전까지는 화폐로 사용되지 않았다.

원주민들에게, 조가비 구슬의 주된 가치는 정신적이며 상징적이었다. 이로쿼이족은 그것이 산 사람들을 죽은 이들과 접촉하게 해줄 수 있다고 믿었다. 알곤킨족은 그 구슬의 색을 중국의 음과 양 개념과 유사한 상징으로 여겼는데, 보라색이 어둠과 죽음을 상징한 반면 흰색은 밝음과 생명을 나타냈다. 일부 문화에서, 조가비 구슬 허리띠는 또한 외교적인 협정을 표시하기 위해 사용되기도 했다. [2]예를 들어, 두 줄의 조가비 구슬 허리띠는 토착민과 네덜란드의 식민지 개척자들 사이의 평화를 상징하기 위해 카누와 유럽의 배를 묘사했다.

유럽인들은 1622년에 한 네덜란드 상인이 원주민을 인질로 잡은 후 그것들을 몸값으로 받기 전까지, 조가비 구슬의 중요성을 거의 알아채지 못했다. 네덜란드인들은 그 인질범을 처벌했지만, 그 후에 조가비 구슬과의 교환에 모피를 제공하기 시작했는데, 그들은 이후 더 많은 모피를 얻기 위해 다른 부족과 그것들을 교환했다. 이러한 방식으로, 네덜란드인들은 프랑스인들보다 먼저 원주민들의 모피를 선점할 수 있었는데, 이는 프랑스인들에게 그것들과 교환할 조가비 구슬이 없었기 때문이다. 1630년에, 영국인 청교도들 또한 조가비 구슬을 화폐로 취급하는 것을 배웠고, 이는 조가비 구슬을 둘러싼 두 식민지 간의 격렬한 대립을 야기했다.

그러나, 결국 유럽 상인들은 모피를 해외에서 거래하는 것이 낫다고 판단했다. [5]조가비 구슬은 유럽의 소비자들에게 가치를 잃기 시작했는데, 이는 그것이 북미 원주민들과 거래하는 데는 훌륭했지만, 아프리카의 노예나 서인도 제도의 담배를 얻으려고 할 때는 가치가 없었기 때문이다. 조가비 구슬의 가치 하락은 토착 부족들에게 중요한 무역 상대국을 없애 버렸다. 비록 조가비 구슬은 화폐로서 단기간 사용되었지만, 그 용어는 오늘날에도 여전히 돈을 뜻하는 속어로 사용된다.

wampum ㈜조가비 구슬 indigenous people 토착민
mollusk ㈜어패류, 연체동물 sand ㈜모래로 닦다, 사포로 닦다
string ㈜실로 꿰다 spiritual ㈜정신적인 significance ㈜중요성
tribal ㈜부족의 currency ㈜화폐, 통화
get involved 개입하다, 연루되다 symbolic ㈜상징적인
represent ㈜나타내다 stand for ~을 상징하다
diplomatic ㈜외교적인 depict ㈜묘사하다, 그리다
colonist ㈜식민지 개척자 oblivious ㈜알아채지 못하는
ransom ㈜(인질·포로의) 몸값 take ~ hostage ~를 인질로 잡다
subsequently ㈜그 후에 obtain ㈜얻다 decline ㈜하락

1 다음 중 글쓴이가 조가비 구슬에 관해 묘사하지 않는 것은?
(A) 그것을 만드는 데 사용된 껍데기를 가진 생물
(B) 그것의 재료가 채집된 장소
(C) 그것을 만드는 과정
(D) 그것을 서로 연결하는 데 사용되는 재료

2 2단락에 따르면, 다음 중 두 줄의 조가비 구슬 허리띠가 상징하는 것은?
(A) 죽은 이들과 소통하는 능력
(B) 밝음과 어둠의 대조
(C) 유럽인들과의 평화 달성
(D) 토착민의 부유함

3 지문의 단어 "oblivious"와 의미가 가장 비슷한 것은?
(A) 무지한
(B) 중독된
(C) 호기심 많은
(D) 신봉하는

4 지문의 단어 "them"이 가리키는 것은?
(A) 네덜란드인들
(B) 프랑스인들
(C) 모피
(D) 조가비 구슬

5 지문에 따르면, 유럽인들이 조가비 구슬의 거래를 중단한 것은 그것이
(A) 원주민에게서 얻는 것이 더욱 어려워졌기 때문이다
(B) 기술 발전으로 인해 기술을 덜 필요로 했기 때문이다
(C) 강제 노역으로 교환될 수 없었기 때문이다
(D) 부족들로부터 모피를 얻는 것에 있어서의 가치가 떨어졌기 때문이다

Reading Practice 3

본문 p.66

1 (B) 2 (B) 3 (C) 4 (C) 5 (D)

Vocabulary Quiz

1 ⓐ 2 ⓒ 3 ⓑ 4 ⓐ

갯줄풀

갯줄풀은 키가 7피트까지 이를 수 있는 긴 다년생 풀이다. [1]그것의 땅 위줄기가 10개에서 40개의 무더기로 자라나며 칼날 같은 잎들로 덮이는 반면, 그것의 땅속줄기는 사방으로 뻗어 나간다. 그것은 가을에 꽃을 피우며, 이 시기에 가시로 덮인 씨앗을 생산한다. 이 종은 다른 식물들은 거의 생존할 수 없는 염수 습지에서 번성한다. 일반적인 서식지는 습지, 해변 및 갯벌이다. 갯줄풀은 한 식물이 일부 생태계에는 긍정적인 영향을 미치고 다른 생태계의 건강은 위협할 수 있음을 보여준다.

메인주에서 텍사스주까지 이르는 미국 동부 해안에서, 갯줄풀은 많은 이점을 제공한다. 농게는 그것이 자라는 부드러운 토양에 굴을 파서 포식자로부터의 은신처를 마련한다. 이것은 산소가 토양 속에 들어가게 해서 배수를 개선한다. 이랑무늬홍합은 그 식물의 줄기와 뿌리에 자신을 부착하는데, 이것 또한 토양에 도움이 된다. 흰기러기는 남동부를 지날 때, 그 식물의 땅속줄기를 먹는 것을 즐긴다. [2]갯줄풀은 또한 대서양의 해변이 침식하는 것을 막으며, 질소와 인과 같은 오염 물질을 물 밖으로 걸러내는 것을 돕고, 습지 생태계에서의 광합성의 많은 부분을 책임진다.

그러나, 서부 해안에서 갯줄풀은 침입종으로 여겨진다. 그것은 1800년대 후반에 워싱턴주에 유입되었으며, 동부 해안에서 온 굴 수송품 안에 있던 반갑지 않은 편승자였다. [4]그것은 또한 서쪽으로 가는 수송품에서 포장재로 도착하기도 했다. 워싱턴에서, 이 종은 멸종 위기에 처한 토착 식물들과의 경쟁에서 이겼고, 그 결과 생물 다양성의 손실을 초래했다. 샌프란시스코만에서 갯줄풀은 보다 최근의 침입자인데, 이곳에서 그것은 미국 공병대에 의해 의도적으로 유입되었다. 그곳에서, 그것은 많은 문제들을 야기해온, 토종 식물들과의 잡종을 형성했다. 예를 들어, 줄풀은 수로를 막아 인접 지역에 홍수를 야기했다. 그것은 또한 생태계의 특성을 바꿈으로써 멸종 위기에 처한 새와 쥐의 토착종들을 위협한다.

서부 해안에서 갯줄풀을 박멸하는 것은 어렵고 비용이 많이 들지만 가능하다. [5C]워싱턴에서, 반복적인 풀베기로 인해 출몰이 줄어들었다. [5A]멸구라고 불리는 곤충 또한 씨앗의 생존을 줄이기 위해 그곳에 방사되었다. [5B]샌프란시스코에서는, 약 700에이커의 갯줄풀이 제초제를 사용하여 제거되었다. 그 침입자가 줄어들자, 이제 토착종들이 그 만에 다시 유입되고 있다.

smooth cordgrass 갯줄풀 perennial ㈜(식물이) 다년생의
clump ㈜무더기 thrive ㈜번성하다 wetland ㈜습지
tidal flat 갯벌, 간석지 demonstrate ㈜보여주다 shelter ㈜은신처
burrow ㈜굴을 파다 drainage ㈜배수 consume ㈜먹다
erode ㈜침식하다 pollutant ㈜오염 물질 nitrogen ㈜질소
phosphorus ㈜인(비금속 원소) photosynthesis ㈜광합성
invasive species (외래) 침입종 outcompete ㈜경쟁에서 이기다

endangered 형 멸종 위기에 처한 biodiversity 명 생물 다양성
intentionally 부 의도적으로 hybrid 명 잡종 adjacent 형 인접한
eradicate 동 박멸하다, 뿌리 뽑다 infestation 명 출몰, 들끓음
herbicide 명 제초제 diminish 동 줄어들다

1 1단락에 따르면, 갯줄풀의 물리적 특징은?
(A) 굵은 뿌리
(B) 무리를 이룬 줄기
(C) 넓은 잎
(D) 큰 씨앗

2 2단락에 따르면, 갯줄풀이 동부 해안에 유익한 것은
(A) 게와 홍합을 위한 식량원을 제공하기 때문이다
(B) 수질 오염 물질의 여과를 개선하기 때문이다
(C) 그것의 긴 잎이 흰기러기에게 은신처를 제공하기 때문이다
(D) 해안가의 모래량을 줄이기 때문이다

3 지문의 단어 "adjacent"와 의미가 가장 비슷한 것은?
(A) 널리 퍼진
(B) 광범위한
(C) 근처의
(D) 근본적인

4 3단락에서 글쓴이가 워싱턴에서의 출몰에 관해 언급한 것으로, 갯줄풀은
(A) 멸종 위기에 처한 쥐 종에 영향을 주었다
(B) 물의 배수를 줄이는 경향이 있었다
(C) 포장에 사용되는 재료로 도착했다
(D) 여러 토착 식물들과 잡종을 형성했다

5 4단락에 따르면, 다음 중 갯줄풀을 줄일 수 있는 방법이 아닌 것은?
(A) 생태계에 벌레를 유입하는 것
(B) 습지에 제초제를 쓰는 것
(C) 여러 차례 풀을 깎는 것
(D) 더 많은 토착 식물 종을 심는 것

Reading Practice 4

본문 p.68

1 (B) 2 (B) 3 (A) 4 (D) 5 (A)

Vocabulary Quiz

1 ⓐ 2 ⓑ 3 ⓑ 4 ⓐ

초기 우주 개발 경쟁

제2차 세계대전 이후 직접적인 우주 탐사가 가능성 있는 일이 되었다. 이전에는, 천문학자들에 의해 수행된 우주 탐사의 대부분을 지상의 광학 및 전파 망원경이 해냈다. 비록 이것들이 귀중한 정보를 축적하기는 했지만, 지구 대기의 간섭은 과학자들이 정확한 정보를 얻는 것을 방해했다.

1957년에 중요한 큰 발전이 일어났다. 그 당시 소비에트 사회주의 연방 공화국(USSR)이었던 러시아는 최초의 인공위성인 스푸트니크 1호를 발사했다. [2]그것은 우주 방사선, 유성체, 온도, 공기 밀도에 관한 정보를 전달했다. 그것의 발사는 우주 시대의 시작을 알렸고 미국의 우주 프로그램이 더 활발해지도록 촉진했으며, 따라서 두 초강대국 사이의 우주 개발 경쟁이 될 것의 기반을 닦았다. 같은 해에 소련에 의해 두 번째 위성이 발사되었다. [3]그 위성은 개를 탑승객으로 태웠는데, 이는 과학자들이 인간이 그 여행을 할 수 있을지 여부를 결정하기 위해 우주 공간에서 살아있는 생명체의 생리학적 정보를 기록할 수 있게 해주었다. 1958년에 미국에 의해 익스플로러 1호가 발사되었으며, 그 이후 우주의 정보에 대한 지속적인 탐구 속에서 양국에 의해 수많은 위성들이 발사되었다. 이러한 위성들이 정보를 얻는 데는 유용했지만, 우주 탐사선은 훨씬 더 생산적이었다.

1960년대에, 러시아와 미국 양국은 대략 50개의 우주 탐사선을 달에 발사했다. 초기의 우주 탐사선은 단지 달을 지나가거나 그것에 충돌하여 착륙하도록 설계되었다. [4A/4B]기술이 발전함에 따라, 우주 탐사선은 부드러운 착륙과 더 정밀한 조종을 하는 것이 가능해졌다. [4C]1960년대 중반까지, 우주 탐사선은 달에 충돌하기 전에 사진을 찍어 전송할 수 있었다. 루나로 알려진 소련의 우주 탐사선은 미국의 대응물인 서베이어에 비해 정보 획득에 있어 몇 개월 앞서 있었다. [5]그러나, 미국의 우주 탐사선에 의해 입수된 정보가 더 상세했다. 시간이 흐르면서, 명확하게 선명한 수천 장의 사진들이 찍혔고, 지구에서 가장 가까운 그 천체에 관한 풍부한 정보를 인류에게 제공했다.

우주 탐사선이 더욱 발전함에 따라, 양국은 인간을 달에 보내는 것을 목표로 삼았다. 양국 모두 이것을 성취하기 위해 맹렬히 경쟁했지만, 미국이 인간을 달에 보낸 유일한 국가였다.

space race (1950~60년대 미국과 소련의) 우주 개발 경쟁
exploration 명 탐사 land-based 형 지상의 optical 형 광학의
radio 형 전파의 accumulate 동 축적하다
interference 명 (전파 등의) 간섭 breakthrough 명 큰 발전
launch 동 (우주선 등을) 발사하다 artificial satellite 인공위성
cosmic ray 우주 방사선 meteoroid 명 유성체 prod 동 촉진하다
pave the way for ~의 기반을 닦다 superpower 명 초강대국
physiological 형 생리학적인 space probe 우주 탐사선
maneuver 명 조종, 조작 equivalent 명 대응물
explicitly 부 명확하게 celestial body 천체 objective 명 목표
fiercely 부 맹렬히

1 지문의 단어 "accumulated"와 의미가 가장 비슷한 것은?
(A) 모의 실험했다
(B) 수집했다
(C) 실험했다
(D) 해결했다

2 2단락에 따르면, 다음 중 최초의 인공위성의 업적인 것은?
(A) 달의 사진을 찍었다.
(B) 유성체에 대한 자료를 제공했다.
(C) 부드럽게 착륙했다.
(D) 달 주위의 궤도를 돌았다.

3 2단락에 따르면, 비행에 개를 투입한 목적은?
(A) 유인 우주선의 실행 가능성을 시험하기 위해
(B) 개의 반응을 인간의 것과 비교하기 위해
(C) 기술이 더 우수하다는 것을 입증하기 위해
(D) 인간 우주 비행사들에게 동행을 제공하기 위해

4 다음 중 달 우주 탐사선의 특징이 아닌 것은?
(A) 정확한 운항
(B) 부드럽게 착륙하는 능력

(C) 사진 촬영 설비
(D) 빠른 비행

5 3단락에 따르면, 미국의 서베이어 탐사선은
(A) 자세한 정보를 수집할 수 있었다
(B) 루나보다 먼저 개발되었다
(C) 완전히 달까지 갈 수 없었다
(D) 그것들이 입수했던 정보 측면에서 제한적이었다

iBT Reading Test

본문 p.70

1 (C) 2 (D) 3 (B) 4 (B)
5 (A) 6 (C) 7 (C) 8 (C)
9 (A) 10 (B), (D), (E)

춤 보존하기

인간이 말이나 글로 의사소통할 수 있기 전에, 몸짓이 있었고, 이 몸짓과 함께 춤이 생겨났다. 그러나 춤의 변하기 쉬운 본질은 그것을 정확하게 보존하는 것을 어렵게 했다. 발가락에서 발가락으로, 손에서 손으로, 눈에서 눈으로, 춤은 대대로 전해졌다. 무용가, 안무가, 그리고 그것의 창작과 공연에 관련된 다른 사람들로 구성된 인간 사슬이 특정 춤에 관한 그들의 지식을 전수해 왔다. 춤이 세월의 시험에서 살아남기 위해서는, 우선 그것의 진가를 알아보고 난 후에 그것을 기꺼이 배우고 기억하고자 하는 사람들이 있어야 한다. [1]심지어 이러한 조건들이 충족되더라도, 매 공연마다 춤이 달라질 수 있기 때문에 정확한 보존은 거의 보장할 수 없다.

춤을 보존하려는 초기의 시도는 몸짓에 대한 글로 된 묘사에 의존했다. 그러나, 상세한 설명은 주관적인 해석을 끌어들이지 않고는 미묘함을 정확하게 포착할 수 없었다. 무용가가 뛰거나 회전할 때 취해야 할 형태를 글로 표현하는 것은 어렵고, 춤을 보지 않고 이 글을 이해하는 것은 더 어렵다. 음악의 것과 유사하게, 춤에 대한 표기 체계를 만들어 내기 위한 여러 시도가 있었다. 최초의 성공적인 표기 체계는 1928년에 무용 이론가 루돌프 폰 라반에 의해 개발된 라바노테이션이었다. [5]그 체계는 미묘한 몸짓에서부터 체중의 이동에 이르기까지 인간 동작의 모든 측면을 표현하기 위해 기호를 사용한다. 모티프 표기와 같은 라바노테이션의 변형 대부분은 이 방법을 간소화한 것이다. 그러나, 서튼 댄스라이팅은 동작을 묘사하기 위해 막대 그림을 사용하는 독특한 체계이다. 이 모든 2차원의 표기 체계들의 문제점은 그것들이 얼마나 정교한지와는 관계없이, 3차원의 동작을 완전하게 포착할 수 없다는 것이다.

춤을 기록하기 위해 그래픽 방식 또한 사용되었다. **처음에는 무용가들에게 표기된 춤에 관한 시각적인 참고를 제공하기 위해 사진이 사용되었다.** 최근에는, 비디오가 춤을 기록하는 표준이 되었는데, 춤 전체가 실시간으로 포착될 수 있기 때문이다. 하지만, 비디오는 한 번에 오직 하나의 관점, 즉 촬영자의 그것만을 제공할 수 있다. 여러 각도에서도, 그 매체는 여전히 본질적으로 2차원이다. 비디오는 또한 값비싼 장비와 세심한 보존이 필요한데, 이는 테이프가 시간이 지나면 변질될 수 있기 때문이다. [8]춤을 기록하는 모든 방식은 춤을 기록하는 사람의 관점에서 이루어지며, 결코 지식이나 경험의 대체물이 될 수는 없다.

preserve 통보존하다 movement 명몸짓, 동작
changeable 형변하기 쉬운 choreographer 명안무가
appreciate 통진가를 알아보다 guarantee 명보장
description 명묘사 detailed 형상세한 account 명설명
subtlety 명미묘함 subjective 형주관적인 interpretation 명해석
assume 통(자세를) 취하다 notation 명표기 theorist 명이론가
transference 명이동 variation 명변형 simplification 명간소화
stick figure 막대 그림 intricate 형정교한
in its entirety 전체로서 perspective 명관점, 시각
medium 명매체, 전달 수단 in essence 본질적으로
deteriorate 통변질되다 viewpoint 명관점 substitute 명대체물

1 1단락에 따르면, 다음 중 춤을 정확하게 기록하는 것의 어려움을 묘사하는 것은?
(A) 춤은 드물게만 공연될 수 있다.
(B) 춤은 이해하기에 너무 복잡할 수 있다.
(C) 춤은 공연마다 바뀔 수 있다.
(D) 춤은 표기하기에는 너무 빠르게 이루어질 수 있다.

2 아래 문장 중 지문 속의 음영된 문장의 핵심 정보를 가장 잘 표현한 것은? 오답은 문장의 의미를 크게 바꾸거나 핵심 정보를 생략한다.
(A) 춤이 보는 사람들에 의해 정확히 묘사될 수 있지 않는 한, 다른 무용수들이 따라하기 어려울 것이다.
(B) 춤을 직접 보는 것은 무용수가 하는 어려운 동작을 더 쉽게 이해하게 해준다.
(C) 춤에 참여한 사람만이 춤의 다양한 동작을 정확하게 설명할 수 있다.
(D) 춤을 묘사하는 것과 관찰하지 않고 그것을 이해하는 것은 둘 다 어려울 수 있다.

3 지문에서 글쓴이는 왜 "Sutton DanceWriting"을 언급하는가?
(A) 3차원의 동작을 포착하는 초기 방법을 제시하기 위해
(B) 독특한 특징을 가진 표기 방법을 소개하기 위해
(C) 무용 표기의 비효율적인 형태를 비판하기 위해
(D) 무용 표기의 아주 오래된 기법을 설명하기 위해

4 지문의 단어 "intricate"와 의미가 가장 비슷한 것은?
(A) 열성적인
(B) 정교한
(C) 결함 있는
(D) 설득력 있는

5 2단락에 따르면, 다음 중 라바노테이션에 관해 사실인 것은?
(A) 몸짓을 기호로 변환한다.
(B) 이전 표기 체계를 단순화한다.
(C) 동작을 나타내기 위해 막대 그림을 사용한다.
(D) 음악 전문가에 의해 개발되었다.

6 지문의 단어 "that"이 가리키는 것은?
(A) 기준
(B) 비디오
(C) 관점
(D) 춤

7 지문의 단어 "deteriorate"와 의미가 가장 비슷한 것은?
(A) 진보하다
(B) 확장하다
(C) 저하되다
(D) 규제하다

8 3단락에 따르면, 다음 중 기록된 춤에 관해 사실인 것은?

(A) 때때로 실시간으로 포착하는 것이 어렵다.
(B) 다양한 관점을 제공하는 효과적인 방법이다.
(C) 경험과 지식을 대체할 수 없다.
(D) 비싼 장비나 관리를 필요로 하지 않는다.

9 네 개의 네모[■]는 다음 문장이 삽입될 수 있는 곳을 나타내고 있다.

처음에는 무용가들에게 표기된 춤에 관한 시각적인 참고를 제공하기 위해 사진이 사용되었다.

이 문장은 어디에 들어가는 것이 가장 적절한가?

10 지시: 지문 요약을 위한 도입 문장이 아래에 주어져 있다. 지문의 가장 중요한 내용을 나타내는 보기 3개를 골라 요약을 완성하라. 어떤 문장은 지문에 언급되지 않은 내용이나 사소한 정보를 나타내므로 요약에 포함되지 않는다. **이 문제는 2점이다.**

춤의 보존은 항상 어려웠다.
- (B) 춤의 스텝을 전달하는 최초의 방법은 동작을 글로 묘사하는 것이었다.
- (D) 춤 표기법 체계는 때때로 꽤 정교했지만, 그것들은 불완전하다.
- (E) 심지어 춤의 비디오 녹화도 그것의 본질을 포착하는 이상적인 방법은 아니다.

(A) 안무가들은 수 세기에 걸쳐 춤을 글의 형태로 옮기는 것을 담당해 왔다.
(C) 라바노테이션은 유명 안무가 루돌프 폰 라반에 의해 개발되었다.
(F) 춤의 비디오 녹화는 기록된 영상들의 평면성에 의해 제한된다.

Vocabulary Review

본문 p.74

1 physiological　2 carnivorous　3 explicitly
4 viewpoints　5 diplomatic　6 devoured
7 (D)　8 (C)　9 (C)　10 (B)
11 (A)　12 (D)　13 (C)　14 (D)

CHAPTER 05
Negative Fact

Example

본문 p.77

1 (A)　2 (D)

에펠탑 밝히기

에펠탑의 원래 조명 장치는 그 당시에 전기를 이용할 수 없었기 때문에 오직 가스등으로만 구성되었다. [1C]1900년에 이 기술이 그럴듯해지자, 전구가 오래된 조명을 대체했고 탑의 구조를 강조하기 위해 뼈대를 따라 설치되었다. 이후, 훨씬 더 창의적인 조명이 특별한 행사들을 위해 설치되었다. [1B]1925년에, 한 프랑스의 산업가는 세계 박람회에서 그의 상표명의 철자를 쓰고 광고하기 위해 그 탑을 임대하여 250,000개의 조명을 달았다. 60년 후, 현대적인 형태의 에펠탑 조명이 탄생했다. [1D]한 기술자가 뼈대 내부에 수백 개의 1000와트 전구를 스포트라이트로 설치했다. 단순히 탑을 밝히는 것이 아니라, 이것들은 탑 그 자체가 아주 멀리서도 보일 수 있는 광원처럼 보이게 했다. 21세기에 여러 추가적인 혁신들이 일어났다. 더욱 효율적인 조명이 이용 가능해지면서, 전구의 전력량이 줄어들었고, 밝기의 손실 없이 에너지를 절약했다. [2A]또한, 탑에 반짝이는 효과나 특정한 색상을 낼 수 있는 조명이 설치되었다. [2B/2C]이러한 개선들은 중요한 행사들이나 기념일을 기념하는 것과 같은 특정 목적을 위한 웅장한 조명 쇼의 제작을 가능하게 해 주었다.

unavailable 형 이용할 수 없는　plausible 형 그럴듯한
replace 동 대체하다　highlight 동 강조하다　install 동 설치하다
industrialist 명 산업가　spell out 철자를 쓰다
illuminate 동 밝히다, 비추다　additional 형 추가적인
innovation 명 혁신　efficient 형 효율적인
available 형 이용 가능한　wattage 명 전력량
be fitted with ~이 설치되다　sparkling 형 반짝이는
magnificent 형 웅장한　commemorate 동 기념하다
anniversary 명 기념일

1 다음 중 1900년대의 에펠탑에 관해 사실이 아닌 것은?

(A) 그것에 달린 많은 조명이 가스로 작동되었다.
(B) 한 기업가가 그의 회사를 광고하는 데 그것을 이용했다.
(C) 그것에 전등이 처음으로 설치되었다.
(D) 스포트라이트가 그것을 아주 멀리서도 보이게 했다.

2 다음 중 21세기에 에펠탑에 일어난 혁신들에 관해 언급되지 않은 것은?

(A) 반짝이는 기능을 가진 조명이 도입되었다.
(B) 개선이 화려한 조명 쇼를 가능하게 했다.
(C) 기념일에 색 전등이 사용되기 시작했다.
(D) 전력량이 더 높은 에너지 절약 조명이 추가되었다.

Reading Practice 1

본문 p.78

1 (B)　2 (A)　3 (D)　4 (C)　5 (A)

Vocabulary Quiz

1 ⓐ　2 ⓑ　3 ⓑ　4 ⓐ

러스트 벨트

러스트 벨트로 알려진, 미국의 북동부 지역은 버려진 공장들, 실업률, 인구 유출로 유명해졌다. 이 경제 지역은 중서부 주인 일리노이, 인디애나, 미시간, 오하이오와 북동부 주 한 곳인 펜실베이니아를 포함한다. 러스트 벨트는 한때 주요한 산업 지역이었다. 그러나, 1950년대에 들어서면서, 제조업체들이 이전하기 시작했고, 이것이 인구와 경제력의 감소를 야기했다. 국가 자동차 산업의 본거지이자 지난날 세계 최대의 제조업 생산지 중 하나였던 디트로이트는 이 하락세에 가장 크게 영향을 받았다.

[1]일반적으로, 미국의 나머지 지역은 서비스 부문의 산업들로 초점을 옮겨 번성했다. 그러나, 러스트 벨트는 자동차와 철강 제조업이 국내외

시장에서 쇠퇴를 겪으면서 1970년대에 계속 악화되었다. 임금이 하락하기 시작했을 뿐만 아니라 실업률도 상승했으며, 복지 지원을 받는 사람들의 수가 증가했다.

1990년대 중반 무렵, 러스트 벨트는 예상치 못한 회복을 이루었다. 3A인구 유출, 임금율 하락, 생산, 범죄율, 실업의 추세가 멈추거나 방향을 바꾸었다. 3C수출은 27퍼센트 증가했는데, 이는 미국 전체보다 5퍼센트 높았다. 3B러스트 벨트의 산업 수도로 불렸던 디트로이트는 급격한 인구 증가를 경험했다. 1990년대 초반의 7년 동안, 대도시 지역의 인구는 거의 5퍼센트 증가했다. 1994년부터 1996년까지의 기간 동안 평균 연봉은 7퍼센트 상승했다. 디트로이트는 또한 이 10년의 첫 5년 동안 비농업 민간 사업체 수의 증가를 경험했다. 러스트 벨트의 다른 지역들, 특히 오하이오의 주요 도시들 또한 이 기간 동안 상승세를 경험했다.

그러나, 이것은 지속적인 회복이라기보다는 단기적인 발전으로 판명되었다. 5B1997년의 아시아 금융 위기는 미국 달러를 상승시켜, 해외에서의 미국 제품에 대한 수요를 감소시켰다. 5C새천년의 첫 10년 동안, 제조업 부문에서 약 160만 개의 일자리가 줄었다. 5D기술 발전과 더 많은 외국 제품을 들여온 개방 무역 정책의 조합은 러스트 벨트 기업들에 부정적으로 영향을 미쳤다.

reputed 형 유명한 abandoned 형 버려진
unemployment 명 실업률, 실업 out-migration 명 인구 유출
dominant 형 주요한 manufacturer 명 제조업체
relocate 동 이전하다 economic strength 경제력
formerly 부 지난날 affect 동 영향을 미치다
downtrend 명 하락세, 하향 추세 prosper 동 번성하다
shift 동 옮기다 domestic 형 국내의 wage 명 임금
welfare 명 (사회) 복지 지원 unexpected 형 예상치 못한
recovery 명 회복 cease 동 멈추다 reverse 동 바꾸다
dramatic 형 급격한, 극적인 notably 부 특히 uptrend 명 상승세
impact 동 영향을 미치다

1 2단락에 따르면, 미국의 다른 지역들은 어떻게 러스트 벨트에서 일어난 경제 하락을 피했는가?
(A) 경제적 협력 관계를 형성함으로써
(B) 다른 산업으로 전환함으로써
(C) 지역 시장을 개발함으로써
(D) 국내의 수요를 늘림으로써

2 지문의 단어 "ceased"와 의미가 가장 비슷한 것은?
(A) 멈추었다
(B) 지연시켰다
(C) 조정했다
(D) 축소했다

3 3단락에 따르면, 다음 중 1990년대에 러스트 벨트에서 일어나지 않은 것은?
(A) 범죄율이 낮아졌다.
(B) 인구가 증가했다.
(C) 수출의 증가가 있었다.
(D) 임금의 감소가 있었다.

4 지문의 단어 "this"가 가리키는 것은?
(A) 러스트 벨트
(B) 오하이오
(C) 상승세
(D) 기간

5 다음 중 새천년 이후 러스트 벨트가 쇠퇴한 원인이 아닌 것은?
(A) 급성장한 아시아 경제
(B) 미국 달러의 가치
(C) 제조업 일자리의 감소
(D) 외국 제품의 입수 가능성

Reading Practice 2 본문 p.80

1 (B) 2 (D) 3 (D) 4 (A) 5 (B)

Vocabulary Quiz

1 ⓑ 2 ⓐ 3 ⓑ 4 ⓐ

대기 먼지

대기 먼지는 미세한 입자들로 나타나는데, 이것들은 가벼운 바람의 흐름에 의해 떠 있다가 천천히 가라앉는다. 이 먼지 입자들은 도시 위 낮은 고도에서 가장 흔하고 바다 위 높은 고도에서 가장 흔하지 않다. 2먼지 입자들은 지름이 1미크론, 즉 1밀리미터의 1,000분의 1 미만으로 매우 작고 너무 가벼워서 한 번에 몇 주 동안 공중에 떠 있을 수 있다. 인도네시아의 크라카타우 같은 화산 폭발에서 나온 먼지는 그 폭발 이후 3년이 지나서도 여전히 공중에 떠 있는 것이 관측되었다.

대기 먼지는 많은 원천에서 생겨난다. 3A건조한 땅 위로 부는 바람은 경작된 밭, 사막, 도로에서 먼지를 싣는다. 연소, 화재로 인한 그을음, 자동차 오염의 산물은 산업화된 지역에서의 일반적인 원천이다. 3B먼 거친 바다에서 나온 바다 소금의 미세 입자, 식물에서 나온 꽃가루, 유성의 입자는 일부 자연적 원천이다. 아프리카 사막, 타클라마칸 사막, 고비 사막에서는 계절에 따른 큰 먼지 폭풍이 발생한다. 3C이 폭풍에서 나온 먼지는 종종 다른 지역들로 이동하는데, 여기에서 그것은 대기질에 부정적으로 영향을 미칠 수 있다.

5A공중에 떠 있는 응결핵은 구름으로 발전하는 구름 방울을 형성한다. 5C이 먼지 입자는 흡습성의 먼지, 즉, 물이 들러붙는 입자로 불리며, 그것들은 너무 작아서 현미경의 사용 없이는 관찰될 수 없다. 구름 속 각 물방울의 응결핵은 이러한 무기물이나 유기물 먼지의 매우 작은 입자들 중 하나이다. 1880년에 공기 중 입자들의 수를 세는 장치를 발명한 스코틀랜드 물리학자 존 에이킨은 처음으로 먼지 입자들과 물방울 사이의 연관성을 밝혔다. 응결핵 주위로 형성되는 구름 방울들이 합쳐지기 시작함에 따라, 그것들은 더 이상 떠 있을 수 없게 된다. 5D그 후에 그것들은 강수의 형태로 땅에 떨어진다. 각각의 빗방울들은 특별히 커보이지 않을 수 있지만, 그것들은 구름 방울들에 비하면 거대한 것이다. 하나의 빗방울은 백만에서 천만 개의 구름 방울과 동등하다.

대기 먼지는 또한 지구의 기후에 다른 방식으로도 영향을 미칠 수 있다. 그것은 온실가스와 유사한 방식으로 기능하여 지구의 기후 체계를 따뜻하게 한다. 그것은 지구 대기로 들어오는 태양 복사열과 지구의 표면에서 나가는 복사열을 모두 흡수하여, 결국 대기에 열을 가둔다.

atmospheric 형 대기의 minute 형 미세한 particle 명 입자
suspend 동 (입자를) 떠 있게 하다 altitude 명 고도
airborne 형 공중에 떠 있는 volcanic 형 화산의
plow 동 (쟁기로) 경작하다 combustion 명 연소 pollution 명 오염
turbulent 형 거친, 격동적인 meteoric 형 유성의
seasonal 형 계절에 따른 nucleus 명 응결핵 droplet 명 방울

hygroscopic 형 흡습성의　adhere 동 들러붙다
correlate 동 ~ 사이의 연관성을 밝히다　condensation 명 물방울, 응결
coalesce 동 합치다　precipitation 명 강수, 강우
particularly 부 특별히　equivalent 형 동등한　absorb 동 흡수하다
solar radiation 태양 복사열　ultimately 부 결국

1 지문에서 글쓴이는 왜 "Krakatoa"를 언급하는가?
(A) 먼지의 주요 원천 중 하나를 언급하기 위해
(B) 먼지가 공기 중에 오래 머무른다는 것을 보여주기 위해
(C) 먼지가 형성되는 과정을 설명하기 위해
(D) 화산과 농지에서 나오는 먼지 배출량을 비교하기 위해

2 1단락에서, 다음 중 글쓴이가 먼지 입자들에 관해 묘사하는 것은?
(A) 가벼운 바람으로 인해 땅에 떨어지는 경향
(B) 바다 표면 바로 위에서의 응집
(C) 도시 환경에서의 축적률
(D) 그것들을 떠다니게 해주는 낮은 질량

3 2단락에서, 다음 중 대기 먼지의 원천으로 언급되지 않은 것은?
(A) 경작으로 흐트러진 토양
(B) 바다에서 나온 소금의 잔여물
(C) 사막에서 불어오는 모래 폭풍
(D) 공장에서 나온 내화성 물질들

4 지문의 단어 "adheres"와 의미가 가장 비슷한 것은?
(A) 달라붙다
(B) 껴안다
(C) 관련이 있다
(D) 사라지다

5 3단락에 따르면, 다음 중 공중에 떠 있는 응결핵에 관해 사실이 아닌 것은?
(A) 구름은 그것들로 이루어진다.
(B) 대부분 무기물이다.
(C) 엄청나게 작다.
(D) 비가 되어 땅에 떨어진다.

Reading Practice 3

본문 p.82

1 (A)　2 (A)　3 (B)　4 (C)　5 (B)

Vocabulary Quiz

1 ⓐ　2 ⓑ　3 ⓑ　4 ⓒ

고대의 테라코타

테라코타는 선사 시대까지 거슬러 올라가며 오늘날에도 여전히 널리 사용되는 도자기의 한 형태이다. 그 이름은 "구운 흙"을 의미하는 이탈리아어로, 그것을 만드는 데 사용되는 과정을 가리키는 것이다. [2B/2C]테라코타는 모양이 잡힌 후 섭씨 1,000도의 온도로 특수한 가마 속에서 굳혀지는 거칠고 구멍이 많은 점토를 가지고 시작한다. 고대 조각가들이 느낀 매력은 이해하기 어렵지 않다. [2D]테라코타는 청동이나 돌에 비해 저렴하고 사용하기 더 쉬운 매체이다. 실제로, 이 재료는 너무 편리해서 전 세계의 많은 초기 문화권에서 사용되었다.

테라코타는 고대 세계의 거의 모든 지역에서 만들어진 것으로 보인다. 최초라고 알려진 테라코타 조각상은 '돌니 베스토니체의 비너스'라고 불리는 4인치의 여인상이다. [3D]오늘날의 체코 공화국인 모라비아에서 재 속에 파묻혀 있다가 발견된 그것은 약 30,000년이 된 것으로 여겨진다. 고대의 테라코타 조각상들은 현대의 터키, 루마니아, 파키스탄, 그리스, 이집트, 이라크에서도 발견되었다. 훨씬 더 멀리 떨어진 테라코타의 표본들은 기원전 1500년부터 그 기법을 사용한 사하라 사막 이남의 녹족과, 문화가 비슷한 시대까지 거슬러 올라가는 오늘날 멕시코의 올멕족의 것으로 여겨진다. [3A]가장 인상적인 테라코타 작품은 '병마용'으로, 8,000개의 실물 크기의 점토 군인 모음이다. 그것은 중국 최초의 황제의 무덤에서 발견되었다. [3C]이 조각상들의 축조는 기원전 246년에 시작되었고, 720,000명의 사람들의 조력을 필요로 했다.

이 모든 다양한 사람들이 개별적으로 테라코타를 발견했을까? 이것은 민감한 질문이다. [5]2016년에, 한 중국인 연구가는 '병마용'을 구성하는 군인들의 실물 같은 외형이 고대 그리스 예술가들의 영향을 시사한다고 제시하여 논란을 불러일으켰다. 한 영국인 미술사학자는 더 나아가, 그 유적지에서 "서양의 DNA"가 발견되었다고 주장했다. 두 사람은 동양과 서양 간 문화 교류가 기존에 인식된 것보다 더 일찍 시작했다고 제시했다. 언론의 광범위한 보도에도 불구하고, 그 이론은 그것을 단독으로 놀라운 예술 작품을 만들어 낼 수 있는 비유럽권 문화의 능력을 의심하는 오래 지속된 경향의 일부로 바라보는 많은 역사 전문가들에 의해 이의를 제기받아왔다.

ceramic pottery 도자기　date back to ~까지 거슬러 올라가다
prehistoric 형 선사의　reference 명 가리키는 것　coarse 형 거친
porous 형 구멍이 많은　comprehend 동 이해하다
medium 명 매체　convenient 형 편리한　far-flung 형 멀리 떨어진
impressive 형 인상적인　life-size 형 실물 크기의
construction 명 축조, 건축　contribution 명 조력, 공헌
independently 부 개별적으로　sensitive 형 민감한
controversy 명 논란　challenge 동 이의를 제기하다
longstanding 형 오래 지속된　remarkable 형 놀라운

1 지문의 단어 "comprehend"와 의미가 가장 비슷한 것은?
(A) 이해하다
(B) 검사하다
(C) 대표하다
(D) 대신하다

2 1단락에서, 글쓴이가 테라코타 제작 과정에 관해 묘사하지 않는 것은?
(A) 상대적인 단단함
(B) 가마의 온도
(C) 점토의 질감
(D) 상대적인 비용

3 2단락에 따르면, 다음 중 초기 테라코타에 관해 사실이 아닌 것은?
(A) 사람의 실물 크기 조각상을 만드는 데 사용되었다.
(B) 아프리카를 제외한 모든 대륙에서 만들어졌다.
(C) 50만 명이 넘는 노동자들이 중국의 프로젝트에 기여했다.
(D) 가장 오래된 작품은 모라비아에서 발견되었다.

4 지문의 단어 "it"이 가리키는 것은?
(A) 보도
(B) 언론
(C) 이론

(D) 역사

5 다음 중 3단락에서 병마용에 관해 추론할 수 있는 것은?
(A) 고대 그리스에 대한 중국인들의 영향을 증명한다.
(B) 타문화의 예술과 유사한 특징을 보여준다.
(C) 동서양이 최초로 교류한 시기를 확인시켜 준다.
(D) 영국계 사람들에 대한 묘사를 포함한다.

Reading Practice 4

본문 p.84

1 (C) 2 (B) 3 (A) 4 (B) 5 (D)

Vocabulary Quiz

1 ⓐ 2 ⓒ 3 ⓒ 4 ⓑ

식물의 무기질 결핍

식물이 생존을 위해 햇빛과 물에 의존한다는 것은 흔히 알려져 있지만, 잘 자라는 식물을 위한 요건은 그것보다 더 광범위하다. 사람과 마찬가지로, 적절한 양분이 부족하면 식물은 건강이 나빠진다. 무기질 양분은 뿌리를 통해 식물로 흡수되어 그 생물의 세포와 조직들로 분배된다. 그것은 토양에 필수 양분이 풍부해야 한다는 것을 의미한다. 토양에 그것들이 부족한 경우에는, 식물의 뿌리가 뻗어간 흙에 부족한 무기질을 쓰는 것이 매우 중요해진다. 식물이 토양으로부터 많은 양분을 필요로 하지만, 가장 일반적인 식물의 결핍은 인, 질소, 철분의 결핍이다. 식물에 이러한 물질들이 부족할 때, 그것들은 예측할 수 있는 특정 증상들을 보인다.

3D부족한 인은 또한 씨앗 발아와 개화를 포함한 식물 발달의 모든 측면에 부정적으로 영향을 미칠 수 있다. 3C식물의 어린잎들이 건강해 보일지도 모르지만, 오래된 잎들은 색소인 안토시아닌의 과도한 축적으로 인해 전형적으로 그것들의 밑면에 보라색을 띠기 시작한다. 3B게다가, 그 잎들의 끝부분은 때때로 메말라지고 탄 것처럼 보인다. 이 증상들은 식물이 토양에서 인을 충분히 얻지 못해, 그것의 광합성 수행 능력이 감소했음을 나타내는 징후이다.

암모늄과 질산염이 과잉의 물에 의해 씻겨 나가면, 식물은 질소 결핍 증상을 경험할 수도 있다. 이 상태의 주된 징후는 오래된 잎들의 황변과 어린잎들의 연한 녹색으로의 변화이다. 어떤 잎들은 심지어 분홍색 빛을 띠게 될 수도 있다. 4성장 또한 느려지고 감소된다. 이러한 증상들이 나타나는 이유는 질소가 식물의 성장과 발육에 필수적이기 때문이다. 그것들은 거름이나 혈분처럼 질소가 많은 비료를 써서 예방될 수 있다.

5B철분은 미량 영양소로, 이는 그것이 식물의 건강에 필수적이지만, 다른 양분에 비해 적은 양이 필요하다는 것을 의미한다. 5C철분은 효소와 엽록체 단백질의 합성을 촉진한다. 5A토양의 pH 수치가 6.5 이상으로 올라가면, 식물은 보통은 토양 내에 풍부하게 있는 철분에 접근할 수 없을 것이다. 잎의 나머지 부분은 색이 옅어지는 반면 잎맥은 짙은 녹색으로 남는다. 이 변색은 잎 전체가 노랗게 될 때까지 진행된다.

mineral 명무기질, 광물 deficiency 명결핍 requirement 명요건
flourishing 형잘 자라는, 무성한 lack 동~이 부족하다
proper 형적절한 nutrition 명양분 absorb 동흡수하다
distribute 동분배하다 deficient 형부족한 crucial 형매우 중요한
missing 형부족한 phosphorus 명인 substance 명물질
predictable 형예측할 수 있는 insufficient 형부족한, 불충분한
germination 명발아 excess 형과도한 accumulation 명축적
pigment 명색소 photosynthesis 명광합성
transition 명변화, 전이 fertilizer 명비료 manure 명거름, 비료
blood meal 혈분(가축의 피를 건조하여 만든 비료)
micronutrient 명미량 영양소 synthesis 명합성
chloroplast 명엽록체 plentiful 형풍부한 pale 동(색이) 옅어지다

1 지문의 단어 "flourishing"과 의미가 가장 비슷한 것은?
(A) 형광의
(B) 끈기 있는
(C) 잘 자라는
(D) 아주 아름다운

2 지문의 단어 "its"가 가리키는 것은?
(A) 징후
(B) 식물
(C) 인
(D) 토양

3 2단락에서, 다음 중 글쓴이가 인 결핍 증상에 관해 언급하지 않은 것은?
(A) 뿌리의 흑변
(B) 잎 끝부분의 줄어든 수분
(C) 잎의 보랏빛 변색
(D) 씨앗 발아의 방해

4 3단락에 따르면, 질소의 부족은
(A) 제한된 번식을 야기한다
(B) 느린 성장을 야기한다
(C) 광합성 감소를 야기한다
(D) 느린 개화를 야기한다

5 4단락에 따르면, 다음 중 철분에 관해 사실이 아닌 것은?
(A) 대부분의 토양에 적절한 양이 존재한다.
(B) 매우 많은 양이 필요하지 않다.
(C) 식물이 단백질과 효소를 처리하는 것을 돕는다.
(D) 잎 전체를 즉시 노란색으로 변하게 한다.

iBT Reading Test

본문 p.86

1 (C) 2 (C) 3 (B) 4 (B)
5 (D) 6 (D) 7 (A) 8 (A)
9 (C) 10 (B), (C), (D)

새의 노래 학습

현존하는 9,000종의 새 중에서 대략 절반이 노래하는 방법을 배운다. 노래하는 새의 학습 과정과 인간의 언어 습득 사이에는 많은 유사점이 있다. 둘 다 사회적 영향에 의해 형성되는 의사소통의 방법을 배우려는 타고난 성향을 수반하는 것으로 보인다.

실험실 내부의 방음실에서 자란 새끼 새들은 정상적인 노래의 것과 유사한 요소들을 포함하는 미숙하지만 알아들을 수 있는 노랫소리를 냈다. 과학자들은 새들이 자기 종의 노래가 어떻게 들려야 하는지에 대한 기본적인 원형을 가지고 태어난다고 가정했다. 그들은 성장하는 동안

그들이 부르는 노래가 완성될 때까지 이 원형을 주변에서 들리는 노래와 맞춰간다. 한 마리의 고립된 새는 정상적인 노래를 듣지 못하므로, 미숙한 원형만을 만들어 낼 수 있다. [4]어린 새들은 부모의 노래를 배우는 것을 선호하지만, 만약 이 중요한 시기 동안 자기 종의 노래를 듣지 못한다면, 다른 종의 노래를 배울 것이다.

[7]카세트테이프와 CD 같은 전자 매체를 통해 노래를 배운 어린 새들이 만약 실제로 노래하는 다른 종 조교의 노래를 듣는다면, 그들은 최종 성체의 노래에서 다른 종에 의해 사용되는 음을 포함시킬 더 큰 경향이 있다. 만약 다른 종의 실제로 노래하는 조교가 같은 환경에 있다면, 그들은 심지어 동일한 종의 전자 노래를 무시하고 다른 종의 노래를 배울 수 있다. 이것은 감각 운동 단계에서 발생하는데, 이때 새는 그것이 이전에 들었던 소리들을 비교하고 연습한다.

많은 연습과 실험 후에, 최종 성체의 노래가 완성된다. 들리는 음들을 흡수하고 기억하는 개체의 능력뿐만 아니라 각 개체의 유전적 능력에 따른 개체 간의 변형이 항상 존재한다. 그들이 적절한 자극에 노출되는 한, 모든 어린 새들은 노래하는 방법을 배운다. **하지만, 오직 소수만이 배운 노래를 완벽하게 재현할 수 있을 것이다.** 학습 과정이 새가 다 자라자마자 끝나는 것이 아니라는 점에 주목하는 것이 중요하다. [8]어떤 경우에는, 완전한 성숙기에 도달한 개체들이 영역을 바꾸었을 때 새로운 노래를 습득하게 된다.

approximately 부 대략, 약　existing 형 현존하는
similarity 명 유사점　acquisition 명 습득
involve 동 수반하다, 포함하다　innate 형 타고난
predisposition 명 성향, 기질　regarding 전 ~에 관하여
soundproofed 형 방음의　crude 형 미숙한, 미완성의, 조악한
recognizable 형 알아들을 수 있는　postulate 동 가정하다
template 명 원형, 견본　isolated 형 고립된
medium 명 매체, 수단　have a tendency to ~하는 경향이 있다
incorporate 동 포함시키다　sensorimotor 형 감각 운동의
phase 명 단계　variation 명 변형　capacity 명 능력
adequate 형 적절한　maturity 명 성숙기　territory 명 영역

1 지문의 단어 "innate"와 의미가 가장 비슷한 것은?
(A) 특별한
(B) 여분의
(C) 타고난
(D) 표준적인

2 지문의 단어 "They"가 가리키는 것은?
(A) 요소들
(B) 과학자들
(C) 새들
(D) 종

3 지문에서 글쓴이는 왜 "isolated bird"를 언급하는가?
(A) 성장하는 동안 혼자 지내는 것의 중요성을 강조하기 위해
(B) 새가 가진 노래의 기본적인 원형의 증거를 제시하기 위해
(C) 노래 학습이 언어 습득과 유사하다고 주장하기 위해
(D) 노래하는 새에 관한 연구의 범위를 설명하기 위해

4 2단락에 따르면, 어린 새는
(A) 자기 종의 다른 새들과 분리되어 있을 때 노래를 가장 잘 배운다
(B) 부모가 같은 환경에 있을 때 노래를 가장 잘 배운다
(C) 다른 종의 노래만을 들을 때 노래를 가장 잘 배운다
(D) 자기 무리가 다른 영역으로 이동했을 때 노래를 가장 잘 배운다

5 지문의 단어 "incorporate"와 의미가 가장 비슷한 것은?
(A) 결정하다
(B) 모으다
(C) 수정하다
(D) 결합시키다

6 아래 문장 중 지문 속의 음영된 문장의 핵심 정보를 가장 잘 표현한 것은? 오답은 문장의 의미를 크게 바꾸거나 핵심 정보를 생략한다.
(A) 그들은 환경이 완벽할 때 다른 새의 의사소통 양식을 받아들일 수 있다.
(B) 서로 다른 새의 종들은 그들이 부르는 노래에 대해 서로 다른 학습 능력을 갖는다.
(C) 다른 새가 있을 때, 전자 녹음은 새에 의해 무시될 수 있다.
(D) 그들은 다른 종의 실제 부르는 노래를 모방하고 자기 종의 녹음을 무시할 수 있다.

7 3단락에서 추론할 수 있는 것으로, 어린 새들은
(A) 녹음보다 실제 새를 모방하는 것을 선호한다
(B) 여러 노래들을 동시에 연습한다
(C) 같은 종의 다른 새들에 의해 불리는 노래만 배운다
(D) 특이한 소리를 내는 새들을 무시한다

8 4단락에 따르면, 다 자란 새는 그들이
(A) 다른 지역으로 이주하면 새로운 노래를 습득할 수 있다
(B) 다른 종의 새와 교류하면 새로운 노래를 습득할 수 있다
(C) 어린 새가 실험하는 것을 들으면 새로운 노래를 습득할 수 있다
(D) 영역을 위한 경쟁자와 직면하면 새로운 노래를 습득할 수 있다

9 네 개의 네모[■]는 다음 문장이 삽입될 수 있는 곳을 나타내고 있다.
하지만, 오직 소수만이 배운 노래를 완벽하게 재현할 수 있을 것이다.
이 문장은 어디에 들어가는 것이 가장 적절한가?

10 **지시:** 지문 요약을 위한 도입 문장이 아래에 주어져 있다. 지문의 가장 중요한 내용을 나타내는 보기 3개를 골라 요약을 완성하라. 어떤 문장은 지문에 언급되지 않은 내용이나 사소한 정보를 나타내므로 요약에 포함되지 않는다. **이 문제는 2점이다.**

새는 인간이 말하는 법을 배우는 것과 비슷한 방식으로 노래하는 법을 배운다.
- (B) 새는 미숙하게 노래하는 능력을 가지고 태어난다.
- (C) 새는 다른 새들의 노래를 들음으로써 자기 노래를 발전시킨다.
- (D) 성숙기에 도달하면 새의 노래가 완성된다.

(A) 새 종의 절반이 노래하는 법을 배운다.
(E) 고립되면, 새는 노래하는 법을 배우지 않는다.
(F) 새는 카세트테이프를 통해 노래하는 법을 배울 수 있다.

Vocabulary Review

본문 p.90

1 insufficient　2 unexpected　3 crude
4 commemorate　5 controversy　6 altitude
7 (D)　8 (C)　9 (B)　10 (B)
11 (A)　12 (C)　13 (D)　14 (C)

CHAPTER 06
Inference

Example

본문 p. 93

1 (B) 2 (D)

고대 이집트의 고양이

고양이는 고대 이집트에서 명예로운 위치를 차지했다. 이집트인들이 그들의 고양이를 너무 사랑해서 그들은 그들의 반려 고양이를 숭배한다고 믿어졌다. 고양이들은 사랑받는 애완동물 이상이어서, 그것들은 고대 이집트인들의 풍부한 문화적 전통 속 어디에나 있었다. 그 시대의 예술은 이집트 사람들이 그토록 동경했던 특징을 드러낸다. [1]고양이는 이집트인들의 집 안으로 위협적인 뱀과 전갈이 들어오지 못하게 하는 보호자로 묘사되었다. 그것들은 종종 앉아 있는 여성의 의자 아래에 그려지는 다산의 상징이었다. [2]그것들이 현세와 내세에서 소중히 여겨지는 동반자였기 때문에, 부유하고 중요한 사람들의 무덤은 흔히 미라로 만들어진 고양이를 포함했다. 그러나, 숭배의 대상이 되기보다는, 고양이는 지능, 속도, 힘과 같은 신적인 특성을 가지고 있다고 믿어졌다. 햇빛을 받으며 자는 습관은 이집트인들에게 그들의 태양신 라를 떠올리게 했다. 또한 형체를 바꾸는 이집트의 신들 중 일부가 사자나 길들여진 고양이의 형태를 취했다고 믿어졌다. 사람들이 고대 이집트에서 고양이가 신으로 여겨졌다는 오해를 어떻게 얻었는지 이해하는 것은 어렵지 않다.

honored 형 명예로운　worship 동 숭배하다; 명 숭배
feline 형 고양이의　companion 명 반려, 동반자
beloved 형 사랑받는　ubiquitous 형 어디에나 있는
threatening 형 위협적인　fertility 명 다산, 비옥함　depict 동 그리다
cherish 동 소중히 여기다　frequently 부 흔히
mummify 동 미라로 만들다　remind 동 떠올리게 하다
shape-shifting 형 형체를 바꾸는　domestic 형 (동물이) 길들여진
acquire 동 얻다　misunderstanding 명 오해

1 글쓴이가 암시하는 것으로, 고대 이집트의 고양이는
(A) 예술 작품에는 거의 등장하지 않았다
(B) 가정의 유해 동물들을 사냥했다
(C) 주로 영향력 있는 귀족 여성들의 마음에 들었다
(D) 종교 지도자들에게 보호받았다

2 다음 중 이집트의 무덤에 관해 추론할 수 있는 것은?
(A) 외부에 종종 고양이 조각상이 있었다.
(B) 이집트인들의 업적을 기념하기 위해 고안되었다.
(C) 일부는 부자들의 죽은 애완동물을 위해 지어졌다.
(D) 안에 있는 것들이 내세로 들어간다고 믿어졌다.

Reading Practice 1

본문 p. 94

1 (C) 2 (D) 3 (A) 4 (A) 5 (B)

Vocabulary Quiz
1 ⓒ 2 ⓑ 3 ⓑ 4 ⓐ

생물 다양성의 중요성

생물 다양성은 유전적 다양성을 통해 가능해진다. 유전자는 환경에 의한 제약 내에서 한 종이 얼마나 다양해질 수 있는지를 조절한다. [2]생물학자들은 새끼를 낳고 번식할 수 있는 자손을 생산할 수 있는 유사한 동족 개체들의 집단을 하나의 종이라고 정의한다. 종의 각 개체는 많은 수의 유전자를 가지고 있다. 예를 들어, 꽃을 피우는 식물이 무려 40만 개의 유전자를 가질 수 있는 반면, 박테리아 하나는 1,000개의 유전자를 가질 수 있다. 각각의 유전자는 엄청난 양의 정보를 담고 있으며, 이 유전 물질은 건강하고 다양한 생태계를 유지하는 데 필요하다.

하나의 군집을 구성하는 종들은 서로에 대한 상호 의존성을 갖게 될 수 있다. 따라서, 한 종의 손실은 전체 생태계에 엄청난 영향을 미칠 수 있다. 이는 그것이 생물 다양성을 유지하는 데 도움이 될 수 있는 엄청난 양의 정보 손실을 의미할 수 있기 때문이다. [3]많고 다양한 개체군의 존재는 환경이 변화할 경우 많은 주어진 종들이 멸종에서 벗어날 수 있도록 유전적 다양성을 갖게 해준다. 그러므로, 한 종의 멸종을 방지함으로써 생물 다양성을 유지하는 것은 지구상 생명체들의 생존에 필수적이다.

그러나 서식지 변화는 항상 멸종을 포함한 혼란을 야기해왔다. 예를 들어, 북미에서는, 자연경관의 풍요로움은 유럽 정착민들로 하여금 그들이 원하는 만큼 토지를 바꿀 수 있다고 잘못 생각하게 했다. 농작물 재배와 동물 사육을 위한 그들의 잘못된 토지와 숲의 이용은 회색늑대와 같은 포식동물의 수가 점차 줄어들게 했다. 동시에, 그들의 야생동물 사냥과 채집은 종들 전체가 사라지게 했다. 살아남은 일부는 그 숫자와 유전적 다양성이 심각하게 제한되었다. 심지어 한때 수억 마리가 존재했던 흔한 들소조차 몇백 마리의 야생 개체로 줄어들었다.

오늘날 현대 환경 과학자들이 생물 다양성의 중요성을 이해하고 있기 때문에, 그들은 점점 더 생태계 보호를 통한 종의 보존을 권장한다. 20세기 후반부터, 환경 보호론자들의 노력은 일부 종들을 그것들이 한때 자유롭게 돌아다녔던 지역에 성공적으로 다시 들여왔다. 이 종들이 생태계에서 그들의 자리를 다시 찾음에 따라, 그들은 최적의 생태적 다양성에 필요한 유전적 균형을 되살려낼 것이다.

biodiversity 명 생물 다양성　genetic 형 유전적인　varied 형 다양한
constraint 명 제약, 제한　related 형 동족의, 관련된
breed 동 (새끼를) 낳다, 번식하다　reproduction 명 번식
offspring 명 자손　diverse 형 다양한　compose 동 구성하다
interdependence 명 상호 의존성　existence 명 존재
extinction 명 멸종　habitat 명 서식지　disturbance 명 혼란, 방해
misguided 형 잘못된　domestication 명 사육, 길들이기
dwindle 동 점차 줄어들다　harvesting 명 채집, 수확
vanish 동 사라지다　severely 부 심각하게
reintroduce 동 다시 들여오다　roam 동 돌아다니다
reestablish 동 자리를 다시 찾다　optimum 형 최적의

1 지문의 단어 "constraints"와 의미가 가장 비슷한 것은?
(A) 목적
(B) 공동체
(C) 제한
(D) 절차

2 1단락에서 추론할 수 있는 것으로, 한 종의 구성원들은
(A) 한 가지 종류의 환경에서만 존재할 수 있다
(B) 정확히 같은 수의 유전자를 소유한다
(C) 건강할 때 더 큰 생물학적 차이를 보인다

(D) 번식 능력이 있는 새끼를 함께 생산할 수 있다

3 2단락에서 추론할 수 있는 것으로, 한 종은

(A) 단일한 개체군 집단으로 구성되면 멸종 위기에 처한다
(B) 다양한 특성을 가진 개체로 구성되면 멸종 위기에 처한다
(C) 다른 종에 의존하게 되면 멸종 위기에 처한다
(D) 너무 많은 유전적 다양성을 갖게 되면 멸종 위기에 처한다

4 지문의 단어 "their"가 가리키는 것은?

(A) 정착민들
(B) 동물
(C) 포식동물
(D) 회색늑대

5 지문에서 글쓴이는 왜 "the common bison"을 언급하는가?

(A) 매우 친숙한 야생동물의 예를 들기 위해
(B) 풍부한 한 종에 미친 유럽인의 영향 규모를 보여주기 위해
(C) 큰 개체군이 한 종의 생존을 도울 수 있다는 것을 설명하기 위해
(D) 유럽인들이 성공적으로 길들인 동물을 확인하기 위해

Reading Practice 2

본문 p.96

1 (C) 2 (A) 3 (B) 4 (D) 5 (A)

Vocabulary Quiz

1 ⓑ 2 ⓒ 3 ⓐ 4 ⓒ

시민권의 발전

시민권의 개념이 시대에 걸쳐 항상 그대로 유지되어온 것은 아니다. 그것은 처음에 고대 그리스에서 중요한 개념이 되었지만, 인구 내 작은 집단으로 제한되었다. 이 개념은 때때로 바뀌었다. 그러나, 인구의 나머지 사람들에게는 허락되지 않았던 권리와 특권들이 시민들에게만 허용된다는 기본 원칙은 계속 적용되었다.

[1]로마 제국 시기 동안, 시민권은 노예도 아니고 외국인도 아닌 모든 거주자들에게 주어졌다. 이탈리아 전체에서는 그 수가 약 70퍼센트였던 반면, 로마에서는 이것이 인구의 약 55퍼센트였다. 이 숫자는 이탈리아의 다른 곳보다 로마에 더 많은 노예와 외국 태생의 거주자들이 있었다는 사실을 반영한다. 이탈리아 밖의 로마 속주들에서는, 로마 시민권이 상당히 덜 흔했다. 속주들에서는 충성의 표시로 로마에 특별한 봉사를 한 특정 사람들만이 자신과 가족의 시민권을 얻었다.

현대의 거의 모든 국가의 법률은 출생 시 한 사람의 시민권을 결정할 때 두 가지 원칙을 따른다. [2]첫 번째 원칙인 '출생지주의'("땅의 권리")는 정해진 영토 내에서 태어난 모든 사람은 자동으로 그 영토의 시민이 된다고 명시하는데, 외국인 외교관의 자녀와 같은 몇몇 예외가 있다. 미국은 출생지주의 원칙을 사용하는 국가의 한 예이다. 그러나, 일부 국가들은 시민권을 두 번째 원칙인 '혈통주의'("혈통의 권리")에 기반한다. 이것은 아이가 어디에서 태어났건 그 혹은 그녀의 부모의 국적을 취득한다고 명시한다. 이 두 번째 원칙은 출생지보다는 혈통에 기초한다.

그러나, 이 원칙들 중 어느 것도 대부분의 국가에서 순수한 형태로 시행되지 않는다. 예를 들어, 캐나다 밖에서 태어난 아이는 출생 시 부모 중 한 명이 캐나다인이며 그 출생이 캐나다 당국에 정식으로 신고되면 캐나다 시민권을 가진다. 게다가, 많은 현대 국가들은 또한 출생이 아닌 이민에 기반을 둔 시민권 취득 경로를 가지고 있다. 이민자들은 외국에 거주를 신청할 수 있고, 일단 그곳에서 자격요건을 충족하면 시민권을 신청할 수 있다. [5B/5C]거주를 확립하는 일반적인 방법은 그 국가에 가족이나 고용 후원자를 갖는 것을 포함한다. [5D]또한, 학대나 전쟁과 같은 극단적인 상황에서 탈출한 난민들이 점점 더 외국으로 이주하고 있다.

citizenship 명 시민권, 시민의 자격 notion 명 개념, 관념
principle 명 원칙 privilege 명 특권 remainder 명 나머지
available 형 (자격이) 주어진 province 명 (로마의) 속주, 지방
considerably 부 상당히 extraordinary 형 특별한
loyalty 명 충성, 충성심 determination 명 결정, 결심
jus soli 출생지주의, 속지주의 automatically 부 자동으로
exception 명 예외 diplomat 명 외교관
base 동 ~에 기반하다 jus sanguinis 혈통주의, 속인주의
ancestry 명 혈통, 가계 authorities 명 당국 immigration 명 이민
residency 명 거주 apply for ~을 신청하다
meet the requirements 자격요건을 충족하다
refugee 명 난민, 망명자 extreme 형 극단적인, 극심한

1 2단락에서 추론할 수 있는 것으로, 로마 제국 시기의 시민권은

(A) 로마에 거주하는 외국인들이 취득할 수 있었다
(B) 로마 영토의 모든 거주자들에게 주어졌다
(C) 노예에게 주어지지 않았다
(D) 로마 속주에서는 허용되지 않았다

2 다음 중 3단락에서 미국에 관해 추론할 수 있는 것은?

(A) 외국인 외교관의 신생아에게 자동으로 시민권을 부여하지는 않는다.
(B) 최근에 혈통주의에서 출생지주의로 변경했다.
(C) 해외에서 태어난 자국민에게 이중 국적을 허용하지 않는다.
(D) 로마 제국의 시민권 모델을 기반으로 한다.

3 지문의 어구 "apply for"와 의미가 가장 비슷한 것은?

(A) 수반하다
(B) 요청하다
(C) 인지하다
(D) 얻다

4 4단락에서 글쓴이는 왜 캐나다에 관해 논하는가?

(A) 부모가 자녀의 출생을 신고할 필요성을 강조하기 위해
(B) 다른 국가들이 따라야 할 시민권 모델을 제안하기 위해
(C) 이민에 대한 특이한 접근법을 가진 국가를 강조하기 위해
(D) 국가들이 여러 시민권 원칙들을 따른다는 것을 보여주기 위해

5 다음 중 4단락에서 거주를 확립하는 방법으로 언급되지 않은 것은?

(A) 교육 기관에 다니기
(B) 그 국가에 친척이 있는 경우
(C) 그 국가에 고용 후원자가 있는 경우
(D) 심각한 상황으로부터의 피난처 찾기

Reading Practice 3

본문 p.98

1 (B) 2 (B) 3 (C) 4 (C) 5 (D)

Vocabulary Quiz

1 ⓒ 2 ⓐ 3 ⓑ 4 ⓒ

마르셀 뒤샹

현대 미술은 혁명에 기반을 두었고, 그것의 중심인물 중 한 사람은 프랑스 예술가 마르셀 뒤샹이었다. [2]뒤샹은 유럽과 미국을 오가며 대부분의 일생을 보냈는데, 이것은 그에게 인상주의, 입체파, 초현실주의와 같은 아방가르드 운동을 목격하게 해주었다. 이것은 그의 예술적 스타일과 예술이 무엇이 될 수 있는지에 대한 비전을 형성하는 데 도움을 주었다. 그가 20대 초반이 되었을 때, 그는 이미 그 자신만의 독특한 예술적 정체성을 발전시키기 시작했다. 이것은 현재 상태에 계속 도전하려는 그의 열망에 의해 정의되었다.

뒤샹은 제1차 세계대전의 참상과 그것에 관련된 다다이즘 운동에 크게 영향받았다. 다다이즘은 심미적 예술, 합리적 사고, 경제적 자본주의에 반대하고자 했는데, 그것의 추종자들은 갈등의 원인으로 그것들 모두를 비난했다. 그것은 유럽에서 시작했지만, 그것에 대한 뒤샹의 경험은 주로 뉴욕에서 일어났는데, 그곳에서 다다이즘 예술가들은 다다이즘의 발생지에서보다 확실히 덜 정치적이었다. 이는 오직 정치적 이유에서만이 아니라 대중의 취향과 수용의 한계를 시험할 목적으로 경계를 넓히는 것에 대한 뒤샹의 관심 증가에서 명백히 보인다.

그의 창의성과 대담함을 보여준 뒤샹의 최초의 작품은 '계단을 내려가는 나부'였다. 이 그림은 파블로 피카소와 조르주 브라크에 의해 발전된 입체파 기법에서 영감을 받았다. 그들처럼 뒤샹은 입체파 형태로 인물을 포착했다. [4]그러나, 그의 작품을 특징짓는 것은 대상의 역동적인 움직임의 명확한 느낌이었다. 비록 이 작품은 오늘날 높이 평가받지만, 당시 예술계는 그것에 대한 준비가 되어 있지 않았다. 특이한 것에 익숙한 파리 미술계에서조차 그것은 부정적인 반응을 불러일으켰다. 심지어 입체파 예술가들도 그것이 너무 초현대적이라고 거부했다.

아마도 더 충격적이었던 것은 뒤샹의 "레디메이드" 예술에서의 선구적인 활동이었을 것이다. 레디메이드 작품은 실생활에서 가져와 예술 작품으로 재사용된 제작물이었다. 뒤샹의 가장 유명한 레디메이드 작품인 '샘'은 그가 1917년의 한 예술 전시회에 익명으로 출품한 소변기였다. 장난처럼 보였을 것이 틀림없는 이 작품은 참가비를 낸 예술가를 거부할 수 없다는 이유만으로 받아들여졌다. [5]하지만, 그것은 결코 감상을 위한 전시장으로 옮겨지지 않았다. 일부 현대 비평가들은 그 원작이 단 한 장의 사진으로만 알려져 있다는 사실에도 불구하고 '샘'을 20세기의 가장 획기적인 예술 작품으로 간주한다.

be founded on ~에 기반을 두다 pivotal 형 중심의, 중추적인
avant-garde movement 아방가르드 운동 identity 명 정체성
challenge 동 도전하다 status quo 현재 상태, 현상 유지
Dada 다다이즘(20세기 초 예술 운동) protest 명 반대하다
aesthetic 형 심미적인, 미학적인 decidedly 부 확실히, 분명히
evident 형 명백한 exclusively 부 오직, 배타적으로
grounds 명 이유 demonstrate 동 보여주다, 입증하다
boldness 명 대담함 distinguish 동 특징짓다, 구분하다
be accustomed to ~에 익숙하다 unusual 형 특이한
futuristic 형 초현대적인, 시대를 앞서는
pioneering 형 선구적인, 개척적인 manufactured 형 제작된
urinal 명 소변기 anonymously 부 익명으로 practical joke 장난
groundbreaking 형 획기적인

1 지문의 단어 "pivotal"과 의미가 가장 비슷한 것은?
(A) 명백한
(B) 중심의
(C) 영향력 있는
(D) 사소한

2 1단락에 따르면, 다음 중 뒤샹의 여행에 관해 사실인 것은?
(A) 주로 그의 20대 초반에 일어났다.
(B) 그에게 많은 다양한 예술 운동을 소개했다.
(C) 그가 미술 공부를 연기하게 했다.
(D) 그가 정치적인 주제에 대한 관심을 발전시키도록 이끌었다.

3 지문에서 글쓴이는 왜 "New York"을 언급하는가?
(A) 뒤샹이 다다이즘의 발생지를 몰랐다는 것을 보여주기 위해
(B) 그 도시가 어떻게 다다이즘 예술의 중심이 되었는지 설명하기 위해
(C) 뒤샹이 유럽의 다다이즘 예술가들과 차별화되는 점을 강조하기 위해
(D) 다다이즘 운동이 유럽에 국한된 것이 아니었음을 강조하기 위해

4 피카소와 브라크의 대상에 관해 추론할 수 있는 것은?
(A) 동시대인들에게 이상하다고 여겨졌다.
(B) 마르셀 뒤샹에 의해 면밀히 복제되었다.
(C) 뒤샹의 작품 속 인물보다 더 정적으로 보였다.
(D) 대부분의 입체파의 것들보다 더 실물처럼 보였다.

5 다음 중 뒤샹의 '샘'에 관해 추론할 수 있는 것은?
(A) 예술가들의 대회에서 수상했다.
(B) 처음에 한 예술 전시회에서 포함되는 것이 거부되었다.
(C) 그것의 창작자는 뒤샹이 아닌 다른 사람이었을 것이다.
(D) 그것의 원래 형태는 대중에게 공개된 적이 없다.

Reading Practice 4

본문 p.100

1 (C) 2 (B) 3 (B) 4 (C) 5 (B)

Vocabulary Quiz

1 ⓐ 2 ⓒ 3 ⓑ 4 ⓑ

아메리카를 발견한 최초의 비원주민

역사가들이 아메리카의 발견을 논할 때, 그들은 일반적으로 아메리카 원주민이 아닌 탐험가들, 특히 대서양을 건너온 이들에 의한 이 땅들의 발견을 가리킨다. 전통적으로, 학교 교과서들은 크리스토퍼 콜럼버스가 최초의 발견자였다는 개념을 영속시켜 왔다. 콜럼버스는 1492년에 인도로 가는 서쪽 항로를 찾던 중 그 대륙을 우연히 발견했기 때문에 아메리카에 도달한 최초의 인물이었다. 오늘날 이 생각은 잘못된 주장으로 널리 인정되고 있지만, 아메리카 땅에 최초로 상륙한 비원주민에 대한 논쟁은 계속되고 있다.

콜럼버스 이전의 아메리카의 발견에 대한 가장 오래된 주장들 중 하나는 그 공을 고대 스칸디나비아인들에게 돌린다. 1800년대 후반에 처음 유행하게 된 이 가설은 원래 빈란드 영웅 전설에 기초했다. 이 영웅 전설은 구전에 기반을 둔 오래된 아이슬란드어 문헌이다. 지리, 토착 풍습, 천연자원에 대한 그 저자들의 묘사는 그들이 아메리카에 대

해 잘 알고 있었다는 것을 보여준다. [3]그러나 그것들이 그들이 묘사한 항해로부터 200년 이상이 지난 후에 기록되었기 때문에, 일부 전문가들은 여전히 회의적이었다. 이 회의론자들은 그것들의 정확성과 아메리카가 그 영웅 전설에서 묘사된 사람들의 목적지였는지에 대해 의심했다. 그럼에도 불구하고, 고고학적 연구들은 캐나다 뉴펀들랜드주에 고대 스칸디나비아인의 정착지가 세워졌다는 것을 확인했다. 그것은 콜럼버스의 항해 훨씬 전인 서기 1000년으로 거슬러 올라간다.

보다 최근의 이론은 대서양 횡단 접근의 연대를 훨씬 더 일찍으로 추정한다. 일부 고고학자들은 2,500년 전에 이미 아프리카인들이 아메리카로 여행했다고 주장한다. [4A]이 관점의 지지자들은 메소아메리카의 조각상들이 외부에서 들여온 디자인을 보여주는 아프리카의 특징들을 가지고 있다고 강조한다. [4D]유사하게, 그들은 마야와 아즈텍 문화의 피라미드가 북아프리카에 위치한 이집트에서 들여온 피라미드 건축 지식을 반영한다고 추정한다. 이 이론을 뒷받침하는 추가적인 물질적 증거는 아메리카가 아닌 이집트에서 온 것이다. [4B]1990년대 몇몇 이집트 미라의 발굴과 분석 후에, 독일의 한 독물학자가 코카인과 니코틴의 존재를 발견했다. 이 두 약물은 모두 아메리카의 식물에서만 생산되는 것으로 알려져 있기 때문에, 전문가들은 그것들이 아메리카에서 이집트로 반입되었다고 추정했다. 게다가, 메소아메리카의 구전은 아메리카에 있는 검은 피부를 가진 사람들을 분명하게 언급한다. [5]증거가 늘어감에 따라, 이전 세대의 역사가들이 고대 아프리카인들의 해양 항해 능력을 크게 과소평가했다는 것이 더욱 분명해진다.

typically 🅟 일반적으로　refer to ~을 가리키다, 언급하다
perpetuate 🅢 영속시키다　stumble across ~을 우연히 발견하다
acknowledge 🅢 인정하다　the Norse 고대 스칸디나비아인
hypothesis 🅜 가설　fashionable 🅗 유행하는
saga 🅜 (중세 북유럽의) 영웅 전설　oral tradition 구전
knowledgeable 🅗 잘 알고 있는　skeptical 🅗 회의적인
destination 🅜 목적지　archaeological 🅗 고고학적인
proponent 🅜 지지자　presume 🅢 추정하다, 간주하다
excavation 🅜 발굴　toxicologist 🅜 독물학자
narcotics 🅜 (마취성의) 약물, 마약　deduce 🅢 추정하다, 추론하다
mount 🅢 늘다, 증가하다　underestimate 🅢 과소평가하다

1 지문의 단어 "those"가 가리키는 것은?
(A) 역사가들
(B) 땅들
(C) 탐험가들
(D) 아메리카 원주민

2 지문의 단어 "perpetuated"와 의미가 가장 비슷한 것은?
(A) 거부했다
(B) 유지했다
(C) 제안했다
(D) 증명했다

3 빈란드 영웅 전설을 기록한 사람들에 관해 추론할 수 있는 것은?
(A) 여행 중에 아메리카의 지리를 기록했다.
(B) 그들이 서술한 여행을 직접 경험하지 못했다.
(C) 캐나다에 있는 고대 스칸디나비아인의 정착지의 존재를 증명했다.
(D) 고고학적 증거를 반박하는 자료를 포함했다.

4 다음 중 아프리카인들의 대서양 횡단 이론을 뒷받침하는 것으로 언급되지 않은 것은?
(A) 아프리카의 특징들을 가진 조각상
(B) 고대 이집트 내 아메리카 약물의 존재
(C) 메소아메리카 구전 속 이집트에 대한 묘사
(D) 고대 이집트의 건축학적 영향

5 3단락에서 이전 세대의 역사학자들에 관해 추론할 수 있는 것은?
(A) 마야인과 아즈텍인이 이집트에서 아메리카로 왔다고 추정했다.
(B) 고대 아프리카 선원들에게 아메리카에 도달할 능력이 있었다는 것을 믿지 않았다.
(C) 스페인 탐험가들이 피라미드에 대해 알고 있었다는 것을 알지 못했다.
(D) 미라 분석의 독성학 결과가 거짓이라고 결론지었다.

iBT Reading Test

본문 p.102

1 (D)　2 (D)　3 (A)　4 (B)
5 (D)　6 (B)　7 (C)　8 (C)
9 (A)　10 (C), (D), (F)

농약의 해로운 영향

농약은 해충을 통제, 박멸 혹은 퇴치하기 위한 모든 물질이다. [2A/2B/2C]세 가지 일반적인 종류의 농약이 있는데, 제초제, 살충제, 살진균제는 각각 잡초, 곤충, 균류를 죽이기 위해 고안되었다. 농약은 한때 기아에 대한 기적의 해결책으로 여겨졌는데, 그 해결책은 농작물에 해충이 생기지 않게 하는 것이었다. 과학자들은 오늘날 이러한 화학 물질들이 사람들에게서 면역 체계 문제, 생식 질환, 선천성 기형 및 더 높은 암 발병률을 초래하고 있다고 우려한다. 지난 50년 동안 20만 개 이상의 화학적 농약이 환경에 유입되었고, 대부분의 사람들은 있으면 안 되는 합성 산업 화학 물질들을 적어도 250가지 이상 체내에 갖고 있다.

이 화학 물질들 중 일부는 20년 전에 미국에서 금지되었지만, 그것들은 여전히 슈퍼마켓의 농산물에서 나타난다. 약 99퍼센트의 농약이 의도된 목표물을 빗나가 주변 환경으로 침투한다. [6]그곳에서, 그 화학 물질들은 물의 흐름, 기류, 또는 먹이 그물을 통한 오랜 여정을 시작할 수 있고, 이것들은 몇 달 동안 지속되어 원래 위치에서 수천 마일 떨어진 곳에서 끝날 수 있다. 이 흩어진 오염 물질의 대부분은 사람에게 즉각적인 영향을 미칠 만큼 충분히 강하지 않지만, 야생 동물을 이러한 오염 물질의 주요 희생자로 만든다. 농약 사용의 증가에도 불구하고, 곤충의 피해로 인한 농작물 손실은 실제로 지난 50년 동안 두 배가 되었다. [5]곤충은 돌연변이를 통해 적응하고 있으며, 이 화학 물질들은 의도치 않게 이러한 곤충의 천적을 죽여서 생태계의 자연 균형과 다양성에 영향을 미치고 있다.

많은 농약은 내분비 교란 물질로서 작용하여, 야생 동물의 호르몬 구성을 변화시키고 행동 및 해부학적으로 그것들에 부정적으로 영향을 미친다. **이 현상은 해양이나 담수 서식지에서 사는 종들 사이에서 흔히 관찰된다.** 여러 갈매기 종에서의 행동 이상이 언급되었고, 흰돌고래에서 면역 억제가 발견되었다. 악어, 바다표범, 악어거북, 서부갈매기에서 생식 문제가 발견되었다. 무지개송어는 미성숙한 생식 기관을 갖고 나타났으며, 서부갈매기와 청어갈매기 각각은 양성의 짝짓기 행동을 보이는 것이 관찰되었다. 1995년에, 미네소타주의 십 대 아이들은 다리가 여섯 개까지 달린 개구리를 발견했는데, 가능성 있는 원인으로 화학적 독소가 언급되어 왔다. [8]전반적으로, 농약이 인간과 야생 동물의 건강에 똑같이 영향을 미치고 있는 것은 분명하지만, 이 문제에 대한 해결책은 불분명하고 전 세계적인 이해와 협력이 필요하다.

pesticide 명 농약, 살충제 repel 동 퇴치하다 herbicide 명 제초제
insecticide 명 살충제 fungicide 명 살진균제, 곰팡이 제거제
respectively 부 각각 chemical 명 화학 물질
immune system 면역 체계 reproductive 형 생식의
ailment 명 질환 birth defects 선천성 기형 synthetic 형 합성의
crop up 나타나다, 발생하다 produce 명 농산물
embark upon ~을 시작하다, 착수하다 dispersed 형 흩어진, 분산된
contaminant 명 오염 물질 adapt 동 적응하다
mutation 명 돌연변이 inadvertently 부 의도치 않게, 무심코
natural predator 천적 endocrine disrupter 내분비 교란 물질
anatomically 부 해부학적으로 abnormality 명 이상, 기형
immune suppression 면역 억제 rudimentary 형 미성숙한, 기초적인
exhibit 동 보이다, 드러내다 toxin 명 독소

1 지문의 단어 "synthetic"과 의미가 가장 비슷한 것은?
(A) 위험한
(B) 불가사의한
(C) 참신한
(D) 인공의

2 1단락에 따르면, 다음 중 농약의 의도된 목표물이 아닌 것은?
(A) 잡초
(B) 곤충
(C) 균류
(D) 화학 물질들

3 지문의 단어 "these"가 가리키는 것은?
(A) 오랜 여정
(B) 물의 흐름
(C) 기류
(D) 먹이 그물

4 지문의 단어 "inadvertently"와 의미가 가장 비슷한 것은?
(A) 고의로
(B) 우연히
(C) 의도적으로
(D) 불행하게도

5 다음 중 2단락에서 곤충에 관해 추론할 수 있는 것은?
(A) 생태계를 균형되게 유지하는 데 더 중요한 역할을 하고 있다.
(B) 남아있는 천적이 없음에 따라 돌연변이하고 있다.
(C) 새로운 화학물질의 개발로 이어지고 있다.
(D) 농약에 대한 내성이 더 강해지고 있다.

6 2단락에 따르면, 다음 중 환경에 유입되는 농약에 관해 사실인 것은?
(A) 장기간의 사용 이후에만 효과가 있다.
(B) 자연적인 경로를 통해 이동할 수 있다.
(C) 야생 동물에게 영향을 줄 만큼 충분히 강하지 않다.
(D) 잡초와 곤충을 효과적으로 죽일 수 있다.

7 지문의 단어 "exhibiting"과 의미가 가장 비슷한 것은?
(A) 가리는
(B) 억누르는
(C) 표현하는
(D) 제한하는

8 3단락에서 추론할 수 있는 것으로, 농약의 사용으로 인한 문제는
(A) 지구의 특정 지역에만 영향을 준다
(B) 점점 덜 심각해지고 있다
(C) 곧 해결될 가능성이 낮다
(D) 사람보다 야생 동물에 더 큰 영향을 끼친다

9 네 개의 네모[■]는 다음 문장이 삽입될 수 있는 곳을 나타내고 있다.
이 현상은 해양이나 담수 서식지에서 사는 종들 사이에서 흔히 관찰된다.
이 문장은 어디에 들어가는 것이 가장 적절한가?

10 **지시:** 지문 요약을 위한 도입 문장이 아래에 주어져 있다. 지문의 가장 중요한 내용을 나타내는 보기 3개를 골라 요약을 완성하라. 어떤 문장은 지문에 언급되지 않은 내용이나 사소한 정보를 나타내므로 요약에 포함되지 않는다. **이 문제는 2점이다.**

한때 혁신적인 농업 도구로 여겨졌던 농약은 환경에 해롭다는 것이 증명되었다.
· (C) 농약은 인간의 많은 건강 문제와 관련되어 왔다.
· (D) 대부분의 농약이 의도치 않게 주변의 생태계로 유입된다.
· (F) 농약은 야생 동물에서 비정상적인 행동과 해부적 구조를 초래했다.

(A) 농업에 사용되는 농약의 적은 비율이 물과 토양으로 들어간다.
(B) 농약 사용의 증가는 곤충의 피해로 인한 더 적은 농작물 손실로 이어졌다.
(E) 동물의 행동 변화 중 일부는 농약 노출의 부정적인 결과보다는 자연적인 적응인 것으로 보인다.

Vocabulary Review
본문 p.106

1 demonstrate		2 optimum	3 privilege
4 exceptions		5 ubiquitous	6 underestimate
7 (C)	8 (A)	9 (C)	10 (C)
11 (C)	12 (B)	13 (A)	14 (D)

CHAPTER 07
Rhetorical Purpose

Example
본문 p.109

1 (C) 2 (D)

지진 발생지 알아내기

지진은 기상학자들이 폭풍을 촬영할 수 있는 방법으로 촬영될 수 없는 요란이다. 지진은 지구 내부의 깊은 곳에서 발생하며 느껴질 수 있을 뿐이다. 따라서, 지진의 위치를 파악하는 것은 특수한 장비를 필요로 한다. 지진은 지면의 운동을 증폭하고 기록하는 지진계 망을 통해 관측될 수 있다. 지진의 발생은 지진의 진원, 즉 진원지에서 초당 수 킬로미

터의 속도로 퍼지는 파면을 발생시킨다. 파면이 진원에서 퍼지면서, 그것은 멀리 떨어져 있는 지진 관측소에 도달한다.

지진학자들은 지진의 위치와 발생 시간을 알아내기 위해 간단한 절차를 사용한다. 그들은 지진파가 관측소에 도착하는 시간을 기록하기 위해 지진계를 사용해서 이 정보를 얻는다. 이 절차는 처음에는 추측을 필요로 하는데, 위치와 발생 시간이 추정된 다음, 이 정보가 관측소에서 관측된 지진파의 도착 시간과 비교된다. 그런 다음, 지진파가 관측소에 도달하기 위해 이동한 속도 및 거리와 일치하는, 가능성이 있는 지진 위치가 파악될 때까지 일련의 계산이 수행된다.

disturbance 명 요란(가벼운 지각 변동), 소란, 방해
meteorologist 명 기상학자 hence 부 따라서, 그러므로
locate 동 ~의 위치를 파악하다 equipment 명 장비
observe 동 관측하다, 관찰하다 seismograph 명 지진계
amplify 동 (전류 등을) 증폭하다 occurrence 명 발생
generate 동 발생시키다 wave front 파면(파동의 연속적인 면)
hypocenter 명 (지진의) 진원 focus 명 진원지
seismic station 지진 관측소 procedure 명 절차
seismic wave 지진파 call for ~을 필요로 하다, 요구하다
guesswork 명 추측, 짐작 consistent 형 일치하는

1 1단락에서 글쓴이는 왜 기상학자들에 의한 폭풍 촬영을 언급하는가?
(A) 지진이 얼마나 깊은 지구 내부에서 발생할 수 있는지를 강조하기 위해
(B) 지진 측정을 위한 장비가 어떻게 생겨났는지 설명하기 위해
(C) 지진의 위치를 파악하는 데 사용되는 방법을 대조하기 위해
(D) 지진학과 기상학 사이의 연관성을 보여주기 위해

2 2단락에서 글쓴이는 왜 "guesswork"를 언급하는가?
(A) 지진학자들이 지진의 위치를 파악하는 방법을 확신하지 못한다는 것을 지적하기 위해
(B) 일반 사람들과 지진학자들이 지진의 위치를 파악하는 방법을 비교하기 위해
(C) 지진이 발생하는 장소를 파악하기 위한 구식의 방법을 설명하기 위해
(D) 지진의 위치를 알아내는 초기 단계를 설명하기 위해

Reading Practice 1

본문 p.110

1 (C) 2 (A) 3 (D) 4 (C), (D) 5 (B)

Vocabulary Quiz

1 ⓑ 2 ⓐ 3 ⓑ 4 ⓒ

모아 멸종

모아는 한때 뉴질랜드에서 번성했던 날지 못하는 큰 새였다. 그것들은 외면적으로 에뮤와 타조와 닮았지만, 일부는 훨씬 더 크게 자랄 수 있었고 실제 날개가 있는 것은 없었다. 인간의 등장 이전의 그것들의 수에 대한 추정치는 다양한데, 과학자들은 대략 6만에서 2백만 마리 이상의 개체가 한때 존재했다고 제시한다. 약 600년 전에 9종의 모아가 모두 멸종했기 때문에, 현재 그것들은 박물관에 있는 몇 개의 뼈와 화석화된 알들을 통해서만 알려져 있다. 3A/3B전통적으로, 과학자들은 기후 변동과 화산 폭발과 같은 요인들이 그 새의 멸종의 원인이 되었는지에 대해 논쟁했다. 3C그러나, 현재의 일치된 의견은 인간이 그것들의 멸종에 일차적으로 책임이 있다는 것이다.

마오리족으로 알려진 폴리네시아인들이 뉴질랜드를 발견했을 때, 모아는 그 섬에서 가장 큰 육지 동물이자 지배적인 초식 동물이었다. 그것들의 유일한 포식자는 하스트독수리였는데, 그것들은 먹잇감으로 모아에 의존했다. 그 외에는 모아는 천적으로부터 비교적 자유로웠다. 그러나, 이것은 그것들에게 자연적 취약성이 없었다는 것을 의미하지는 않는다. 4C예를 들어, 그것들의 거대한 알은 지금까지의 모든 새들 중에서 가장 컸다. 4D하지만, 달걀보다 80배나 더 컸음에도 불구하고, 그것들은 훨씬 더 깨지기 쉬웠다. 그리고 암컷 모아는 한 번에 하나의 알만 낳았기 때문에, 한 개의 깨진 알은 중대한 손실을 의미했다. 게다가, 새로 부화한 모아는 성숙기에 도달하는 데 거의 10년이 걸려서, 모아의 개체군은 전반적으로 번식률이 낮았다.

하지만, 인간의 등장 이전에 모아는 살아남았을 뿐만 아니라 번성했다. 유전 연구는 마지막 개체군이 유전적으로 다양했다는 것을 보여주는데, 이는 강한 생물학적 적합성의 표시이다. 아마도 더 중요한 것은, 마오리족의 구전에 따르면, 모아는 한때 수가 많았으며 그들의 조상에게 중요한 음식 공급원이었다는 것이다. 5그들의 많은 속담들 또한 하스트독수리의 멸종과 더불어 그것의 멸종을 언급한다. 모아가 마오리족에 의해 멸종 위기까지 사냥당하였다는 증거가 뉴질랜드 전역의 수많은 고고학적 유적지에서 발견되었다. 그것들의 고기는 섭취되었고, 깃털과 가죽은 옷으로 만들어졌으며, 뼈는 낚싯바늘과 장신구로 만들어졌다. 마오리족이 알을 훔치고 모아가 살던 숲을 불태웠을 때 그 멸종은 앞당겨졌다. 인간이 정착한 지 200년 만에 모아는 영원히 사라졌다.

flightless 형 날지 못하는 thrive 동 번성하다, 잘 자라다
superficially 부 외면적으로 resemble 동 닮다, 비슷하다
fossilized 형 화석화된 die out 멸종하다 fluctuation 명 변동
demise 명 멸종, 소멸 consensus 명 일치된 의견
extinction 명 멸종 herbivore 명 초식동물 relatively 부 비교적
vulnerability 명 취약성 be prone to ~하기 쉽다
hatch 동 부화하다 maturity 명 성숙기 reproductive 형 번식의
diverse 형 다양한 fitness 명 적합성 archaeological 형 고고학적인
hasten 동 앞당기다 vanish 동 사라지다

1 글쓴이는 왜 "a few skeletons and fossilized eggs"를 언급하는가?
(A) 모아의 행동에 대해 알려진 것이 거의 없다는 것을 암시하기 위해
(B) 모아의 원래 수를 확인하는 것이 가능하지 않다는 것을 보여주기 위해
(C) 오늘날 살아 있는 모아 표본이 남아 있지 않다는 것을 강조하기 위해
(D) 과학자들이 모아의 생김새에 관해 어떻게 알게 되었는지를 나타내기 위해

2 지문의 단어 "demise"와 의미가 가장 비슷한 것은?
(A) 멸종
(B) 감소
(C) 진화
(D) 출발

3 1단락에 따르면, 다음 중 모아의 멸종 이유로 제시되지 않은 것은?
(A) 기후 변화
(B) 화산 폭발
(C) 인간 활동

(D) 초식 동물과의 경쟁

4 2단락에 따르면, 모아 알의 두 가지 특징은? 두 개의 정답을 고르시오.

(A) 포식자로부터 지속적인 보호가 필요했다.
(B) 부화하는 데 유난히 오랜 시간이 걸렸다.
(C) 역사상 모든 새들 중에서 가장 컸다.
(D) 달걀보다 훨씬 더 깨지기 쉬웠다.

5 다음 중 3단락에서 하스트독수리에 관해 추론할 수 있는 것은?

(A) 마오리족의 속담에 언급된 적이 없다.
(B) 마오리족 활동의 간접적인 결과로 멸종했다.
(C) 마오리족에 의해 사육되었다.
(D) 다양한 다른 생물을 잡아먹었다.

Reading Practice 2

본문 p.112

1 (D) 2 (B) 3 (C) 4 (A) 5 (A)

Vocabulary Quiz

1 ⓑ 2 ⓐ 3 ⓑ 4 ⓑ

북아메리카 암각화

암각화는 수천 년 동안 행해져 온 암석 미술의 한 형태이다. [1A]암각화는 암벽화와 구별되는데, 전자가 암석 표면에 새겨져 있는 반면, 후자는 암석 표면 위에 그려져 있다는 점에서 그러하다. [1B]그 조각은 돌로 된 끌을 이용하여 만들어졌는데, 그것은 맨 위층 아래에 있는 암석의 대비되는 색상을 드러내기 위해 돌을 긁어낸다. [1C]암각화는 씻겨질 수 없기 때문에 매우 오래 지속된다. 전 세계에 암각화가 있지만, 북아메리카에는 이 고대 미술 형식의 특히 주목할 만한 표본들이 있다.

북아메리카에서 가장 오래된 것으로 알려진 암각화는 10,000년에서 14,800년 전에 네바다주의 리노에서 새겨졌다. 이 암각화는 거대한 바위 더미에 새겨진 나무 같은 모양과 함께 원과 다이아몬드 같은 기하학적인 무늬들로 구성되어 있다. 2013년에 과학자들에 의해 이 고대 무늬들의 연대가 측정되었을 때, 그 결과는 놀라웠는데, 북아메리카 최초의 인류가 약 14,000년 전에 도착했다고 생각되어 왔기 때문이다. 이 예술 작품은 그 대륙 내 인간 등장에 관한 이전 최선의 추정치가 부정확할 수도 있다는 것을 나타내는 것으로 보인다. 암각화는 북아메리카의 최초 거주민들이 남긴 유일한 예술 작품들 중 하나일 수 있다.

또 다른 주목할 만한 암석 미술의 모음은 뉴멕시코주의 앨버커키에 있는 암각화 국립 기념물에서 찾을 수 있다. 이 기념물의 경계 안에는 24,000여 점의 그림들이 새겨져 있다. 그것들 대부분은 서기 1300년 이후에 끌로 새겨졌을 가능성이 높지만, 일부는 기원전 2000년까지 거슬러 올라갈 수 있다. 비록 뉴멕시코주의 초기 스페인 정착민 중 일부가 1700년대부터 새긴 무늬를 추가했지만, 예술가들은 대부분 고대 푸에블로인들이었다. [5]스페인인의 영향이 1680년 이후 암각화 제작 관행을 종식시켰을 수도 있는데, 이는 가톨릭 사제들이 푸에블로인들로 하여금 암각화가 제작될 가능성이 높은 종류의 전통 의식에 참여하지 못하게 했기 때문이다. 그럼에도 불구하고, 동물, 사람, 별, 나선형, 기하학적 형태에 대한 이러한 묘사는 푸에블로인들의 사회적 관습과 종교의식의 측면을 반영하며, 그것들은 그들의 문화에 대한 귀중한 기록으로서 기능한다.

petroglyph 명 암각화 distinct 형 구별되는 pictograph 명 암벽화
chisel 명 끌; 동 끌로 새기다 uncover 동 드러내다
contrasting 형 대비되는 specimen 명 표본, 견본
geometric 형 기하학적인 boulder 명 바위 astounding 형 놀라운
estimate 명 추정치 inaccurate 형 부정확한 inhabitant 명 거주민
terminate 동 종식시키다, 끝내다 discourage 동 ~을 못하게 하다
engage in ~에 참여하다 spiral 명 나선형 religious rite 종교의식

1 다음 중 1단락에서, 글쓴이가 암각화에 관해 묘사하지 않는 것은?

(A) 그것들과 다른 형태의 암석 미술의 차이
(B) 암석 무늬를 새기는 데 사용되는 도구
(C) 그것들이 수천 년을 견디는 이유
(D) 고대의 새긴 무늬에 묘사된 그림 유형

2 지문의 단어 "astounding"과 의미가 가장 비슷한 것은?

(A) 만족스러운
(B) 충격적인
(C) 설득력 있는
(D) 주목할 만한

3 2단락에서 글쓴이는 왜 리노 암각화가 제작된 연대에 관해 논하는가?

(A) 이 작품들의 오랜 시대와 보다 최근의 암각화를 대조하기 위해
(B) 리노 암각화가 세계 최초의 암각화라는 증거를 제공하기 위해
(C) 암각화가 북아메리카 내 인간의 등장 시기에 대한 추정치에 이의를 제기했음을 강조하기 위해
(D) 리노 암각화의 연대를 측정하는 데 사용된 방법의 정확성에 의문을 제기하기 위해

4 지문의 단어 "they"가 가리키는 것은?

(A) 묘사
(B) 측면
(C) 관습
(D) 의식

5 3단락에서 추론할 수 있는 것으로, 스페인인들이 푸에블로인의 의식을 하지 못하게 한 것은

(A) 그 의식이 가톨릭 신앙과 충돌한다고 여겨졌기 때문이다
(B) 그들에 대한 전쟁을 계획하는 데 그 의식이 이용되는 것을 스페인인들이 두려워했기 때문이다
(C) 스페인인들이 암각화를 만드는 유일한 집단이 되기를 원했기 때문이다
(D) 그 의식이 스페인 정착민들에게 공공연하게 적대적이었기 때문이다

Reading Practice 3

본문 p.114

1 (B) 2 (D) 3 (A) 4 (B) 5 (C)

Vocabulary Quiz

1 ⓐ 2 ⓒ 3 ⓐ 4 ⓒ

유아의 대상 영속성

아기들은 자기 보고를 할 수 없기 때문에 유아의 심리적 특성을 연구하는 것은 성인에게서 동일한 특성을 연구하는 것보다 명백히 더 어렵

다. 연구자는 부모가 아직 말을 못 하는 아이의 생각과 감정을 해석하려고 시도할 때 직면하는 것과 같은 딜레마에 직면한다. 즉, 유아는 자신이 생각하는 것을 말할 수 없다. 따라서, 유아 행동이나 정신 작용에 대한 오래되고 충분히 검증된 이론조차도 비판의 대상이 될 수 있다. 1954년의 인지 발달 이론의 핵심 측면인, 장 피아제의 유명한 대상 영속성 개념이 그러한 경우이다.

아기와 놀면서 시간을 보내본 사람들은 사물이 사라지면 어린 유아가 자연스럽게 슬퍼한다는 것을 알고 있다. "까꿍 놀이" 또는 "이제 보이지만, 이제 안 보이지" 게임은 피아제가 관찰했던 정신적 취약을 증명하는 것이다. 그는 그것들이 아이의 시야를 벗어나면 신생아들은 그 사물들이 존재하는 것을 멈추지 않는다는 것을 깨닫지 못한다고 의심했다. 몇 개월의 기간이 지나야 어린아이는 사물이 시야에서 사라져도 영속한다는 것을 깨닫는 데 필요한 '스키마'(지식의 기본 단위)를 발전시킨다.

피아제는 대상 영속성에 관한 유아의 능력을 실험하기 위한 꽤 간단한 방법을 가지고 있었다. 그는 아기의 시선에 장난감을 둔 다음에 그것을 숨겼다. 그런 다음 그는 장난감이 사라진 것처럼 보이는 것에 대한 그 아이의 반응을 관찰하고 기록했다. [4]만약 아이가 없어진 장난감을 찾는다면, 피아제는 그 아이가 대상 영속성에 대한 이해를 습득했다고 가정했다. 반면에, 아이가 잃어버린 사물에 대해 속상해한다면, 그는 이 중요한 발달의 단계가 아직 달성되지 않았다고 가정했다.

피아제의 결론에 대한 비평가들은 그가 아주 어린 유아의 정신 능력을 과소평가했다고 주장했다. [5A]그들은 겉보기에는 부재한 사물의 지속적인 존재를 인식하지 못한 유아가 단지 그 사물에 대한 탐색을 시작하기에 운동 신경이 부족한 것일지도 모른다고 지적했다. [5D]아니면 아마도 그들의 기억력이 탐색을 했던 아이들의 기억력만큼 잘 발달되지 않았을지도 모른다. [5B]심지어 장난감에 대한 관심 부족이 문제였을 가능성도 있다. 다시 말해, 모든 유아의 정신 속에 대상 영속성이 존재할 수 있지만 특정 변수에 의해 숨겨질 수 있다. 오늘날 연구자들은 이러한 취약점을 바로잡기 위한 새로운 실험을 고안하고 있지만, 불가피한 사실은 유아가 연구하기 어렵다는 것이다.

object permanence 대상 영속성　characteristic 명특성
obviously 부명백히, 분명히　challenging 형어려운
self-report 동자기 보고를 하다　attempt to ~하려고 시도하다
preverbal 형아직 말을 못 하는　abundantly 부충분히, 매우
criticism 명비판, 비난　cognitive 형인지의
distressed 형슬퍼하는, 괴로워하는　demonstration 명증명, 입증
deficit 명취약, 부족　cease 동멈추다　assume 동가정하다
pivotal 형중요한　milestone 명(중요한) 단계　attain 동달성하다
seemingly 부겉보기에는　absent 형부재한
insufficient 형부족한, 불충분한　motor skills 운동 신경, 운동 기능
variable 명변수　vulnerability 명취약점
unavoidable 형불가피한, 피할 수 없는

1 1단락에서 글쓴이는 왜 "parents"를 언급하는가?
(A) 사람들이 심리학자들이 할 수 있는 것보다 그들의 자녀를 더 잘 안다고 시사하기 위해
(B) 아기들을 이해하기 위한 고된 노력의 보편성을 보여주기 위해
(C) 피아제가 그가 연구한 아이들과 타고난 유대감을 가졌다는 것을 암시하기 위해
(D) 성인들도 때때로 대상 영속성이 부족하다고 주장하기 위해

2 지문의 단어 "they"가 가리키는 것은?
(A) 게임
(B) 증명
(C) 신생아들
(D) 사물들

3 지문의 단어 "attained"와 의미가 가장 비슷한 것은?
(A) 달성되다
(B) 보증되다
(C) 승인되지 않다
(D) 확인되다

4 3단락에 따르면, 피아제가 아이가 대상 영속성을 갖고 있다는 증거로 믿었던 것은?
(A) 장난감 분실에 대한 부정적인 감정 반응
(B) 갑자기 없어진 사물을 찾기 위한 노력
(C) 방금 획득한 사물을 숨기려는 시도
(D) 연구자의 기대에 대한 명확한 이해

5 4단락에 따르면, 다음 중 유아의 대상 영속성 결여를 설명하지 않는 것은?
(A) 신체 조정 능력의 부족
(B) 사라진 물건에 대한 무관심
(C) 신체 움직임을 제한하는 과잉 자극
(D) 없어진 장난감을 기억하지 못하는 것

Reading Practice 4

본문 p.116

1 (C)　2 (B)　3 (B)　4 (D)　5 (A)

Vocabulary Quiz

1 ⓑ　2 ⓑ　3 ⓒ　4 ⓑ

폼페이 발굴

서기 79년 베수비오 산의 폭발 이후, 폼페이의 도시는 말 그대로 사라져 버렸다. 세월이 흐르면서, 그 지역은 '키비타스' 또는 그 도시라고 알려지게 되었다. 따라서, 그곳 도시의 존재가 결코 완전히 잊히지는 않았다. 하지만, 폼페이의 문화적, 경제적 중요성과 심지어 그것의 이름은 그러했다. 현지인들조차도 고대 로마의 생활 방식이 그 표면 아래에 보존되어 왔다는 것을 깨닫지 못했다. 일련의 발굴이 폼페이를 다시 한 번 드러낼 때까지 그 유적은 수 세기 동안 대체로 온전히 남아 있었다.

폼페이의 첫 번째 주요 재발견은 1592년에 우연히 일어났다. 도메니코 폰타나라는 이름의 한 이탈리아 건축가가 그 지역에 지하 수로를 건설하던 중에, 그는 그림과 비문이 있는 고대 벽을 발견했다. 이후 몇 년 동안 일부 작업이 진행되었으나, 1631년에 파괴적인 지진이 진행을 중단시켰다. 1680년대에, 'Decurio Pompeiis'(폼페이의 시의원)라는 문구가 새겨진 돌의 발견은 로마 황제 폼페이우스를 가리키는 것으로 잘못 믿어졌다. [3]그 후, 1699년에 이탈리아 고고학자 주세페 마크리니는 그 유적지가 사실은 폼페이라고 주장했지만, 그의 주장은 대체로 회의적으로 받아들여졌다. 1763년이 되어서야 폰타나가 무엇을 발견했는지 확실히 알게 되었다. 1763년에, 고고학 발굴이 그 고대 도시의 이름이 폼페이라는 것을 분명히 확인할 수 있는 비문을 발견했다.

초기 발굴 중 많은 부분은 폼페이에 대해 거의 밝혀내지 못했다. 스페인의 카를로스 3세는 한때 그의 궁전을 장식할 고대 유물을 찾기 위해

잔해의 제거를 명령했다. 그러나, 금이나 귀중품이 발견되지 않자, 그 구덩이는 메워져 내버려 졌다. [4]이러한 유형의 보물찾기는 일반적이었고 상당한 피해를 입혔다. 심지어 고고학의 아버지라고 불리는 빙켈만과 칼 베버의 발굴조차 엉망진창으로 만드는 것을 피하지는 못했다. 하지만, 베버는 대리석 기둥과 제단이 있는 예배 장소인 포르투나 아우구스타 신전을 발견했다.

1800년대와 1900년대에는, 발굴이 더 신중하고 체계적이 되었다. 그것들은 일상에 대한 놀라울 정도로 상세한 정보들을 밝혀냈고 폼페이가 번영하는 도시였다는 것을 보여주었다. 그곳은 부자들이 사는 곳이었고, 여가와 오락 시설이 많은 곳이었다. [5B/5C/5D]검투사 싸움과 다른 대회를 위한 2만 명의 관중을 수용할 수 있었던 경기장, 희극과 비극이 공연된 극장, 수많은 공중 및 개인 목욕탕의 존재로 증명된다.

eruption 명 (화산의) 폭발, 분화　literally 부 말 그대로, 문자 그대로
existence 명 존재　significance 명 중요성　locals 명 현지인, 주민
preserve 동 보존하다　remains 명 유적　intact 형 온전한
excavation 명 발굴　by accident 우연히, 뜻밖에
aqueduct 명 수로　inscription 명 비문, 새겨진 것
halt 동 중단시키다　inscribe 동 새기다　councillor 명 시의원
skepticism 명 회의, 의심　with certainty 확실히
archaeological 형 고고학적인　debris 명 잔해, 쓰레기
artifact 명 유물　valuables 명 귀중품　typical 형 일반적인
substantial 형 상당한　unearth 동 밝혀내다
evidence 동 (증거로) 증명하다　spectator 명 관중

1 지문에서 글쓴이는 왜 "*Civitas*"를 언급하는가?

(A) 폼페이가 문화적 및 경제적으로 중요했다는 것을 보여주기 위해
(B) 지역 주민들이 폼페이의 생활 방식에 익숙했다는 것을 암시하기 위해
(C) 폼페이의 이름이 잊혔다는 것을 강조하기 위해
(D) 수 세기 동안 발굴이 이루어지지 않은 이유를 설명하기 위해

2 지문의 단어 "halted"와 의미가 가장 비슷한 것은?

(A) 줄였다
(B) 중지했다
(C) 재촉했다
(D) 수정했다

3 2단락에서 이탈리아 고고학자 주세페 마크리니에 관해 추론할 수 있는 것은?

(A) 수로의 건설에 참여했다.
(B) 그의 폼페이에 대한 주장의 증거는 결정적이지 않았다.
(C) 그의 발굴은 중요한 비문이 새겨진 돌을 드러냈다.
(D) 다른 전문가들이 폼페이의 유적지를 조사하도록 영감을 주었다.

4 3단락에 따르면, 다음 중 폼페이의 초기 발굴에 관해 사실인 것은?

(A) 많은 귀중한 유물의 발견을 가져왔다.
(B) 비용 때문에 포기되었다.
(C) 이탈리아 고고학자들에 의해 수행되었다.
(D) 그 고대 유적지에 많은 피해를 입혔다.

5 4단락에서 폼페이가 많은 예술 및 오락 시설을 가지고 있었다는 것을 뒷받침하는 것으로 언급되지 않은 것은?

(A) 부유한 관광객을 위한 고급 리조트
(B) 2만 명의 관중을 수용할 수 있을 만큼 큰 경기장
(C) 연극 공연을 위한 장소
(D) 공중 및 개인 목욕 시설

iBT Reading Test

본문 p.118

1 (B)　2 (C)　3 (C)　4 (D)
5 (C)　6 (D)　7 (C)　8 (C)
9 (D)　10 (A), (B), (D)

뇌간의 역할

인간의 뇌는 신체의 다양한 기능을 제어하는 여러 부분으로 구성된다. 우리의 신체로 들어오고 나가는 모든 정보는 뇌간을 지나간다. [2]몇몇 동물들이 완전히 뇌간으로만 구성된 뇌를 갖고 있기 때문에 일부 과학자들은 그것을 뇌의 간단한 일부라고 여긴다. 하지만, 뇌간이 중요한 생명 기능들을 담당하기 때문에, 그것의 역할은 결코 간단하지 않다.

뇌간의 윗부분은 중뇌라고 불리며, 그것은 무의식적인 행동을 통제한다. [4]뒷부분이 대뇌 피질과 결합하여 작동하며 의식적 운동 기능들에 중요한 반면 중뇌의 앞부분은 시각 및 청각 지각 같은 기능들에 영향을 미친다. 교뇌 또한 뇌간의 일부이며 고속도로 체계의 중심과 비슷하다. 예를 들어, 귀에서 온 정보는 먼저 교뇌를 통해 뇌로 들어가고, 그것은 이 정보를 중뇌로, 그 후에 뇌의 다른 부분들로 전달한다. 교뇌는 또한 의식에 영향을 미치며 깊은 수면 동안 매우 중요하다. **이는 그것이 근육들을 이완시켜 사람들이 꿈꾸는 동안 그것들이 과잉 반응하지 않도록 하는 것을 책임지기 때문이다.**

교뇌 아래에 척수와 이어지는 연수가 있는데, 그것은 척수와 뇌 사이에서 신경 신호를 전달한다. 연수는 뇌의 반사 중추이며 재채기와 같은 자동 반응을 통제한다. [5B/5D]마찬가지로, 그것은 호흡과 심장 수축과 같은 무의식적 근육 운동을 관리한다. [5A]따라서, 그것은 혈액 화학을 조절하는 데 매우 중요하다. 예를 들어, 만약 혈액이 너무 산성화되면, 연수는 근육 조직에 화학 신호를 전달하여 그것들을 수축시키고 혈액에 더 많은 산소를 공급하게 한다. [6]뇌졸중으로 이어지는 혈관의 막힘은 연수를 손상시켜 신체 일부의 촉각 상실을 초래할 수 있다.

뼈 조직에 대한 그것의 근접성 때문에, 뇌간은 충격에 의한 손상에 취약하다. 뇌간의 신경 섬유는 쉽게 재생되지 않으므로, 부상은 영구적인 기능 상실을 초래할 수 있다. 뇌 손상을 입은 환자는 회복될 수 있지만 뇌간의 심각한 손상은 극복하기 어렵다. [8]이러한 상황에서, 뇌간은 생명 유지에 필요한 기능을 통제할 수 없으며, 사실상 생존 가능성이 없다.

brain stem 뇌간　be comprised of ~으로 구성되다
by no means 결코 ~이 아닌　vital 형 중요한, 생명 유지에 필요한
involuntary 형 무의식적인　auditory 형 청각의
perception 명 지각, 인지　rear 형 뒤의
interface 동 결합하여 작동하다　cerebral cortex 대뇌 피질
voluntary 형 의식적인　pons 명 교뇌, 다리뇌
subsequently 부 그 후에　spinal cord 척수
medulla 명 (뇌의) 연수　reflex 명 반사 (작용)　respiration 명 호흡
contraction 명 수축　regulate 동 조절하다
acidic 형 산성화된, 산성의　stroke 명 뇌졸중
proximity 명 근접성, 가까움　susceptible 형 취약한
readily 부 쉽게, 손쉽게　regenerate 동 재생되다, 재건되다
permanent 형 영구적인　virtually 부 사실상

1 지문의 어구 "by no means"와 의미가 가장 비슷한 것은?

(A) 거의
(B) 거의 ~않는
(C) 늘
(D) 약간

2 일부 과학자들이 뇌간을 간단하다고 여기는 것은

(A) 뇌의 모든 부분에서 가장 기본적인 정보를 전달하기 때문이다.
(B) 복잡하지 않은 기능만 수행하기 때문이다.
(C) 일부 생물들의 뇌 전체를 구성하기 때문이다.
(D) 인류 진화의 초기 단계 동안에 형성되었기 때문이다.

3 글쓴이는 왜 "a hub for a highway system"을 언급하는가?

(A) 뇌의 일부분의 중요성을 강조하기 위해
(B) 뇌의 물리적 생김새를 묘사하기 위해
(C) 뇌 구성 요소의 기능을 설명하기 위해
(D) 뇌가 정보를 저장하는 방법을 묘사하기 위해

4 2단락에 따르면, 다음 중 중뇌의 앞부분에 관해 사실인 것은?

(A) 대뇌 피질과 연결되어 있다.
(B) 깊은 수면과 관련이 있다.
(C) 수면과 의식에 매우 중요하다.
(D) 청각과 시각에 중요하다.

5 3단락에 따르면, 다음 중 연수의 직접적인 기능이 아닌 것은?

(A) 혈액의 화학 균형 조절
(B) 호흡 조절
(C) 의식적인 근육 운동 관리
(D) 심장 박동 조절

6 3단락에 따르면, 다음 중 연수 손상의 가능한 결과는?

(A) 일부 기억 기능이 중단될 수 있다.
(B) 혈관의 막힘이 뇌졸중을 일으킬 수 있다.
(C) 체내 혈액이 너무 산성화될 수 있다.
(D) 일부 신체 부위가 촉각을 잃을 수 있다.

7 지문의 단어 "readily"와 의미가 가장 비슷한 것은?

(A) 어쩔 수 없이
(B) 점차적으로
(C) 쉽게
(D) 빠르게

8 다음 중 4단락에서 뇌간의 심각한 손상에 관해 추론할 수 있는 것은?

(A) 보통 의학적 치료를 통해 나을 수 있다.
(B) 다른 형태의 뇌 손상보다 덜 심각하다.
(C) 환자의 사망을 초래할 가능성이 매우 높다.
(D) 일반적으로 신경 섬유의 재생이 뒤따른다.

9 네 개의 네모[■]는 다음 문장이 삽입될 수 있는 곳을 나타내고 있다.

이는 그것이 근육들을 이완시켜 사람들이 꿈꾸는 동안 그것들이 과잉 반응하지 않도록 하는 것을 책임지기 때문이다.

이 문장은 어디에 들어가는 것이 가장 적절한가?

10 **지시:** 지문 요약을 위한 도입 문장이 아래에 주어져 있다. 지문의 가장 중요한 내용을 나타내는 보기 3개를 골라 요약을 완성하라. 어떤 문장은 지문에 언급되지 않은 내용이나 사소한 정보를 나타내므로 요약에 포함되지 않는다. **이 문제는 2점이다.**

뇌간은 신체 기능에서 필수적인 역할을 한다. · (A) 연수는 뇌와 척수 사이에서 정보를 전달하는 뇌간의 부분이다. · (B) 뼈 조직에 대한 뇌간의 근접성 때문에 갑작스러운 충격은 그것을 손상시키고 심각한 결과를 초래할 수 있다. · (D) 중뇌와 교뇌는 각각 뇌간에서 다양한 중요한 역할을 한다.

(C) 의식적인 운동 기능은 주로 대뇌 피질에 의해 제어된다.
(E) 뇌간 손상은 환자들에게서 가장 흔한 유형의 뇌 손상이다.
(F) 연수 바로 아래의 뇌 부분은 교뇌이다.

Vocabulary Review

본문 p.122

1 fluctuations		2 generate	3 inaccurate
4 artifacts		5 discouraged	6 assumed
7 (B)	8 (A)	9 (D)	10 (B)
11 (D)	12 (A)	13 (A)	14 (C)

CHAPTER 08

Sentence Insertion

Example

본문 p.125

1 (D) 2 (C)

감기

대부분의 감기가 여름보다 가을과 겨울에 더 빈번하게 발생하는 것은 사실이다. 그러나, 대부분의 사람들이 생각하는 것과 달리, 추운 날씨는 감기의 발병이나 중증도에 거의 혹은 전혀 직접적인 영향을 미치지 않는다. 사람들이 겨울에 감기에 걸리는 주요 원인은 그들이 나쁜 날씨를 피하기 위해 실내에서 더 많은 시간을 보내기 때문이다. 따라서, 그들은 서로 더 가까이 있고, 이는 감염 위험의 가능성을 높인다. 게다가, 감기를 유발하는 바이러스들은 습도가 낮을 때 더 잘 생존하는데, 일 년 중 더 추운 몇 개월 동안이 그러하다. **공기의 적은 수분은 또한 비강의 내벽을 건조하게 하는 경향이 있으며, 이는 사람을 바이러스 감염에 더 취약하게 한다.**

일 년 동안, 미국의 개인들은 약 10억 번 감기에 걸린다. 그중 상당 비율은 바이러스 감염에 대한 저항력이 낮고, 또한 어린이집과 학교에서 다른 아이들과 더 많이 접촉하는 아이들에서 기인한다. 실제로, 아이들은 매년 6번에서 10번 감기에 걸리며, 이는 매년 1억 9천만 일의 결석의 원인이 된다. 게다가, 부모는 그들의 아이들을 돌보기 위해 집에 머무르며 1억 2천만 일을 결근하게 된다. **이러한 인력의 상실은 국가 경제에 부정적인 영향을 미친다.** 실제로, 감기의 경제적 비용은 전국적으로 200억 달러를 초과한다.

common cold (유행성이 아닌 보통의) 감기 frequently 부 빈번하게
severity 명 중증도, 심각성 catch 동 ~에 걸리다

indoors 부 실내에서 get away from ~을 피하다
proximity 명 가까움, 근접 likelihood 명 가능성 infection 명 감염
humidity 명 습도 be attributed to ~에서 기인하다, ~ 때문이다
resistance 명 (감염 등에 대한) 저항력 viral 형 바이러스의
daycare center 어린이집 account for ~의 원인이 되다
missed school day 결석 annually 부 매년
economic 형 경제적인 exceed 동 초과하다, 넘다

1 1단락에서 네 개의 네모[■]는 다음 문장이 삽입될 수 있는 곳을 나타내고 있다.

공기의 적은 수분은 또한 비강의 내벽을 건조하게 하는 경향이 있으며, 이는 사람을 바이러스 감염에 더 취약하게 한다.

이 문장은 어디에 들어가는 것이 가장 적절한가?

2 2단락에서 네 개의 네모[■]는 다음 문장이 삽입될 수 있는 곳을 나타내고 있다.

이러한 인력의 상실은 국가 경제에 부정적인 영향을 미친다.

이 문장은 어디에 들어가는 것이 가장 적절한가?

Reading Practice 1

본문 p.126

1 (D) 2 (B) 3 (A) 4 (B) 5 (B)

Vocabulary Quiz

1 ⓐ 2 ⓐ 3 ⓑ 4 ⓒ

필기도구의 발전

모든 인간의 발명 중에서, 필기는 가장 위대한 것 중 하나이다. 그것은 모든 사람들이 생각, 신념, 발견을 기록하고 국경과 시대를 넘어 그것들을 공유하는 것을 가능하게 한다. 그러나, 무언가를 적는 것이 항상 종이에 펜을 대는 것만큼 쉬웠던 것은 아니다. 맨 처음에는, 필기에 사용된 도구들이 우리가 오늘날 알고 있는 것과 상당히 달랐다.

사실, 최초의 필기도구들은 안료를 전혀 사용하지 않았다. 예를 들어, 중국인들은 거북이 등껍질이나 동물의 뼈에 단어를 새겼다. 고대 수메르인들은 재사용되거나 내구성을 위해 구워질 수 있는 부드러운 점토판에 무늬를 내기 위해 철필을 사용했다. 로마인들은 밀랍판을 사용하는 유사한 체계를 가지고 있었는데, 그것은 쉽게 지워지고 다시 사용될 수 있었다. **그것들 자체로 꽤 혁신적이었지만, 이 방법들에는 단점이 있었다.** 뼈에 새긴 무늬는 지워질 수 없었고, 점토는 깨지기 쉬워 다루기 어려웠으며, 밀랍판은 열에 강하지 못했다. 시간이 지남에 따라, 사람들은 그들의 역사를 기록하기 위한 더 나은 방법들을 찾았다.

잉크로 필기를 한 최초의 증거는 기원전 3000년경의 고대 이집트에서 나왔다. 이집트인들은 파피루스라 불리는 필기 재료를 발명했는데, 이것은 갈대의 얇은 층들로 만들어졌다. 그것은 진정으로 실용적이며 안정적인 최초의 표면 중 하나였다. 이에 걸맞게, 그들은 또한 갈대 펜을 발명하였는데, 그것은 촉이 뾰족하게 깎인, 잉크에 적셔졌던 갈대 마디였다. 이러한 기초적인 도구는 유용했지만, 만드는 데 시간이 오래 걸리고 사용하기가 번거로웠다. 이때 유럽에서 발전의 도약이 일어났는데, 그것은 바로 깃펜이었다. 깃펜은 큰 새의 깃털로 만들어졌으며, 깃털의 속이 빈 줄기는 촉으로 흐르는 잉크로 채워질 수 있었다. 이것은 촉을 적시는 번거로움 없이 더 긴 필기 시간을 가능하게 했고, 이는 그것들이 천년이 넘는, 역사상 가장 긴 기간 동안 필기를 지배한 이유이다.

5A또 다른 중요한 발전은 19세기에 산업혁명의 기술 발전의 결과로 일어났다. 철과 같은 자원의 이용 가능성과 기계의 확산은 새로운 유형의 펜이 제작될 수 있다는 것을 의미했다. 영국인 제임스 페리가 1819년에 최초의 금속 펜촉 펜을 생산했고, 1835년까지, 그의 회사는 일 년에 500만 개 이상을 생산하고 있었다. 5C/5D이 단순하고, 저렴하며, 내구성이 있는 펜은 만년필, 볼펜, 샤프펜슬을 위한 기반을 닦았고, 필기를 훨씬 더 편리하게 만들었다.

invention 명 발명 jot down ~을 적다, 쓰다 pigment 명 안료, 물감
stylus 명 철필(끝이 철로 된 펜) permanence 명 내구성, 영속성
wax 명 밀랍 brittle 형 깨지기 쉬운 resistant 형 ~에 강한
document 동 기록하다 reed 명 갈대 practical 형 실용적인
stable 형 안정적인 fittingly 부 걸맞게, 적합하게
rudimentary 형 기초적인 serviceable 형 유용한
time-consuming 형 시간이 오래 걸리는 annoying 형 번거로운
leap 명 도약 quill (pen) 깃펜 hollow 형 속이 빈 shaft 명 줄기
hassle 명 번거로움 proliferation 명 확산
durable 형 내구성이 있는 pave the way for ~을 위한 기반을 닦다

1 네 개의 네모[■]는 다음 문장이 삽입될 수 있는 곳을 나타내고 있다.

그것들 자체로 꽤 혁신적이었지만, 이 방법들에는 단점이 있었다.

이 문장은 어디에 들어가는 것이 가장 적절한가?

2 지문의 단어 "rudimentary"와 의미가 가장 비슷한 것은?

(A) 모범적인
(B) 기본적인
(C) 강박적인
(D) 세련된

3 지문의 단어 "they"가 가리키는 것은?

(A) 깃펜
(B) 새
(C) 시간
(D) 촉

4 3단락에서, 글쓴이는 왜 깃펜에 속이 빈 줄기가 있었다고 언급하는가?

(A) 불편했던 그것들의 디자인의 특징을 비판하기 위해
(B) 그것들이 오랜 기간 사용된 이유를 설명하기 위해
(C) 그것들을 제작하는 데 많은 시간이 걸렸다는 것을 강조하기 위해
(D) 다른 종류의 유럽 펜들과 비교하기 위해

5 4단락에 따르면, 다음 중 금속 펜에 관해 사실이 아닌 것은?

(A) 산업혁명 동안 발명되었다.
(B) 1819년까지 수백만 개가 생산되었다.
(C) 만년필과 볼펜의 전신이었다.
(D) 비싸거나 허술하지 않았다.

Reading Practice 2

본문 p.128

1 (C) 2 (D) 3 (A) 4 (B) 5 (D)

Vocabulary Quiz

1 ⓑ 2 ⓐ 3 ⓒ 4 ⓑ

수생 환경의 이점

우리 행성의 약 70퍼센트는 물로 덮여 있고, 이는 그것에 거주하는 수생 생물에 많은 이점을 제공한다. [1A]기온은 하루에 20도까지 변동할 수 있지만, 수온은 비교적 안정적으로 유지되며 하루에 단 몇 도만 변화한다. 계절적 변동 또한 완만하여, 일 년 내내 안정적인 환경을 조성한다. 물은 끊임없이 수생 생물의 내부와 외부의 표면을 적신다. 그 결과, 수생 생물은 육상 생물처럼 복잡한 체온 유지 체계를 발달시키거나 많은 양의 수분을 섭취할 필요가 없다. 그것들은 또한 기체의 발산을 위한 정교한 호흡 구조를 필요로 하지 않는다. [1B/1D]게다가, 물의 밀도와 점도는 무척추동물에게 유리한 환경을 조성하는데, 척추가 척추동물에게 제공하는 버팀대를 물이 제공해줄 수 있기 때문이다.

많은 양분과 염분이 이미 물에 용해되어 있고 수생 생물에 의해 쉽게 흡수될 수 있다. 미세한 동식물 또한 물에 떠다닌다. 따라서, 많은 해양 생물, 특히 무척추동물은 부유물 섭식을 통해 움직이지 않는 방식으로 먹이를 잡는다. [3]이 방법은 대단한 수준의 노력을 필요로 하지 않는다. 해파리와 같은 생물은 떠다니다가 물에서 먹이를 걸러낸다. 이러한 섭식 행동은 육지 환경에서는 극히 드문데, 여기에서는 거미줄을 치는 거미가 주목할 만한 예외이다. 거미줄은 그것이 수동적으로 곤충을 잡는 데 사용되어 거미가 적극적으로 먹이를 찾을 필요가 없다는 점에서 그물망과 매우 유사하게 기능한다. 수생 부유물 섭식자는 유사한 방식으로 기능하는 여과 장치를 그들의 체내에 가지고 있으며, 이는 그들에게 육지의 부유물 섭식자 이상의 이점을 제공한다.

번식 또한 육지보다 물속에서 상당히 더 쉽다. 해면동물은 무성 생식하여, 아구, 즉 다양한 세포들의 작은 뭉치들을 만든다. 이 뭉치들은 수개월 내에 결국 해면동물 성체로 성장한다. 유성 생식에서, 암컷은 특정 종의 경우 수백만 개에 이를 정도로 많은 알을 낳고, 그것들이 수컷에 의해 수정되기를 기다린다. 이 수정란들은 발달하기까지 홀로 물속에 남겨지는 반면, 육상 동물은 체내에서 수정하여 태아를 여러 달 동안 임신해야 한다. **결과적으로, 육상 동물은 새로운 자손을 낳기 위해 더 많은 물리적 비용을 지불한다.**

aquatic 형 수생의, 물속에 사는 fluctuate 동 변동하다
moderate 형 완만한, 적당한 intricate 형 복잡한
maintenance 명 유지 terrestrial 형 육상 생물의; 명 육상 생물
elaborate 형 정교한 respiratory 형 호흡의 diffusion 명 발산
density 명 밀도 viscosity 명 점도, 점성 favorable 형 유리한
invertebrate 명 무척추동물 vertebrate 명 척추동물
dissolve 동 용해하다, 녹이다 microscopic 형 미세한
stationary 형 움직이지 않는, 정지한
suspension-feeding 명 부유물 섭식 exertion 명 노력
notable 형 주목할 만한 exception 명 예외 function 동 기능하다
reproduction 명 번식, 생식 sponge 명 해면동물
asexually 부 무성으로 gemmule 명 (해면동물의) 아구
eventually 부 결국 fertilize 동 수정시키다 mature 동 발달하다

1 다음 중 생명 유지에 유리한 물의 특징이 아닌 것은?
(A) 온도
(B) 밀도
(C) 투명도
(D) 점도

2 지문의 단어 "stationary"와 의미가 가장 비슷한 것은?
(A) 활동적인
(B) 조직적인
(C) 영구적인
(D) 움직이지 않는

3 2단락에서 추론할 수 있는 것으로, 수생 부유물 섭식자는
(A) 먹이를 찾는 데 적은 에너지를 소비한다
(B) 먹이를 잡기 위해 거미줄 같은 구조를 만든다
(C) 거미보다 덜 효과적인 방법을 사용한다
(D) 미세한 식물만 섭취한다

4 지문의 단어 "them"이 가리키는 것은?
(A) 해면동물
(B) 알
(C) 수백만 개
(D) 종

5 네 개의 네모[■]는 다음 문장이 삽입될 수 있는 곳을 나타내고 있다.
결과적으로, 육상 동물은 새로운 자손을 낳기 위해 더 많은 물리적 비용을 지불한다.
이 문장은 어디에 들어가는 것이 가장 적절한가?

Reading Practice 3

본문 p. 130

1 (B) 2 (D) 3 (A) 4 (C) 5 (D)

Vocabulary Quiz

1 ⓑ 2 ⓐ 3 ⓑ 4 ⓒ

이누이트족의 생활 방식

이누이트족은 그린란드, 캐나다, 미국의 북극 지방에 사는 토착민이다. 수천 년 동안, 그들은 혹독한 환경에서 사는 어려움을 겪었다. 특정 영역에서 벗어나지 않으면서, 가족 집단의 무리들은 생존하기 위해 기술과 창의력을 활용했다. 북극의 더 생산적인 지역에 있는 다른 집단들이 수백 명에 이르렀던 반면, 몇몇 집단은 단 십여 명으로 이루어져 있었다. 이들은 모든 결정을 내리는 공식적인 정부 형태와 단일 지도자가 없는 정치적 자치 집단이었다.

이누이트족 활동의 대부분은 바다에 집중되었는데, 그것이 그들에게 많은 자원을 제공했기 때문이었다. 가끔, 그들은 내륙으로 진출했지만, 이것들은 특정한 계절 동안 오직 카리부 고기와 같은 주식을 얻기 위해서만 행해졌다. 이누이트족이 살았던 방식은 그들이 스스로를 환경의 일부로 여겼고, 그 결과 자연을 존중했다는 것을 드러냈다. [3]그들은 오직 필요한 것만을 취했고, 그들이 죽인 동물은 음식, 옷, 연장 및 다른 비축물이 되었다.

그러나, 18세기에 유럽의 탐험가들이 그들의 영역으로 여행하기 시작했을 때 그들의 삶의 방식은 도전받았다. 그 새로 온 사람들은 자연이 정복되어야 하는 것이라고 믿었고, 비옥한 땅과 바다는 그들이 이용하고 싶어 했던 풍부한 자원을 제공했다. [4]그것이 매우 광활했기 때문에, 포경업자와 다른 상인들이 그 지역을 착취하는 것은 어렵지 않았다. 따라서, 북극 사람들은 새로운 정착자들의 유입과 그들의 활동에 대처할 수밖에 없다는 것을 알게 되었다.

20세기가 시작할 무렵, 이누이트족의 삶은 급격하게 변화했다. 그들은 어류의 남획과 과도한 사냥으로 인해 더 이상 식량을 찾을 수 없었고 서양의 상인들과 상품을 물물 교환할 수밖에 없었다. 다른 사람들

에 점점 더 의존하게 된다는 것은 그들이 이전의 자급자족의 상당 부분을 상실했음을 의미했다. 더욱이, 그 지역에 새로 설립된 정부는 이누이트족을 야만적이고 단순하다고 여겼다. **따라서, 그들은 보다 "문명화된" 문화로의 이누이트족의 동화를 촉진하는 많은 다양한 종류의 프로그램들을 수립했다.** 이것은 더 나은 의료서비스와 취업 기회를 제공하는 등 일부 측면에서는 이누이트족에게 이득을 주었지만, 그들의 전통적인 생활 방식과 문화유산의 대부분은 불행하게도 소실되었다.

indigenous people 토착민, 원주민 the Arctic region 북극 지방
challenge 명 어려움; 동 도전을 받다 severe 형 혹독한
cluster 명 무리 ingenuity 명 창의력 autonomous 형 자치의
make a foray 진출하다 inland 부 내륙으로 conduct 동 행하다
food staples 주식 newcomer 명 새로 온 사람
conquer 동 정복하다 abundance 명 풍부함 whaler 명 포경업자
exploit 동 착취하다 expansive 형 광활한
cope with ~에 대처하다 influx 명 유입 drastically 부 급격하게
overfishing 명 남획 overhunting 명 과도한 사냥
barter 동 물물 교환하다 self-sufficiency 명 자급자족
barbaric 형 야만적인, 미개한 naive 형 단순한, 순진한

1 지문의 단어 "ingenuity"와 의미가 가장 비슷한 것은?
(A) 낙천주의
(B) 영리함
(C) 힘
(D) 유산

2 지문에서 글쓴이는 왜 이누이트족의 "forays inland"를 언급하는가?
(A) 이누이트족의 무지함을 설명하기 위해
(B) 이누이트족의 회복력을 보여주기 위해
(C) 이누이트족이 직면했던 어려움의 사례를 제시하기 위해
(D) 이누이트족의 또 다른 식량원을 확인하기 위해

3 2단락에서 이누이트족과 동물에 관해 추론할 수 있는 것은?
(A) 이누이트족은 동물 전체를 낭비 없이 사용했다.
(B) 이누이트족이 가장 좋아했던 동물은 육지의 것들이었다.
(C) 이누이트족은 그들이 필요했던 것보다 많은 동물을 죽였다.
(D) 동물은 이누이트족에게 가장 신성한 존재였다.

4 3단락에 따르면, 다음 중 사실인 것은?
(A) 이누이트족은 많은 초기 유럽 탐험가들의 길잡이 역할을 했다.
(B) 이누이트족은 환경을 패배시켜야 할 적으로 여겼다.
(C) 포경업자와 상인들은 북극 지역의 광대함 때문에 이익을 얻을 수 있었다.
(D) 북극 지역의 새로운 정착민들은 이누이트족에게 상당한 혜택을 제공했다.

5 네 개의 네모[■]는 다음 문장이 삽입될 수 있는 곳을 나타내고 있다.
따라서, 그들은 보다 "문명화된" 문화로의 이누이트족의 동화를 촉진하는 많은 다양한 종류의 프로그램들을 수립했다.
이 문장은 어디에 들어가는 것이 가장 적절한가?

Reading Practice 4

본문 p.132

1 (A) 2 (C) 3 (C) 4 (C) 5 (B)

Vocabulary Quiz

1 ⓒ 2 ⓐ 3 ⓑ 4 ⓑ

산업 혁명의 환경적 영향

1760년경, 세계는 돌이킬 수 없는 변화를 겪기 시작했다. 증기력과 직물 및 철을 생산하는 새로운 방법들을 포함해서, 다수의 중요한 혁신들이 산업 혁명을 촉발시켰다. 농업 경제에서 산업 경제로의 이동은 사회의 근본적인 구조, 즉 사람들이 일하고, 살고, 노는 방식을 변화시켰다. 하지만 사회의 변화와 함께, 산업 혁명은 또한 지구를 더 나쁜 쪽으로 급격하게 변화시켰다. 한 역사가가 말했듯이, "몇 가지 예외를 제외하면, 세계의 현대 환경 문제는 산업 혁명과 함께 시작했거나 산업 혁명에 의해 크게 악화되었다."

[3A]가장 큰 결과 중 하나는 대기질의 저하였고, 가장 큰 원인은 석탄이었다. 산업 혁명은 그것에 의해 동력을 공급받았는데, 이는 엄청난 양의 매연이 대기 속으로 쏟아지게 했다. 엄청난 양의 미세 먼지가 급격하게 증가하여, 도시 위에 끊임없는 안개를 만들어 냈다. [3B]호흡기 질환과 사망률 증가가 그 모든 스모그에 뒤이어 빠르게 나타났다. [3D]게다가, 석탄 연소의 부산물인 이산화탄소가 지구 온도의 비정상적인 상승을 야기했다. 물론, 지구는 과거에도 냉각기와 온난기를 거쳤지만, 이 변화들은 대개 수천 년에 걸쳐 점진적이고 자연스럽게 일어났다. **그 결과, 지구의 생명체는 새로운 기후 조건에 필요한 적응을 할 충분한 시간을 가지고 있었다.** 그러나, 산업 혁명은 급작스러운 화석 연료의 연소를 도입했고, 매우 짧은 시기 동안 기후의 극적인 온난화를 촉발시켰다. 이러한 변화는 대량 멸종, 해수면 상승, 예측 불가능한 악천후 패턴을 가져왔다.

석유와 가스처럼, 연료로 사용되었던 또 다른 재생 불능 자원들에는 그것들만의 문제가 있었다. 이 에너지 원천들이 지각 아래에서 추출되었기 때문에, 지상의 생태계는 대체로 그것들의 부재 속에서 진화해 왔다. 그러나, 시추로 인해 지표면으로 그것들이 유입되면서, 방출된 독소는 본질적으로 생물권을 오염시켰고, 동식물 모두에서 생물 다양성의 엄청난 손실을 초래했다. [5]오염된 토양과 물은 또한 농작물에 심각하게 해를 입혔다.

최초의 공장이 문을 연 이래로, 지구는 점점 더 환경적인 정점으로 향하고 있다. 만약 그것이 한계점에 도달하면, 모든 자연계의 붕괴가 되돌릴 희망 없이 일어날 수 있다. 그러한 영향은 단지 육지, 바다, 공기뿐만 아니라, 언젠가 살 수 없는 행성을 물려받게 될 미래 세대에까지 뻗어 나간다.

irrevocable 형 돌이킬 수 없는 steam power 증기력
spark 동 촉발시키다 agricultural 형 농업의
fundamental 형 근본적인 alteration 명 변화
radically 부 급격하게 exacerbate 동 악화시키다
consequence 명 결과 culprit 명 원인 pump 동 쏟아지다
copious 형 엄청난 particulate matter 미세 먼지
perpetual 형 끊임없는 byproduct 명 부산물
trigger 동 촉발시키다 mass extinction 대량 멸종
nonrenewable resources 재생 불능 자원
absence 명 부재 in essence 본질적으로 biosphere 명 생물권
tipping point 정점 threshold 명 한계점 inherit 동 물려받다
unlivable 형 살 수 없는

1 지문의 단어 "exacerbated"와 의미가 가장 비슷한 것은?
(A) 악화되다
(B) 안정되다
(C) 측정되다
(D) 진행되다

2 네 개의 네모[■]는 다음 문장이 삽입될 수 있는 곳을 나타내고 있다.
그 결과, 지구의 생명체는 새로운 기후 조건에 필요한 적응을 할 충분한 시간을 가지고 있었다.
이 문장은 어디에 들어가는 것이 가장 적절한가?

3 다음 중 2단락에서 증가된 석탄 사용의 결과로 언급되지 않은 것은?
(A) 대기질의 악화
(B) 호흡기 질환의 증가
(C) 도시 인구 규모의 감소
(D) 지구 온도의 상승

4 지문의 단어 "their"가 가리키는 것은?
(A) 연료
(B) 문제
(C) 원천들
(D) 생태계

5 3단락에 따르면, 다음 중 석유와 가스 시추에 관해 사실인 것은?
(A) 많은 양의 에너지를 소비한다.
(B) 농업 활동에 부정적인 영향을 미친다.
(C) 동물보다 식물에 더 큰 영향을 미친다.
(D) 한 지역의 사용 가능한 물의 공급을 줄인다.

iBT Reading Test

본문 p.134

1 (B) 2 (A) 3 (C) 4 (A)
5 (D) 6 (C) 7 (A) 8 (C)
9 (D) 10 (A), (C), (F)

메디치가와 르네상스

르네상스에 대한 언급만으로도 사진 같은 초상화를 그릴 수 있었던 정교한 기법을 가진 예술가들을 떠올리게 한다. [2]15세기와 16세기 동안 다른 어떤 곳보다 이탈리아 피렌체에서 예술이 가장 비약적으로 발전했다는 것을 부인할 수는 없다. 그러나, 이 시기 동안의 예술이 어느 정도 불가피하게 돈, 종교, 정치와 연결되어 있었다는 것은 간과하기 쉽다. 이것은 메디치가의 복잡한 유산으로, 그들은 자신들의 지배를 견고하게 하는 데 도움이 되는 예술품 의뢰에 그들의 재산을 사용했던 피렌체 출신의 은행 가문이다.

메디치가는 1937년 지오반니 데 메디치에 의해 설립된 가문의 은행을 위한 홍보 전략의 일부로 르네상스 예술에 자금을 지원했다. 지오반니의 아들인 코시모는 피렌체를 유럽의 문화 중심지로 만들었고, 이는 사업에 도움이 되었다. [3A]레오나르도 다빈치와 미켈란젤로와 같은 예술가들이 메디치가의 저택을 방문하여, 그 은행가들에게 선도적인 지식인으로서의 정통성을 부여했다. [3D]그 은행가들이 의뢰했던 예술품은 호화로웠고, 종종 귀한 재료로 만들어졌다. **예를 들어, 조각가 첼리니의 코시모 청동 흉상은 대단히 귀한 은으로 된 눈을 특징으로 한다.** [3B]가문 일원들의 초상화가 일반적이었으며, 이는 그 가문의 명성을 널리 퍼지게 했다.

메디치가에 의해 의뢰된 르네상스 예술품의 대부분은 종교적인 주제를 가지고 있었고, 이를 하는 것은 종교적으로 문제 되는 은행 영업을 만회하는 목적으로 이용되었다. 대출에 이자를 부과하는 것은 종교 지도자들의 가르침에 의해 금지되어 있었다. [6]네 명의 가톨릭 교황을 배출한 메디치가는 법적으로 기독교의 법을 준수했지만, 해외 무역에서의 환전으로 이득을 취함으로써 그것들의 제한을 넘었다. 그들 스스로를 종교적인 원칙을 위반할 수 없는 경건한 가문으로 묘사하는 것이 그 가문의 최대 관심사였다. 게다가, 메디치가의 몇몇 이들은 천국에서의 그들의 입지에 대해 확신이 없었을지도 모르는데, 이는 신학자들이 그들의 은행 방침의 도덕성에 관해 의견이 엇갈렸기 때문이었다. 이 두 가지 이유로, 메디치 가문 일원들이 삽입된 성서화를 의뢰하는 것은 합리적이었다.

메디치 가는 또한 여러 세대에 걸쳐 피렌체를 통치한 강력한 정치적 인물들이었는데, 이는 예술에 크게 투자할 또 다른 이유였다. 메디치가의 대모였던 톨레도의 엘레노오라가 메디치 왕조의 후계자인 그녀의 아들을 옆에 두고 자세를 취한 그림들과 같은 가족 초상화는 정치적 선전으로서 기능했다. [8]그것들은 가문의 권력을 보여주었고, 그 왕조가 지속될 것임을 암시했으며, 문화적 교양이라는 정치적으로 유리한 평판을 강화했다.

mention 명 언급, 거론 meticulous 형 정교한, 세심한
photorealistic 형 사진 같은 portraiture 명 초상화
by leaps and bounds 비약적으로 overlook 동 간과하다
inevitably 부 불가피하게 complicated 형 복잡한
commission 동 (예술 작품을) 의뢰하다 cement 동 견고하게 하다
dominance 명 지배 legitimacy 명 정통성, 정당성
opulent 형 호화로운 reputation 명 명성
compensate for ~을 만회하다, 보상하다
questionable 형 문제 되는, 의심스러운 forbid 동 금지하다
technically 부 법적으로 obey 동 준수하다 pious 형 경건한
morality 명 도덕성 sensible 형 합리적인
matriarch 명 대모, 여자 가장 propaganda 명 선전
bolster 동 강화하다 refinement 명 교양, 고상함

1 지문의 단어 "meticulous"와 의미가 가장 비슷한 것은?
(A) 인상적인
(B) 세심한
(C) 표현력 있는
(D) 화려한

2 1단락에 따르면, 15세기와 16세기의 예술은
(A) 상당한 발전을 이루었다
(B) 심미적인 가치가 제한적이었다
(C) 예술가들에게 큰 부를 창출했다
(D) 종교 지도자들에 의해 비판받았다

3 다음 중 2단락에서 메디치가의 문화적 명성의 증거로 언급되지 않은 것은?
(A) 메디치가를 직접 방문한 유명한 예술가들
(B) 자신들의 그림을 의뢰하는 메디치가의 경향
(C) 메디치가에 의해 부담된 피렌체 건축 개선
(D) 메디치가의 후원을 받은 예술품의 비싸고 인상적인 품질

4 아래 문장 중 지문 속의 음영된 문장의 핵심 정보를 가장 잘 표현한 것은? 오답은 문장의 의미를 크게 바꾸거나 핵심 정보를 생략한다.

(A) 메디치가는 의심스러운 사업 방식을 만회하기 위해 종교 예술을 의뢰했다.
(B) 메디치가는 거의 신뢰받지 못하는 의심스러운 인물들이었기 때문에, 그들은 성서화에 크게 투자했다.
(C) 메디치가가 종교 예술품 제작에 참여했다는 것은 그들을 더 좋아 보이게 했다.
(D) 메디치가는 은행 영업에 있어 그들이 기독교 원칙을 위반하고 있지 않다고 확신하지 못했다.

5 지문의 단어 "their"가 가리키는 것은?

(A) 대출
(B) 지도자들
(C) 교황
(D) 법

6 3단락에 따르면, 메디치가는

(A) 부유한 미술관에 예술품을 팔아 이익을 얻었다
(B) 피렌체 주민에 대한 세금을 인상하여 이익을 얻었다
(C) 다른 국가들과 환전하여 이익을 얻었다
(D) 가톨릭 교회의 공식 은행을 설립하여 이익을 얻었다

7 지문의 단어 "bolstered"와 의미가 가장 비슷한 것은?

(A) 신장시켰다
(B) 의존했다
(C) 성공했다
(D) 정의했다

8 4단락에서 추론할 수 있는 것으로, 메디치가가 톨레도의 엘레노오라의 초상화를 의뢰한 것은

(A) 그녀가 유난히 아름다웠기 때문이다
(B) 그들은 그녀가 피렌체를 다스리기를 원했기 때문이다
(C) 그들은 그들의 가족이 권력을 유지하기를 원했기 때문이다
(D) 그녀가 그 가문의 남자들에게 그렇게 하도록 설득했기 때문이다

9 네 개의 네모[■]는 다음 문장이 삽입될 수 있는 곳을 나타내고 있다.

예를 들어, 조각가 첼리니의 코시모 청동 흉상은 대단히 귀한 은으로 된 눈을 특징으로 한다.

이 문장은 어디에 들어가는 것이 가장 적절한가?

10 **지시:** 지문 요약을 위한 도입 문장이 아래에 주어져 있다. 지문의 가장 중요한 내용을 나타내는 보기 3개를 골라 요약을 완성하라. 어떤 문장은 지문에 언급되지 않은 내용이나 사소한 정보를 나타내므로 요약에 포함되지 않는다. **이 문제는 2점이다.**

메디치가는 그들의 재산으로 르네상스에 힘을 실어준 피렌체 가문이었다.
- (A) 메디치가의 은행은 예술과의 연관성으로 긍정적인 평판을 얻었다.
- (C) 메디치가는 피렌체에서 그들의 정치적 지배를 발전시키기 위해 초상화를 사용했다.
- (F) 종교적인 그림을 후원하는 것은 메디치가의 비도덕적인 사업을 만회하는 한 가지 방법이었다.

(B) 미켈란젤로는 메디치가 저택의 손님이었고 그 가문을 위한 예술품을 창작하도록 고용되었다.
(D) 르네상스 예술가들은 부유한 은행가들과 직업적으로 관련되는 것을 꺼려했다.
(E) 기독교법은 메디치가가 대출에 이자를 부과하는 것을 막았다.

Vocabulary Review

본문 p.138

1 naive		2 proximity	3 absence
4 byproduct		5 resistance	6 pave
7 (A)	8 (B)	9 (C)	10 (B)
11 (A)	12 (D)	13 (D)	14 (B)

CHAPTER 09

Summary

Example

본문 p.141

1 (A), (C), (E)

제브라피시로 실험하기

제브라피시는 피라미와 밀접한 관련이 있는 남아시아 토종의 작은 줄무늬 물고기이다. 그들은 인간과 특징을 거의 공유하지 않는 것처럼 보이지만, 사실, 제브라피시와 인간은 그들 유전자의 약 70퍼센트를 공유한다. 이 지느러미를 가진 작은 생물체는 또한 인간에서 발견되는 동일한 신체 기관을 많이 가지고 있다. 이러한 유사성 때문에, 제브라피시는 의학 실험에서 가장 선호되는 동물 종으로서 쥐를 대체하고 있다. 진화론적 관점에서 쥐는 인간과 더 밀접하게 관련이 있는데, 두 종 모두 포유류라는 점에서 그렇다. 그러나 제브라피시는 수집하여 보관하기에 훨씬 더 저렴하고, 인간과 그들의 유전적 유사성은 인간의 질병과 치료제를 연구하기 위한 노력으로 그들의 유전자를 조작하는 것을 비교적 쉽게 만든다. 게다가, 제브라피시는 몇 가지 유용한 인간과의 차이점이 있다. 그들은 빠르게 많은 수로 번식하여, 빠른 다세대 연구를 가능하게 해준다. 그들의 반투명한 신체는 배아의 성장이 그것이 일어나는 대로 목격하는 것을 가능하게 해준다. 물론, 제브라피시는 폐와 같은 장기에 영향을 미치는 인간의 질병에 대해서는 불충분한 모형인데, 이는 이 작은 물고기에게 그러한 기관이 없기 때문이다. 하지만 유전자 변형에 있어서, 제브라피시는 약의 효능을 평가할 수 있는 대단히 풍부한 시험대를 제공한다. 그들은 빠르게 생물 의학 분야 연구를 위한 인기 있는 모형이 되고 있으며, 다른 동물에 대한 실험을 줄이면서 새로운 약물 개발을 촉진하는 데 기여하고 있다.

minnow 명 피라미 characteristic 명 특징
finned 형 지느러미를 가진 similarity 명 유사성
replace 동 대체하다 evolutionary 형 진화론적인
perspective 명 관점 mammal 명 포유류
resemblance 명 유사성 comparatively 부 비교적
manipulate 동 조작하다 reproduce 동 번식하다
multigenerational 형 다세대의 translucent 형 반투명한
embryo 명 배아 organ 명 장기 genetic mutation 유전자 변형
fertile 형 풍부한, 많이 산출하는 efficacy 명 효능
facilitate 동 촉진하다

1 지시: 지문 요약을 위한 도입 문장이 아래에 주어져 있다. 지문의 가장 중요한 내용을 나타내는 보기 3개를 골라 요약을 완성하라.

제브라피시는 실험용 종으로 쥐보다 더 나을 수 있다.

(A) 제브라피시는 인간과 놀라운 유전적 유사성을 가지고 있다.
(B) 쥐는 포유류이기 때문에 인간 유전체를 더 밀접하게 반영한다.
(C) 사람과의 유전적인 유사성은 제브라피시 유전자 변형을 유용하게 만든다.
(D) 인간은 제브라피시보다 쥐와 더 가까운 진화론적 관계를 가지고 있다.
(E) 제브라피시는 사람과의 차이에도 불구하고 연구에 적합한 많은 특징을 가지고 있다.
(F) 제브라피시 연구는 그들이 덜 진화되었기 때문에 설치류 연구보다 더 윤리적이다.

Reading Practice 1

본문 p.142

1 (A) 2 (C) 3 (B) 4 (B), (D), (F)

Vocabulary Quiz

1 ⓐ 2 ⓒ 3 ⓒ 4 ⓐ

'하위헌스'가 타이탄에 착륙하다

타이탄은 토성의 궤도를 도는 가장 큰 위성이다. 2005년 1월 14일에 미국항공우주국(NASA)이 설계한 '하위헌스'라는 탐사선이 그곳의 표면에 착륙할 때까지, 과학자들은 그것의 지구로부터의 거리와 그것의 지질학적 특성을 가리는 두껍고 흐린 대기 때문에 타이탄에 관해 거의 알지 못했다. 접근 비행은 타이탄을 연구하는 데 쓸모가 거의 없기에, 그 위성을 탐사하는 가장 좋은 방법은 그것의 표면으로 낙하하는 우주선을 보내는 것이다. '하위헌스'의 비행은 타이탄의 수수께끼를 풀기 위한 대단히 성공적인 첫걸음이었다.

타이탄의 표면 지형에 관한 미국항공우주국(NASA)의 불확실성은 성공적인 착륙이 필연적 결론과는 거리가 멀다는 것을 의미했다. 실제로, 그 계획은 '하위헌스'가 타이탄의 대기를 통과하는 2시간 반 동안의 하강 도중에 그것의 데이터의 대부분이나 전체를 수집하는 것이었다. 비록 전파 망원경은 착륙할 단단한 표면이 존재할 수도 있음을 보여주었지만, 미국항공우주국(NASA)의 공학자들은 그 표면이 탐사선을 지탱할지 혹은 그것이 얼마나 많은 잠재적 위험에 직면할지에 대해 예측할 수 없었다. 과학자들은 '하위헌스'가 타이탄에서 무엇을 발견할 것인지를 두고 내기를 했다. 얼음? 액체? 타르? 한 참가자는 농담 삼아 "바다 괴물에게 잡아먹힌다"에 걸었다.

타이탄 상공으로의 자유 낙하는 '하위헌스'가 그곳 대기의 화학적 구성을 확인하게 해주었다. [3C]그 탐사선은 대부분 질소와 메탄을 발견하여, 과학자들의 예측을 확인시켜 주었다. 그것은 태양에서 훨씬 더 풍부한 기체인 아르곤을 소량만 발견했는데, 이는 미국항공우주국(NASA)이 타이탄이 태양계 초기에 형성되지 않았다고 추측하게 했다. [3D]오히려, 타이탄이 처음 형성될 때 그것으로의 운석 충돌로부터 타이탄은 그것의 대기를 얻었을 가능성이 있다. 지구도 같은 방식으로 형성되었을 수 있다. [3A]'하위헌스'는 또한 생명체의 화학적 기본 요소가 타이탄의 대기에 존재한다는 것을 시사하는 톨린이라는 분자를 발견했다. 비록 타이탄 자체에는 생명체가 존재하지 않지만, 그곳의 톨린의 존재는 타이탄이 아닌 다른 곳에서의 생명체 탐색에 있어 긍정적인 신호이다.

결국, '하위헌스'는 부드러운 물질 위에 완만하게 착륙했고, 해변 같은 지형의 놀라운 이미지 100장을 돌려보냈다. 타이탄은 태양계에서 액체를 포함하는 유일한 천체임이 밝혀졌다. 비록 물은 없지만, 액체 탄화수소는 분명히 타이탄 표면에 새겨진 강을 통해 흐른다. '하위헌스'는 이 액체를 직접 발견하지는 못했지만, 구불구불한 강바닥의 사진을 찍었다. 타이탄의 표면은 메탄 비의 침식뿐만 아니라 홍수의 흔적을 보여준다. 유감스럽게도, '하위헌스'는 그것의 배터리가 꺼지기 전까지 단 72분 동안만 타이탄을 탐사할 수 있었다.

moon 명 위성 orbit 동 궤도를 돌다 probe 명 탐사선
obscure 동 가리다 unravel 동 풀다 uncertainty 명 불확실성
foregone conclusion 필연적 결론, 뻔한 결과 descent 명 하강
radio telescope 전파 망원경 encounter 동 직면하다
potential 형 잠재적인 place a bet on ~에 내기를 걸다
peril 명 위험 freefall 명 자유 낙하 airspace 명 상공, 영공
ascertain 동 확인하다 abundant 형 풍부한
probable 형 가능성 있는 molecule 명 분자
building block 기본 요소 remarkable 형 놀라운
hydrocarbon 명 탄화수소 apparently 부 분명히
spot 동 발견하다 erosion 명 침식 expire 동 꺼지다, 만료되다

1 지문의 단어 "its"가 가리키는 것은?

(A) 타이탄
(B) 토성
(C) 미국항공우주국(NASA)
(D) '하위헌스'

2 글쓴이는 왜 "radio telescopes"를 언급하는가?

(A) 지구에서 타이탄의 표면을 연구하려는 시도가 무의미함을 입증하기 위해
(B) 개발되지는 않았지만 유용할 수 있는 기술에 대해 논하기 위해
(C) 과학자들이 타이탄에 착륙할 표면이 있는지에 대해 의심한 이유를 설명하기 위해
(D) 타이탄에 액체가 있다는 과학자들의 지식의 출처를 밝히기 위해

3 다음 중 '하위헌스'가 타이탄의 대기를 통과해 하강하는 동안 발견되지 않은 것은?

(A) 생명체의 화학적 기본 요소가 타이탄에 존재한다.
(B) 액체 탄화수소가 타이탄의 강을 통해 흐른다.
(C) 대기에는 질소와 메탄이 가장 두드러진다.
(D) 타이탄의 대기는 운석과의 충돌에 의해 생겨났다.

4 지시: 지문 요약을 위한 도입 문장이 아래에 주어져 있다. 지문의 가장 중요한 내용을 나타내는 보기 3개를 골라 요약을 완성하라.

'하위헌스'의 비행은 멀리서 얻을 수 없는 타이탄의 표면에 대한 정보를 제공했다.

(A) 타이탄은 지구에서 약 10억 마일 떨어져 있어, 유인 비행에 의해 도달하는 것이 불가능하다.
(B) 타이탄은 구름으로 덮여 있어, '하위헌스' 탐사선의 착륙 계획을 세우는 것을 어렵게 만들었다.
(C) 과학자들은 '하위헌스'가 타이탄에서 직면할 가능성이 있는 표면의 특성에 대해 내기를 했다.
(D) '하위헌스'는 대기를 통과해 하강하는 동안 타이탄의 기체에 관한 데이터를 수집했다.
(E) 타이탄의 기체는 태양계 역사 초기의 지구 형성에 대한 정보를 제공한다.
(F) 착륙 후, '하위헌스'는 타이탄이 지구를 제외하고 액체를 포함하는 유일한 천체임을 밝혀냈다.

Reading Practice 2

본문 p.144

1 (A) 2 (D) 3 (C) 4 (A), (C), (E)

Vocabulary Quiz

1 ⓒ 2 ⓑ 3 ⓒ 4 ⓑ

초기 은행업

은행이 존재하기 전에, 은행업이 존재했다. 문명이 다양한 형태의 화폐에 의존하기 시작하면서, 금융 자원의 대출, 기록 관리, 보관의 세 가지 주요 은행 서비스에 대한 필요가 생겨났다. 이러한 서비스들을 제공한 최초의 기관들은 대개 본질적으로 종교적이었다. 고대 바빌로니아인들은 개인, 심지어 왕족도 신에게 정기적인 성금을 낼 것을 요구했고, 이 헌금은 곡물과 가축의 형태로 지불할 수 있었다. [1]사원들이 이 생산물들의 잉여분을 모았을 때, 그들은 그것들을 빌려주기 시작했다. 기원전 2000년경, 사원들은 또한 금을 예금으로 받았고, 그 서비스의 대가로 예금의 일정 비율을 청구했다.

은행업을 사원에서 벗어나 개인 건물로 옮긴 최초의 문명은 로마인들이었다. 기원전 352년에, 특히 전쟁 중 사회 불안을 방지하기 위한 노력의 일환으로 로마의 공공 은행이 가난한 이들의 부채를 관리하기 위해 설립되었다. '멘사리이'라고 알려진 이 공공 은행가들은 정부 공무원들로부터 시민들이 그들의 부채를 갚지 못할 때 토지를 몰수할 권한을 받았다. 멘사리이는 또한 예금을 받았고 동전의 진위와 가치를 평가했다.

중세 은행업의 대부분은 상업 은행에 의해 제공되었다. 이탈리아의 롬바르디아 지역은 이 산업의 중심지가 되었다. [3B]이 시기 동안 많은 은행가들은 스페인인들에 의한 박해를 피하기 위해 이탈리아로 건너온 유대인 상인들이었다. [3A]대출해준 사람이 대출에 이자를 부과하는 것을 막는 기독교의 고리대금 금지법에 그들이 구속되지 않았기 때문에 그것은 그들에게 천부적인 직업이었다. [3D]이것은 그들에게 고위험 대출을 맡고 곡물이 수확되기 전에 그것을 판매할 권리를 구입할 자유를 주었다.

로마의 멸망 이후 쇠퇴했던 공공 은행업은 12세기 중에 서유럽에서 재등장했다. 1157년에 설립된 베네치아 은행은 최초의 현대적인 의미의 공공 은행 기관이었다. 잉글랜드의 헨리 2세는 십자군 원정을 지원하기 위해 백성들에게 세금을 부과하기 시작했다. 시간이 지남에 따라, 유럽의 왕권은 그들 스스로 정한 금액으로 대출을 제공하기 시작했다. 이러한 관행은 18세기에 이르러 현대 은행업으로 천천히 발전했다.

banking 명 은행업 currency 명 화폐, 통화 institution 명 기관
religious 형 종교적인 contribution 명 성금
payable 형 지불할 수 있는 surplus 명 잉여분
loan 동 빌려주다; 명 대출 deposit 명 예금 debt 명 부채
social unrest 사회 불안 empower 동 권한을 주다
government official 정부 공무원 confiscate 동 몰수하다
evaluate 동 평가하다 authenticity 명 진위 persecution 명 박해
profession 명 직업 be bound to ~에 구속되다
usury laws 고리대금 금지법 interest 명 이자
recede 동 쇠퇴하다, 감소하다 reemerge 동 재등장하다
the Crusades 십자군 원정 dictate 동 정하다

1 1단락에 따르면, 은행업이 고대 바빌론에서 처음으로 시작된 것은
(A) 종교 지도자들이 신에게 기증된 물품들을 빌려주기 시작했기 때문이다
(B) 사원이 그곳에서 예배하는 사람들이 가지고 있었던 곡물의 기록을 보관했기 때문이다
(C) 사람들이 그들이 여행하는 동안 금을 보관할 장소를 필요로 했기 때문이다
(D) 종교 박해를 피한 외국인들이 사원에서 대출을 제공했기 때문이다

2 지문의 단어 "their"가 가리키는 것은?
(A) 공공 은행가들
(B) 멘사리이
(C) 정부 공무원들
(D) 시민들

3 3단락에 따르면, 중세의 유대인 상인들에 관해 사실이 아닌 것은?
(A) 대출에 대한 이자를 징수할 수 있었다
(B) 종교적 차별로부터 벗어났다
(C) 고리대금 금지법 위반으로 처벌받았다
(D) 미리 곡물에 대한 권리를 샀다

4 지시: 지문 요약을 위한 도입 문장이 아래에 주어져 있다. 지문의 가장 중요한 내용을 나타내는 보기 3개를 골라 요약을 완성하라.

은행 서비스의 제공은 최초의 은행 기관보다 먼저 이루어졌다.

(A) 초기 문명의 사원들은 최초의 은행 기관의 역할을 했다.
(B) 고대 바빌론에서, 왕족은 곡물과 동물을 공물로 바쳐야 했다.
(C) 최초의 정부 운영 은행은 로마인들에 의해 설립되었다.
(D) 멘사리이는 시민들에게 지불할 수 없는 부채가 있는 경우 토지를 인수할 수 있었다.
(E) 중세에는 상업 은행이 은행업의 기능을 수행했다.
(F) 헨리 2세는 십자군 원정 동안 발생한 비용을 지불하기 위해 세금에 의지했다.

Reading Practice 3

본문 p.146

1 (C) 2 (C) 3 (B) 4 (B), (D), (F)

Vocabulary Quiz

1 ⓒ 2 ⓐ 3 ⓐ 4 ⓑ

래쿤의 점령

매력적인 검은 얼굴 마스크, 총명한 눈, 숱이 많은 줄무늬 꼬리를 가진 래쿤은 상대방을 무장 해제시키듯 사랑스러운 북미 태생의 동물이다. 매혹된 인간들은 이 동물을 전 세계 다양한 지역들로 옮겨왔고, 항상 그 결정을 후회한다. 래쿤은 그들의 독특한 털을 좋아하는 사람들에 의해 1930년대에 독일로 전해졌다. 그들은 이제 유럽의 각지로, 그리고 중동의 일부 지역에도 퍼져나가고 있다. 1970년대에, 귀여운 만화 래쿤이 텔레비전에서 인기를 끌게 된 후에, 일본 아이들은 그들의 부모를 설득하여 매달 이 동물의 약 1,500마리를 수입하게 했다. 대부분의 애완용 래쿤들은 위험한 행동으로 주인을 위협한 이후 야생에 방출되었다. 현재 그들은 매년 일본에서 30만 달러 상당의 농업 피해를 입힌다.

래쿤은 놀라울 정도로 환경에 쉽게 적응하는 동물이라는 것을 스스로 입증해왔다. 본래, 그들은 강 주변에서 살았는데, 이는 먹이를 먹기 전에 물에 적시는 그들의 이상한 습관을 설명한다. 그들은 이제 시골, 도시, 교외 지역을 똑같이 쉽게 따라잡으며 도처에서 살고 있다. [2A]이 잡식성 동물은 견과류와 열매에서부터 설치류와 거북까지 거의 모든 것을 먹을 수 있다. 그들은 쓰레기 봉지를 찢어 온갖 종류의 인간의 맛있

는 음식을 먹는 것을 걱정스러울 정도로 좋아한다. [2B/2D]래쿤은 비슷한 크기의 다른 동물들보다 똑똑하고, 다락과 굴뚝에 쉽게 접근할 수 있는 날렵한 앞발을 가지고 있으며, 다양한 기후 조건을 견딜 수 있다. 그들은 따뜻한 날씨를 편안해하고, 겨울이 오면 그저 지방을 축적한다.

래쿤은 일단 한 지역에 들어오면 제거하기 어려운 것으로 악명 높다. 토론토 시는 래쿤이 뚫을 수 없을 것이라고 생각되는 쓰레기통을 설계하고 생산하는 데 수백만 달러를 썼지만, 그 동물들이 그것들 안으로 들어갈 수 있다는 것을 알게 되었을 뿐이었다. 그들이 포획과 사냥을 통해 제거되면, 그 종의 개체 수는 1년 내에 회복하는 경향이 있다. 이는 암컷이 1년에 8번까지 출산하는 그들의 빠른 번식 능력 때문이다.

[3]지구 온난화로 인해, 래쿤은 전 세계에서 심지어 더 흔해질 가능성이 크다. 그들은 캐나다 북부, 유럽, 아시아의 취약한 숲에 침입할 것으로 예상된다. 이 회복력 있는 청소 동물이 모든 것을 먹어 치우고 그들이 마주치는 모든 토착종들과의 경쟁에서 이기는 경향이 있기 때문에 그것은 생태학적 관점에서 파멸적일 수 있다. 그들이 귀엽기는 하지만, 래쿤은 세계가 아직 효과적인 해결책을 찾지 못한 딜레마를 제기한다.

captivating 형 매력적인 bushy 형 숱이 많은
disarmingly 부 상대방을 무장 해제시키듯 adorable 형 사랑스러운
charmed 형 매혹된 convince 동 설득하다
wreak 동 (피해 등을) 입히다 adaptable 형 (환경 등에) 쉽게 적응하는
dunk 동 적시다 omnivore 명 잡식성 동물 rodent 명 설치류
disturbingly 부 걱정스러울 정도로 tear 동 찢다
delicacy 명 맛있는 음식 nimble 형 날렵한 withstand 동 견디다
accumulate 동 축적하다 notoriously 부 악명 높게
rebound 동 회복하다, 다시 돌아오다 capacity 명 능력
ubiquitous 형 흔한, 어디에나 있는 invade 동 침입하다
catastrophic 형 파멸적인 perspective 명 관점
resilient 형 회복력 있는 scavenger 명 (죽은 고기를 먹는) 청소 동물
outcompete 동 ~과의 경쟁에서 이기다

1 지문의 단어 "They"가 가리키는 것은?
(A) 인간들
(B) 지역들
(C) 래쿤
(D) 좋아하는 사람들

2 2단락에 따르면, 다음 중 래쿤에 관해 사실이 아닌 것은?
(A) 식물과 동물을 둘 다 먹는다.
(B) 다양한 기온에서 생존할 수 있다.
(C) 시골 지역보다 도시를 더 좋아한다.
(D) 비슷한 크기의 종들보다 더 똑똑하다.

3 지문에 따르면, 래쿤이 캐나다 북부의 숲으로 퍼져나갈 것이라 예상되는 것은
(A) 그들이 여름 동안 북쪽으로 이동하기 때문이다
(B) 평균 기온이 상승할 것이기 때문이다
(C) 북부 주민들이 그들을 애완동물로 즐겨 키우기 때문이다
(D) 숲에 많은 강이 있는 경향이 있기 때문이다

4 지시: 지문 요약을 위한 도입 문장이 아래에 주어져 있다. 지문의 가장 중요한 내용을 나타내는 보기 3개를 골라 요약을 완성하라.

래쿤은 인간에게 사랑받아 북미에서 퍼져나갔다.

(A) 일본의 한 텔레비전 프로그램은 래쿤을 캐릭터로 등장시켰다.
(B) 래쿤은 다양한 환경에서 생존할 수 있다.
(C) 래쿤은 구조물에 접근하는 데 사용되는 민첩한 앞발을 가지고 있다.
(D) 래쿤의 영구적 제거는 아직까지 실현되지 않은 과제이다.
(E) 토론토는 효과가 없는 값비싼 쓰레기통에 많은 돈을 썼다.
(F) 래쿤은 취약한 생태계로 더 확산될 것으로 예상된다.

Reading Practice 4

본문 p. 148

1 (C) 2 (B) 3 (D) 4 (C), (D), (F)

Vocabulary Quiz

1 ⓒ 2 ⓑ 3 ⓐ 4 ⓒ

아크로폴리스

'아크로폴리스'의 문자 그대로의 의미는 "마을에서 가장 높은 지점"이고, 고대 그리스의 거의 모든 도시가 하나씩 가지고 있었다. 그러나, 이 용어는 현대에는 일반적으로 아테네의 아크로폴리스를 가리키는 데 사용되며, 그것은 아테네 시를 내려다보는 네 개의 언덕을 차지하는 고대 신전 및 다른 건물들의 집합체이다. 아크로폴리스는 20여 개의 고고학 유적을 특징으로 하는데, 여기에는 아테나 여신에게 헌정된 23,000 제곱피트의 신전인 파르테논 신전과, 그리스의 위대한 비극 시인들의 작품들이 상연된 공연 장소인 디오니소스 극장이 포함된다.

아크로폴리스의 건축 개발에 대한 최초의 기록들은 미케네인들의 청동기 문명으로 거슬러 올라간다. 기원전 1400년경에 미케네의 왕들은 그곳에 26피트의 성벽으로 요새화된 궁전들을 지었다. 그 성벽들 중 하나의 유적은 아크로폴리스의 남서쪽 끝에 서 있으며, 오늘날까지 남아 있는, 이 시기를 대표하는 가장 중요한 것이다. 왕의 거주지로서 기능하는 것에 더해, 아크로폴리스는 또한 다산과 자연의 여신인 데메테르의 숭배를 위한 중심지를 제공했다.

아크로폴리스에 있는 대부분의 건축물은 기원전 480년에 페르시아인들에 의해 심하게 훼손되었지만, 약 30년 후 아테네의 황금기 동안 아테네의 통치자 페리클레스가 그 요새를 재건했다. 일련의 군사적 승리 이후, 에게해 지역의 약 200개의 도시들은 그들을 지키기 위해 아테네에 막대한 금액을 지급했고, 그 부는 거대한 건설 활동에 자금을 지원했다. 아크로폴리스의 꽃인 파르테논 신전이 세워진 것이 바로 이 시기 동안이었다. [1]그 신전은 축구장의 절반 크기였고, 46개의 높은 대리석 기둥으로 둘러싸여 있었다.

아크로폴리스는 기원전 146년 고대 그리스의 멸망 이후 이어진 수 세기에 걸친 전쟁과 정치적 상황 변화를 견뎌냈다. [3A/3B]신성 로마 제국의 지배하에서, 그곳의 많은 신전들은 기독교 교회가 되었다. 튀르크의 지배하에서, 그것들은 모스크가 되었고 군수품을 보관하는 데 사용되었다. [3C]1687년에 베네치아인들은 아크로폴리스를 공격했으며, 이는 파르테논 신전을 약탈과 기물 파괴에 노출되게 했다. 1822년이 되어서야 그리스는 독립 국가가 되었고 발굴과 복원이라는 시간이 많이 소요되는 작업을 시작했다. 오늘날, 아크로폴리스는 인기 있는 관광 명소이다.

literal 형 문자 그대로의 occupy 동 차지하다
overlook 동 내려다보다 feature 동 특징으로 하다
archaeological 형 고고학의, 고고학적인 remains 명 유적
dedicated to ~에게 헌정된 architectural 형 건축의
date back to ~으로 거슬러 올라가다 fortify 동 요새화하다
significant 형 중요한 representation 명 대표하는 것
function 동 기능하다 residence 명 거주지 worship 명 숭배
fertility 명 다산 decimate 동 심하게 훼손하다 citadel 명 요새, 성채

crown jewel (상징적 의미의) 꽃, 가장 매력적인 것 endure 동 견디다
circumstances 명 상황 ammunition 명 군수품 looting 명 약탈
vandalism 명 기물 파괴 excavation 명 발굴 restoration 명 복원
tourist attraction 관광 명소

1 글쓴이가 파르테논 신전에 관해 묘사하는 것은?
(A) 축구장보다 넓은 면적을 차지한다
(B) 데메테르를 숭배하는 데 사용되었다
(C) 거의 50개의 외부 기둥을 특징으로 한다
(D) 페르시아인들에 의해 파괴되었다

2 지문의 단어 "they"가 가리키는 것은?
(A) 상황
(B) 신전들
(C) 수 세기
(D) 튀르크

3 4단락에 따르면, 다음 중 아크로폴리스에 관해 사실이 아닌 것은?
(A) 그것의 신전들은 수세기에 걸쳐 여러 종교에 의해 사용되었다.
(B) 그곳의 건축물은 군수품을 보관하는 데 사용되었다.
(C) 다른 유럽 강대국과의 전쟁 중에 손상되었다.
(D) 그 유적지는 튀르크의 지배 아래 있는 동안 발굴되었다.

4 지시: 지문 요약을 위한 도입 문장이 아래에 주어져 있다. 지문의 가장 중요한 내용을 나타내는 보기 3개를 골라 요약을 완성하라.
아크로폴리스에는 수많은 신전과 고고학적으로 흥미로운 다른 건축물들이 있다.
(A) 파르테논 신전은 아테나 여신 숭배를 위해 설계되었다.
(B) 고대 그리스의 극작가들은 아크로폴리스에서 작품을 공연했다.
(C) 아크로폴리스의 역사는 미케네 문명에서 시작되었다.
(D) 아테네의 황금기 동안, 많은 건물이 아크로폴리스에 지어졌다.
(E) 군사적 승리는 황금기 동안 아테네에 큰 부를 창출했다.
(F) 아크로폴리스는 그리스가 멸망한 후 여러 차례 종교 지도자와 주인을 바꾸었다.

iBT Reading Test

본문 p.150

1 (B) 2 (C) 3 (B) 4 (C)
5 (B) 6 (A) 7 (C) 8 (B)
9 (B) 10 (A), (B), (D)

발레의 역사

[2]르네상스 시대의 이탈리아 귀족들은 음악, 무언극, 무용으로 중요한 방문객들을 즐겁게 해주었다. '스펙터클'이라고 불리는 이 궁중 공연은 종종 수백 명의 공연자를 포함하는 웅장한 기념행사였다. 피렌체의 귀족 여성인 캐서린 데 메디치는 그녀가 앙리 2세와 결혼했을 때 궁중 무용을 프랑스로 가져왔다. 이 시기 동안, 캐서린은 주예즈 공작과 로렌의 마르게리트와의 결혼식 기념행사를 위해 스펙터클을 의뢰했다. 이것은 발레의 탄생으로 여겨진다. [3]그것은 5시간이 넘는 대작으로, 현대 발레와는 달리 음성 공연의 요소들을 포함했다.

[6D]발레의 발전에서 또 다른 영향력 있는 인물은 프랑스의 루이 14세로, 그는 궁중 오락에서 전문 직업으로의 무용의 전환을 시작했다. [6B]어린 시절부터 발레에 관심이 있었던 루이는 다른 이들이 그 예술을 완성시키고 무용을 존경할 만한 것으로 만들도록 장려했다. [7]루이는 발레단에서 그의 높은 신분에 걸맞은 것으로 여겨지는 역을 맡아 공연했다. 그것들 중 가장 중요한 것은 '밤의 발레'로, 여기서 그는 태양왕으로 등장했는데, 이것은 그가 스스로에게 붙인 별명이기도 했다. 그의 궁정은 많은 에너지를 무용에 쏟았고, 안무와 구성 두 가지 모두에서 더 대단한 기량을 성취했다. [6C]1661년에, 루이는 세계 최초의 발레 학교인 왕립무용학교를 세우며 발레를 전문적인 연극 예술로서 확립했다. 신체적인 전성기가 지나, 루이는 1669년에 은퇴했는데, 이는 보다 유능하고 재능 있는 무용수들이 주인공 역할을 맡을 수 있게 해주었다.

17세기 후반까지, 현대 발레의 토대가 확립되었다. 발레의 대가들은 발레의 다섯 가지 발의 자세를 체계화하고 음악의 것과 유사한 무용 표기법을 만드는 시도를 통해 그들의 교수법을 체계화하기 시작했다. 게다가, 의상은 더 복잡한 발놀림을 가능하게 하도록 개조되었고, 여성 무용수인 발레리나가 더욱 명성을 얻었다. **최초의 발레리나 중 한 명인 마리 데 카마르고는 그녀의 점프와 혁신적인 동작들로 유명했다.** 이 시기까지, 발레 예술에는 많은 제약이 있었다. 자유롭게 흐르는 동작, 점프, 들어 올리기는 사회적으로 용납되지 않는 것으로 여겨졌다. 효과를 위한 변형은 오직 바닥의 무늬나 속도 변화를 통해서만 이루어질 수 있었다. 이 시기에, 발레는 춤, 노래, 음악의 조합으로 유지되었고, 주로 노래에 중점을 두었다. 그러나, 1760년에 이르러, 발레의 대가들은 궁중 오락의 일부였던 시절로부터 남겨진 불필요한 제한과 엄격한 규약을 문제 삼기 시작했다.

nobility 명 귀족 magnificent 형 웅장한 celebration 명 기념행사
commission 동 의뢰하다 epic 형 대작의, 서사시의
influential 형 영향력 있는 transition 명 전환
profession 명 전문 직업 respectable 형 존경할 만한
exalted 형 높은, 고귀한 devote 동 (노력·시간을) 쏟다, 바치다
proficiency 명 기량, 능숙 choreography 명 안무
composition 명 구성 theatrical 형 연극의 prime 명 전성기
codify 동 체계화하다 notation 명 표기법 intricate 형 복잡한
restriction 명 제약 unwanted 형 불필요한 rigid 형 엄격한
protocol 명 규약

1 지문의 단어 "This"가 가리키는 것은?
(A) 기간
(B) 스펙터클
(C) 결혼식
(D) 공작

2 1단락에 따르면, 다음 중 '스펙터클'에 관해 사실인 것은?
(A) 왕족만 참석하는 것이 허용되었다.
(B) 무언극이 거기에서 처음으로 공연되었다.
(C) 매우 다양한 프로그램들을 특징으로 했다.
(D) 캐서린 데 메디치에 의해 처음 만들어졌다.

3 1단락에서 발레에 관해 추론할 수 있는 것은?
(A) 발레는 종종 결혼식에서 공연된다.
(B) 오늘날의 발레는 노래를 포함하지 않는다.
(C) 발레는 이탈리아에서 인기 있는 오락의 형태였다.
(D) 평균적으로 발레는 5시간 이상 지속된다.

4 지문의 단어 "transition"과 의미가 가장 비슷한 것은?
(A) 기대
(B) 비교
(C) 변화

(D) 기념행사

5 지문의 단어 "proficiency"와 의미가 가장 비슷한 것은?
(A) 퇴보
(B) 능력
(C) 유행
(D) 리듬

6 다음 중 루이 14세에 관해 사실이 아닌 것은?
(A) 질병 때문에 무용계에서 은퇴했다.
(B) 무용에 대한 그의 사랑은 어린 시절에 시작되었다.
(C) 최초의 발레 학교를 설립했다.
(D) 발레를 전문 직업으로 발전시키는 데 도움을 주었다.

7 2단락에서 추론할 수 있는 것으로, 루이 14세는
(A) 은퇴할 때까지 왕립무용학교에서 가르쳤다
(B) 최초의 전문 무용수였다
(C) 그의 발레단에서 주인공 역할을 맡았다
(D) '밤의 발레'의 안무를 짜고 음악을 작곡했다

8 아래 문장 중 지문 속의 음영된 문장의 핵심 정보를 가장 잘 표현한 것은? 오답은 문장의 의미를 크게 바꾸거나 핵심 정보를 생략한다.
(A) 일부 무용수들에게 발레의 동작들은 너무 제한적이었다.
(B) 무용 전문가들은 발레가 그것의 기원 때문에 너무 제한적이라고 느꼈다.
(C) 18세기 중반에 발레는 무용 팬들 사이에서 인기를 잃었다.
(D) 궁중의 일원들을 위한 발레 공연에는 제한이 있었다.

9 네 개의 네모[■]는 다음 문장이 삽입될 수 있는 곳을 나타내고 있다.
최초의 발레리나 중 한 명인 마리 데 카마르고는 그녀의 점프와 혁신적인 동작들로 유명했다.
이 문장은 어디에 들어가는 것이 가장 적절한가?

10 지시: 지문 요약을 위한 도입 문장이 아래에 주어져 있다. 지문의 가장 중요한 내용을 나타내는 보기 3개를 골라 요약을 완성하라. 어떤 문장은 지문에 언급되지 않은 내용이나 사소한 정보를 나타내므로 요약에 포함되지 않는다. **이 문제는 2점이다.**

> **발레는 이탈리아 사회에서 귀족들을 위한 오락으로 시작되었다.**
> · (A) 캐서린 데 메디치에 의해 마련된 공연은 발레의 기원으로 여겨진다.
> · (B) 발레의 예술 형식은 루이 14세 통치하에서 더 중요해졌다.
> · (D) 발레의 동작들은 1600년대에 체계화되었다.

(C) 루이는 '밤의 발레'에서 주역을 맡았을 때 별명을 얻었다.
(E) 19세기 후반까지 대부분의 여성 역할은 남자들이 추었다.
(F) 표기법 체계의 발달은 발레 안무에 제약을 두었다.

Vocabulary Review

본문 p.154

1 similarities　2 attraction　3 efficacy
4 overlooked　5 persecution　6 captivating
7 (C)　8 (D)　9 (B)　10 (A)
11 (A)　12 (C)　13 (D)　14 (C)

CHAPTER 10
Category Chart

Example

본문 p.157

1 Tectonic Lakes: (B), (D), (G)　Glacial Lakes: (E), (F)

호수의 형성

호수는 육지로 둘러싸인 큰 수역이다. 그것들은 매우 다양한 크기, 모양, 깊이로 발견될 수 있고, 염수뿐만 아니라 담수도 포함할 수 있다. 그것들이 형성된 방식에 따라 그것들을 분류하는 것이 가능하다. 예를 들어, 구조호는 지각을 형성하는 판의 움직임이 지면에 나중에 물로 채워지는 균열이나 함몰을 만들 때 형성된다. 구조호는 대개 경사가 가파르다. 그것들은 무리 지어 형성되는 경향이 있고, 일반적으로 다른 호수들에 비해 매우 깊다. 구조호의 예시에는 카스피해와 아랄해가 포함된다. 구조호가 매우 깊을 수 있는 반면, 빙하 활동으로 형성된 호수들은 종종 더 넓은 지역을 덮는다. 북미의 오대호는 마지막 빙하기에 형성된 빙하호로, 그 시기에 빙하라고 불리는 큰 얼음덩어리들이 지형 위로 서서히 이동하여, 분지와 계곡을 남겼다. 호수가 형성되는 다른 방법은 화산 활동, 땅꺼짐, 산사태, 강에 의한 침식을 포함한다. 게다가, 일부 호수는 우주에서 온 운석이 땅에 충돌한 후 형성된다. 이 화구호는 퀘벡의 언게이바 호를 포함한다.

body of water (강·호수 등의) 수역　surrounded 형 둘러싸인
classify 동 분류하다　tectonic lake 구조호(지각 변동으로 생성된 호수)
rift 명 균열, 갈라진 틈　depression 명 함몰, 움푹한 곳
subsequently 부 나중에　steep 형 가파른　slope 명 경사
compared to ~에 비해　glacial 형 빙하의　gradually 부 서서히, 점차
landscape 명 지형　basin 명 분지　valley 명 계곡, 골짜기
volcanic 형 화산의　sinkhole 명 땅꺼짐　landslide 명 산사태
erosion 명 침식　meteorite 명 운석
crater lake 화구호(화산의 화구에 생성된 호수)

1 지시: 주어진 선택지에서 적절한 어구를 선택하여 관계있는 호수의 종류에 연결하시오.

<table>
<tr><th>선택지</th><th>구조호</th></tr>
<tr><td rowspan="3">(A) 화산에서 형성되었다
(C) 산사태로 인해 생겼다</td><td>· (B) 가파른 경사를 특징으로 한다
· (D) 무리 지어 형성되는 경향이 있다
· (G) 매우 깊다</td></tr>
<tr><td>빙하호</td></tr>
<tr><td>· (E) 보다 넓은 지역을 차지한다
· (F) 오대호를 포함한다</td></tr>
</table>

Reading Practice 1

본문 p. 158

1 (A) 2 (C) 3 (D)
4 Applied Arts: (A), (E), (G) Fine Arts: (C), (F)

Vocabulary Quiz

1 ⓑ 2 ⓐ 3 ⓑ 4 ⓒ

예술 분류하기

'예술'이라는 단어는 매우 다양한 인간 노력의 모음을 하나의 넓은 포괄적인 용어로 분류하려는 시도이다. 따라서, '예술'이라는 단어의 정확한 정의는 존재하지 않는다. 그 단어가 묘사하기 원하는 것을 결정하는 것은 사람들에게 달려 있다. [1]이것을 어렵게 만드는 것은 사람들이 그 단어가 묘사하기 원하는 것에 대해 동의하지 못하는 것처럼 보인다는 사실인데, 그들은 그것이 공통점이 거의 없는 것처럼 보이는 많은 것들을 묘사하기를 원한다는 점에만 동의한다. 모네의 그림, 모차르트의 교향곡, 조이스의 '율리시스', 셰익스피어의 '리어왕'을 묘사하는 데 한 단어가 사용될 수 있을까? 그러한 단어는 이미 너무 폭넓게 쓰여서 거의 의미가 없어지게 된 것처럼 보일 것이다. 그럼에도 불구하고 우리는 가령, 소풍 바구니, 화장지, 메이플 시럽 사이에서는 아니지만, 이 모든 것들 사이에 공유되는 무언가가 있다고 본능적으로 느낀다. 예술의 정의를 강구할 때, 순수 예술과 응용 예술을 구별하는 것은 유용하다.

순수 예술의 유일한 목적은 심미적 즐거움을 주는 것이다. 레오나르도 다빈치의 가장 유명한 그림인 '모나리자'에 대해 생각해보자. 그것은 아무런 실용적 기능을 하지 않는다. 사람들은 그것의 아름다움, 실물과 같은 정확성, 능숙한 붓놀림을 감상하는 것 외에는 그것으로 아무것도 할 수 없다. 이제, 사람들이 박물관 기념품점에서 찾을법한 '모나리자'의 그림이 있는 커피 머그잔에 대해 생각해보자. 그 머그잔에 있는 그림은 그 그림의 정확한 복제품일 수는 있지만, 그 머그잔은 뜨거운 음료를 위한 용기를 제공하도록 의도된 것이기에 순수 예술이 아니다. 그것은 심미적 아름다움의 표현 외의 다른 목적을 갖는다.

[3B]'모나리자' 커피 머그잔은 응용 예술의 한 사례이다. 이 예술 범주는 특정한 기능을 하도록 고안된다. 일반적으로 이 분류에 있는 물건들은 상업적인 목적으로 판매되도록 의도된다. 그것들은 아름다울 수 있지만, 또한 실용적이기도 하다. 예를 들어, 고급 자동차는 "예술 작품"으로 묘사될 수 있지만, 분명 그것의 주된 목적은 사람들을 운송하는 것이다. [3A]패션이 같은 범주에 들어가는데, 그것이 예술 디자이너들에 의해 제작되어 구매자의 신체를 심미적으로 보기 좋은 방식으로 감싸기 위해 판매되기 때문이다. [3C]제작 예술 또한 응용 예술에 속하는데, 그것은 영화와 같은 대량 생산된 상업 작품의 제작과 의상 디자인, 특수 효과, 무대 디자인처럼 그것들을 가능하게 하는 요소 분야를 포함한다.

endeavor 명 노력 umbrella 형 포괄적인 definition 명 정의
describe 동 묘사하다 symphony 명 교향곡 apply 동 쓰다
broadly 부 폭넓게 meaningless 형 의미가 없는
instinctively 부 본능적으로 pursue 동 강구하다, 추구하다
distinguish 동 구별하다 fine arts 순수 예술
applied arts 응용 예술 aesthetic 형 심미적인, 미학적인
utilitarian 형 실용적인 appreciate 동 감상하다
accuracy 명 정확성 masterful 형 능숙한
reproduction 명 복제품 container 명 용기, 그릇
commercial 형 상업적인 discipline 명 (학문 등의) 분야

1 1단락에 따르면, 예술을 정의하기가 어려운 것은
(A) 사람들이 서로 다른 것들을 묘사하기 위해 그 단어를 사용하기 때문이다
(B) 특정한 대상들이 분명하게 예술의 어떠한 정의에도 들어맞지 않기 때문이다
(C) 그 용어가 심미적으로 보기 좋지 않은 대상을 포함하지 않기 때문이다
(D) 순수 예술이 응용 예술과 종종 혼동되기 때문이다

2 지문의 단어 "them"이 가리키는 것은?
(A) 순수 예술
(B) 응용 예술
(C) 영화
(D) 분야

3 지문에 따르면, 다음 중 응용 예술이 아닌 것은?
(A) 의복
(B) 기념품점의 커피 머그잔
(C) 무대 디자인
(D) 교향곡

4 지시: 주어진 선택지에서 적절한 어구를 선택하여 관계있는 예술의 종류에 연결하시오.

선택지	응용 예술
(B) 금전적 가치가 거의 없다 (D) 복제하기 어렵다	· (A) 실용적인 용도로 쓰인다 · (E) 대개 상업적인 이유로 만들어진다 · (G) 영화와 다른 제작 예술을 포함한다
	순수 예술
	· (C) 순수한 심미적 즐거움을 주기 위해 고안된다 · (F) 실용적인 기능을 제공하지 않는다

Reading Practice 2

본문 p. 160

1 (C) 2 (A) 3 (A)
4 Placental Mammals: (C), (D), (G) Marsupials: (B), (E)

Vocabulary Quiz

1 ⓐ 2 ⓒ 3 ⓑ 4 ⓑ

태반 포유류와 유대류

[1B/1D]포유류는 척추가 있고, 머리카락이나 털로 덮여 있으며, 일반적으로 알을 낳는 대신 새끼를 출산하는 동물이다. [1A]이 넓은 분류에는 두 개의 더 작은 집단이 있는데, 바로 태반 포유류와 유대류이다. 이 두 포유류 집단의 중요한 차이점은 그것들의 새끼가 성장하는 방식이다.

태반 포유류는 그것들이 잘 발달된 태반을 가지고 있다는 사실에 의해 구분되는데, 그것은 성장하는 태아에 양분을 공급하는 어미의 자궁 속

장기이다. 태반 포유류는 자궁 속 새끼에게 더 많은 양분을 공급하기 때문에, 그것들은 유대류의 상대보다 잘 발달된, 어미에게 덜 의존적인 더 큰 새끼를 낳는다. 태반 포유류는 유대류에 비해 더 적은 이빨을 가지고 태어나며, 평생 하나가 아닌 두 열의 이빨을 갖는다. 그것들은 또한 더 높은 신진대사율을 가지고 있다. 그것들은 오늘날 살아 있는 현대 포유류 종의 대다수를 차지한다. 인간은 태반 포유류이며, 고래, 고양이, 말 또한 그렇다.

비록 유대류 또한 태반을 가지고 있지만, 그것들의 새끼는 몸 밖의 주머니 속에서 성장한다. [3]유대류의 태반은 임신 초기에 영양분을 제공하며, 태아는 매우 짧은 기간 동안만 그것에 붙어 있다. 그것들이 태어날 때, 유대류 새끼들은 귀나 뒷다리가 없고 눈이 보이지 않는데, 이 특징들은 그것들이 어미의 주머니 속에 있는 동안 생긴다. 겨우 몇 달 동안만 젖을 먹이는 태반 포유류에 비해 유대류는 오랫동안 모유를 먹는다. 유대류의 새끼가 어미의 출산 통로에서 주머니로 들어가는 길을 찾기 위해 강한 앞발과 예민한 후각을 사용한다는 것은 주목할 만하다. 캥거루가 모든 유대류 중에서 가장 유명하며, 다른 것들로는 주머니쥐와 코알라가 있다. 화석 기록이 그것들이 한때 더 널리 퍼져 있었다는 것을 보여주기는 하지만, 그것들은 주로 호주에서 발견된다.

그것들의 차이점에도 불구하고, 태반 포유류와 유대류는 상당한 공통점을 가지고 있다. 두 집단 모두 새끼를 위해 모유를 생산하는 온혈의, 공기를 호흡하는 동물들로 이루어져 있다. 그것들 사이의 주요한 차이점은 유대류가 바깥세상에 보이는 새끼를 키우기 위해 주머니를 사용한다는 것이다.

mammal ⓜ포유류 marsupial ⓜ유대류; ⓗ유대류의
spine ⓜ척추 offspring ⓜ새끼, 자손 classification ⓜ분류
placental ⓗ태반의; ⓜ태반 포유류 distinguish ⓥ구분하다
placenta ⓜ태반 organ ⓜ장기 womb ⓜ자궁
nourishment ⓜ양분 fetus ⓜ태아 counterpart ⓜ상대, 대응물
metabolic rate 신진대사율 account for ~을 차지하다
pouch ⓜ주머니 lactate ⓥ젖을 먹이다 keen ⓗ예민한
opossum ⓜ주머니쥐 warm-blooded ⓗ온혈의
distinction ⓜ차이점 visible ⓗ보이는

1 1단락에 따르면, 다음 중 유대류와 태반 포유류 둘 다에 관해 사실이 아닌 것은?
(A) 둘 다 포유류이다.
(B) 둘 다 털로 덮여 있다.
(C) 둘 다 적은 수의 새끼만 낳는다.
(D) 둘 다 척추가 있다.

2 아래 문장 중 지문 속의 음영된 문장의 핵심 정보를 가장 잘 표현한 것은?
(A) 태반 포유류는 유대류보다 더 크고, 더 잘 발달되었고, 더 독립적인 새끼를 낳는다.
(B) 태반 포유류가 자궁에서 더 많이 먹기 때문에, 그것들은 유대류의 상대보다 더 크게 자란다.
(C) 태반 포유류가 자궁에서 새끼에게 양분을 공급하는 데 반해 유대류는 의존적인 새끼를 낳는다.
(D) 태반 포유류의 자궁은 유대류의 자궁보다 더 많은 양분을 함유한다.

3 글쓴이가 유대류에 관해 묘사하는 것은?
(A) 태반에의 짧은 부착
(B) 자궁 내에서의 긴 수유 기간
(C) 새끼일 때의 튼튼하고 뭉툭한 뒷다리
(D) 어미가 주머니로 운반하는 방법

4 지시: 주어진 선택지에서 적절한 어구를 선택하여 관계있는 동물의 종류에 연결하시오.

선택지	태반 포유류
(A) 냉혈 동물이다 (F) 일생 동안 세 열의 치아가 발달한다	· (C) 더 큰 새끼를 출산한다 · (D) 긴 기간 동안 자궁 속의 새끼에게 양분을 공급한다 · (G) 일생 동안 두 열의 치아가 발달한다
	유대류
	· (B) 미성숙한 새끼를 낳는다 · (E) 주머니 속 새끼에게 양분을 공급한다

Reading Practice 3

본문 p.162

1 (C) 2 (D) 3 (C)
4 Veblen Goods: (A), (D), (G) Giffen Goods: (B), (E)

Vocabulary Quiz
1 ⓒ 2 ⓐ 3 ⓑ 4 ⓑ

베블런재와 기펜재

수요의 법칙은 재화의 가격과 소비자가 구매하는 양 사이에 반비례 관계가 존재한다고 명시한다. 다시 말해서, 만약 재화의 가격이 높다면, 더 적은 재화가 팔릴 것이다. 그리고, 이에 상응하여, 가격이 가장 낮을 때 재화는 사실상 날개 돋친 듯 팔린다. 물론 이것이 상점이 상품을 할인하는 이유이다. 판매하는 물품의 수가 늘어남에 따라 그들의 총수익이 커질 것이기 때문에 그들은 기꺼이 개별 물품에서 일부 수익을 희생한다. 그러나, 베블런재와 기펜재는 이 법칙의 예외이다.

베블런재는 수요의 법칙을 거스르는데, 이는 일부 아주 고가의 제품 구매에 일정 수준의 지위가 붙기 때문이다. 그 현상은 19세기의 경제학자 소스타인 베블런에 의해 발견되었다. 그는 비싼 가격이 높은 품질의 증거로 인식되기 때문에 특정 사치품이 구매된다는 이론을 제시했다. 새로운 스포츠카 모델이 소형차의 가격과 경쟁할 수 있는 가격으로 출시된다고 가정해보자. 처음에, 그 차는 저렴한 정가에 반응해 판매량이 증가하면서 수요의 법칙을 따라간다. 그런 다음, 그 자동차의 품질이 인정받게 됨에 따라, 제조업체는 가격을 올리기 시작한다. [2]가격이 특정 한계점에 도달하면, 그 자동차는 부유한 소비자들에게 명성을 얻기 시작하고, 가격에 따라 수요가 늘어난다. 베블런재는 위치재인데, 이는 그것들이 레오나르도 다빈치의 그림처럼 제한된 이용 가능한 공급 때문에 가치 있게 여겨진다는 것을 의미한다.

이 영역의 반대쪽 끝에는 기펜재가 있는데, 이는 통계학자 로버트 기펜의 이름을 따서 명명되었다. 그는 필수 상품이 필요하고 더 저렴한 대안이 없을 때는 수요의 법칙이 적용되지 않는다는 점에 주목했다. 이러한 경우, 가격이 올라가면 소비자는 이 종류의 제품을 더 적게가 아니라 더 많이 살 것이다. 주로 빵과 고기를 소비하는 한정된 식비 예산을 가지고 있는 가정을 생각해보자. 빵이 고기보다 훨씬 더 저렴하기 때문에, 그것은 예산의 대부분을 차지할 것이다. [3]만일 빵의 가격이 올라가

면, 그 가정은 그것이 여전히 충분한 음식을 갖도록 보장해야 한다. 이렇게 하기 위해, 그것은 가장 저렴한 필수 상품에 대한 지출을 늘리고 더 비싼 것에 대한 지출을 줄여야 할 것이다. 사실상, 빵 가격의 상승이 그 가정이 어쩔 수 없이 그것을 더 많이 사도록 만들 것이다.

law of demand 수요의 법칙 inverse 형반비례의
correspondingly 부이에 상응하여 virtually 부사실상
fly off the shelves 날개 돋친 듯 팔리다 sacrifice 동희생하다
revenue 명수익 defy 동거스르다 exceptionally 부아주
phenomenon 명현상 theorize 동이론을 제시하다
perceive 동인식하다 indication 명증거
affordable 형저렴한 sticker price (자동차의) 정가, 권장 소매 가격
inflate 동(가격을) 올리다 threshold 명한계점, 문턱
prestige 명명성, 위신 affluent 형부유한
staple goods (주식 등의) 필수 상품 alternative 명대안

1 지문의 단어 "They"가 가리키는 것은?
(A) 재화
(B) 선반
(C) 상점들
(D) 물품

2 2단락에 따르면, 스포츠카 제조업체가 더 많은 차를 판매하는 것은
(A) 중산층 소비자가 자동차를 지위의 상징으로 간주하기 때문이다
(B) 자동차의 공급이 가격과 함께 상승하기 때문이다
(C) 소비자가 자동차를 살 수 있을 때까지 가격이 내려가기 때문이다
(D) 더 비싼 상품이 더 지위가 높다고 여겨지기 때문이다

3 다음 중 3단락에서 기펜재에 관해 추론할 수 있는 것은?
(A) 가격이 심하게 변동하는 경향이 있다
(B) 불경기에 가격이 상승한다.
(C) 가난한 소비자들에게 더 인기가 있다.
(D) 보통 제한된 수량만 이용 가능하다.

4 지시: 주어진 선택지에서 적절한 어구를 선택하여 관계있는 재화의 종류에 연결하시오.

<table>
<tr><th>선택지</th><th>베블런재</th></tr>
<tr><td rowspan="3">(C) 수요의 법칙을 따른다
(F) 자주 할인되는 경향이 있다</td><td>· (A) 일반적으로 사치품이다
· (D) 품질이 높다고 인식된다
· (G) 제한된 공급 때문에 가치 있게 여겨진다</td></tr>
<tr><td>기펜재</td></tr>
<tr><td>· (B) 더 저렴한 대안이 없다
· (E) 일반적으로 필수 상품이다</td></tr>
</table>

Reading Practice 4

본문 p.164

1 (A) 2 (C) 3 (C)
4 Freud: (B), (C), (G) Jung: (D), (F)

Vocabulary Quiz

1 ⓑ 2 ⓒ 3 ⓐ 4 ⓐ

꿈의 해석자들

오스트리아의 정신과 의사 지그문트 프로이트는 정신 분석학의 아버지로 여겨지며, 한때 그는 그의 젊은 동료 칼 융을 직업상의 후계자로 인정했다. 1907년에 두 사람이 처음 만났을 때, 그들은 13시간 동안 정신 분석에 대한 공통된 관심사에 관해 이야기를 나누었다. 여기에는 환자의 무의식의 비밀을 푸는 도구로 꿈을 이용하는 것이 포함되었다. [1]두 사람 모두에게, 꿈은 환자들이 정신적인 문제를 해결하도록 도울 수 있는 상징들을 포함했다. 그러나, 융이 여러 중요한 방식에서 스승의 이론과 의견을 달리하면서, 1913년 경에 그들의 상호 존경은 약해졌다.

프로이트는 주로 무의식적인 욕망의 억압에 의해 꿈이 발생한다고 생각했다. 그것들은 '이드'의 발현이었다. 이는 프로이트가 '자아'라고 불렀던, 의식에게는 대체로 알려지지 않는 기본 욕망에 의해 이끌리는 인간 정신의 구성 요소이다. 이드의 격렬한 갈망은 현실에서는 도덕적 판단을 하는 '초자아'에 의해 억압되었는데, 초자아는 그것의 욕구를 사회적으로 용인되는 행동으로 바꾸었다. 꿈속에서, 이드는 암호화된 이미지로 그것의 소망을 자유롭게 성취했다. 이러한 이미지들은 모든 사람에게 일관된 인식 가능한 상징이었다. 예를 들어, 만약 아내가 한 남자를 쏴 죽이는 꿈을 꾼다면, 프로이트는 그녀가 남모르게 남편을 미워하고 있다고 그녀에게 말할 것이다.

융은 꿈의 기능에 더 관심이 있었다. [3A]이 더 젊은 정신과 의사는 꿈이 의식과 무의식 사이의 다리라고 생각했다. [3D]꿈의 고정된 상징에 대한 일종의 사전을 만들고자 했던 프로이트의 시도를 무시하면서, 융은 꿈에서 나타나는 상징들이 사람과 맥락에 따라 의미가 다양할 수 있다고 생각했다. [3B]게다가, 융에게는 무의식의 영적인 능력이 중요했던 반면, 프로이트는 모든 유심론을 망상이라고 생각했다. 위의 사례에서, 융은 그 여성의 총 쏘는 꿈이 아마도 남편에 대해 숨겨진 욕망을 표현하는 것이 아니라고 말할 것이다. 대신, 그녀의 영혼이 자신에게 느끼는 감정에 관한 메시지를 보내오는 중이었을지도 모른다. 결국, 융은 프로이트로부터 스스로를 분리시켰고, 자신만의 불후한 정신 분석 학파를 발전시켰다.

psychiatrist 명정신과 의사 psychoanalysis 명정신 분석학
heir 명후계자, 상속자 unconscious mind 무의식, 잠재의식
resolve 동해결하다 mutual 형상호의 admiration 명존경
dim 동약해지다 diverge from ~과 의견을 달리하다
repression 명억압 manifestation 명발현 raging 형격렬한
craving 명갈망 repress 동억압하다 waking life 현실
judgmental 형도덕적 판단을 하는 channel 동(어떤 방향으로) 바꾸다
acceptable 형용인되는 coded 형암호화된
identifiable 형인식 가능한 disdain 동무시하다, 경멸하다
emerge 동나타나다 spiritualism 명유심론, 정신주의
delusional 형망상의 enduring 형불후한, 영속적인

1 1단락에 따르면, 프로이트와 융 둘 다 꿈을
(A) 환자를 치료하는 데 유용하다고 여겼다
(B) 영성과 양립할 수 없다고 여겼다
(C) 사회적 관습에 의해 억압된다고 여겼다
(D) 보편적인 상징을 포함한다고 여겼다

2 지문의 단어 "its"가 가리키는 것은?
(A) 정신
(B) 자아
(C) 이드
(D) 초자아

3 글쓴이가 꿈에 대한 융의 관점에 관해 묘사하지 않는 것은?

(A) 무의식과 의식의 연결
(B) 유심론에 대한 강조
(C) 개인적 욕망의 원인
(D) 상징의 맥락적 성격

4 지시: 주어진 선택지에서 적절한 어구를 선택하여 관계있는 심리학자에 연결하시오.

선택지	프로이트
(A) 꿈이 부도덕하다고 생각했다 (E) 꿈이 미래의 범죄 행위를 예측한다고 말했다	· (B) 꿈이 억압된 욕망을 성취한다고 생각했다 · (C) 꿈의 원인에 초점을 맞추었다 · (G) 특정 이미지들의 의미를 발견했다
	융
	· (D) 꿈의 목적에 초점을 맞추었다 · (F) 상징의 고정된 해석에 반대했다

iBT Reading Test

본문 p.166

1 (B) 2 (C) 3 (A) 4 (C)
5 (C) 6 (A) 7 (B) 8 (C)
9 (B) 10 Earth's Atmosphere: (B), (C), (F)
Mars's Atmosphere: (D), (E)

지구와 화성의 대기

대기는 행성을 둘러싸고 있는 겹겹의 기체로 된 덮개이다. [3]행성의 표면에서 뻗어 나온 이 기체 거품은 중력에 의해 유지된다. 대기가 생명체를 위한 필요 조건으로 보이지만, 대기가 있다고 해서 생명체가 발달할 것임을 보장하지는 않는다. 특정 행성에서 생명체의 생존 가능성을 결정하는 데 있어서 대기의 온도, 기체의 구성, 밀도는 몇 가지 중요한 고려 사항이다. 이 요인들은 지구가 생명체로 가득한 이유와 이웃의 화성은 불모지로 보이는 이유를 설명하는 데 도움을 준다.

지구가 지표면에서 발산하는 열을 가두는 온실 효과의 대기를 가지고 있기 때문에 귀중한 온기를 유지하는 반면, 화성은 훨씬 더 약한 온실 효과를 갖는다. 화성은 생명체가 살 수 없는 화씨 영하 80도가 평균인 반면, 지구는 결과적으로 그것의 지표면에서 평균 59도의 기온을 유지한다. 화성의 기온은 또한 지구의 것보다 훨씬 더 크게 변동하는데, 적도에서는 범위가 낮 동안 70도에서 밤에는 영하 100도까지 이른다.

온실 효과는 행성 대기의 존재에 의해 만들어진다. [5A]이산화탄소같은 온실가스는 태양 방사선을 흡수하여, 마치 행성을 덮은 담요처럼 열을 흡수한다. **그것들은 햇빛은 투과시키지만 적외 방사선은 투과시키지 않기 때문에 이것을 할 수 있다.** 이 기체들이 온실 효과를 만들어 내기 위해 대기 성분에서 가장 많을 필요는 없다. 화성의 대기는 온실가스인 이산화탄소가 95퍼센트이고, 지구의 대기는 질소가 71퍼센트인데, 질소는 온실가스가 아니다. [5B]그렇다면 왜 화성이 더 온실 효과가 약할까? [5D]그 이유는 화성 대기의 밀도인데, 그것은 지구의 것보다 100배 더 희박하다. 이 희박한 대기는 태양풍 및 우주 방사선과 같은 우주 입자들의 끊임없는 충돌로부터 오는 방사선에 대한 보호를 거의 제공하지 못한다. 그러나, 이것이 수십억 년 전에는 그렇지 않았을지도 모른다. 로봇 및 항공 우주 비행으로 축적된 증거는 한때 화성의 표면에 물이 흘렀다는 가설을 뒷받침한다. 만약 그렇다면, 화성은 아마도 태양풍이나 거대한 우주 물체와의 충돌로 인해 제거된 더 빽빽한 대기가 있었을 것이다. [8]지구상 870만 개의 종에게는 다행스럽게도, 우리의 대기는 강력한 자기장에 의해 태양풍으로부터 보호되는데, 이는 화성에는 없는 특징이다.

atmosphere 명 대기 layered 형 겹겹의, 층을 이룬
envelope 명 덮개, 외피 guarantee 동 보장하다
determine 동 결정하다 viability 명 생존 가능성
consideration 명 고려 사항 gaseous 형 기체의
composition 명 구성, 성분 density 명 밀도
be teeming with ~으로 가득하다 barren 형 불모지인
retain 동 유지하다 emanate 동 발산하다, 내뿜다
deadly 형 생명체가 살 수 없는 fluctuate 동 변동하다
range from A to B 범위가 A에서 B까지 이르다 equator 명 적도
absorb 동 흡수하다 radiation 명 방사선
dominate 동 (~중에서) 가장 많다 impact 명 충돌
cosmic rays 우주 방사선 accumulate 동 축적하다
aerial 형 항공의 space mission 우주 비행
hypothesis 명 가설 strip away ~을 제거하다 collision 명 충돌
robust 형 강력한 magnetic field 자기장

1 아래 문장 중 지문 속의 음영된 문장의 핵심 정보를 가장 잘 표현한 것은? 오답은 문장의 의미를 크게 바꾸거나 핵심 정보를 생략한다.

(A) 생명체는 행성의 대기가 없어도 나타날 수 있는데, 이 두 가지가 상호 의존적이지 않기 때문이다.
(B) 일부 행성은 대기가 있고 생명체가 없지만, 생명체는 있지만 대기가 없는 행성은 없다.
(C) 생명체에 대한 보장은 어느 행성에도 존재하지 않지만, 대기는 그것의 존재를 불가능하게 한다.
(D) 생명체는 때때로 대기와 함께 나타나지만, 그러한 필요 조건은 존재하지 않는다.

2 지문의 단어 "teeming"과 의미가 가장 비슷한 것은?

(A) 비어 있는
(B) 섬세한
(C) 풍부한
(D) 합리적인

3 1단락에 따르면, 행성을 둘러싼 기체가 유지되는 것은

(A) 그것들에게 중력이 가해지기 때문이다
(B) 그것들이 대기의 태양 방사선을 가두기 때문이다
(C) 대기가 그것들을 유지할 정도로 충분히 빽빽하기 때문이다
(D) 그것들이 여러 층으로 분포되어 있기 때문이다

4 지문의 단어 "its"가 가리키는 것은?

(A) 화성
(B) 효과
(C) 지구
(D) 기온

5 다음 중 지구의 온실 효과에 관해 사실이 아닌 것은?

(A) 대기를 따뜻하게 한다.
(B) 화성의 그것보다 더 강하다.
(C) 질소의 존재에 의해 만들어진다.
(D) 대기의 밀도 때문에 가능하다.

6 지문의 단어 "impact"와 의미가 가장 비슷한 것은?

(A) 충돌
(B) 연속
(C) 노출
(D) 결과

7 4단락에서 글쓴이는 왜 화성의 물에 관해 논하는가?

(A) 희박한 대기에도 불구하고 화성이 한때 생명체를 수용했다는 증거를 제시하기 위해
(B) 화성 대기의 과거 상태에 관한 가설의 근거를 설명하기 위해
(C) 화성 생명체의 가능성에 관한 지문의 앞선 진술을 반박하기 위해
(D) 수십억 년 동안 화성의 대기가 변하지 않았다는 것을 입증하기 위해

8 4단락에 따르면, 지구가 화성보다 더 빽빽한 대기를 갖는 것은

(A) 온실가스가 더 적기 때문이다
(B) 대기가 태양풍을 흡수하기 때문이다
(C) 자기장으로 둘러싸여 있기 때문이다
(D) 화성보다 어린 행성이기 때문이다

9 네 개의 네모[■]는 다음 문장이 삽입될 수 있는 곳을 나타내고 있다.

그것들은 햇빛은 투과시키지만 적외 방사선은 투과시키지 않기 때문에 이것을 할 수 있다.

이 문장은 어디에 들어가는 것이 가장 적절한가?

10 **지시:** 주어진 선택지에서 적절한 어구를 선택하여 관계있는 종류에 연결하시오. **이 문제는 3점이다.**

선택지	지구의 대기
(A) 주로 산소로 구성되어 있다 (G) 날씨를 지탱하기에는 너무 희박하다	· (B) 자기장에 의해 보호된다 · (C) 화씨 59도의 평균 기온을 가지고 있다. · (F) 강력한 온실 효과를 가지고 있다
	화성의 대기
	· (D) 이산화탄소가 가장 많다 · (E) 100배 더 희박하다

Vocabulary Review

본문 p.170

1 ranging 2 sacrificed 3 mutual
4 meaningless 5 aesthetic 6 appreciated
7 (A) 8 (C) 9 (B) 10 (D)
11 (C) 12 (B) 13 (D) 14 (A)

Actual Test 1

Passage 1

본문 p.172

1 (C) 2 (D) 3 (B) 4 (A)
5 (A) 6 (C) 7 (C) 8 (D)
9 (B) 10 (C), (D), (F)

농업 노동에서의 말

기원전 4000년경 가축화 이후로, 말은 음식, 운송, 농업을 포함하는 다양한 목적으로 인간에 의해 이용되어 왔다. 몸에 나무와 금속으로 된 장치가 부착된 이 커다란 포유류는 인간의 능력을 능가하는 속도로 농경지를 경작할 수 있다. 그들의 강한 견인력은 밭이 갈리거나 수확될 수 있는 속도를 크게 높인다. 그러나, 농기구로서 그들의 이용은 점진적으로 이루어졌고 시간이 지남에 따라 변화했다.

처음, 인간이 농경 사회로 전환함에 따라 소가 전통적으로 인간들에게 선호되었다. [4]소는 상당히 더 느리기는 하지만, 더 많은 근육량을 가지고 있어서 말보다 무거운 무게를 끌 수 있다. 이러한 초기의 선호로 인해, 밭일을 위한 멍에는 말의 그것보다는 소의 신체 구조에 맞게 설계되었다. 말에 더 적합한 멍에를 만들려는 시도는 기원전 481년 중국의 가슴 끈 발명과 함께 시작되었는데, 그것은 결국 유럽에 도입되어 목을 완전히 덮는 어깨띠로 변형된 혁신이었다. 서기 1100년에 이르러서, 이 목을 완전히 덮는 어깨띠는 원래의 몸통 끈이 없고 대신 가죽으로 묶인 한 쌍의 구부러진 나무 조각으로 구성되었다. 이것들은 아래에 두텁게 솜을 넣어, 당기는 하중의 무게를 어깨에 고르게 분산시켜 동물의 숨통에 가해지는 압력을 줄였다. 이러한 변화들은 말이 이전의 어깨띠에 비해 주어진 작업에 50퍼센트 더 많은 힘을 가할 수 있게 해주었다.

중세 유럽에서 이러한 발전의 사회적, 경제적 영향은 광범위했다. 직접적인 결과는 소작농의 효율성과 농작물 수확량의 증가였다. 말은 그들의 발굽이 잘 맞는 굽과 세심한 세척을 필요로 했기 때문에 시간이 오래 걸리는 보살핌을 필요로 했지만, 그들의 빠른 속도는 소보다 더 큰 이익이 되었다. 농부들이 부유해지고 상업과 같은 다른 분야를 전문으로 하기 시작하면서, 이러한 개선은 유럽 경제를 자극했다. [6]게다가, 작은 농장들이 과거 시대보다 더 많은 사람들을 부양할 수 있었기 때문에 더 많은 농작물 수확량으로 인한 잉여 식량은 인구 증가를 가능하게 했다.

그것의 이점에도 불구하고, 효율적인 말 중심 농업의 시대는 결국 끝이 났다. [7]처음에 이것은 1840년대 영국에서 증기 기관의 등장 때문이었다. 시간이 지남에 따라, 증기 동력 수확기가 인기를 얻었다. **그 결과, 영국 농장에서 일하는 말의 수가 97퍼센트 감소했다.** 마찬가지로, 트랙터는 1940년대에 기계화의 확산과 함께 미국 농가에서 빠르게 우위를 점했고 말을 대체하기 시작했다. 저렴한 연료비와 저금리의 연방 정부 대출로 미국 농부들은 현대 기술에 투자할 수 있게 되었고, 그 결과 동물은 거의 완전히 농업에서 사라지게 되었다.

최근 몇 년간, 환경 보호와 에너지 절약에 관한 관심 확산에 따라 소규모 농장주들이 말을 농기구로 다시 사용하면서 말 기반의 농업이 부활하고 있다. 지지자들은 말이 풀을 먹고 관리를 덜 필요로 하기 때문에 저렴하다고 주장한다. [8A/8C]대조적으로 트랙터는 지속적인 재급유, 반복적인 관리가 필요하고 값비싼 부품 교체가 필요하다. [8B]게다가, 비록 동물이 트랙터보다 효율은 낮지만, 그들은 유해 가스를 배출하지 않는다.

employ 동 이용하다, 고용하다　device 명 장치　mammal 명 포유류
cultivate 동 경작하다　surpass 동 능가하다　tractive force 견인력
significantly 부 크게, 상당히　boost 동 높이다, 증대시키다
gradually 부 점진적으로　agrarian 형 농경의, 농업의
preference 명 선호　yoke 명 (소에 씌우는) 멍에　bovine 형 소의
anatomy 명 (해부학적) 신체 구조　collar 명 (말의) 어깨띠
padded 형 솜을 넣은　pressure 명 압력　windpipe 명 숨통, 기관
evenly 부 고르게　far-reaching 형 광범위한　efficiency 명 효율성
crop yields 농작물 수확량　peasant farmer 소작농
necessitate 동 필요로 하다　profitable 형 이익이 되는
specialize in ~을 전문으로 하다　surplus 명 잉여, 과잉
advent 명 등장, 출현　dominance 명 우위, 우세
mechanization 명 기계화　low-interest 형 저금리의
federal 형 (미국) 연방 정부의　be phased out of ~에서 사라지다
recurrent 형 반복적인

1 지문의 단어 "surpass"와 의미가 가장 비슷한 것은?
(A) 지지하다
(B) 발견하다
(C) 넘다
(D) 넓히다

2 지문의 단어 "that"이 가리키는 것은?
(A) 선호
(B) 멍에
(C) 밭일
(D) 신체 구조

3 지문의 단어 "modified"와 의미가 가장 비슷한 것은?
(A) 설계되다
(B) 수정되다
(C) 속다
(D) 특징지어지다

4 2단락에 따르면, 농사에 있어서 본래 소가 말보다 선호된 것은
(A) 더 큰 무게를 끌 수 있었기 때문이다
(B) 승객을 더 먼 거리로 실어 나를 수 있었기 때문이다
(C) 더 빠른 속도로 훈련될 수 있었기 때문이다
(D) 더 빠르게 성장하는 것이 증명되었기 때문이다

5 아래 문장 중 지문 속의 음영된 문장의 핵심 정보를 가장 잘 표현한 것은? 오답은 문장의 의미를 크게 바꾸거나 핵심 정보를 생략한다.
(A) 말은 더 많은 노력을 필요로 했지만, 소보다 더 높은 수익을 창출했다.
(B) 말이 물건을 옮길 수 있었지만, 소가 운반에 더 효율적이었다.
(C) 농부들은 말을 선호했지만, 소보다 유지비가 더 비쌌다.
(D) 말 농사는 소가 필요로 하지 않는 신발을 포함했다.

6 3단락에 따르면, 목을 완전히 덮는 어깨띠는 중세 유럽에 어떤 영향을 미쳤는가?
(A) 소작농들이 농장 규모를 확장할 수 있게 해주었다.
(B) 부유한 농부들이 더 많은 소를 구매하게 했다.
(C) 인구의 증가로 이어졌다.
(D) 농부들 간의 말 거래를 촉진했다.

7 4단락에서 증기 기관 기계에 관해 추론할 수 있는 것은?
(A) 영국 내에서만 인기가 있었다.
(B) 그것의 발명가는 말의 작업에서 영감을 받았다.
(C) 농경에서의 사용은 영국에서 처음 일어났다.
(D) 발명 직후 농부들에 의해 거부되었다.

8 5단락에 따르면, 다음 중 트랙터 농업의 부정적 측면이 아닌 것은?
(A) 반복적인 연료비
(B) 유해 가스 배출
(C) 값비싼 수리
(D) 제한된 효율성

9 네 개의 네모[■]는 다음 문장이 삽입될 수 있는 곳을 나타내고 있다.
그 결과, 영국 농장에서 일하는 말의 수가 97퍼센트 감소했다.
이 문장은 어디에 들어가는 것이 가장 적절한가?

10 **지시:** 지문 요약을 위한 도입 문장이 아래에 주어져 있다. 지문의 가장 중요한 내용을 나타내는 보기 3개를 골라 요약을 완성하라. 어떤 문장은 지문에 언급되지 않은 내용이나 사소한 정보를 나타내므로 요약에 포함되지 않는다. **이 문제는 2점이다.**

> **말 농업 방식은 시간이 지나면서 발전하여 20세기에 이르러 구식이 되었지만 그것들은 환경 문제로 인해 부활했다.**
> · (C) 멍에의 발전은 말 기반 농업의 역사에서 중요했다.
> · (D) 현대의 소규모 농장은 말 농업으로 돌아감으로써 많은 이점을 얻을 수 있다.
> · (F) 증기 기관 기계가 농업 노동에서 말을 대체하기 시작했다.

(A) 말은 농업 생산성을 향상시키는 데 이용된 최초의 동물이 아니었다.
(B) 중국인들이 5세기에 최초로 말을 최대한 활용했다.
(E) 말 경작으로 창출된 부는 농부들이 상인이 되는 것을 가능하게 했다.

Passage 2

본문 p. 176

11 (C)　12 (C)　13 (D)　14 (B)
15 (C)　16 (A)　17 (B)　18 (C)
19 (A)　20 (A), (C), (E)

산불을 확산시키는 원인

기후 변화로 인해 더 많은 산불에 직면하게 됨에 따라 산불에 대한 과학적 정밀 조사가 강화되어 왔다. 그러나, 그것들의 빈도와 관계없이, 그것들의 확산 속도는 항상 같은 요소에 의해 결정된다. 이것들 중 첫 번째이자 가장 중요한 것은 연료의 이용 가능성이다. 자연 환경에서 연소하기 쉬운 모든 것이 연료가 될 수 있다. 이것은 사람이 만든 많은 구조물과 물건들뿐만 아니라 나무와 덤불도 포함한다. 모든 물질은 불이 타오르는 온도를 가지고 있다. 이 온도는 인화점으로 알려져 있다. 13 예를 들어, 나무가 섭씨 300도의 인화점까지 가열되면, 그것은 공기의 산소와 섞여 연소하는 무색의 탄화수소 가스를 방출하기 시작한다. 일단 최초의 연소가 발생하면, 불은 그것을 둘러싸고 있는 추진 연료의 종류에 따라 확산된다. 제한된 연료 공급원은 새로운 산불이 천천히 번지고 낮은 강도로 타오르게 할 것이다. 그러나, 풍부한 것은 빠른 움직임과 매우 강한 열을 발생시킬 것이다.

기상 조건 역시 산불이 얼마나 빨리 확산되는지에 중요한 역할을 하며, 가장 관련성이 높은 두 가지 변수는 습도와 바람이다. 가뭄 기간에는, 작은 불꽃이나 단 한 번의 번개만으로도 산불이 시작될 수 있다. 그러

나, 더 습한 조건에서는, 더 많거나 지속적인 열원이 산불 확산에 필요하다. 마찬가지로, 더 강한 바람은 더 빠른 확산과 관련이 있다. **이는 바람이 산불에 추가적인 산소를 공급하여 더 빨리 움직이게 하기 때문이다.** 게다가, 바람은 불의 방향을 정할 수 있고 때로는 가장 큰 파괴가 일어날 수 있는 지역으로 그것을 옮긴다. 1990년대 초 연구진에 의해 처음 언급된 산불의 특징은 크고 격렬한 산불이 불 회오리라고 알려진 바람을 스스로 일으킬 수 있다는 것이다. 불 회오리는 불의 열에 의해 생성된 소용돌이에서 발생한다. [15]이것들은 불을 키울 수 있으며 종종 물질을 멀리까지 퍼뜨릴 수 있을 정도로 충분히 강하다.

거기에 더해, 지형 그 자체가 산불이 발달하는 속도의 중요한 결정 요인이다. 특히, 평평하거나 완만하게 경사진 지형은 심하게 경사진 지형보다 산불을 지속시킬 가능성이 훨씬 적다. 열이 상승하기 때문에, 불은 내리막길이나 평지를 가로지르기보다 오르막으로 훨씬 빠르게 이동하는 경향이 있고, 화염의 길이가 더 길다. 산불의 진전 정도는 또한 그것이 마주하는 방향의 경사 방향에 영향을 받는데, 북쪽을 향한 경사면은 남쪽을 향한 경사면보다 더 느리게 건조해지고 가열되기 때문이다. 이러한 사실은 산불에 취약한 지역에 건축할 때 주변에서 이용될 수 있는 연료에 대한 이해와 함께 고려되어야 한다. 전문가들은 토지의 경사에 따라 나무와 관목을 다양한 간격으로 심을 것을 추천한다. [18]평평한 지형에서는 연료 공급원 사이의 몇 미터면 방화대를 만들기에 충분한 공간이 될 수 있지만, 가파른 경사는 보호 장벽을 제공하기 위해 최소 10미터가 필요하다.

scrutiny 명 정밀 조사 intensify 동 강화되다
encounter 동 직면하다, 만나다 regardless of ~와 관계없이
frequency 명 빈도 be dependent on ~에 의해 결정되다
availability 명 이용 가능성 combustible 형 연소하기 쉬운, 가연성의
flash point 인화점 hydrocarbon gas 탄화수소 가스
combust 동 연소하다 propellant 명 추진 연료 intensity 명 강도
plentiful 형 풍부한 relevant 형 관련성이 높은 variable 명 변수
humidity 명 습도 drought 명 가뭄 lightning strike 번개, 낙뢰
substantial 형 많은 fire whirls 불 회오리 vortex 명 소용돌이
disperse 동 퍼뜨리다 determinant 명 결정 요인
topography 명 지형 sloping 형 경사진
perpetuate 동 지속시키다 aspect 명 방향, 쪽
be prone to ~에 취약하다 fire break 방화대 barrier 명 장벽

11 지문의 단어 "scrutiny"와 의미가 가장 비슷한 것은?
(A) 합의
(B) 지식
(C) 조사
(D) 논쟁

12 지문의 단어 "one"이 가리키는 것은?
(A) 종류
(B) 추진 연료
(C) 연료 공급원
(D) 새로운 산불

13 1단락에 따르면, 나무가 인화점까지 가열되면 일어나는 것은?
(A) 탄화수소를 저장하기 시작한다.
(B) 연기가 나기 시작한다.
(C) 공기 중의 산소를 소모한다.
(D) 무색의 기체를 방출한다.

14 지문에서 글쓴이는 왜 "a small spark or a single lightning strike"를 언급하는가?
(A) 자연 환경에서 산불의 가장 흔한 두 가지 원인을 나타내기 위해
(B) 낮은 습도 조건에서 산불이 쉽게 발생할 수 있음을 강조하기 위해
(C) 대부분의 산불을 유지하기 위해 지속적인 열원이 필요함을 강조하기 위해
(D) 지역의 조건이 극도로 건조하지 않는 한 산불은 거의 발생하지 않음을 시사하기 위해

15 2단락에 따르면, 다음 중 불 회오리에 관해 사실인 것은?
(A) 산불의 중심에서 발생한다.
(B) 불을 훨씬 더 뜨겁게 만들 수 있다.
(C) 물질을 멀리 흩어지게 할 수 있다.
(D) 불에 산소 공급을 제한한다.

16 아래 문장 중 지문 속의 음영된 문장의 핵심 정보를 가장 잘 표현한 것은? 오답은 문장의 의미를 크게 바꾸거나 핵심 정보를 생략한다.
(A) 북쪽 경사면은 남쪽 경사면보다 더 느리게 건조해지고 뜨거워지기 때문에 경사의 방향도 산불이 얼마나 멀리 번지는지에 영향을 미친다.
(B) 산불의 진전에 대한 또 다른 영향은 경사가 어느 쪽을 향하는지이다.
(C) 북향과 남향 경사면이 산불에 미치는 영향의 차이 때문에 특정 산불이 어디까지 진행될지 가늠하는 것은 어렵다.
(D) 경사의 북쪽 또는 남쪽 방향은 산불의 형성 여부에 어느 정도 영향을 미치지만, 확산되는 방식에는 거의 영향을 미치지 않는다.

17 지문의 단어 "prone"과 의미가 가장 비슷한 것은?
(A) 면역의
(B) 취약한
(C) 위험한
(D) 탄력적인

18 3단락에서 건축 지역의 관목과 나무에 관해 추론할 수 있는 것은?
(A) 그것들 중 일부를 통제된 방식으로 태우면 산불 발생 빈도를 줄일 것이다.
(B) 산불이 흔한 지역에는 절대 심으면 안 된다.
(C) 가파른 경사면에서 10미터 미만의 간격을 두면 화재 위험을 증가시킬 수 있다.
(D) 평평한 지형에서는 최대 3미터 간격으로 배치되어야 한다.

19 네 개의 네모[■]는 다음 문장이 삽입될 수 있는 곳을 나타내고 있다.
이는 바람이 산불에 추가적인 산소를 공급하여 더 빨리 움직이게 하기 때문이다.
이 문장은 어디에 들어가는 것이 가장 적절한가?

20 **지시:** 지문 요약을 위한 도입 문장이 아래에 주어져 있다. 지문의 가장 중요한 내용을 나타내는 보기 3개를 골라 요약을 완성하라. 어떤 문장은 지문에 언급되지 않은 내용이나 사소한 정보를 나타내므로 요약에 포함되지 않는다. **이 문제는 2점이다.**

산불의 확산 속도는 여러 가지에 의해 결정된다.
· (A) 토지의 특징은 산불이 확산되는 속도에 기여한다.
· (C) 연료의 가용성은 산불의 확산 여부를 결정하는 가장 중요한 요소이다.
· (E) 산불이 얼마나 빨리 진행되는지는 바람과 습도 같은 날씨 관련 요인에 달려 있다.

(B) 기후 변화는 자연 환경에서 더 많은 산불에 직면하게 되는 결과를 낳았다.

(D) 바람은 산불에 산소를 공급하기 때문에 강한 바람은 더 빠른 움직임을 낳는다.
(F) 산불은 경사를 올라갈 때보다 내리막으로 더 빠르게 이동하는 경향이 있다.

Passage 3

본문 p. 180

21 (D) 22 (C) 23 (A) 24 (C)
25 (C) 26 (B) 27 (B) 28 (C)
29 (D) 30 (C), (D), (F)

미국 정부의 발전

1763년은 영국과 미국 식민지 사이의 우호 관계의 정점을 찍었다. 150년 이상에 걸쳐, 식민지들은 그들만의 사회, 경제, 정부 기관들을 발전시켜 왔다. 그러나, 1764년을 기점으로 영국 의회의 의원들이 식민지 주민들에 대한 수많은 규제를 가하는 여러 법안들을 통과시켰고 그들에 의한 격렬한 항의를 초래했다. 그 결과, 1774년 가을에, 조지아 주를 제외한 13개 주 식민지의 대표들이 필라델피아에서 열린 제1차 대륙회의에서 만났다. 그런 다음, 1776년 7월 4일, 제2차 대륙회의는 독립선언문에서 영국으로부터의 그것의 자유를 선언했다. 독립이 선언되면서, 새로운 주들은 일종의 중앙 권력을 형성할 필요가 있었지만, 그럼에도 불구하고 강력한 정부에 대한 정서는 크지 않았다.

이전의 식민지 주민들은 강력한 국가 정부를 설립하는 것을 꺼려했다. [24]새로운 독립을 조심스럽게 수호하면서, 대륙회의의 대표들은 국가를 희생하면서 개별적인 주의 자유를 보장하는 느슨한 구조의 입법부를 만들었다. 이 시점까지, 유일한 중앙 정부 기관은 대륙회의뿐이었다. 1781년에, 이 기구는 최초의 진정한 국가 정부로 대체되었다. 그것은 연합규약이라고 알려진 협정 하에 조직되었는데, 그것은 모든 주에 의해 승인되었다. **그러나, 그 협정이 단순히 대륙회의가 이미 하고 있던 활동을 합법화했기 때문에 의미 있는 변화는 일어나지 않았다.**

그 규약에 의해 만들어진 무질서한 연방정부는 몇 가지 확연한 약점을 빠르게 보여주었다. 강력한 중앙 권력의 부재는 그 정부를 사실상 독립적인 국가들이었던 주들의 느슨하게 묶인 연맹에 불과하게 했다. [26A/26C/26D]의회는 세금을 걷거나, 상업을 규제하거나, 주 사이의 분쟁을 해결할 수 없었다. 국가적 단결에 대한 국민들의 인식 부족으로 인해 그것의 작업은 더욱 불리해졌다. [25]대부분의 미국인들은 여전히 그들의 고향 주에 대한 첫 애국심을 품고 있었다. 게다가, 새로운 국가의 거의 4백만 명의 주민들은 메인주에서부터 조지아주까지 널리 흩어져 있었다. 정착지 사이의 교통과 통신은 열악했고 주 사이에서는 더 심했다. 중앙 정부는 또한 외교 문제에 대한 통제력이 부족하여, 개별적인 주가 다른 국가에 외교 사절을 파견할 수 있었다.

정부의 약점을 해결하기 위해, 각 주의 대표들이 1787년에 헌법 제정 회의를 위해 필라델피아로 파견되었다. 그들은 미국 헌법의 초안을 작성했고, 국가는 그 이후로 줄곧 그것에 따라 통치되어 왔으며, 영구적인 미국 헌법이 되었다. [28]1788년 6월까지, 13개 주 중 9개 주가 그 헌법을 비준하여 국가의 새로운 법률이 되었다. 현재까지도 그 헌법의 원래의 7개 조항이 그대로 남아 있다. 그러나 27개의 수정 조항이 추가되어 그것의 범위가 크게 확장되었다.

institution 명 기관 British Parliament 영국 의회
place a restriction on ~에 규제를 가하다 colonist 명 식민지 주민
bitter 형 격렬한 protest 명 항의 representative 명 대표
the Declaration of Independence (미국) 독립선언문
sentiment 명 정서, 감정 reluctant 형 꺼려하는, 주저하는
legislature 명 입법부 at the expense of ~을 희생하면서
the Articles of Confederation 연합규약 sanction 동 승인하다
disorganized 형 무질서한 glaring 형 확연한, 두드러진
virtually 부 사실상 dispute 명 분쟁 handicap 동 불리하게 하다
owe 동 (감정을) 품고 있다 loyalty 명 애국심, 충성심
settlement 명 정착지 envoy 명 외교 사절, 외교관
delegate 명 대표, 대리인
the Constitutional Convention 헌법 제정 회의
draft 동 초안을 작성하다 permanent 형 영구적인 ratify 동 비준하다
intact 형 그대로인, 바뀌지 않은 amendment 명 (미국 헌법) 수정 조항

21 글쓴이는 왜 영국 의회에 의해 통과된 여러 법안들을 언급하는가?
(A) 식민지 주민들이 항의 행위에 있어 과잉반응했음을 암시하기 위해
(B) 식민지들이 그들만의 문화와 경제를 발전시켜 온 이유를 설명하기 위해
(C) 새로운 미국 정부가 기초한 원래의 모델을 강조하기 위해
(D) 제1차 대륙회의의 소집 이유를 밝히기 위해

22 지문의 단어 "them"이 가리키는 것은?
(A) 의원들
(B) 규제들
(C) 식민지 주민들
(D) 항의

23 지문의 단어 "sanctioned"와 의미가 가장 비슷한 것은?
(A) 승인되다
(B) 거절되다
(C) 지명되다
(D) 의심받다

24 2단락에 따르면, 다음 중 대륙회의의 입법부에 관해 사실인 것은?
(A) 1781년까지 정부를 장악하는 데 실패했다.
(B) 모든 주에 투표권을 주는 것을 거부했다.
(C) 국가를 희생하면서 주의 자유를 지켰다.
(D) 강력한 중앙 집권적 정부를 수립했다.

25 3단락에 따르면, 다음 중 18세기 대다수의 미국인들에 관해 사실인 것은?
(A) 그들의 연합규약에 대한 신뢰가 낮았다.
(B) 연방 지도자들이 부패했다고 믿었다.
(C) 그들의 주된 애국심은 그들의 주에 대한 것이었다.
(D) 열악한 교통수단에 대해 불평했다.

26 3단락에 따르면, 다음 중 주들을 다루는 데 있어서 의회가 어려움을 겪지 않았던 것은?
(A) 세금 징수
(B) 군대 구축
(C) 상업 관리
(D) 분쟁 해결

27 지문의 단어 "permanent"와 의미가 가장 비슷한 것은?
(A) 잦은
(B) 영속적인
(C) 의도적인
(D) 일시적인

28 다음 중 미국 헌법에 관해 추론할 수 있는 것은?

(A) 미국인에게 다양한 시민의 권리를 보장했다.
(B) 그것에 대해 제안된 대다수의 수정 조항이 통과되었다.
(C) 그것을 법으로 만들기 위해 모든 주의 지지가 필요했던 것은 아니다.
(D) 그 국가 대부분 지역의 사람들에게 인기가 없었다.

29 네 개의 네모[■]는 다음 문장이 삽입될 수 있는 곳을 나타내고 있다.

그러나, 그 협정이 단순히 대륙회의가 이미 하고 있던 활동을 합법화했기 때문에 의미 있는 변화는 일어나지 않았다.

이 문장은 어디에 들어가는 것이 가장 적절한가?

30 지시: 지문 요약을 위한 도입 문장이 아래에 주어져 있다. 지문의 가장 중요한 내용을 나타내는 보기 3개를 골라 요약을 완성하라. 어떤 문장은 지문에 언급되지 않은 내용이나 사소한 정보를 나타내므로 요약에 포함되지 않는다. **이 문제는 2점이다.**

150년의 영국 통치 후에, 미국의 식민지 주민들은 독립된 정부를 구성했다.
- (C) 식민지 주민들은 그들의 독립을 보장하기를 원했기 때문에 매우 강력한 정부를 세우는 것을 경계했다.
- (D) 대표단이 정부의 문제 해결을 시도하며 필라델피아에 있었을 때, 그들은 미국 헌법을 만들었다.
- (F) 연합규약에 의해 정부가 수립된 후, 곧 새 정부의 약점이 명백해졌다.

(A) 미국의 식민지 주민들은 영국 정부가 그들에게 부과한 제한에 대한 반응으로 항의했다.
(B) 1763년, 영국과 13개의 미국 식민지 사이에 우호적인 관계가 있었다.
(E) 헌법의 원래의 7개 조항 중 일부만이 변경되거나 삭제되지 않았다.

Actual Test 2

Passage 1

본문 p.184

1 (A)	2 (D)	3 (C)	4 (D)
5 (D)	6 (B)	7 (B)	8 (D)
9 (D)	10 (B), (C), (F)		

미국 의회 도서관의 역사

설립 이래로, 미국 의회 도서관은 미국 정부의 입법부의 일부여 왔다. 그 기관은 신생 공화국이 수도를 필라델피아에서 워싱턴 DC로 이전할 준비를 하던 중에 그것에 의해 설립되었다. 1800년 4월 18일, 존 애덤스 대통령은 의회의 사용에 필요하다고 여겨지는 책을 구입하는 데 자금을 책정하는 법안을 승인했다. [2]첫 소장품은 영국에서 주문되어 1801년에 도착한 740권의 책들과 3개의 지도로 구성되었다. [3]그것들은 그 도서관의 첫 번째 시설인 미국 국회 의사당 건물에 보관되었다.

이 도서관의 철학과 이상은 토머스 제퍼슨으로 거슬러 올라갈 수 있는데, 그는 지성의 힘이 자유롭고 민주적인 사회를 형성할 수 있다고 생각했다. 책 없이는 살 수 없다고 말한 사람으로서, 그는 대통령으로 재임하는 동안 미국 의회 도서관과 그것의 소장품에 열렬한 관심을 가졌다. 대통령 임기 내내, 그는 개인적으로 도서관에 책을 추천했으며, 최초의 의회 사서 두 명을 임명했다. 1814년, 영국군이 워싱턴 시를 침공하여 국회 의사당을 불태웠고, 그 과정에서 미국 의회 도서관과 그것의 3,000권의 책들을 파괴했다. 제퍼슨은 새 도서관을 설립할 수 있도록 국가 최대 규모이자 최고 수준인 자신의 개인 장서를 팔겠다고 의회에 제안했다. 제퍼슨의 6,487권의 책들의 구입은 1815년에 승인되었다. **이는 당초 손실된 장서보다 두 배 이상 늘어난 것이었다.**

시간이 지남에 따라, 미국 의회 도서관의 관리와 운영은 다양한 법률에 의해 좌우되었다. 이 중 첫 번째는 1802년에 수립되었다. [5B]1802년의 법안은 의회 사서직을 신설하고 의회에 도서관의 예산뿐만 아니라 그것의 규칙과 규정을 제정할 수 있는 권한을 부여했다. [5A/5C]그것은 또한 공식적으로 의회 사서의 임명을 대통령의 책임으로 만들었고 대통령과 부통령이 책을 빌릴 수 있도록 허용했다. 이후, 이 특권은 사법부를 포함한 대부분의 정부 기관으로 확대되었다. 1832년에 미국 대법원장의 지도 아래 법률 서적을 구입할 예산과 함께 별도의 법률 부서가 승인되었다. 1887년, 새로운 법률이 의회에 대통령의 의회 사서 선출을 승인하는 권한을 부여했다. [6]더불어, 사서에게 도서관의 규칙과 규정을 만들고 그것의 직원을 임명하는 것에 대한 단독 책임을 주었다.

20세기 중반 이후, 그 도서관은 상당한 확장과 다양화를 겪었다. 주된 이유는 두 번의 세계 대전 이후의 국제 문제에 대한 강한 관심과 세계에 대해 더 알고자 하는 관련된 열망이었다. 늘어난 예산은 도서관이 다양한 외국 자료들을 축적하는 것을 시작하게 해주었다. 그것의 아시아 언어 소장품만 해도 거의 2백만 개의 항목을 포함하며, 이는 아시아 이외의 지역에서 가장 큰 것이다. 그것의 방대한 자료 소장품에 더해, 그 도서관은 수많은 디지털 자료 소장품을 보유하고 있으며, 그 중 일부는 온라인으로 이용할 수 있다. 그것은 또한 연설과 콘서트와 같은 특별 행사를 주최하며 국가의 공식 저작권 사무소의 역할을 한다.

legislative branch 입법부 fledgling ⓗ신생의
republic ⓜ공화국 legislation ⓜ법안, 법률
appropriate ⓢ(돈의 사용처를) 책정하다 deem ⓢ여기다, 생각하다
consist of ~으로 구성되다 US Capitol 미국 국회 의사당
philosophy ⓜ철학 intellect ⓜ지성 keen ⓗ열렬한
presidency ⓜ(대통령의) 임기 administration ⓜ관리, 행정
operation ⓜ운영 measure ⓜ법안 appointment ⓜ임명
privilege ⓜ특권 government agency 정부 기관
judiciary ⓜ사법부 chief justice 대법원장 substantial ⓗ상당한
diversification ⓜ다양화 international affairs 국제 문제
amass ⓢ축적하다 copyright ⓜ저작권

1 지문의 단어 "fledgling"과 의미가 가장 비슷한 것은?

(A) 초기의
(B) 민주적인
(C) 성숙한
(D) 독특한

2 다음 중 미국 의회 도서관의 최초 소장품에 관해 추론할 수 있는 것은?

(A) 그것의 지도는 희귀하고 가치가 있었다.
(B) 그것의 책은 존 애덤스에 의해 선택되었다.
(C) 필라델피아에 보관되어 있었다.
(D) 해외에서 배송되었다.

3 1단락에서 추론할 수 있는 것으로, 미국 의회 도서관은
(A) 원래 존 애덤스의 아이디어였다
(B) 대통령이 사용하기 위해 만들어졌다
(C) 더 이상 미국 국회 의사당 건물에 위치하지 않는다
(D) 정부의 사법부의 일부가 되었다

4 지문의 단어 "its"가 가리키는 것은?
(A) 미국
(B) 의회
(C) 사서
(D) 도서관

5 3단락에 따르면, 다음 중 1802년의 법률이 포함하지 않은 법안은?
(A) 대통령에게 의회 사서를 임명할 수 있는 권한을 주는 것
(B) 의회에게 그 도서관의 예산을 책정할 권리를 주는 것
(C) 대통령과 부통령이 책을 빌리는 것을 허용하는 것
(D) 사법부로 대여 권한을 확장하는 것

6 다음 중 1887년 법률에 관해 사실인 것은?
(A) 대법원장에게 도서 구입 예산을 책정할 권한을 부여했다.
(B) 의회 사서에게 규칙과 규정에 대한 통제권을 넘겼다.
(C) 도서관 직원을 더 많이 고용하기 위한 추가 자금을 제공했다.
(D) 의회 사서를 입법부의 일원으로 확정했다.

7 지문의 단어 "amass"와 의미가 가장 비슷한 것은?
(A) 버리다
(B) 축적하다
(C) 회복하다
(D) 통합하다

8 지문에서 글쓴이는 왜 도서관의 "Asian-languages collection"을 언급하는가?
(A) 일부 소장품을 온라인으로 이용할 수 없는 이유를 설명하기 위해
(B) 그것의 최대 디지털 소장품 중 하나를 예로 들기 위해
(C) 아시아 이외의 지역에서 가장 큰 규모의 도서관임을 강조하기 위해
(D) 그것의 광범위한 해외 자료 소장품을 강조하기 위해

9 네 개의 네모[■]는 다음 문장이 삽입될 수 있는 곳을 나타내고 있다.
이는 당초 손실된 장서보다 두 배 이상 늘어난 것이었다.
이 문장은 어디에 들어가는 것이 가장 적절한가?

10 **지시**: 지문 요약을 위한 도입 문장이 아래에 주어져 있다. 지문의 가장 중요한 내용을 나타내는 보기 3개를 골라 요약을 완성하라. 어떤 문장은 지문에 언급되지 않은 내용이나 사소한 정보를 나타내므로 요약에 포함되지 않는다. **이 문제는 2점이다.**

> **미국 의회 도서관은 설립 이래로 미국 입법부의 일부여 왔다.**
> · (B) 토마스 제퍼슨은 그 도서관의 이념을 확립하는 데 도움을 주었고 그것을 크게 지원했다.
> · (C) 미국 의회 도서관은 1900년대 중반 이후 크게 성장했고 훨씬 더 다양해졌다.
> · (F) 수년에 걸쳐 다양한 규정이 그 도서관의 기능과 관리를 형성해 왔다.

(A) 세계 대전 이후 국제 정세에 대한 관심이 줄어들면서 그 도서관의 역할도 축소되었다.
(D) 도서관을 설립하기 위한 자금 지원은 1800년에 존 애덤스가 대통령이었을 때 승인되었다.
(E) 당초에, 이 도서관은 정부 구성원들에게만 개방되었지만, 이후 일반인들에게 개방되었다.

Passage 2

본문 p. 188

11 (A) 12 (C) 13 (D) 14 (C)
15 (A) 16 (B) 17 (A) 18 (C)
19 (C) 20 (B), (D), (F)

미국 연극의 발전

미국 연극은 극단들이 뉴욕 도심에서 쇼를 제작했던 18세기 중반에서 그 기원을 찾을 수 있다. 이러한 초기 연극들은 일반적으로 윌리엄 셰익스피어의 희곡과 몇 편의 오페라 공연을 포함했다. 부동산 가격이 너무 비싸지자, 극장주들은 맨해튼의 중간 지대로 이주하기 시작했고, 그곳에서 극장가가 형성되었다. 이 지역은 줄거리를 전달하기 위해 춤과 독창적인 음악을 추가한 유명한 브로드웨이 뮤지컬을 탄생시켰다. 일단 자리를 잡자, 연극은 빠르게 미국인들의 삶에 널리 퍼진 일부가 되었다.

뉴욕의 브로드웨이는 19세기에 미국 연극 산업의 중심지로 자리잡았다. [13A/13B]늘어나는 수요를 충족시키기 위해 대형 극장들이 지어졌고, 이러한 성장은 더 대형의 작품들과 더 유명한 배우들을 끌어들였다. [13C]많은 사업체들이 극장가로 이전함으로써 이 성공에 편승하고자 했고, 이는 그 산업의 성장을 더욱 촉진했다. 20세기 초까지, 타임스 스퀘어는 극장, 식당, 상점들로 가득 찼으며, 이것은 예술 오락과 상업 기업의 완벽한 융합이었다.

그러나 브로드웨이 극장이 점점 인기 있는 오락 매체가 됨에 따라, 그곳에서 공연하는 것 또한 매우 비싸졌다. 제작자가 극장을 빌렸을 때, 그는 오직 좌석과 설비가 있는 건물만을 얻었다. 조명, 소품, 의상, 음향 장비, 무대 장치는 모두 확보되어야 했다. [15]재정적 부담은 필연적으로 착수되는 제작 유형에 영향을 미쳤고, 그래서 브로드웨이는 주로 검증된 연극과 화려한 뮤지컬을 제작했다. 그 결과, 뉴욕 극장은 오프 브로드웨이 공연장을 개발했는데, 이곳에서는 작품들이 작은 극장에서 공연되었다. 이러한 보다 친밀한 공연장은 육체 노동자 관객들을 끌어들였고, 이전에 그들은 브로드웨이 극장에서는 더 저렴한 발코니 좌석만을 이용할 수 있었다. 오프 브로드웨이는 또한 더 폭넓은 공연을 제작했고 잘 알려지지 않은 배우들에게 전문 배우가 될 기회를 제공했다. 그럼에도 불구하고, 어떤 경우에는, 성공적인 오프 브로드웨이 쇼가 결국 브로드웨이로 옮겨졌다. [14]이러한 이동은 그것들의 배우들과 제작자들이 권위 있는 토니상의 후보로 고려될 자격이 있게 만들었다.

급속한 성장과 얼마간의 성공에도 불구하고, 오프 브로드웨이 작품들과 공연자들은 계속해서 상당한 어려움을 겪었다. 게다가, 브로드웨이와 오프 브로드웨이 작품들 사이의 예술적 가치의 격차에 대한 인식이 증가하고 있었다. 예를 들어, 인기 있는 록 밴드가 모차르트 콘서트보다 더 많은 표를 팔더라도, 그들이 모차르트보다 예술적으로 더 중요하게 여겨질 가능성은 없었다. [18]오프 브로드웨이 작품들에 대한 수요가 많을 때조차, 그것들은 종종 입장권 판매만으로는 스스로를 지탱할 수 없었다. 따라서 1965년에, 국립 예술 기금(NEA)이 연방 정부의 독립 기관으로 설립되었다. **그 기관은 예술성이 뛰어난 프로젝트를 인정하고 지원하기 위해 설립되었다.** 연극 산업, 특히 소규모 오프 브로드웨이 작품들의 출연자들은 국립 예술 기금으로부터 자금을 지원받았고,

그것은 다시 기부금과 세금에서 자금을 지원받았다. 국립 예술 기금은 또한 브로드웨이와 오프 브로드웨이 양쪽 모두에게 보조금을 지급했다. 그 결과, 두 공연장은 그들의 공연 입장권을 구매하는 관객을 계속해서 끌어들였고, 미국 연극 산업 내에서 고유한 정체성을 유지했다.

give rise to ~을 탄생시키다 pervasive 형 널리 퍼진
cash in on ~에 편승하다 fuel 동 촉진하다
seamless 형 완벽하게 결합된 merger 명 융합, 합병
utilities 명 설비 props 명 (연극의) 소품
acquire 동 확보하다, 획득하다 inevitably 부 필연적으로
undertake 동 착수하다 extravagant 형 화려한
blue-collar 형 육체 노동자의 eligible 형 지격이 있는
prestigious 형 권위 있는 challenge 명 어려움
recognition 명 인식 disparity 명 격차, 불균형
sustain 동 지탱하다 specifically 부 특히 donation 명 기부금
subsidize 동 보조금을 지급하다 identity 명 정체성

11 지문의 단어 "pervasive"와 의미가 가장 비슷한 것은?
(A) 광범위한
(B) 한정적인
(C) 목적 있는
(D) 따끔따끔한

12 지문의 단어 "fueling"와 의미가 가장 비슷한 것은?
(A) 유지했다
(B) 철회했다
(C) 자극했다
(D) 보상했다

13 다음 중 브로드웨이의 초기 성장의 요인이 아닌 것은?
(A) 연극에 대한 높은 수요
(B) 대형 작품
(C) 사업체의 유입
(D) 더 큰 예술적 가치

14 3단락에 따르면, 다음 중 토니상에 관해 언급된 것은?
(A) 거액의 상금이 수반되었다.
(B) 가장 인기 있는 뮤지컬의 제작자에게 주어졌다.
(C) 브로드웨이 작품에만 수여되었다.
(D) 잘 알려지지 않은 배우들이 나오는 쇼를 위한 것이었다.

15 브로드웨이 작품들과 비교했을 때, 오프 브로드웨이 작품들에 관해 추론할 수 있는 것은?
(A) 제작하기가 더 저렴했다
(B) 더 많은 관객들을 끌어들였다
(C) 더 자주 공연되었다
(D) 더 많은 배우들이 출연했다

16 지문에서 글쓴이는 왜 "a popular rock band"를 언급하는가?
(A) 오프 브로드웨이에서 일반적으로 등장했던 공연 유형을 설명하기 위해
(B) 상업적 성공과 예술적 가치 사이에 직접적인 연관성이 없었다는 것을 보여주기 위해
(C) 대중 사이에서 클래식 음악에 대한 줄어드는 관심을 강조하기 위해
(D) 브로드웨이 작품에서 대중음악에 대한 증가하는 수요를 강조하기 위해

17 지문의 단어 "their"가 가리키는 것은?
(A) 공연장
(B) 관객
(C) 입장권
(D) 공연

18 4단락에 따르면, 국립 예술 기금은 왜 오프 브로드웨이 작품들에 자금을 지원했는가?
(A) 오프 브로드웨이 작품들은 인기가 없었다.
(B) 오프 브로드웨이 입장권 가격이 너무 비쌌다.
(C) 오프 브로드웨이 작품들은 스스로를 지탱할 수 없었다.
(D) 브로드웨이 작품들은 오프 브로드웨이 작품들에 자금을 지원하기를 거부했다.

19 네 개의 네모[■]는 다음 문장이 삽입될 수 있는 곳을 나타내고 있다.
그 기관은 예술성이 뛰어난 프로젝트를 인정하고 지원하기 위해 설립되었다.
이 문장은 어디에 들어가는 것이 가장 적절한가?

20 지시: 지문 요약을 위한 도입 문장이 아래에 주어져 있다. 지문의 가장 중요한 내용을 나타내는 보기 3개를 골라 요약을 완성하라. 어떤 문장은 지문에 언급되지 않은 내용이나 사소한 정보를 나타내므로 요약에 포함되지 않는다. **이 문제는 2점이다.**

18세기부터, 연극은 미국인들의 삶에 중요한 역할을 해왔다.
- (B) 브로드웨이는 19세기에 미국 연극의 중심지가 되었고, 그곳에서 번성하는 예술 오락 산업이 발달했다.
- (D) 오프 브로드웨이 작품들은 얼마간의 성공에도 불구하고 계속해서 어려움에 직면했고, 그래서 정부의 재정적 지원이 필요했다.
- (F) 브로드웨이 작품 상연의 큰 비용은 소규모 오프 브로드웨이 공연장의 개발로 이어졌다.

(A) 미국 연극의 초기 작품들은 극장들이 주로 오페라와 셰익스피어의 연극에 초점을 맞추었기 때문에 제한적이었다.
(C) 국립 예술 기금의 자금 지원에도 불구하고, 오프 브로드웨이 작품들은 재정적으로 실용적이 될 수 없었다.
(E) 임대료가 매우 비쌌기 때문에 극소수의 극단들만 브로드웨이에서 운영될 수 있었다.

Passage 3

본문 p.192

21 (B) 22 (D) 23 (D) 24 (A)
25 (B) 26 (A) 27 (C) 28 (A)
29 (C) 30 (A), (C), (D)

별의 생성과 소멸

별은 가스와 먼지의 거대한 구름으로 시작한다. 별의 형성은 그 구름이 자체의 중력에 의해 응축되기 시작할 때 발생한다. 구름 조각들은 원시성으로 알려진 별의 구름으로 융합된다. [22]만약 원시성의 질량이 충분히 크면, 가스와 먼지는 결국 거대한 구체로 모이고 중심부의 온도가 약 1,500만 도에 이른다. 이 시점에, 핵융합이 시작되고 가스와 먼지의 구체가 빛나기 시작한다. 핵융합은 수소 원자를 결합하여 헬륨을 형성함으로써 별에 연료를 공급한다.

새로운 별이 일생을 시작한 후, 그것의 발전을 완전히 예측할 수는 없지만, 그것의 운명은 보통 질량에 의해 결정된다. [24]가장 무거운 별은, 또한 가장 크고 가장 뜨거운데, 단 수백만 년 동안만 존속한다. 이는 그것들이 연료원을 더 빨리 고갈시키는 경향이 있기 때문이다. 태양과 같은 중간 크기의 별은 심지어 수십억 년 동안 생존할 수 있으며, 적색왜성 같은 작은 별은 연료를 다 쓰기 전에 수백억 년 동안 타기도 한다. 별의 색은 온도에 달려 있는데, 뜨거운 별은 더 푸르며 차가운 별은 더 붉다.

일생 동안, 별은 중력의 내부로의 당김을 핵 반응에 의해 생성된 외부로의 압력으로 상쇄시킨다. 별이 수소의 약 10퍼센트를 태우면, 헬륨 원자는 수소 융합을 방해하기 시작하고, 핵반응이 멈춘다. [25]중력을 상쇄하기 위한 이 반응에서 생성된 외부로의 압력이 없으면, 별의 외부 층은 내부로 붕괴하기 시작하여, 온도와 압력을 증가시킨다. 이것은 헬륨을 융합시키고, 별의 외부 층이 바깥으로 밀려나는 동안 새로 발생한 열이 일시적으로 중력을 상쇄시킨다. 별은 그것의 원래 크기보다 백 배 더 크게 팽창할 수 있다. 이것이 일어나면, 별은 적색거성이 된다. 다행히도, 태양은 앞으로 50억 년 동안 이 단계에 도달하지 않을 것이다.

일단 별이 적색거성 단계에 도달하면, 그것은 천천히 혹은 빠르게 붕괴한다. [28]태양 크기의 별의 경우, 이 단계는 약 20억 년 동안 지속될 것이다. 느린 붕괴는 행성상성운을 생성하고, 핵이 식어 백색왜성이 된다. **이 차가운 별의 핵의 잔해는 가시광선을 거의 생성하지 않기 때문에 망원경으로도 관측하기 어렵다.** [27A]만약 별이 태양보다 5배 이상 무겁다면, 그 적색거성은 빠르게 붕괴되어 초신성이라고 불리는 굉장한 폭발을 일으킨다. [27B/27D]초신성의 핵은 밀도가 높은 중성자별이나 심지어 밀도가 더 높은 블랙홀을 형성할 수 있다. 별의 진화에 대한 대부분의 과학적 지식은 관측보다는 이론에서 비롯되기 때문에 어떤 것이 형성되는지가 항상 명확하지는 않다. 별의 일생의 모든 단계는 현재 우주에 존재하며, 천문학 연구는 매일 별에 대한 더 많은 실마리를 계속해서 밝혀내고 있다.

condense 통 응축되다　fragment 명 조각, 파편　fuse 통 융합되다
protostar 명 원시성　nuclear fusion 핵융합　hydrogen 명 수소
foreseeable 형 예측할 수 있는　exhaust 통 고갈시키다
red dwarf 적색왜성　counteract 통 상쇄시키다
get in the way of ~을 방해하다　collapse 통 붕괴하다
temporarily 부 일시적으로　red giant 적색거성
planetary nebula 행성상성운　spectacular 형 굉장한
supernova 명 초신성　neutron star 중성자별
be derived from ~에서 비롯되다　astronomical 형 천문학의

21 지문의 단어 "condense"와 의미가 가장 비슷한 것은?

(A) 증폭시키다
(B) 압축하다
(C) 연장하다
(D) 진화하다

22 1단락에 따르면, 별의 형성은

(A) 같은 양의 수소와 먼지를 필요로 한다
(B) 중력을 가하는 근처의 별을 필요로 한다
(C) 수소 원자의 충분한 공급을 필요로 한다
(D) 충분히 큰 질량의 원시성을 필요로 한다

23 지문의 단어 "foreseeable"과 의미가 가장 비슷한 것은?

(A) 믿을 수 있는
(B) 믿을 만한
(C) 이용 가능한
(D) 예측 가능한

24 다음 중 2단락에서 별의 일생에 관해 추론할 수 있는 것은?

(A) 가장 크고 뜨거운 별은 수명이 일반적으로 가장 짧다.
(B) 태양은 수십억 년 후에 결국 적색왜성이 될 것이다.
(C) 적색왜성은 연료가 바닥나기 시작하면 크기가 커진다.
(D) 대부분의 별들은 크기가 커지기 전에 연료를 모두 소모한다.

25 3단락에 따르면, 별의 핵반응이 멈춘 후에 일어나는 것은?

(A) 중력이 다수의 핵반응을 일으킨다.
(B) 별의 외부 층이 무너지기 시작한다.
(C) 온도와 압력이 낮아진다.
(D) 별의 수소가 헬륨으로 변한다.

26 지문의 단어 "derived"와 의미가 가장 비슷한 것은?

(A) 추출되다
(B) 모욕당하다
(C) 방해되다
(D) 수송되다

27 4단락에 따르면, 다음 중 초신성에 관해 사실이 아닌 것은?

(A) 그것은 적색거성의 붕괴에서 비롯된다.
(B) 그것의 핵은 중성자별이 될 수도 있다.
(C) 그것은 행성상성운에서 생겨난다.
(D) 그것의 핵은 블랙홀을 형성할 수도 있다.

28 4단락에 따르면, 태양은 대략 20억 년 동안 어떤 단계에 머무르게 되는가?

(A) 적색거성
(B) 백색왜성
(C) 중성자별
(D) 블랙홀

29 네 개의 네모[■]는 다음 문장이 삽입될 수 있는 곳을 나타내고 있다.

이 차가운 별의 핵의 잔해는 가시광선을 거의 생성하지 않기 때문에 망원경으로도 관측하기 어렵다.

이 문장은 어디에 들어가는 것이 가장 적절한가?

30 **지시:** 지문 요약을 위한 도입 문장이 아래에 주어져 있다. 지문의 가장 중요한 내용을 나타내는 보기 3개를 골라 요약을 완성하라. 어떤 문장은 지문에 언급되지 않은 내용이나 사소한 정보를 나타내므로 요약에 포함되지 않는다. **이 문제는 2점이다.**

별들은 가스와 먼지로 이루어진 거대한 구름으로부터 형성되며, 조건이 맞으면 핵융합을 시작한다.

- (A) 별의 적색거성 단계의 길이는 그것의 붕괴가 느린지 빠른지에 달려 있다.
- (C) 별의 핵 반응은 별의 일생 동안 중력의 내부로의 힘에 대항하는 외부로의 압력을 만들어낸다.
- (D) 별이 태어나면, 그것의 발달을 완전히 예측할 수는 없지만, 그것의 운명은 보통 질량에 의해 결정된다.

(B) 보통 그것의 색을 관찰함으로써 별의 대략적인 온도를 알 수 있다.
(E) 별의 핵에 에너지가 아무리 많더라도, 영원히 중력을 이길 수 없어 결국 소멸한다.
(F) 태양의 크기와 나이 때문에, 그것은 아마도 그것의 일생 동안 절대 적색거성이 될 수 없을 것이다.

MEMO

MEMO

MEMO

HACKERS

APEX READING for the TOEFL iBT®

Intermediate

Answer Book